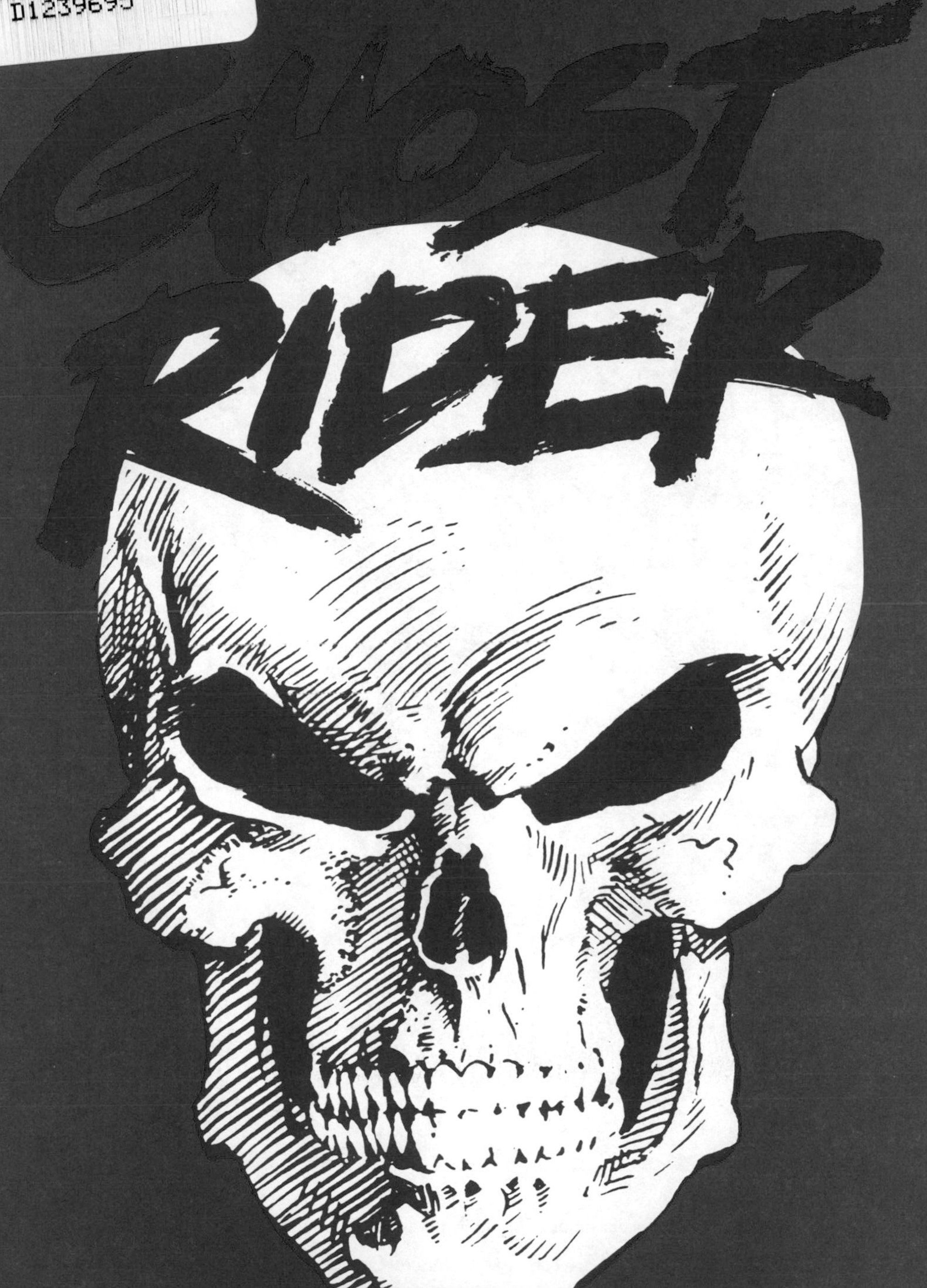
GHOST
RIDER

HOWARD MACKIE
writer

JAVIER SALTARES
penciler, issues 1-6

MARK TEXEIRA
inker, issues 1-6
artist, issue 7

MICHAEL HEISLER
letterer, issues 1-5

JANICE CHIANG
letterer, issues 6&7

GREGORY WRIGHT
colorist

JIM LEE
cover artist, issue 5

BOBBIE CHASE
editor

CHRIS COOPER
assistant editor

TOM DeFALCO
editor in chief

DAWN GEIGER
designer

Ghost Rider®: Resurrected. Originally published in magazine form as GHOST RIDER Vol. 2, Nos. 1-7.

Published by Marvel Comics, 387 Park Avenue South, New York, N.Y. 10016.

Printed in the United States of America.   First Printing: November 1991
ISBN #0-87135-803-4   GST #R127032852

10 9 8 7 6 5 4 3 2

LIFE'S BLOOD
5

DO BE AFRAID OF THE DARK!
52

DEATHWATCH
75

**YOU CAN RUN,
BUT YOU CAN'T HYDE!**
98

GETTING PAID!
121

DO OR DIE!
144

OBSESSION
167

afterword by
HOWARD MACKIE
189

cover & pin-up by
**MARK TEXEIRA
& JAMES PALMIOTTI**
190

pin-up by
JAVIER SALTARES
191

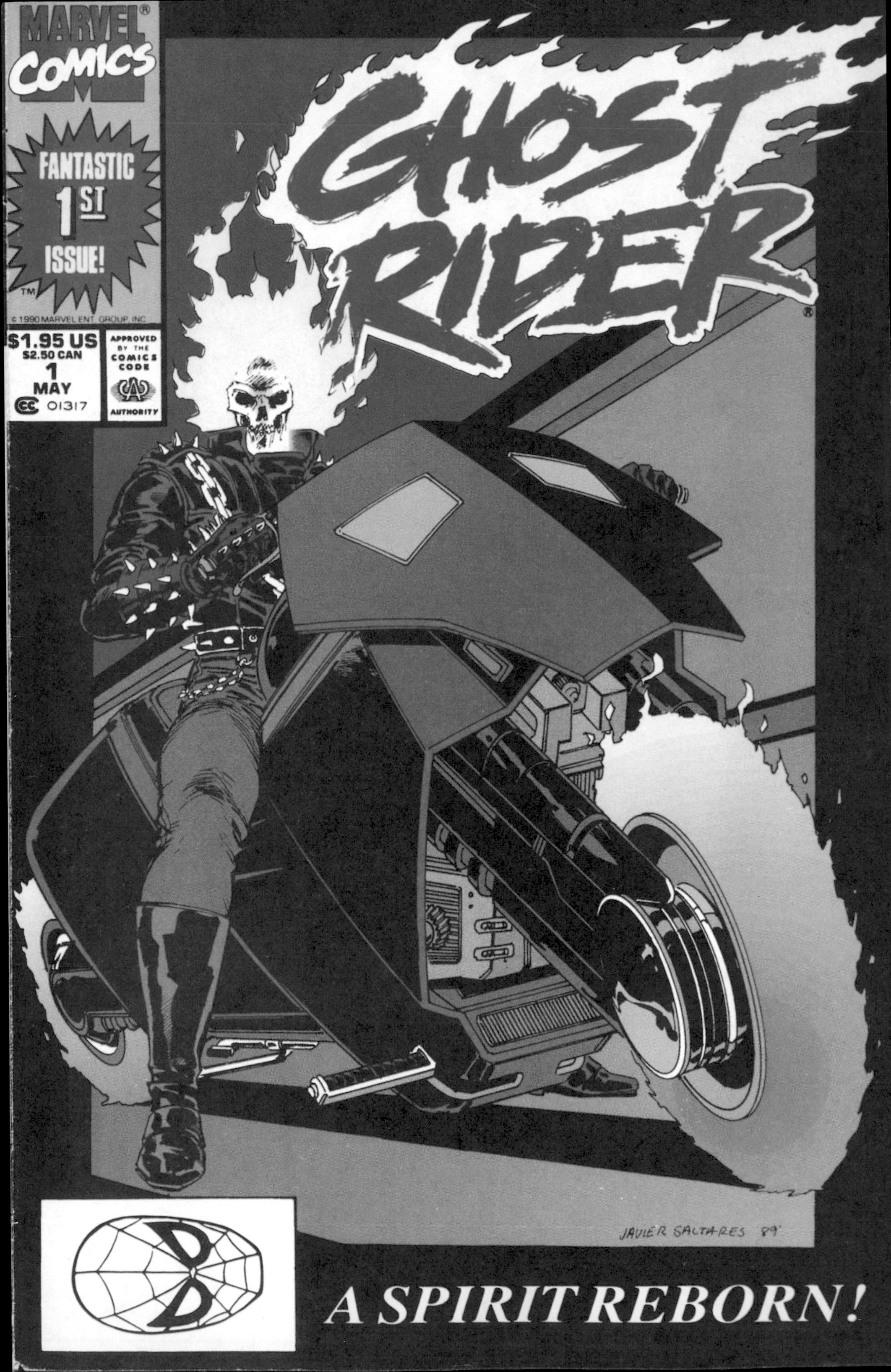
MARVEL COMICS
FANTASTIC 1ST ISSUE!
TM
© 1990 MARVEL ENT. GROUP, INC.
$1.95 US
$2.50 CAN
1
MAY
CC 01317
APPROVED BY THE COMICS CODE AUTHORITY
GHOST RIDER
JAVIER SALTARES '89
A SPIRIT REBORN!

WHEN INNOCENT BLOOD IS SPILLED, A SPIRIT OF VENGEANCE IS BORN, AND DANNY KETCH FINDS HIMSELF TRANSFORMED INTO THE

GHOST RIDER

STAN LEE PRESENTS:

LIFE'S BLOOD

writer: **HOWARD MACKIE**
penciler: **JAVIER SALTARES**
inker: **MARK TEXEIRA**
letterer: **MICHAEL HEISLER**
colorist: **GREGORY WRIGHT**
editor: **BOBBIE CHASE**
editor in chief: **TOM DeFALCO**

"Revenge proves its own executioner."
—John Ford

"I am the spirit of vengeance. Nothing will stop me from inflicting pain on all those who have inflicted it on innocent beings."
—Ghost Rider

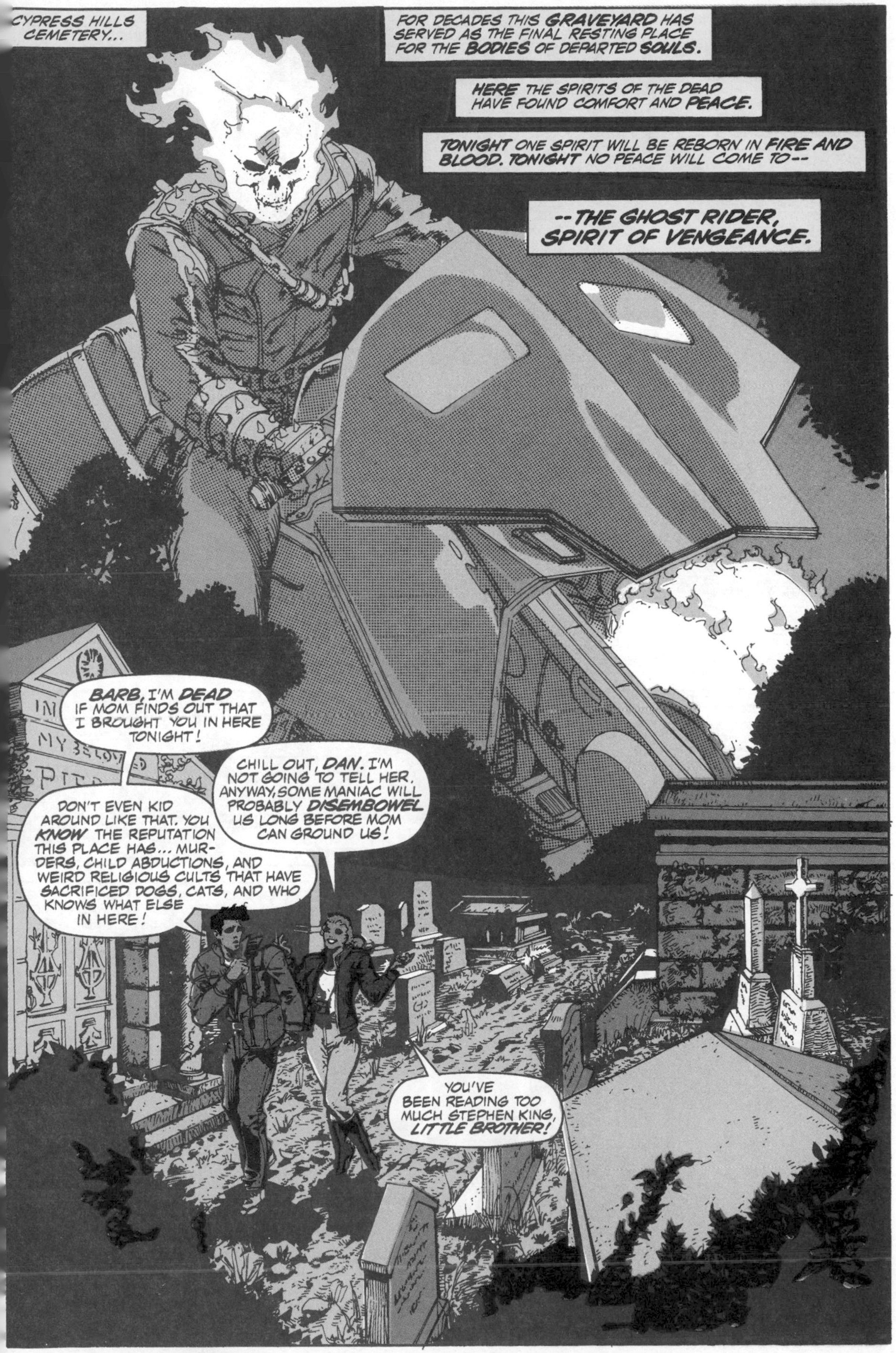

CYPRESS HILLS CEMETERY...
FOR DECADES THIS GRAVEYARD HAS SERVED AS THE FINAL RESTING PLACE FOR THE BODIES OF DEPARTED SOULS.
HERE THE SPIRITS OF THE DEAD HAVE FOUND COMFORT AND PEACE.
TONIGHT ONE SPIRIT WILL BE REBORN IN FIRE AND BLOOD. TONIGHT NO PEACE WILL COME TO--
--THE GHOST RIDER, SPIRIT OF VENGEANCE.
BARB, I'M DEAD IF MOM FINDS OUT THAT I BROUGHT YOU IN HERE TONIGHT!
CHILL OUT, DAN. I'M NOT GOING TO TELL HER. ANYWAY, SOME MANIAC WILL PROBABLY DISEMBOWEL US LONG BEFORE MOM CAN GROUND US!
DON'T EVEN KID AROUND LIKE THAT. YOU KNOW THE REPUTATION THIS PLACE HAS... MURDERS, CHILD ABDUCTIONS, AND WEIRD RELIGIOUS CULTS THAT HAVE SACRIFICED DOGS, CATS, AND WHO KNOWS WHAT ELSE IN HERE!
YOU'VE BEEN READING TOO MUCH STEPHEN KING, LITTLE BROTHER!

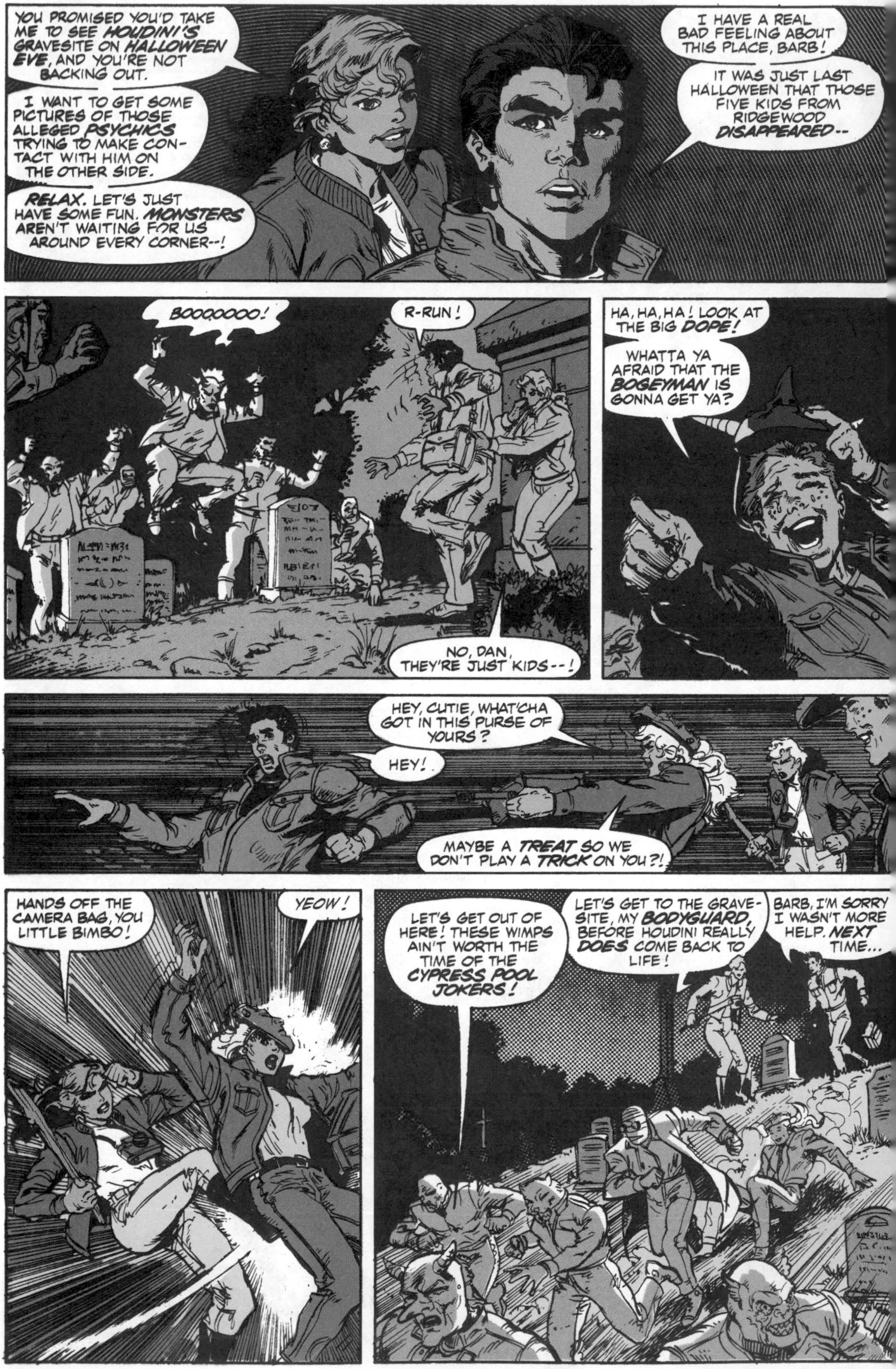
YOU PROMISED YOU'D TAKE ME TO SEE HOUDINI'S GRAVESITE ON HALLOWEEN EVE, AND YOU'RE NOT BACKING OUT.
I WANT TO GET SOME PICTURES OF THOSE ALLEGED PSYCHICS TRYING TO MAKE CONTACT WITH HIM ON THE OTHER SIDE.
RELAX. LET'S JUST HAVE SOME FUN. MONSTERS AREN'T WAITING FOR US AROUND EVERY CORNER--!
I HAVE A REAL BAD FEELING ABOUT THIS PLACE, BARB!
IT WAS JUST LAST HALLOWEEN THAT THOSE FIVE KIDS FROM RIDGEWOOD DISAPPEARED--
BOOOOOOO!
R-RUN!
NO, DAN, THEY'RE JUST KIDS--!
HA, HA, HA! LOOK AT THE BIG DOPE!
WHATTA YA AFRAID THAT THE BOGEYMAN IS GONNA GET YA?
HEY, CUTIE, WHAT'CHA GOT IN THIS PURSE OF YOURS?
HEY!
MAYBE A TREAT SO WE DON'T PLAY A TRICK ON YOU?!
HANDS OFF THE CAMERA BAG, YOU LITTLE BIMBO!
YEOW!
LET'S GET OUT OF HERE! THESE WIMPS AIN'T WORTH THE TIME OF THE CYPRESS POOL JOKERS!
LET'S GET TO THE GRAVESITE, MY BODYGUARD, BEFORE HOUDINI REALLY DOES COME BACK TO LIFE!
BARB, I'M SORRY I WASN'T MORE HELP. NEXT TIME...

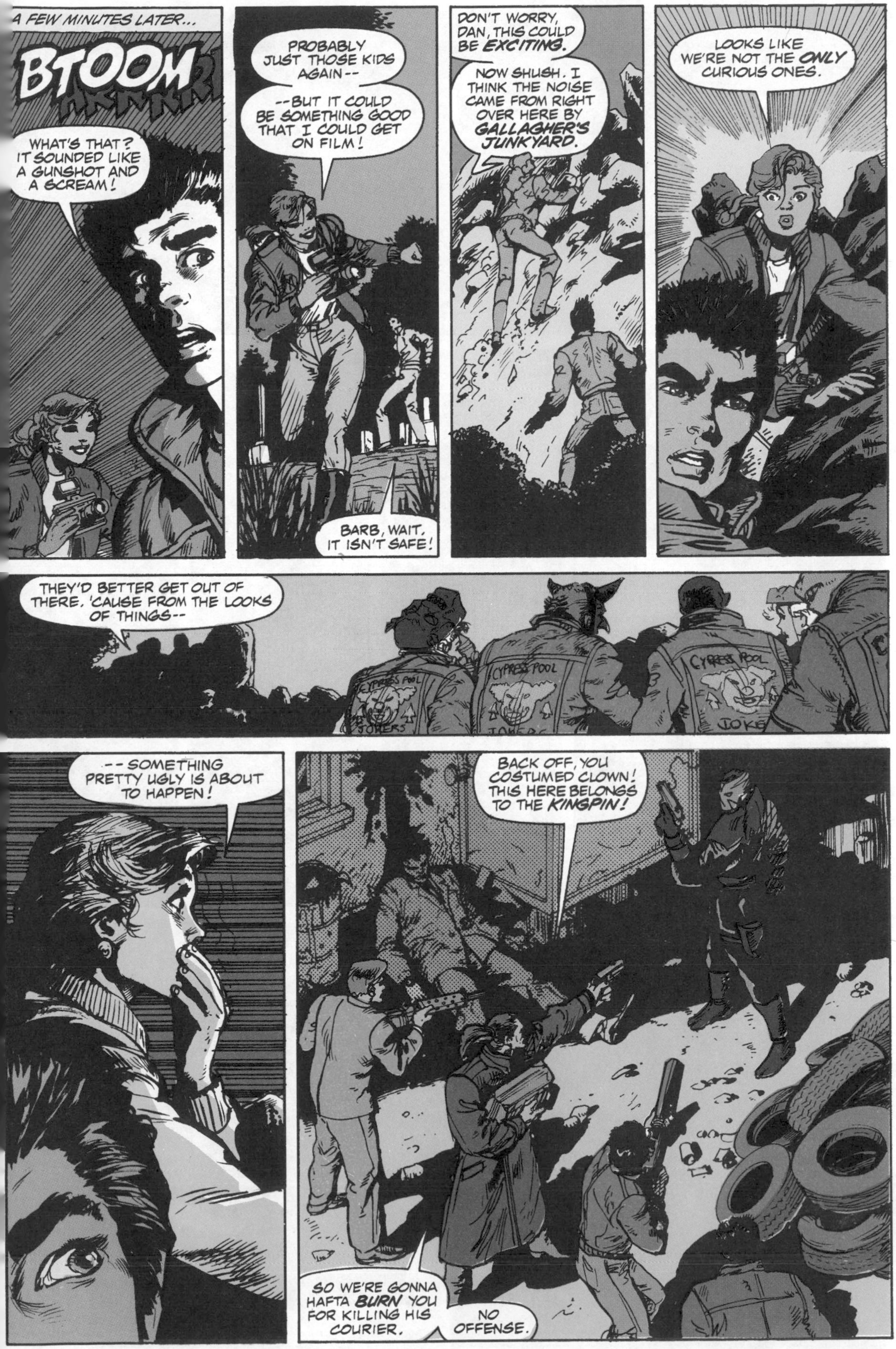
A FEW MINUTES LATER...
BTOOM
AKKKK
WHAT'S THAT? IT SOUNDED LIKE A GUNSHOT AND A SCREAM!
PROBABLY JUST THOSE KIDS AGAIN--
--BUT IT COULD BE SOMETHING GOOD THAT I COULD GET ON FILM!
BARB, WAIT. IT ISN'T SAFE!
DON'T WORRY, DAN, THIS COULD BE EXCITING.
NOW SHUSH. I THINK THE NOISE CAME FROM RIGHT OVER HERE BY GALLAGHER'S JUNKYARD.
LOOKS LIKE WE'RE NOT THE ONLY CURIOUS ONES.
THEY'D BETTER GET OUT OF THERE. 'CAUSE FROM THE LOOKS OF THINGS--
CYPRESS POOL
JOKERS
--SOMETHING PRETTY UGLY IS ABOUT TO HAPPEN!
BACK OFF, YOU COSTUMED CLOWN! THIS HERE BELONGS TO THE KINGPIN!
SO WE'RE GONNA HAFTA BURN YOU FOR KILLING HIS COURIER.
NO OFFENSE.

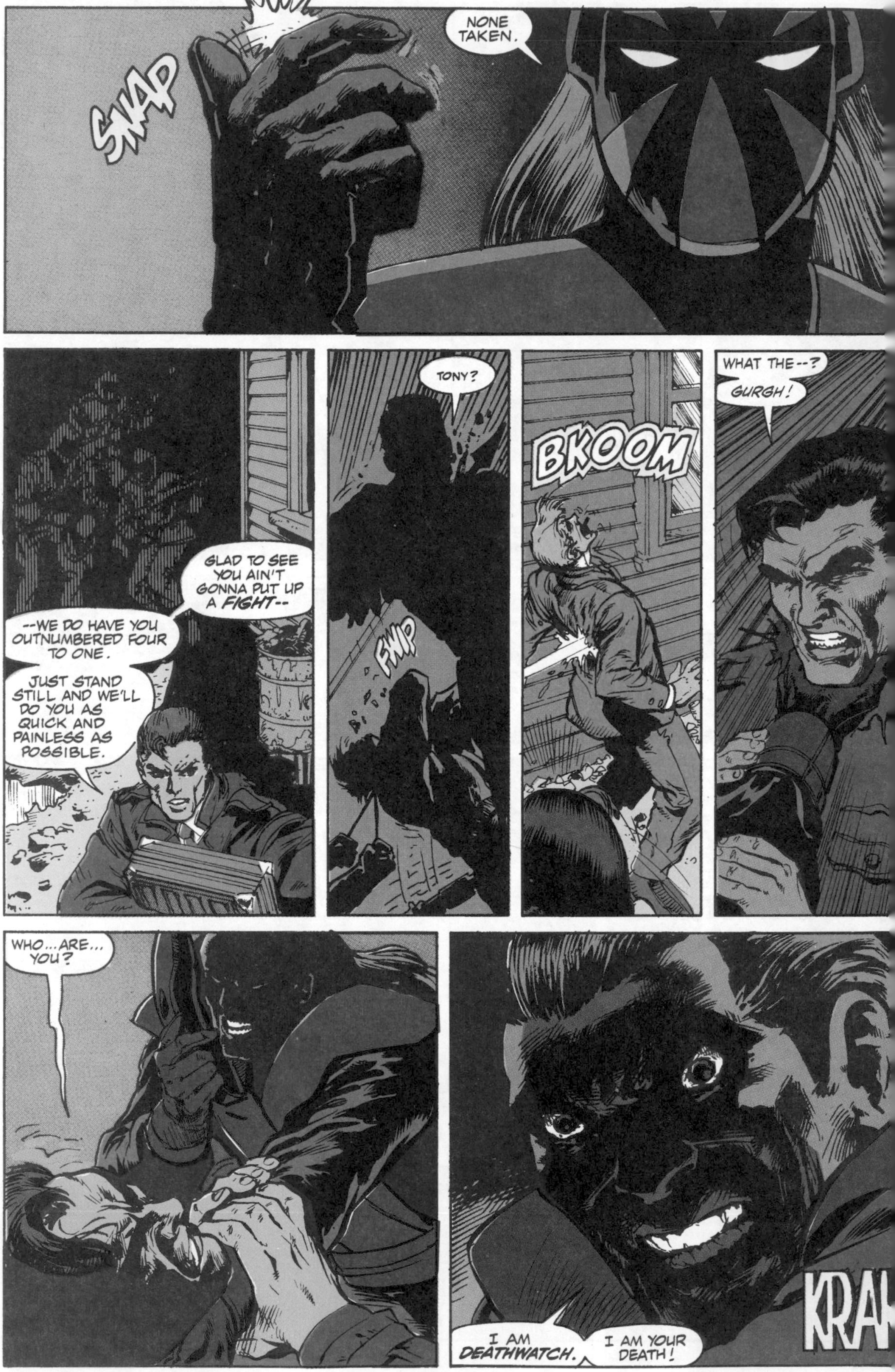

SNAP
NONE TAKEN.
GLAD TO SEE YOU AIN'T GONNA PUT UP A FIGHT--
--WE DO HAVE YOU OUTNUMBERED FOUR TO ONE.
JUST STAND STILL AND WE'LL DO YOU AS QUICK AND PAINLESS AS POSSIBLE.
TONY?
FWIP
BKOOM
WHAT THE--? GURGH!
WHO...ARE... YOU?
I AM DEATHWATCH.
I AM YOUR DEATH!
KRAK

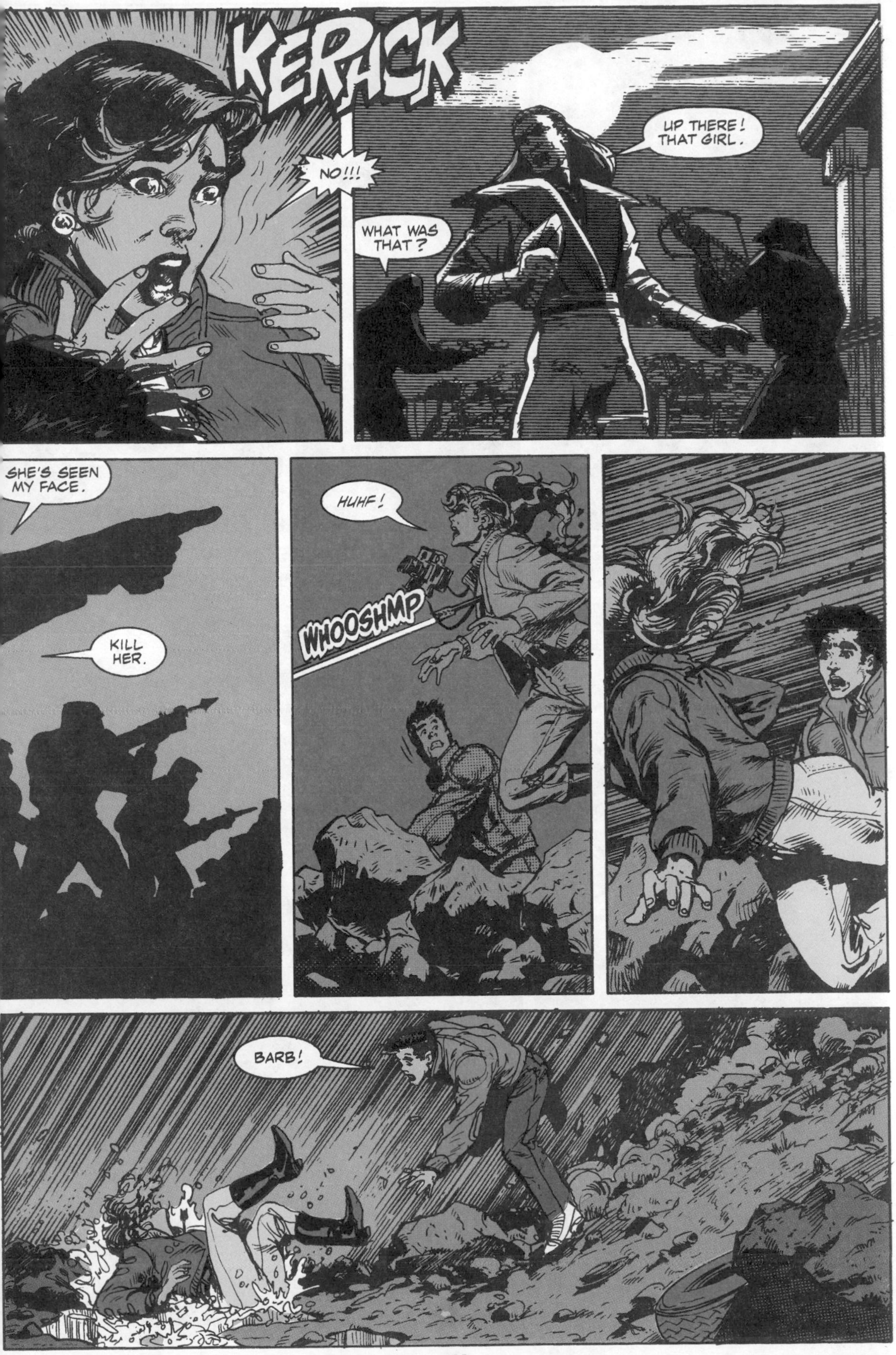
KERACK
NO!!!
UP THERE! THAT GIRL.
WHAT WAS THAT?
SHE'S SEEN MY FACE.
KILL HER.
HUHF!
WHOOSHMP
BARB!

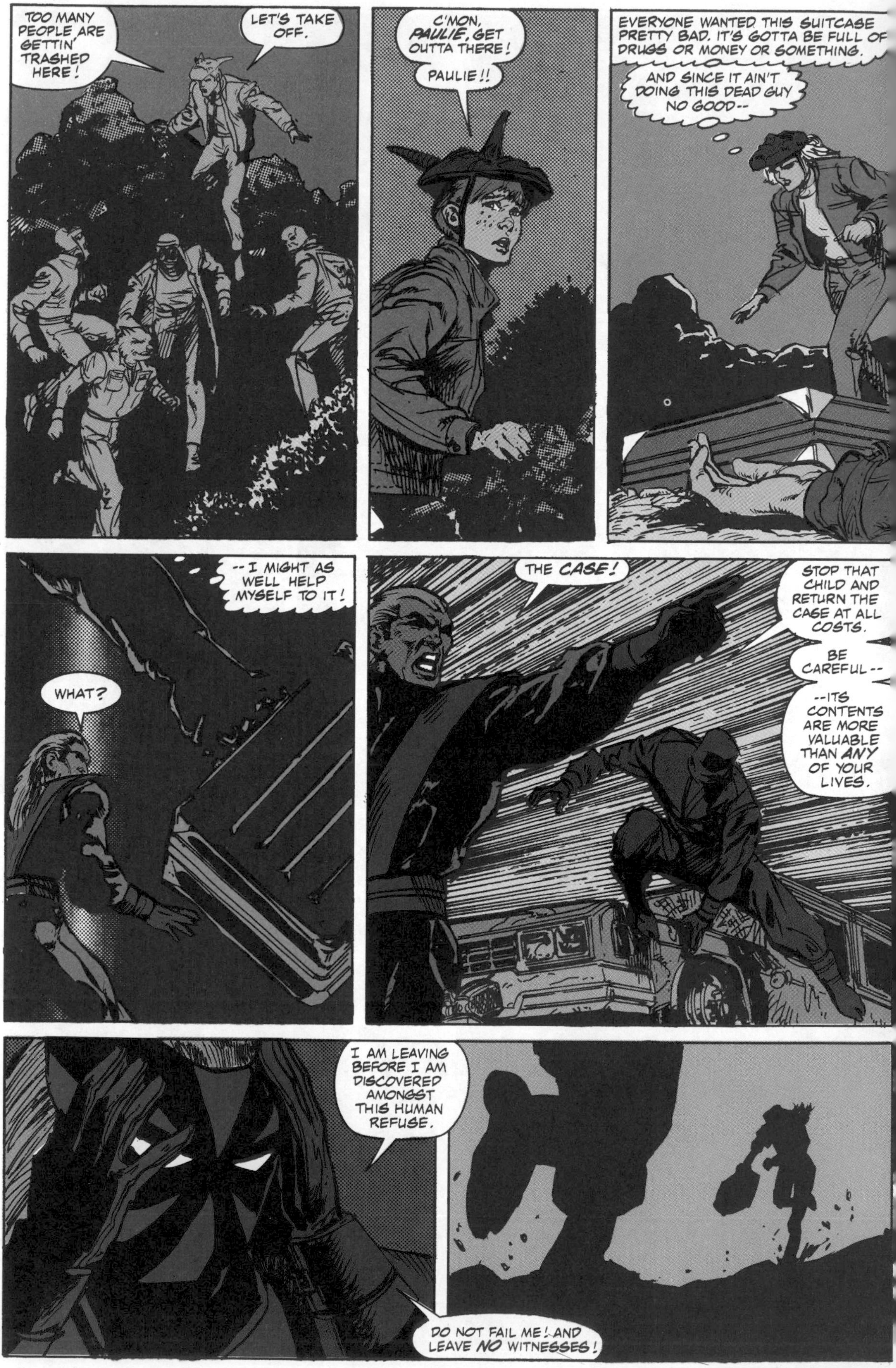
TOO MANY PEOPLE ARE GETTIN' TRASHED HERE!
LET'S TAKE OFF.
C'MON, PAULIE, GET OUTTA THERE!
PAULIE!!
EVERYONE WANTED THIS SUITCASE PRETTY BAD. IT'S GOTTA BE FULL OF DRUGS OR MONEY OR SOMETHING.
AND SINCE IT AIN'T DOING THIS DEAD GUY NO GOOD--
--I MIGHT AS WELL HELP MYSELF TO IT!
WHAT?
THE CASE!
STOP THAT CHILD AND RETURN THE CASE AT ALL COSTS.
BE CAREFUL--
--ITS CONTENTS ARE MORE VALUABLE THAN ANY OF YOUR LIVES.
I AM LEAVING BEFORE I AM DISCOVERED AMONGST THIS HUMAN REFUSE.
DO NOT FAIL ME! AND LEAVE NO WITNESSES!

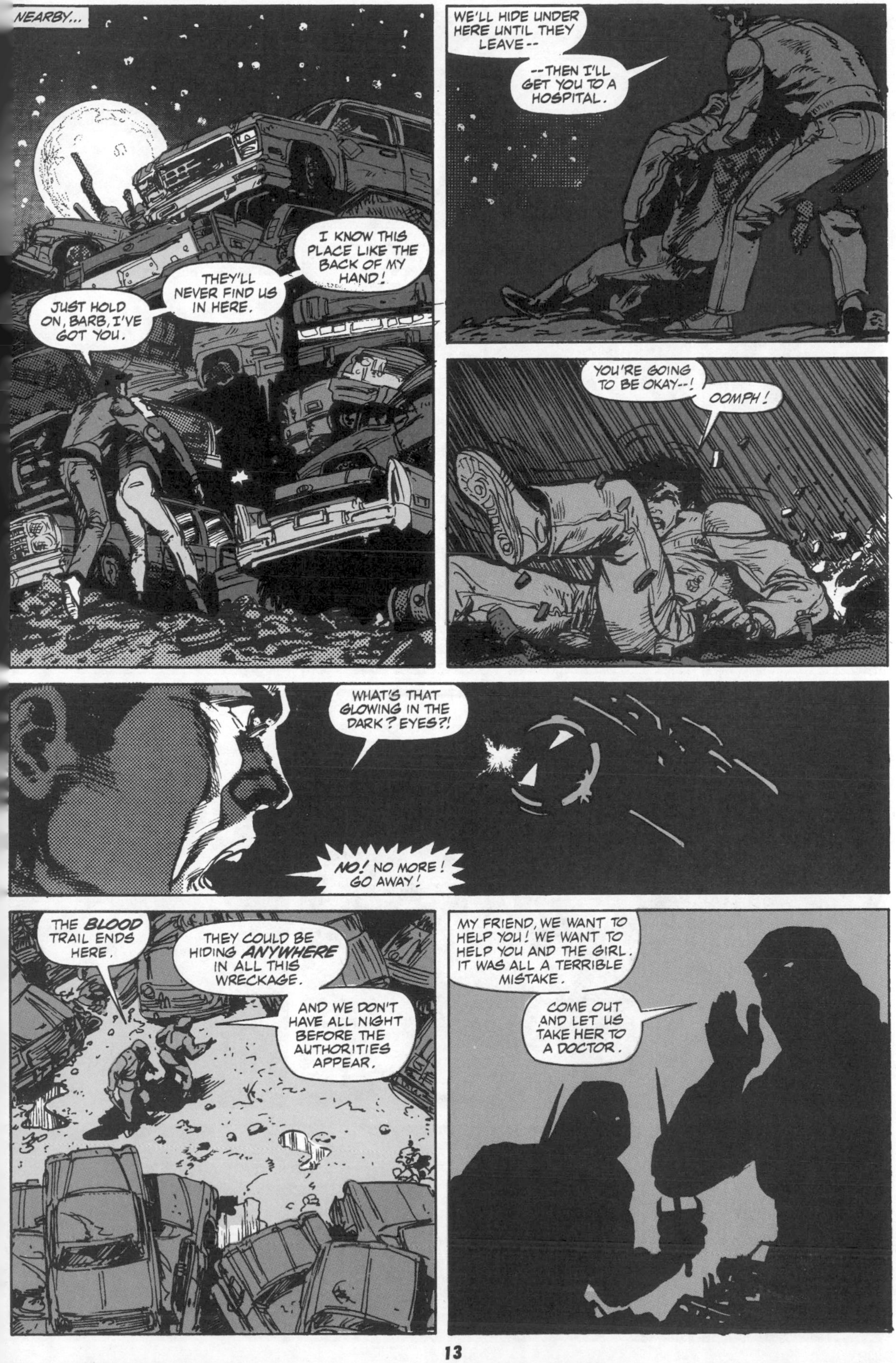

NEARBY...
I KNOW THIS PLACE LIKE THE BACK OF MY HAND!
THEY'LL NEVER FIND US IN HERE.
JUST HOLD ON, BARB, I'VE GOT YOU.
WE'LL HIDE UNDER HERE UNTIL THEY LEAVE --
--THEN I'LL GET YOU TO A HOSPITAL.
YOU'RE GOING TO BE OKAY--!
OOMPH!
WHAT'S THAT GLOWING IN THE DARK? EYES?!
NO! NO MORE! GO AWAY!
THE BLOOD TRAIL ENDS HERE.
THEY COULD BE HIDING ANYWHERE IN ALL THIS WRECKAGE.
AND WE DON'T HAVE ALL NIGHT BEFORE THE AUTHORITIES APPEAR.
MY FRIEND, WE WANT TO HELP YOU! WE WANT TO HELP YOU AND THE GIRL. IT WAS ALL A TERRIBLE MISTAKE.
COME OUT AND LET US TAKE HER TO A DOCTOR.

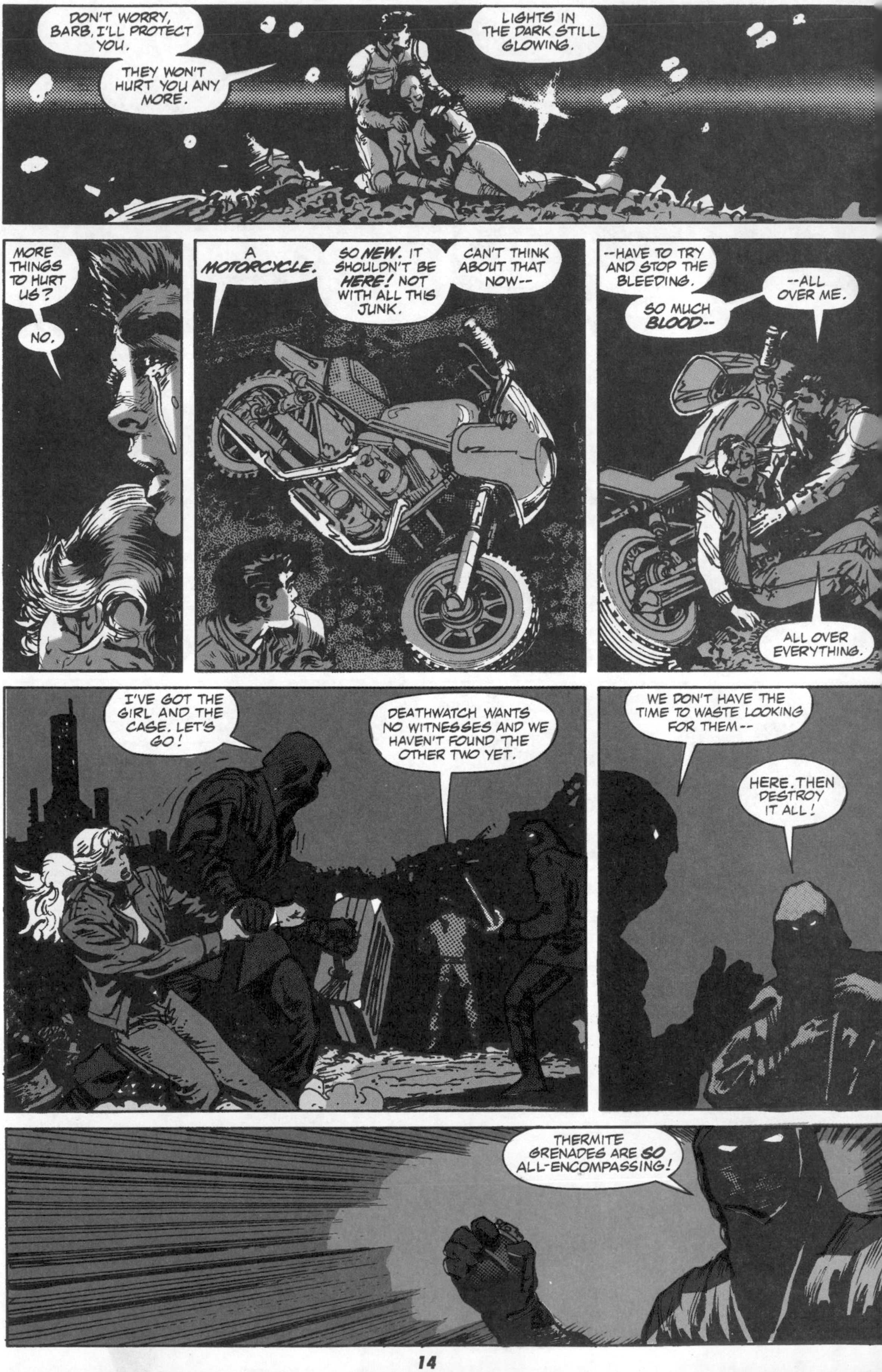
DON'T WORRY, BARB, I'LL PROTECT YOU.
THEY WON'T HURT YOU ANY MORE.
LIGHTS IN THE DARK STILL GLOWING.
MORE THINGS TO HURT US?
NO.
A MOTORCYCLE.
SO NEW. IT SHOULDN'T BE HERE! NOT WITH ALL THIS JUNK.
CAN'T THINK ABOUT THAT NOW--
--HAVE TO TRY AND STOP THE BLEEDING.
SO MUCH BLOOD--
--ALL OVER ME.
ALL OVER EVERYTHING.
I'VE GOT THE GIRL AND THE CASE. LET'S GO!
DEATHWATCH WANTS NO WITNESSES AND WE HAVEN'T FOUND THE OTHER TWO YET.
WE DON'T HAVE THE TIME TO WASTE LOOKING FOR THEM--
HERE. THEN DESTROY IT ALL!
THERMITE GRENADES ARE SO ALL-ENCOMPASSING!

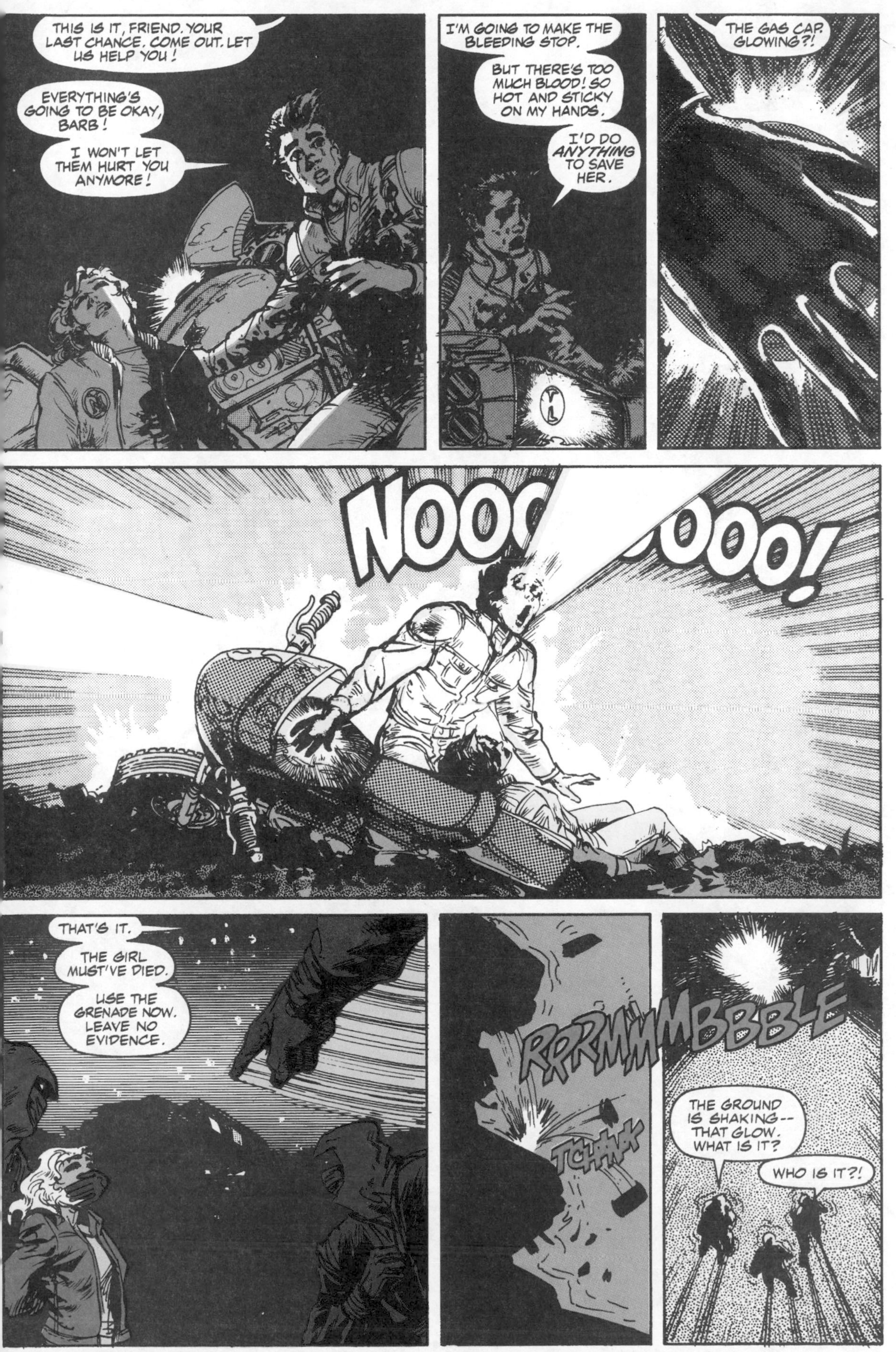
THIS IS IT, FRIEND. YOUR LAST CHANCE. COME OUT. LET US HELP YOU!
EVERYTHING'S GOING TO BE OKAY, BARB!
I WON'T LET THEM HURT YOU ANYMORE!
I'M GOING TO MAKE THE BLEEDING STOP.
BUT THERE'S TOO MUCH BLOOD! SO HOT AND STICKY ON MY HANDS.
I'D DO *ANYTHING* TO SAVE HER.
THE GAS CAP. GLOWING?!
NOOO
OOOO!
THAT'S IT.
THE GIRL MUST'VE DIED.
USE THE GRENADE NOW. LEAVE NO EVIDENCE.
RRRMMMMBBBLE
TCHANK
THE GROUND IS SHAKING-- THAT GLOW. WHAT IS IT?
WHO IS IT?!

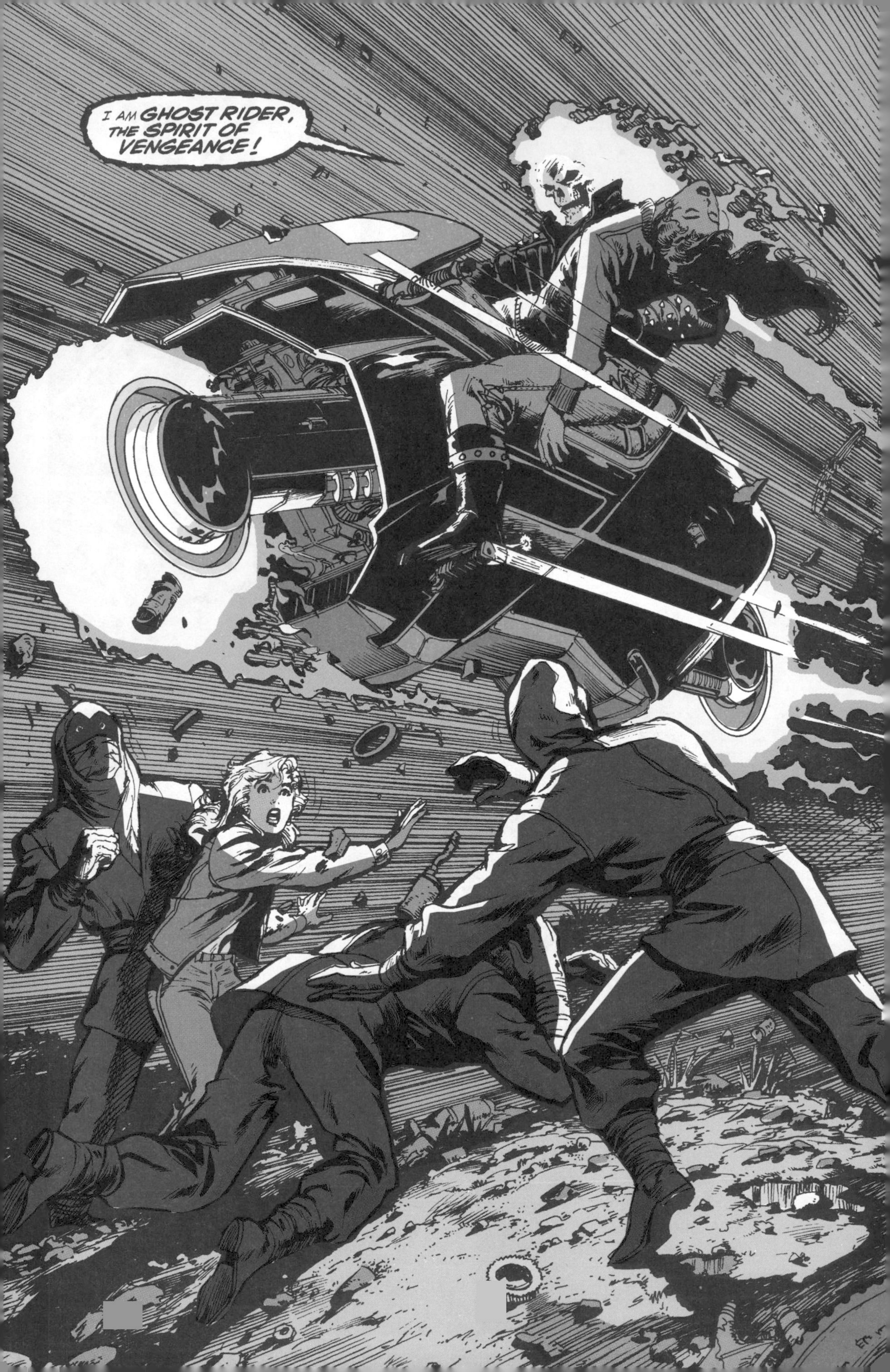
I AM GHOST RIDER, THE SPIRIT OF VENGEANCE!

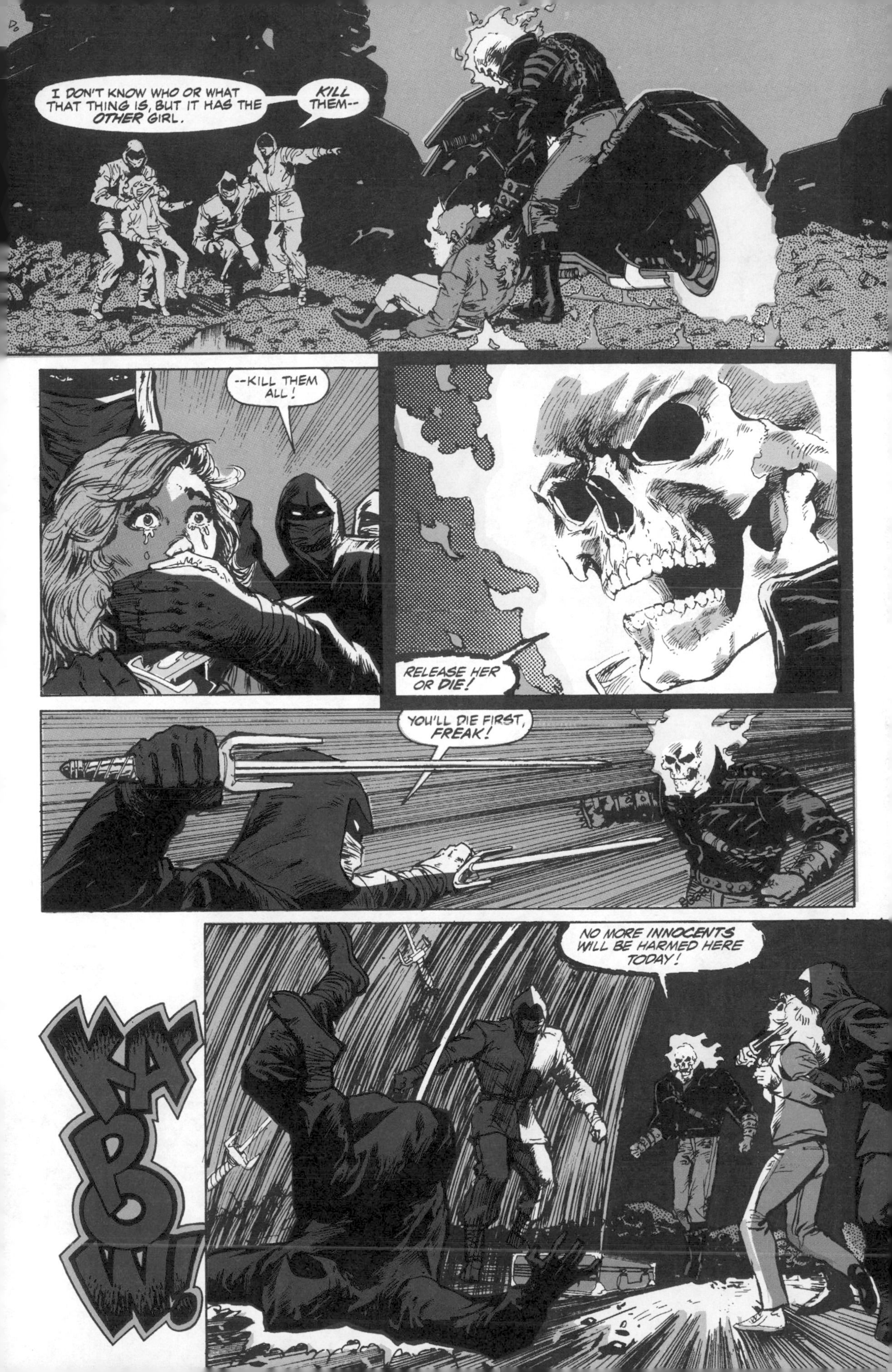
I DON'T KNOW WHO OR WHAT THAT THING IS, BUT IT HAS THE OTHER GIRL.
KILL THEM--
--KILL THEM ALL!
RELEASE HER OR DIE!
YOU'LL DIE FIRST, FREAK!
NO MORE INNOCENTS WILL BE HARMED HERE TODAY!
KA-BOW!

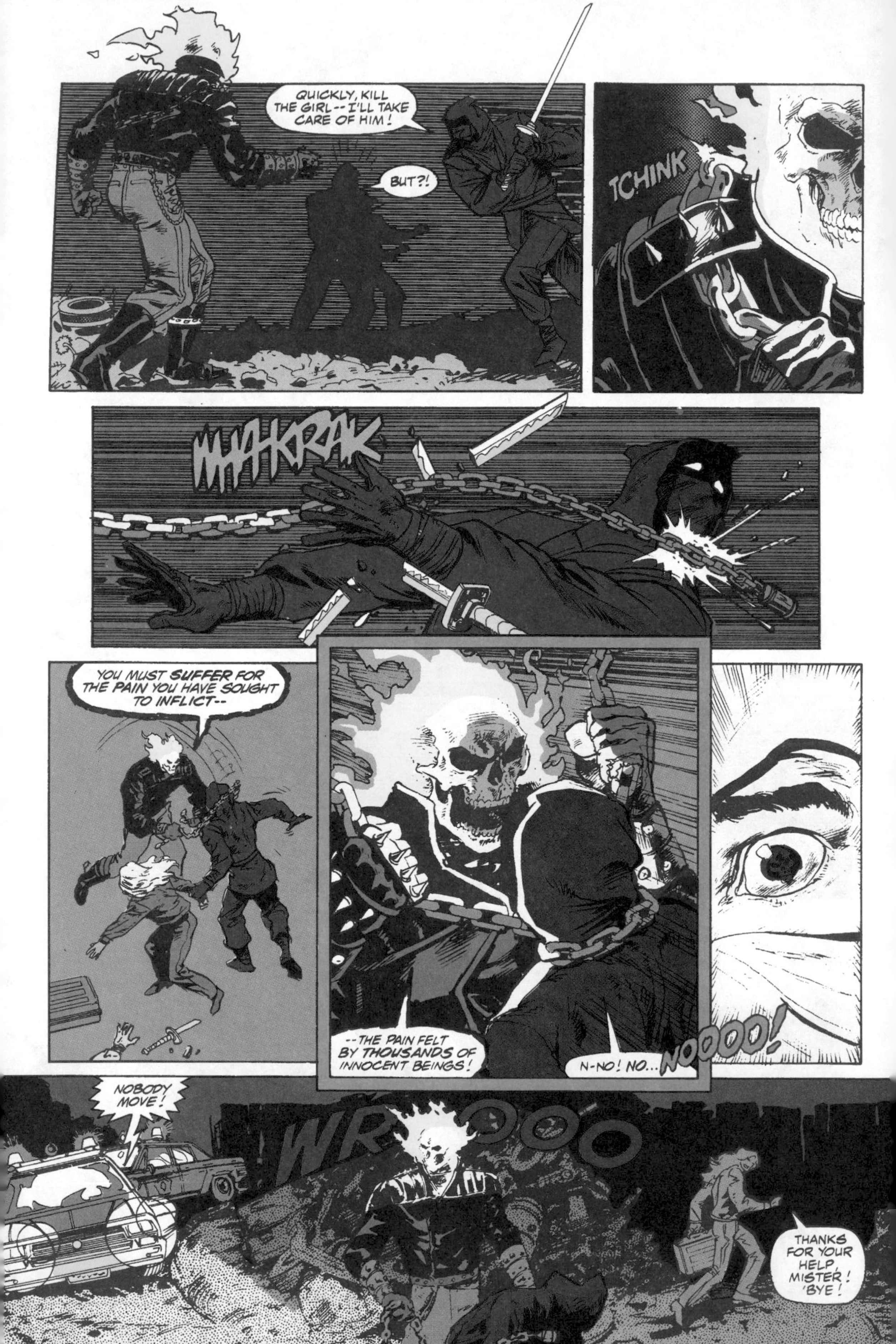
QUICKLY, KILL THE GIRL--I'LL TAKE CARE OF HIM!
BUT?!
TCHINK
WHAKRAK
YOU MUST SUFFER FOR THE PAIN YOU HAVE SOUGHT TO INFLICT--
--THE PAIN FELT BY THOUSANDS OF INNOCENT BEINGS!
N-NO! NO... NOOOO!
NOBODY MOVE!
WROOOO
THANKS FOR YOUR HELP, MISTER! 'BYE!

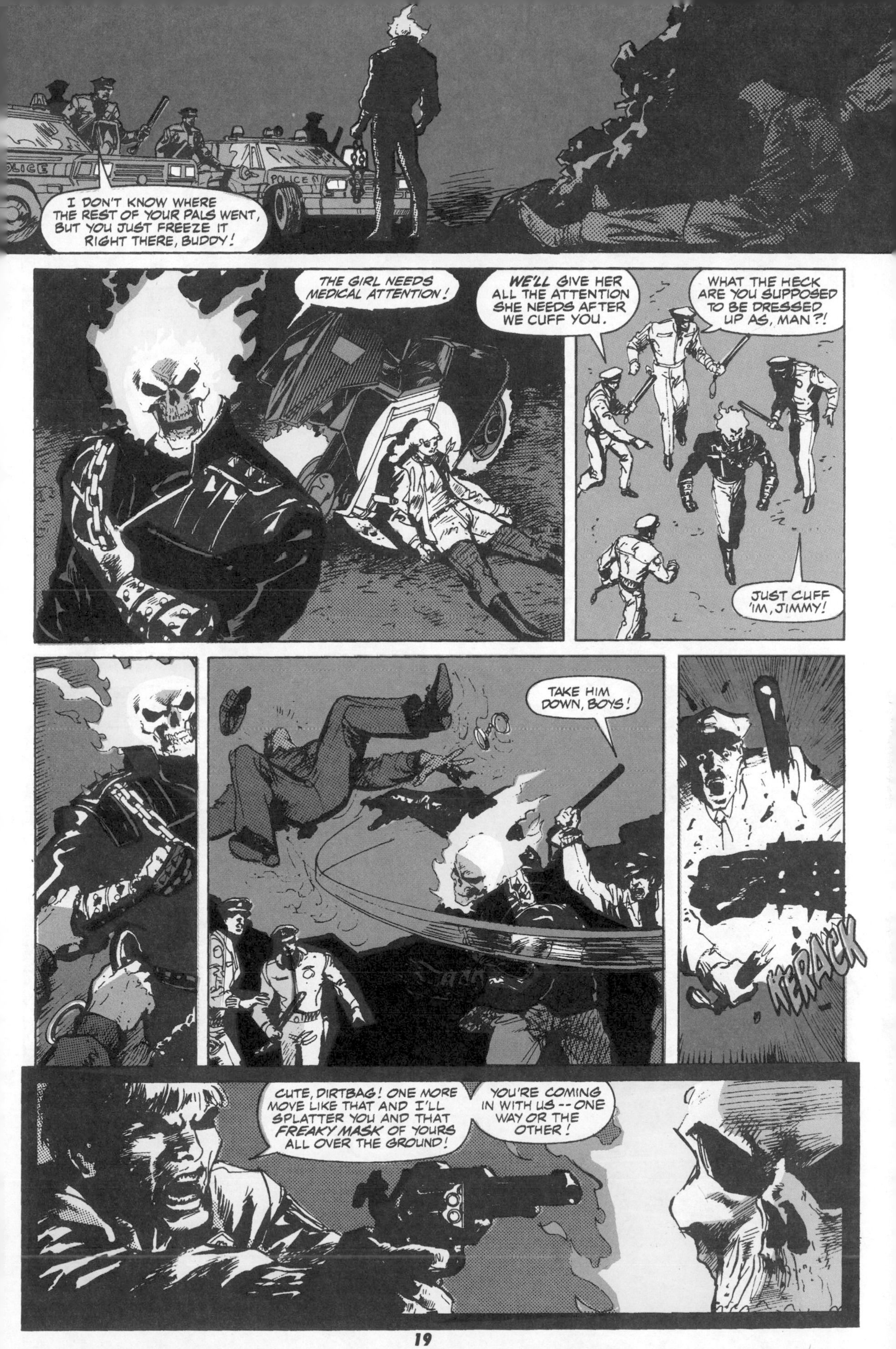

I DON'T KNOW WHERE THE REST OF YOUR PALS WENT, BUT YOU JUST FREEZE IT RIGHT THERE, BUDDY!
THE GIRL NEEDS MEDICAL ATTENTION!
WE'LL GIVE HER ALL THE ATTENTION SHE NEEDS AFTER WE CUFF YOU.
WHAT THE HECK ARE YOU SUPPOSED TO BE DRESSED UP AS, MAN?!
JUST CUFF 'IM, JIMMY!
TAKE HIM DOWN, BOYS!
KERACK
CUTE, DIRTBAG! ONE MORE MOVE LIKE THAT AND I'LL SPLATTER YOU AND THAT FREAKY MASK OF YOURS ALL OVER THE GROUND!
YOU'RE COMING IN WITH US -- ONE WAY OR THE OTHER!

THE INNOCENT BLOOD SPILLED HERE TONIGHT MUST BE AVENGED!

OOF!

IT IS MY SOLEMN DUTY.

DO HIM!

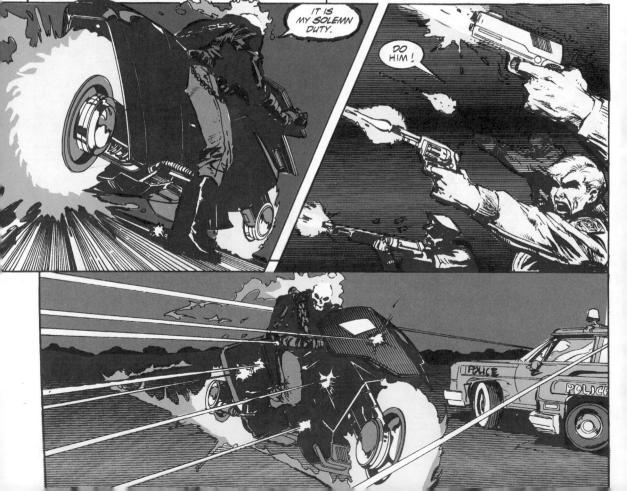

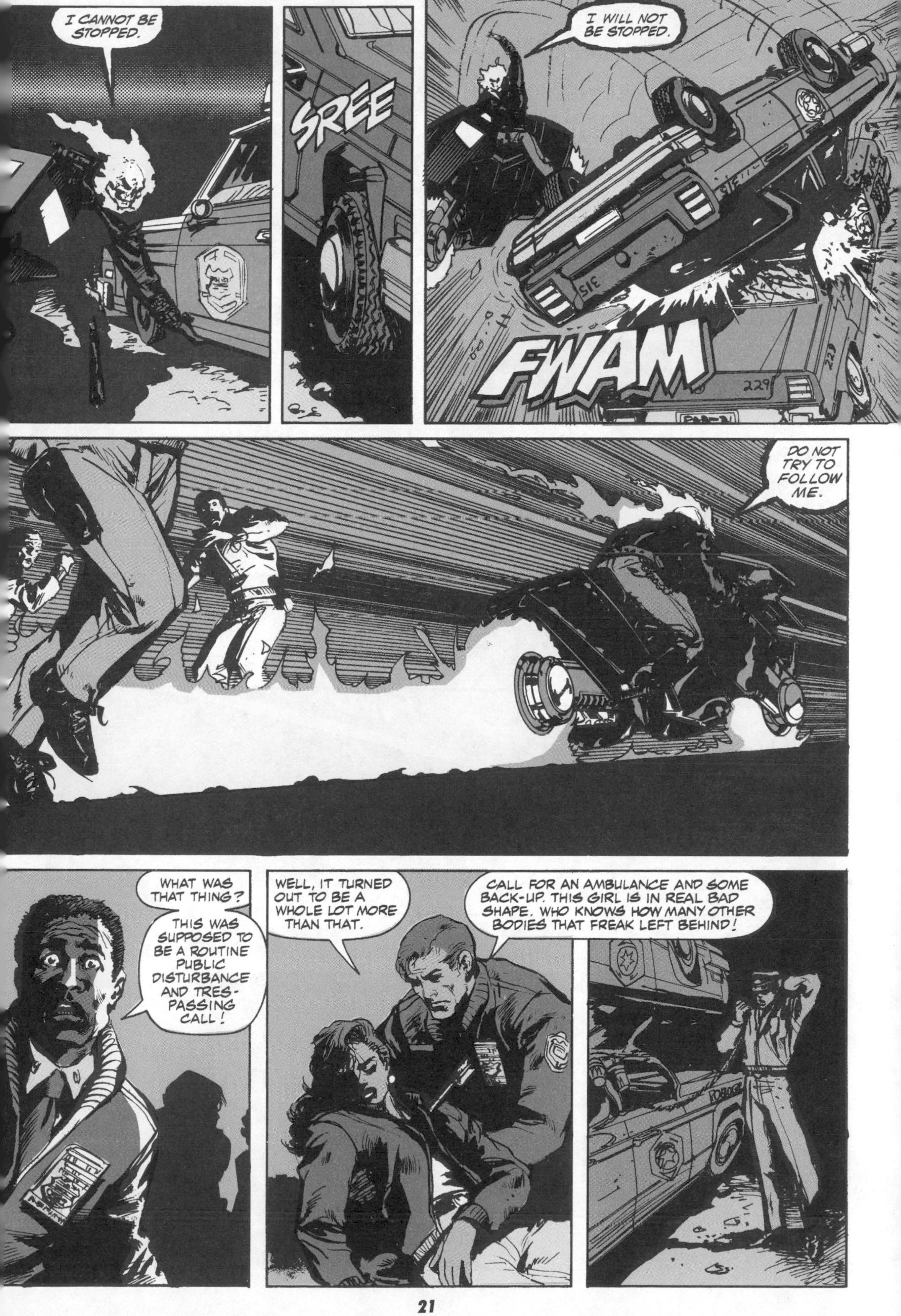
I CANNOT BE STOPPED.
SREE
I WILL NOT BE STOPPED.
FWAM
DO NOT TRY TO FOLLOW ME.
WHAT WAS THAT THING?
THIS WAS SUPPOSED TO BE A ROUTINE PUBLIC DISTURBANCE AND TRES-PASSING CALL!
WELL, IT TURNED OUT TO BE A WHOLE LOT MORE THAN THAT.
CALL FOR AN AMBULANCE AND SOME BACK-UP. THIS GIRL IS IN REAL BAD SHAPE. WHO KNOWS HOW MANY OTHER BODIES THAT FREAK LEFT BEHIND!

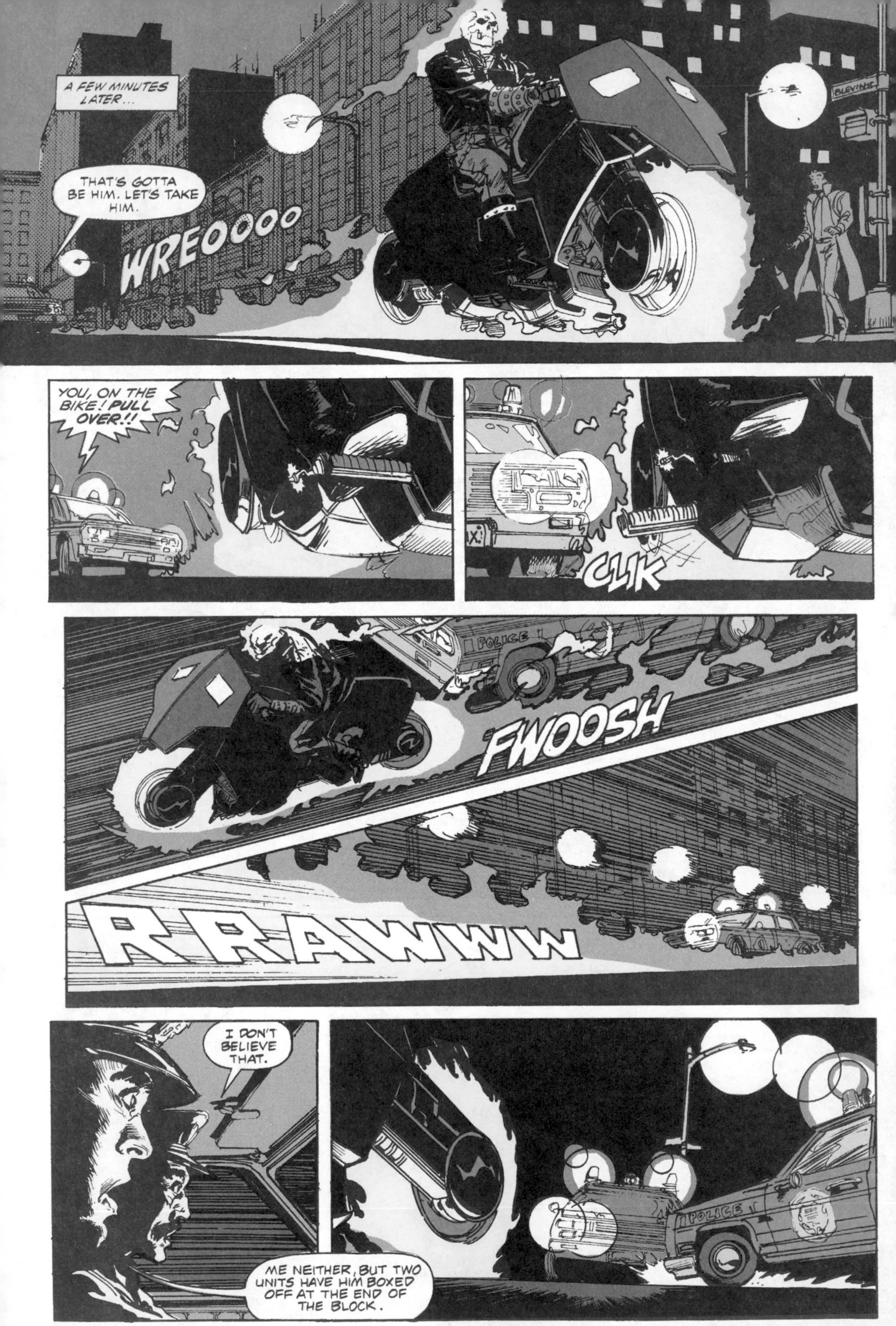

A FEW MINUTES LATER...
THAT'S GOTTA BE HIM. LET'S TAKE HIM.
WREOOOO
BLEVINS
YOU, ON THE BIKE! PULL OVER!!
CLIK
POLICE
FWOOSH
RRAWWW
I DON'T BELIEVE THAT.
ME NEITHER, BUT TWO UNITS HAVE HIM BOXED OFF AT THE END OF THE BLOCK.
POLICE

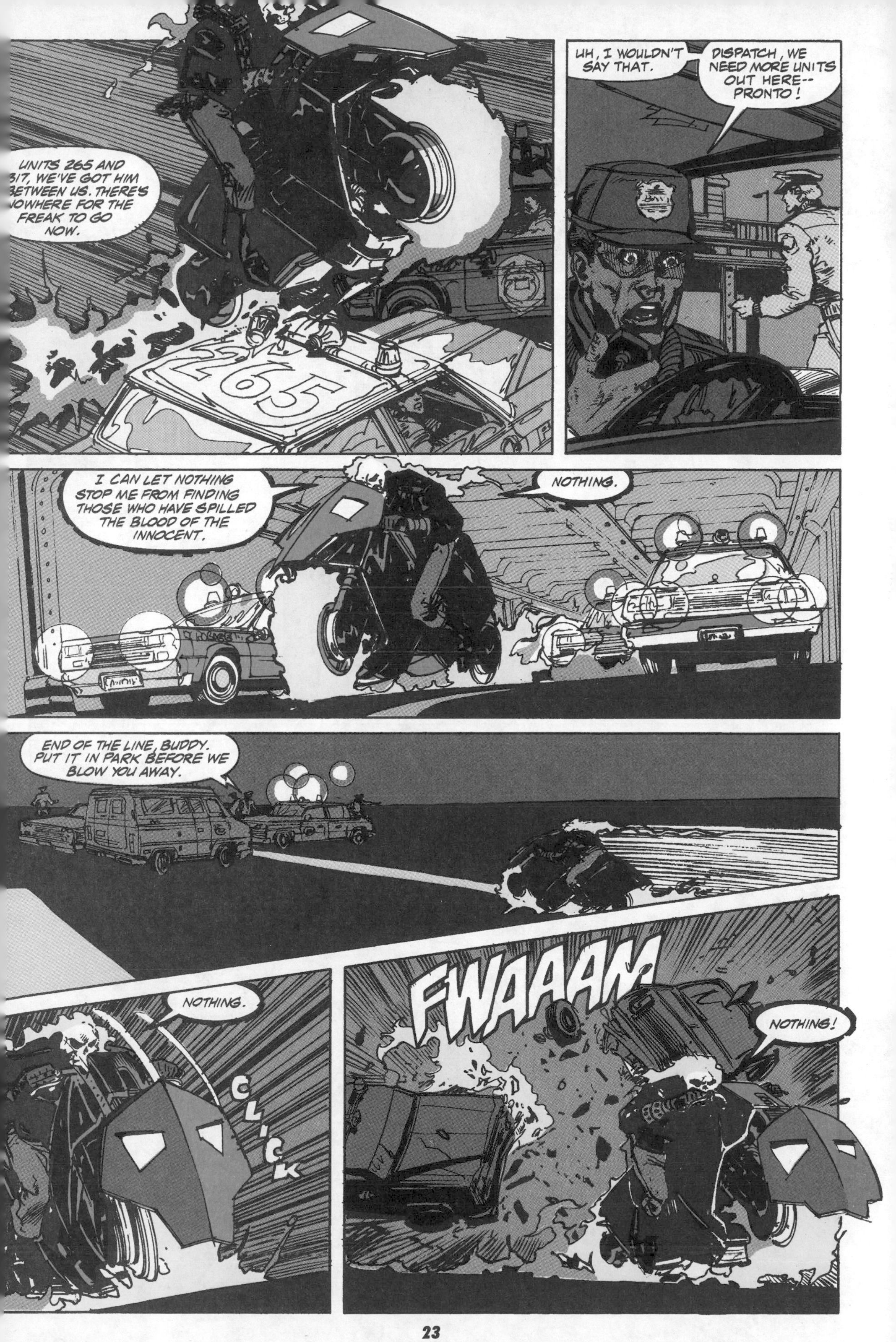
UNITS 265 AND 317, WE'VE GOT HIM BETWEEN US. THERE'S NOWHERE FOR THE FREAK TO GO NOW.
265
UH, I WOULDN'T SAY THAT.
DISPATCH, WE NEED MORE UNITS OUT HERE-- PRONTO!
I CAN LET NOTHING STOP ME FROM FINDING THOSE WHO HAVE SPILLED THE BLOOD OF THE INNOCENT.
NOTHING.
END OF THE LINE, BUDDY. PUT IT IN PARK BEFORE WE BLOW YOU AWAY.
NOTHING.
CLICK
FWAAAM
NOTHING!

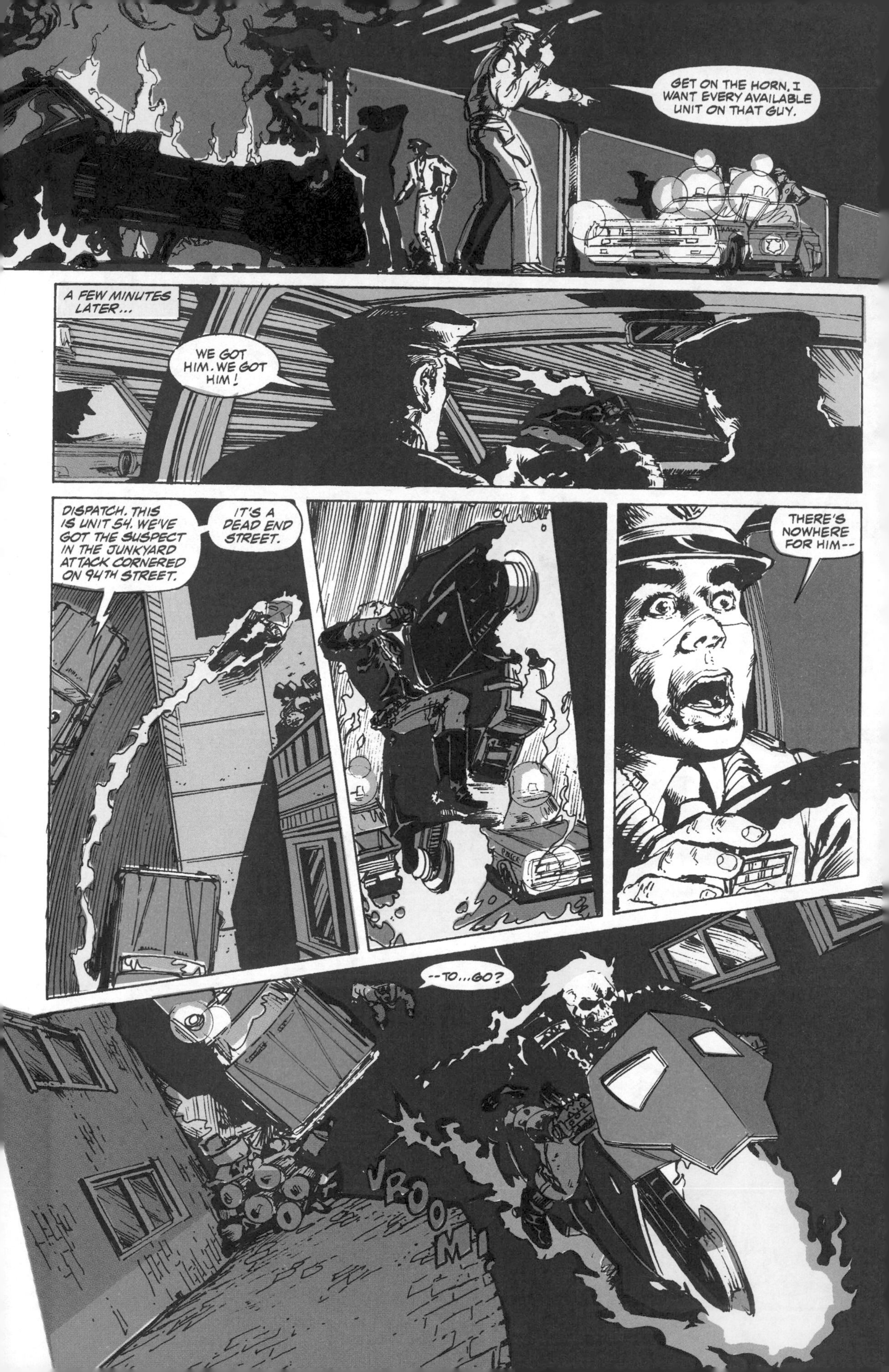
GET ON THE HORN. I WANT EVERY AVAILABLE UNIT ON THAT GUY.
A FEW MINUTES LATER...
WE GOT HIM. WE GOT HIM!
DISPATCH. THIS IS UNIT 54. WE'VE GOT THE SUSPECT IN THE JUNKYARD ATTACK CORNERED ON 94TH STREET.
IT'S A DEAD END STREET.
THERE'S NOWHERE FOR HIM--
--TO...GO?
VROOOM!

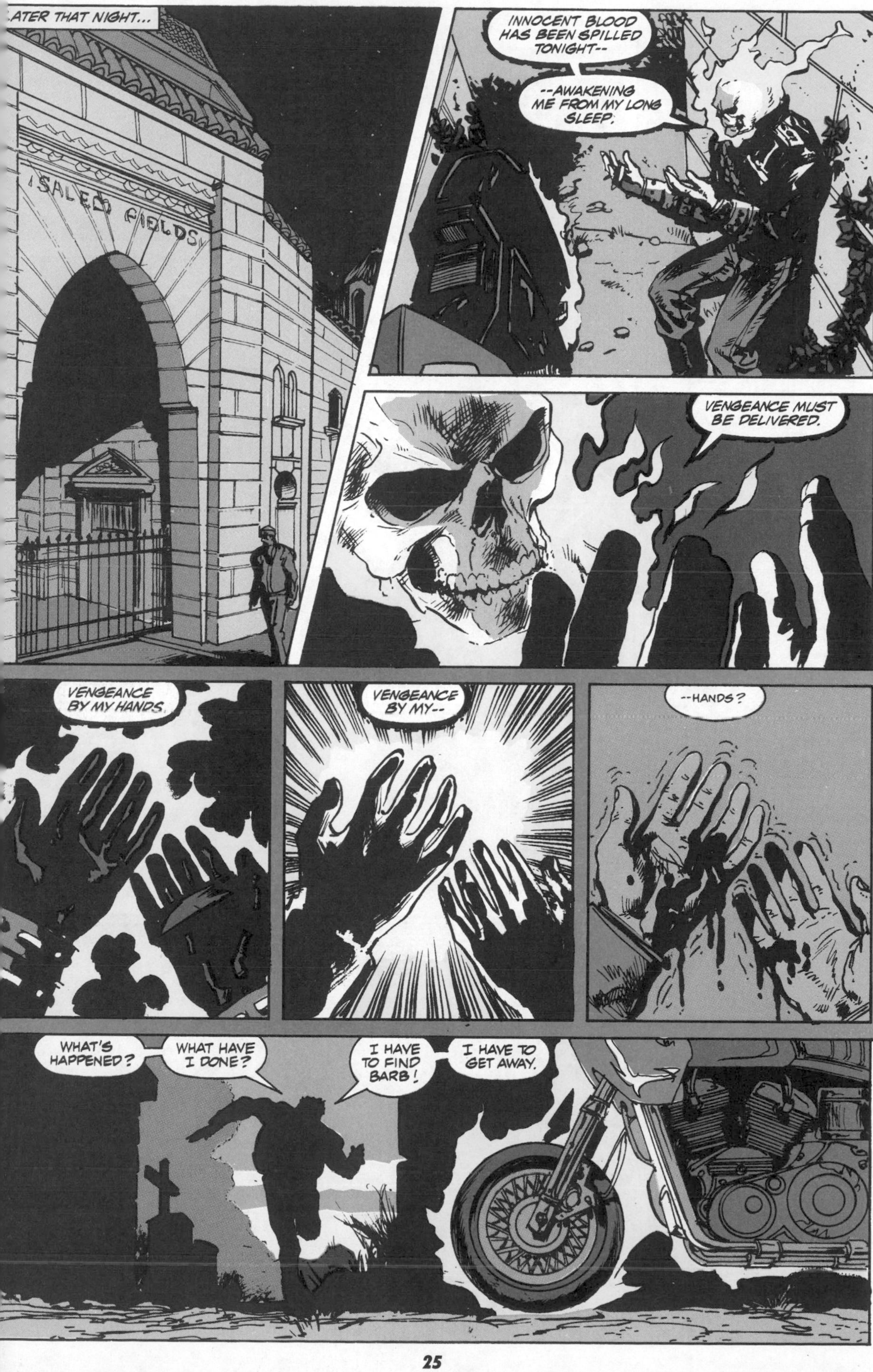
LATER THAT NIGHT...
SALEM FIELDS
INNOCENT BLOOD HAS BEEN SPILLED TONIGHT--
--AWAKENING ME FROM MY LONG SLEEP.
VENGEANCE MUST BE DELIVERED.
VENGEANCE BY MY HANDS.
VENGEANCE BY MY--
--HANDS?
WHAT'S HAPPENED?
WHAT HAVE I DONE?
I HAVE TO FIND BARB!
I HAVE TO GET AWAY.

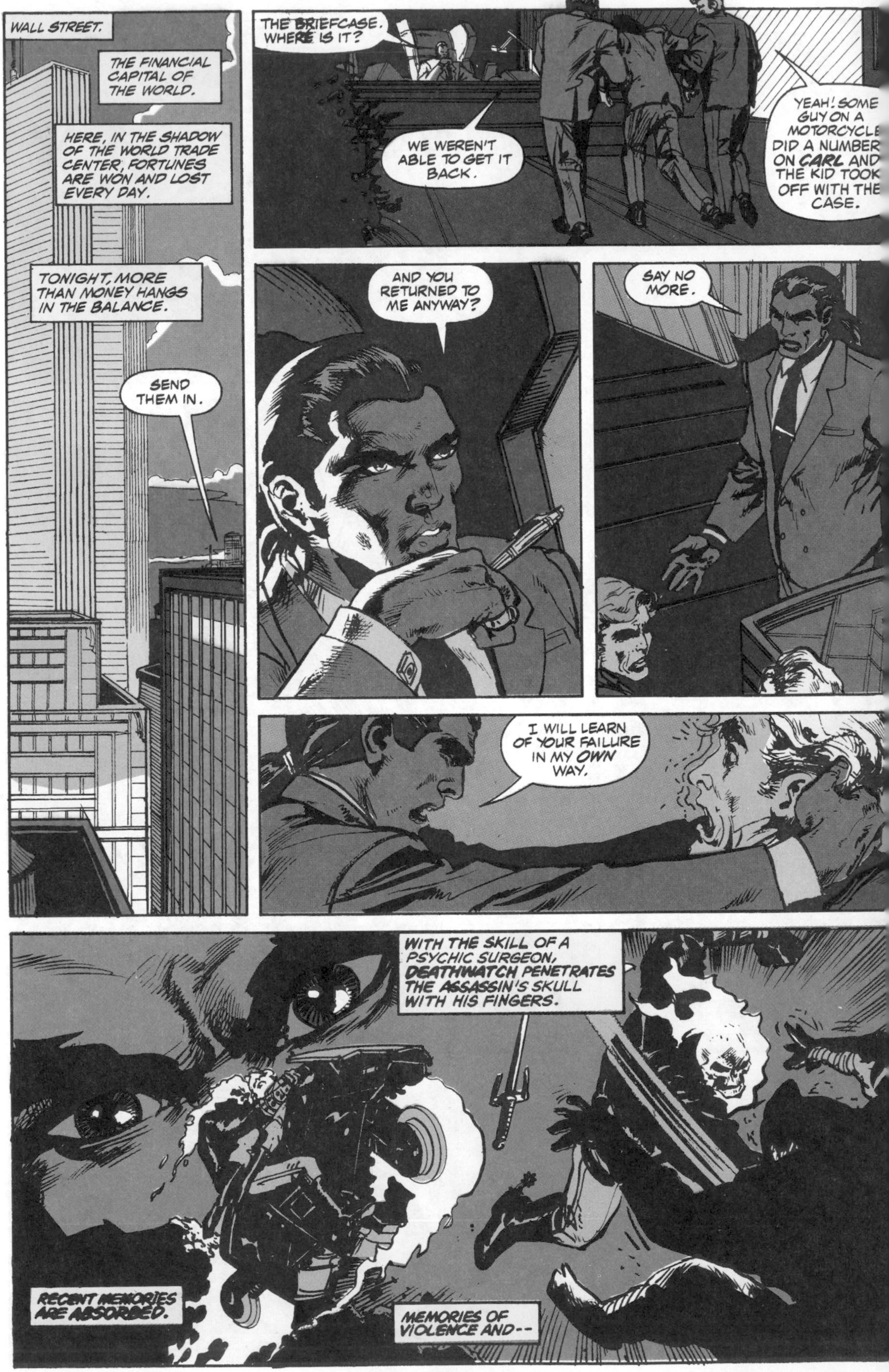
WALL STREET.
THE FINANCIAL CAPITAL OF THE WORLD.
HERE, IN THE SHADOW OF THE WORLD TRADE CENTER, FORTUNES ARE WON AND LOST EVERY DAY.
TONIGHT, MORE THAN MONEY HANGS IN THE BALANCE.
SEND THEM IN.
THE BRIEFCASE. WHERE IS IT?
WE WEREN'T ABLE TO GET IT BACK.
YEAH! SOME GUY ON A MOTORCYCLE DID A NUMBER ON CARL AND THE KID TOOK OFF WITH THE CASE.
AND YOU RETURNED TO ME ANYWAY?
SAY NO MORE.
I WILL LEARN OF YOUR FAILURE IN MY OWN WAY.
WITH THE SKILL OF A PSYCHIC SURGEON, DEATHWATCH PENETRATES THE ASSASSIN'S SKULL WITH HIS FINGERS.
RECENT MEMORIES ARE ABSORBED.
MEMORIES OF VIOLENCE AND--

--PAIN.

RR--ENOUGH! YOU HAVE FAILED ME--

--AND YOU KNOW THE PENALTY FOR FAILURE.

NO! I'M NOT PLAYING ANY MORE OF YOUR SICK GAMES.

I'LL KILL YOU FIRST!

BLAM

HUUCKK!

NICE OF YOU TO VOLUNTEER YOUR LIFE, SO THAT YOUR FRIENDS CAN CONTINUE LIVING.

THANK CARL, GENTLEMEN!

THANKS, CARL.

KRAK

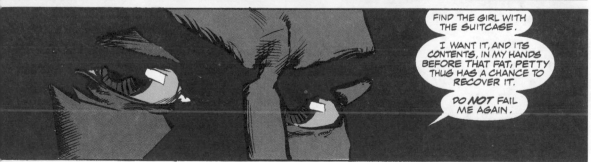

FIND THE GIRL WITH THE SUITCASE.

I WANT IT, AND ITS CONTENTS, IN MY HANDS BEFORE THAT FAT, PETTY THUG HAS A CHANCE TO RECOVER IT.

DO **NOT** FAIL ME AGAIN.

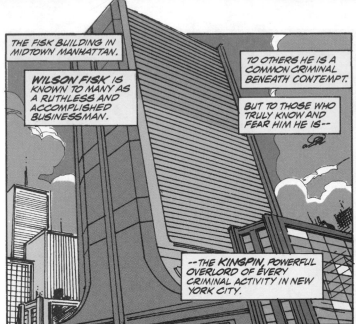

THE FISK BUILDING IN MIDTOWN MANHATTAN.

WILSON FISK IS KNOWN TO MANY AS A RUTHLESS AND ACCOMPLISHED BUSINESSMAN.

TO OTHERS HE IS A COMMON CRIMINAL BENEATH CONTEMPT.

BUT TO THOSE WHO TRULY KNOW AND FEAR HIM HE IS--

--THE KINGPIN, POWERFUL OVERLORD OF EVERY CRIMINAL ACTIVITY IN NEW YORK CITY.

THE KINGPIN'S POWER IS NOT ONLY FIGURATIVE.

WHAK WHAK

SWAK

SLAM

YOU CALL YOURSELVES MARTIAL ARTS MASTERS?

SWOOSH

FINISH ME.

28

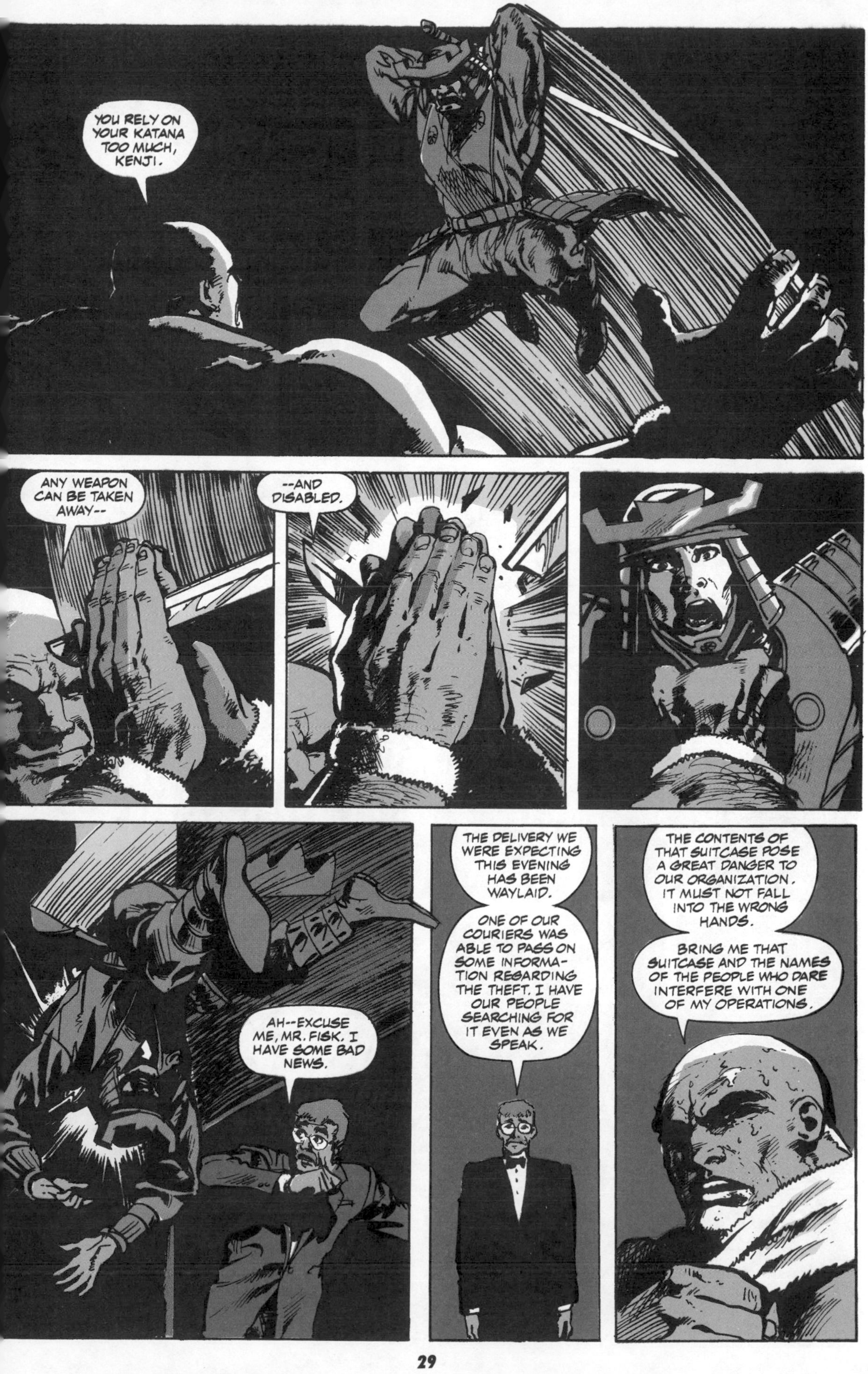
YOU RELY ON YOUR KATANA TOO MUCH, KENJI.
ANY WEAPON CAN BE TAKEN AWAY--
--AND DISABLED.
AH--EXCUSE ME, MR. FISK, I HAVE SOME BAD NEWS.
THE DELIVERY WE WERE EXPECTING THIS EVENING HAS BEEN WAYLAID.
ONE OF OUR COURIERS WAS ABLE TO PASS ON SOME INFORMATION REGARDING THE THEFT. I HAVE OUR PEOPLE SEARCHING FOR IT EVEN AS WE SPEAK.
THE CONTENTS OF THAT SUITCASE POSE A GREAT DANGER TO OUR ORGANIZATION. IT MUST NOT FALL INTO THE WRONG HANDS.
BRING ME THAT SUITCASE AND THE NAMES OF THE PEOPLE WHO DARE INTERFERE WITH ONE OF MY OPERATIONS.

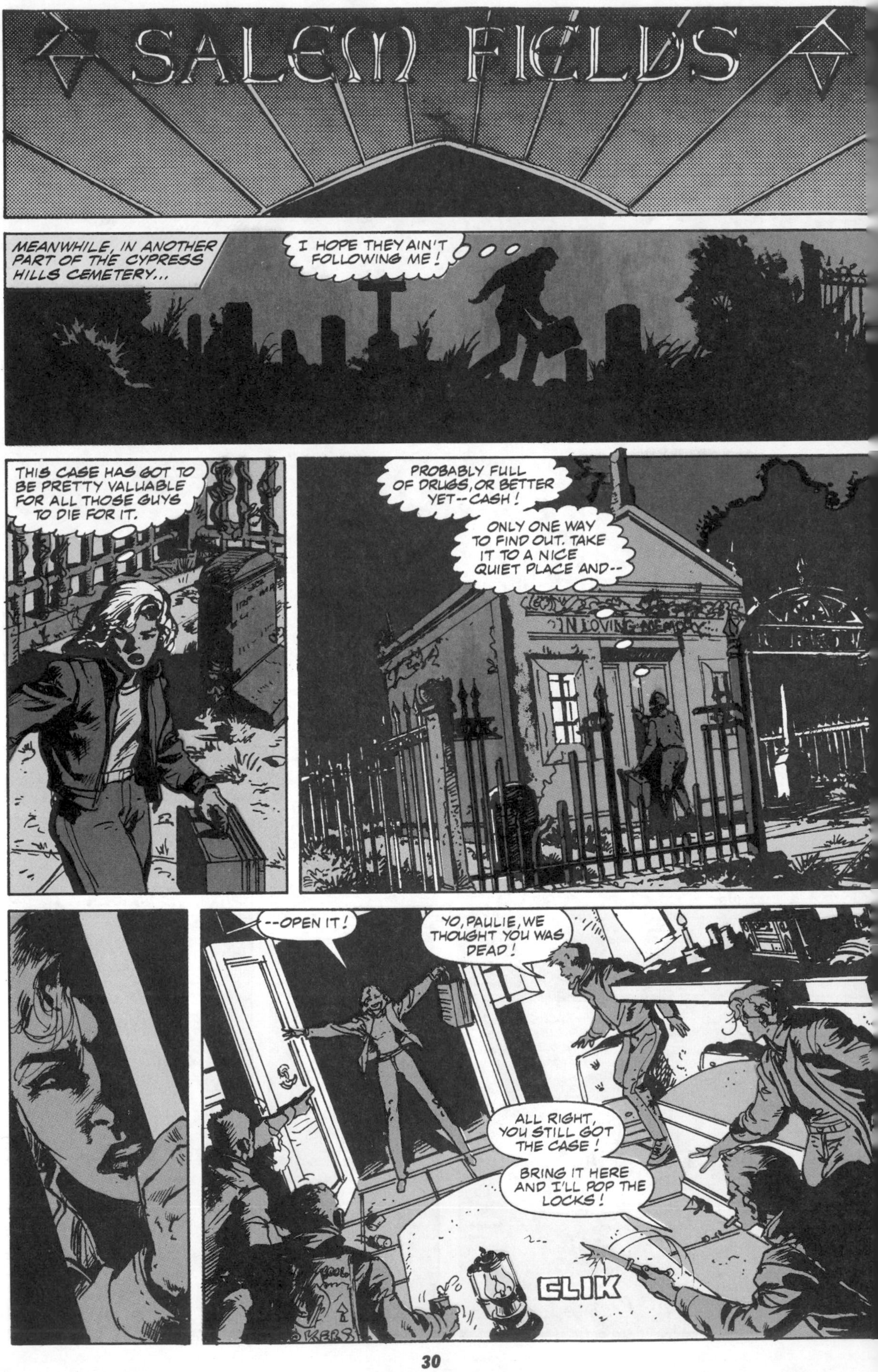
SALEM FIELDS
MEANWHILE, IN ANOTHER PART OF THE CYPRESS HILLS CEMETERY...
I HOPE THEY AIN'T FOLLOWING ME!
THIS CASE HAS GOT TO BE PRETTY VALUABLE FOR ALL THOSE GUYS TO DIE FOR IT.
PROBABLY FULL OF DRUGS, OR BETTER YET--CASH!
ONLY ONE WAY TO FIND OUT. TAKE IT TO A NICE QUIET PLACE AND--
IN LOVING MEMORY
--OPEN IT!
YO, PAULIE, WE THOUGHT YOU WAS DEAD!
ALL RIGHT, YOU STILL GOT THE CASE!
BRING IT HERE AND I'LL POP THE LOCKS!
CLIK

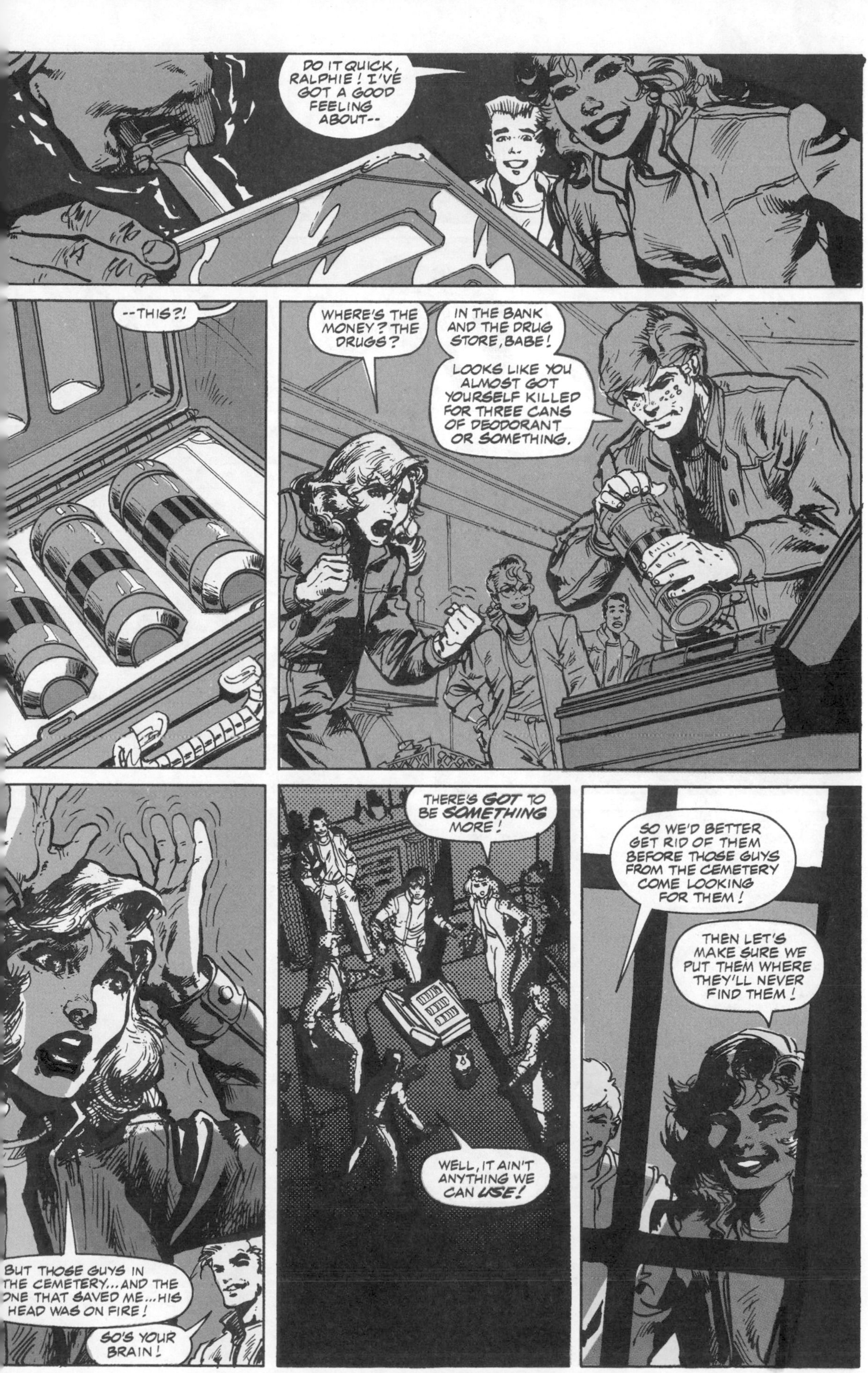
DO IT QUICK, RALPHIE! I'VE GOT A GOOD FEELING ABOUT--
--THIS?!
WHERE'S THE MONEY? THE DRUGS?
IN THE BANK AND THE DRUG STORE, BABE!
LOOKS LIKE YOU ALMOST GOT YOURSELF KILLED FOR THREE CANS OF DEODORANT OR SOMETHING.
BUT THOSE GUYS IN THE CEMETERY... AND THE ONE THAT SAVED ME... HIS HEAD WAS ON FIRE!
SO'S YOUR BRAIN!
THERE'S GOT TO BE SOMETHING MORE!
WELL, IT AIN'T ANYTHING WE CAN USE!
SO WE'D BETTER GET RID OF THEM BEFORE THOSE GUYS FROM THE CEMETERY COME LOOKING FOR THEM!
THEN LET'S MAKE SURE WE PUT THEM WHERE THEY'LL NEVER FIND THEM!

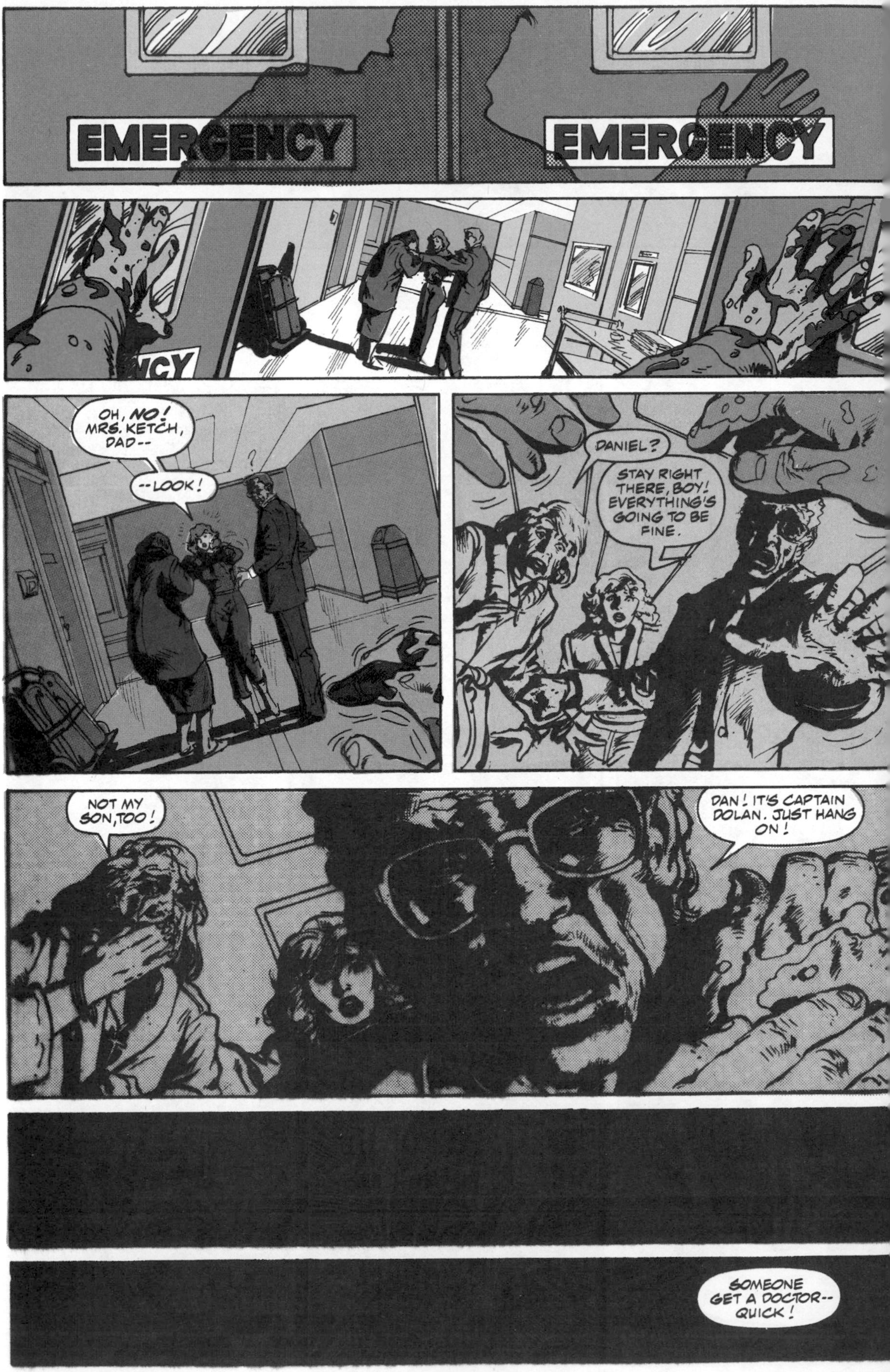
EMERGENCY
EMERGENCY
OH, NO! MRS. KETCH, DAD--
--LOOK!
DANIEL?
STAY RIGHT THERE, BOY! EVERYTHING'S GOING TO BE FINE.
NOT MY SON, TOO!
DAN! IT'S CAPTAIN DOLAN. JUST HANG ON!
SOMEONE GET A DOCTOR-- QUICK!

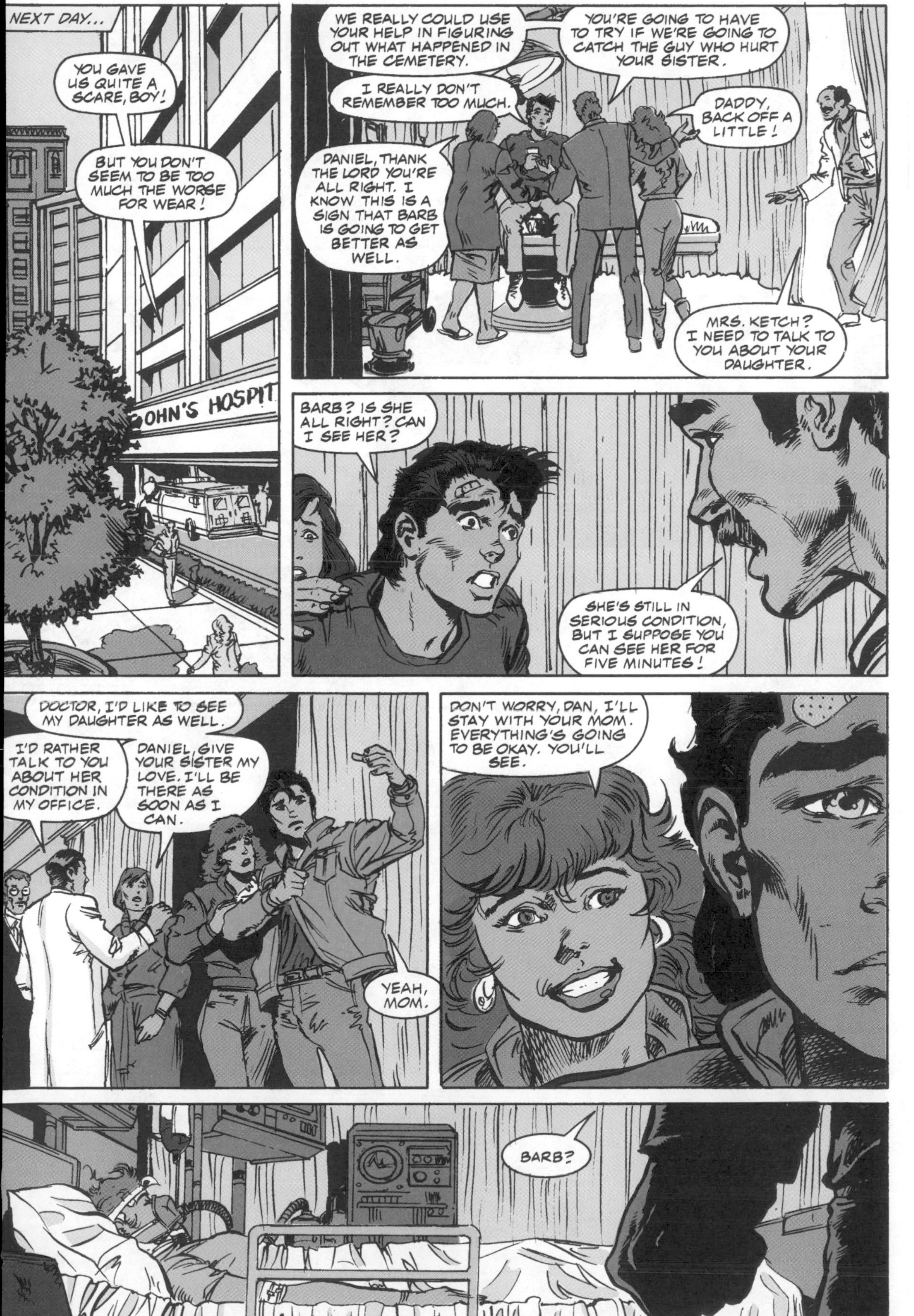
NEXT DAY...
YOU GAVE US QUITE A SCARE, BOY!
BUT YOU DON'T SEEM TO BE TOO MUCH THE WORSE FOR WEAR!
OHN'S HOSPIT
WE REALLY COULD USE YOUR HELP IN FIGURING OUT WHAT HAPPENED IN THE CEMETERY.
I REALLY DON'T REMEMBER TOO MUCH.
YOU'RE GOING TO HAVE TO TRY IF WE'RE GOING TO CATCH THE GUY WHO HURT YOUR SISTER.
DADDY, BACK OFF A LITTLE!
DANIEL, THANK THE LORD YOU'RE ALL RIGHT. I KNOW THIS IS A SIGN THAT BARB IS GOING TO GET BETTER AS WELL.
MRS. KETCH? I NEED TO TALK TO YOU ABOUT YOUR DAUGHTER.
BARB? IS SHE ALL RIGHT? CAN I SEE HER?
SHE'S STILL IN SERIOUS CONDITION, BUT I SUPPOSE YOU CAN SEE HER FOR FIVE MINUTES!
DOCTOR, I'D LIKE TO SEE MY DAUGHTER AS WELL.
I'D RATHER TALK TO YOU ABOUT HER CONDITION IN MY OFFICE.
DANIEL, GIVE YOUR SISTER MY LOVE. I'LL BE THERE AS SOON AS I CAN.
YEAH, MOM.
DON'T WORRY, DAN, I'LL STAY WITH YOUR MOM. EVERYTHING'S GOING TO BE OKAY. YOU'LL SEE.
BARB?

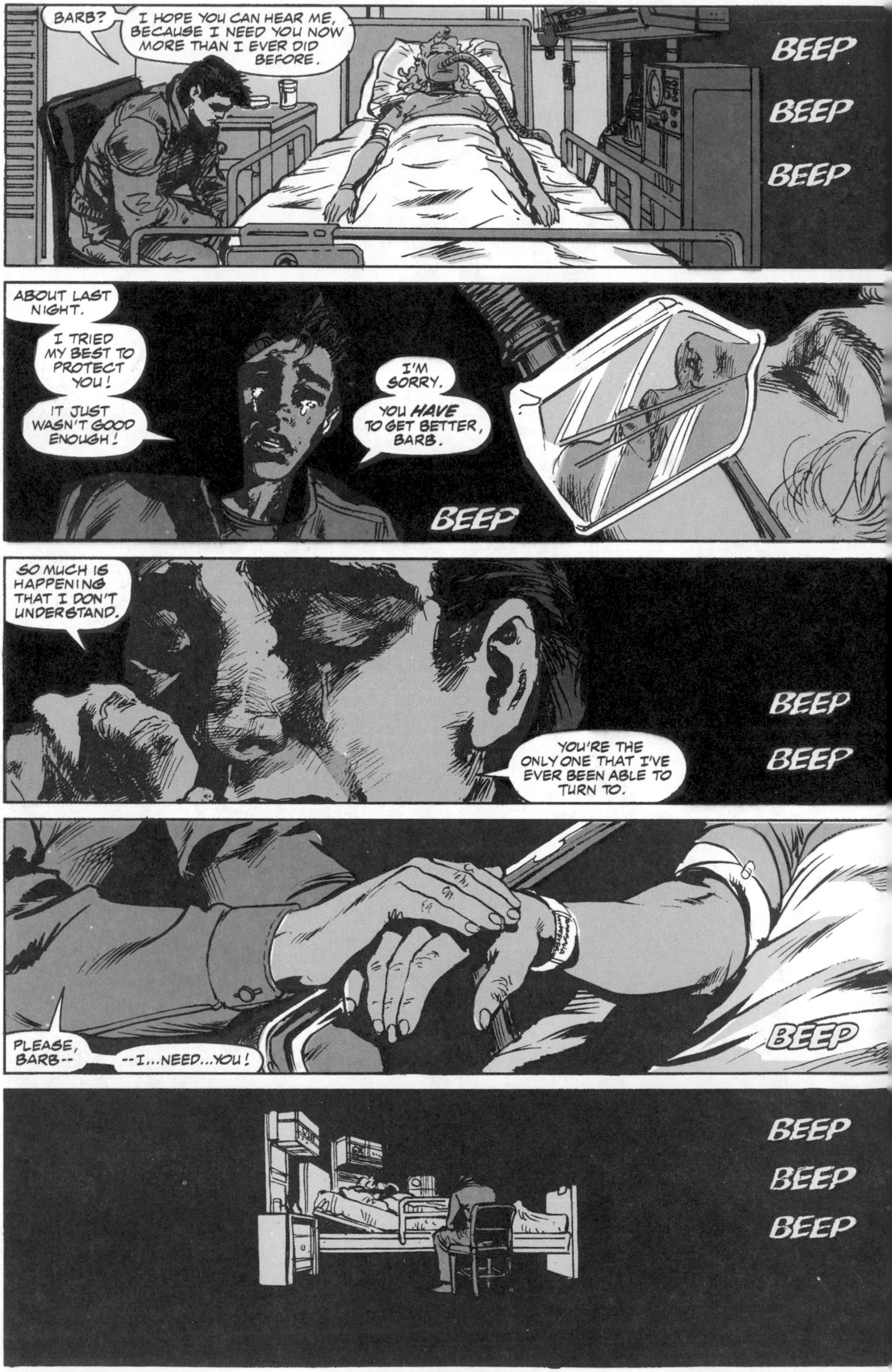
BARB?
I HOPE YOU CAN HEAR ME, BECAUSE I NEED YOU NOW MORE THAN I EVER DID BEFORE.
BEEP
BEEP
BEEP
ABOUT LAST NIGHT.
I TRIED MY BEST TO PROTECT YOU!
IT JUST WASN'T GOOD ENOUGH!
I'M SORRY.
YOU HAVE TO GET BETTER, BARB.
BEEP
SO MUCH IS HAPPENING THAT I DON'T UNDERSTAND.
BEEP
BEEP
YOU'RE THE ONLY ONE THAT I'VE EVER BEEN ABLE TO TURN TO.
PLEASE, BARB--
--I...NEED...YOU!
BEEP
BEEP
BEEP
BEEP

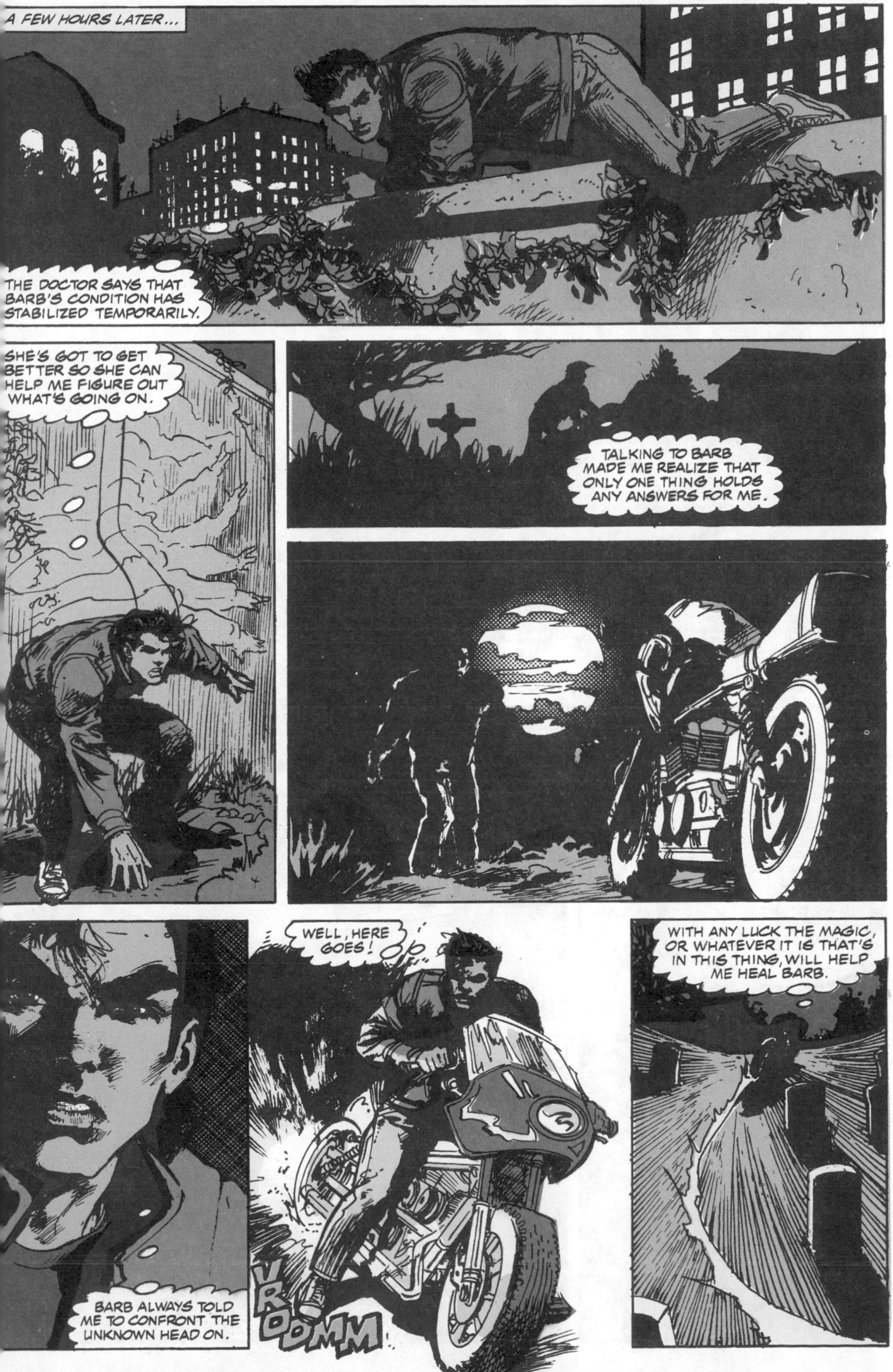
A FEW HOURS LATER...
THE DOCTOR SAYS THAT BARB'S CONDITION HAS STABILIZED TEMPORARILY.
SHE'S GOT TO GET BETTER SO SHE CAN HELP ME FIGURE OUT WHAT'S GOING ON.
TALKING TO BARB MADE ME REALIZE THAT ONLY ONE THING HOLDS ANY ANSWERS FOR ME.
BARB ALWAYS TOLD ME TO CONFRONT THE UNKNOWN HEAD ON.
WELL, HERE GOES!
VROOMM
WITH ANY LUCK THE MAGIC, OR WHATEVER IT IS THAT'S IN THIS THING, WILL HELP ME HEAL BARB.

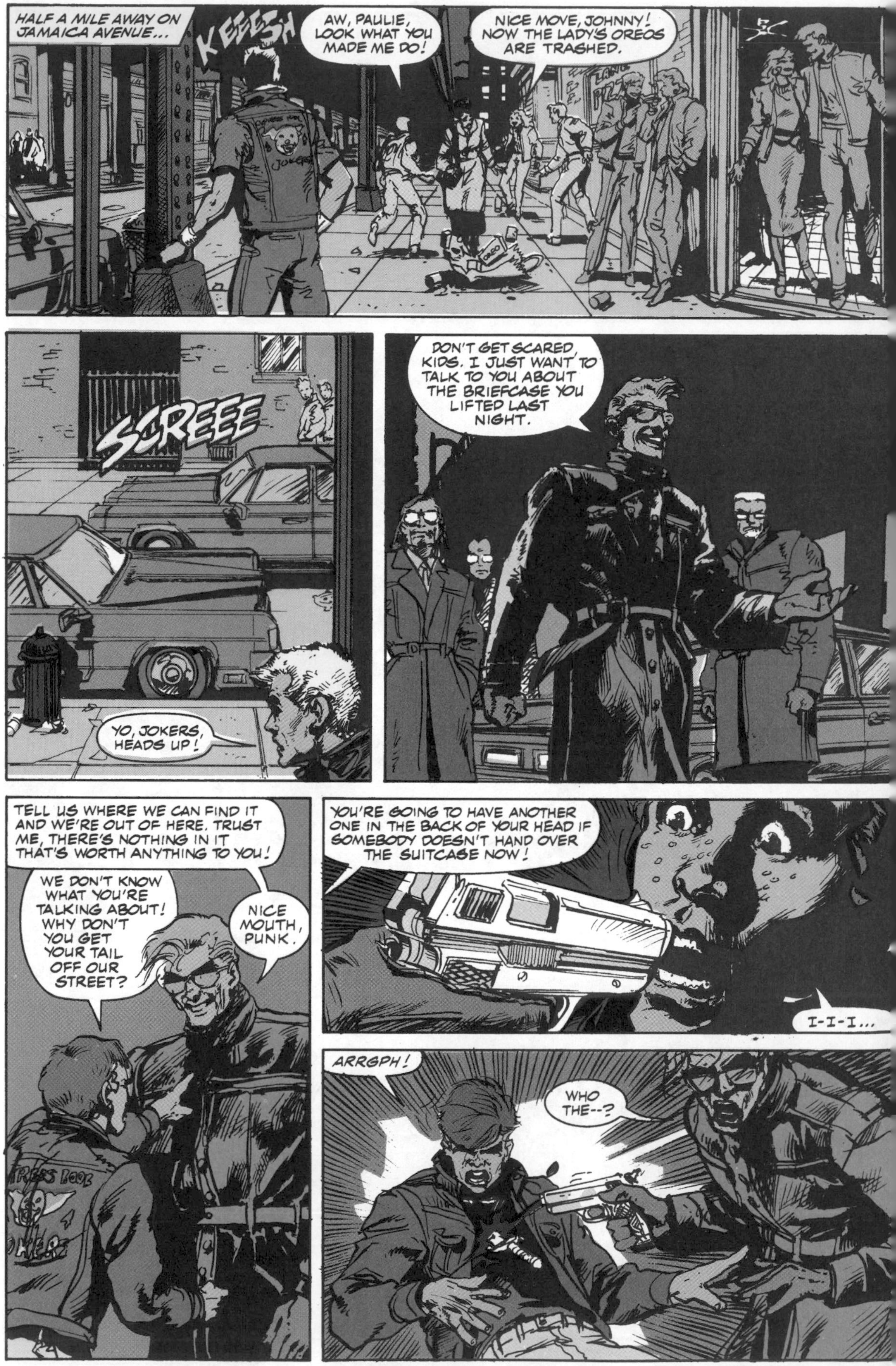
HALF A MILE AWAY ON JAMAICA AVENUE...
KEEESH
AW, PAULIE, LOOK WHAT YOU MADE ME DO!
NICE MOVE, JOHNNY! NOW THE LADY'S OREOS ARE TRASHED.
SCREEE
DON'T GET SCARED, KIDS. I JUST WANT TO TALK TO YOU ABOUT THE BRIEFCASE YOU LIFTED LAST NIGHT.
YO, JOKERS, HEADS UP!
TELL US WHERE WE CAN FIND IT AND WE'RE OUT OF HERE. TRUST ME, THERE'S NOTHING IN IT THAT'S WORTH ANYTHING TO YOU!
WE DON'T KNOW WHAT YOU'RE TALKING ABOUT! WHY DON'T YOU GET YOUR TAIL OFF OUR STREET?
NICE MOUTH, PUNK.
YOU'RE GOING TO HAVE ANOTHER ONE IN THE BACK OF YOUR HEAD IF SOMEBODY DOESN'T HAND OVER THE SUITCASE NOW!
I-I-I...
ARRGPH!
WHO THE--?

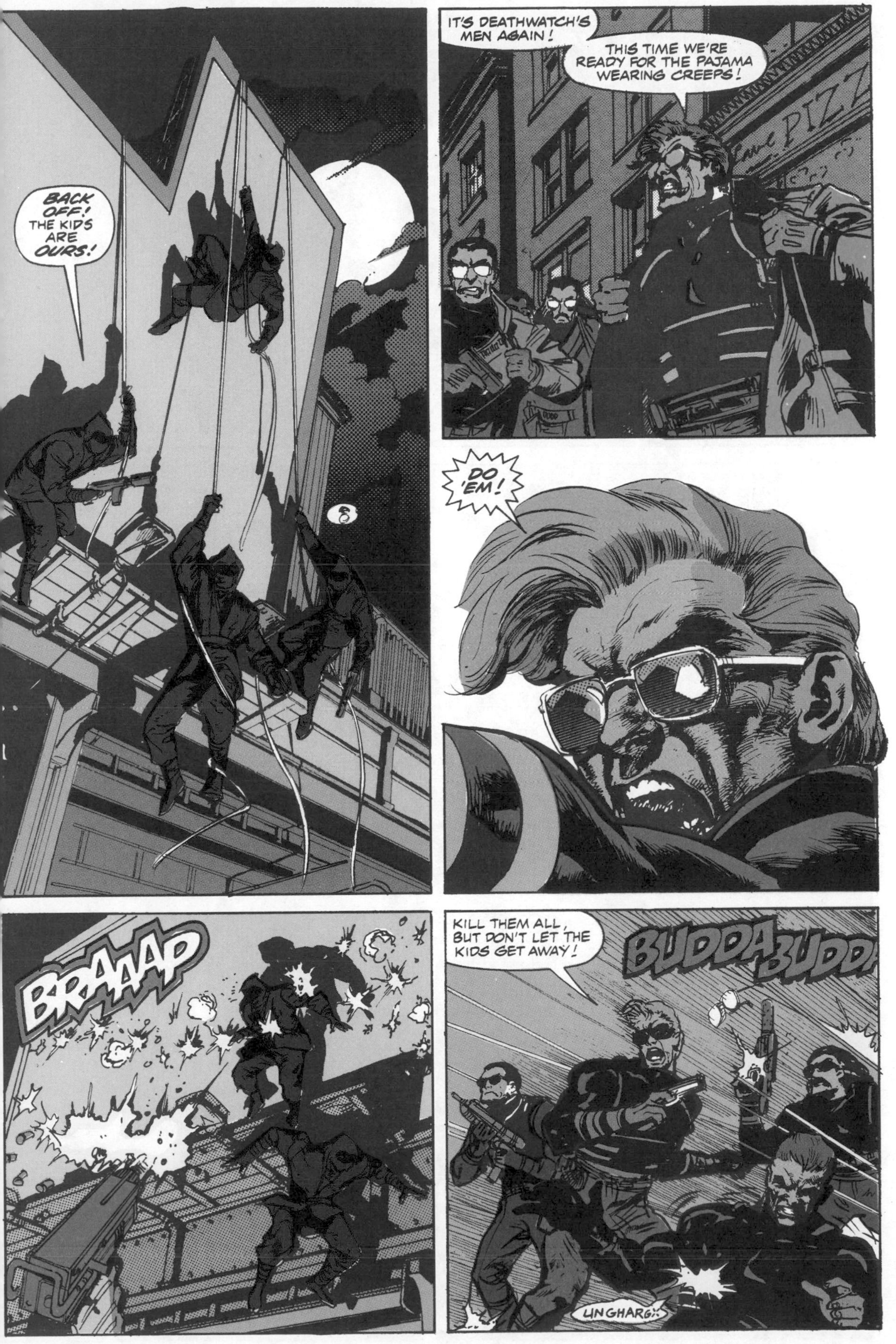

BACK OFF! THE KIDS ARE OURS!
IT'S DEATHWATCH'S MEN AGAIN!
THIS TIME WE'RE READY FOR THE PAJAMA WEARING CREEPS!
DO 'EM!
BRAAAP
KILL THEM ALL, BUT DON'T LET THE KIDS GET AWAY!
BUDDA BUDDA
UNGHARG!

BUDDA BUDDA
BRAAAP
PTING
PAULIE, GET DOWN!
NO! WE'VE GOT TO GET AWAY! COME ON, RALPHIE, GET UP! WE'VE GOTTA RUN!
PTING
THERE DOESN'T SEEM TO BE ANYTHING WEIRD ABOUT THIS BIKE!
I WONDER IF I IMAGINED THE WHOLE THING AFTER BARB GOT HURT?
AIEEEEE!
BUDDA
BRAAAP
SOMETHING'S GOING ON DOWN NEAR THE EL!
BUDDA BUDDA
BRAAAP
NO... NOT AGAIN!

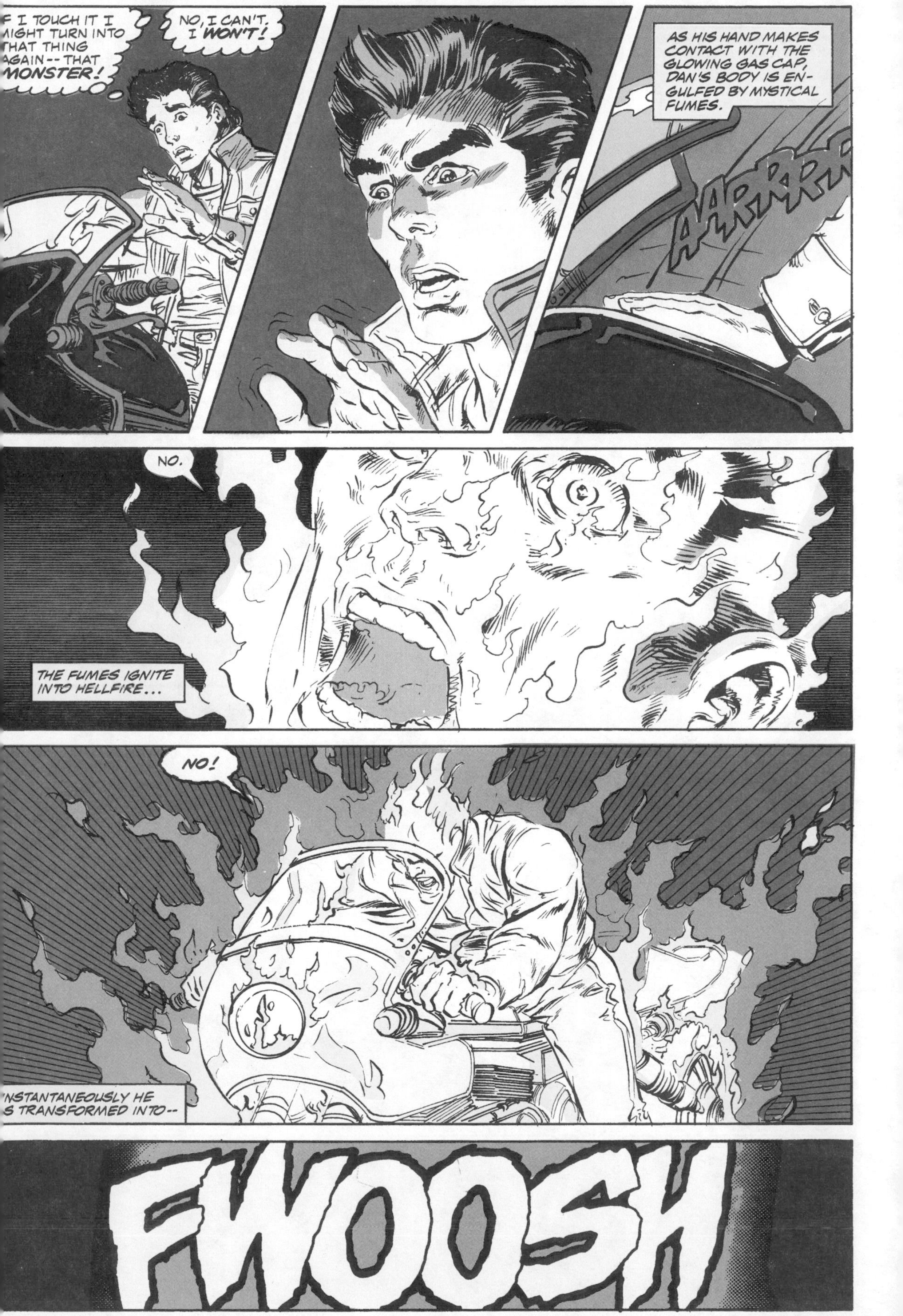
F I TOUCH IT I MIGHT TURN INTO THAT THING AGAIN -- THAT MONSTER!
NO, I CAN'T. I WON'T!
AS HIS HAND MAKES CONTACT WITH THE GLOWING GAS CAP, DAN'S BODY IS EN-GULFED BY MYSTICAL FUMES.
AARRRR
NO.
THE FUMES IGNITE INTO HELLFIRE...
NO!
NSTANTANEOUSLY HE S TRANSFORMED INTO--
FWOOSH

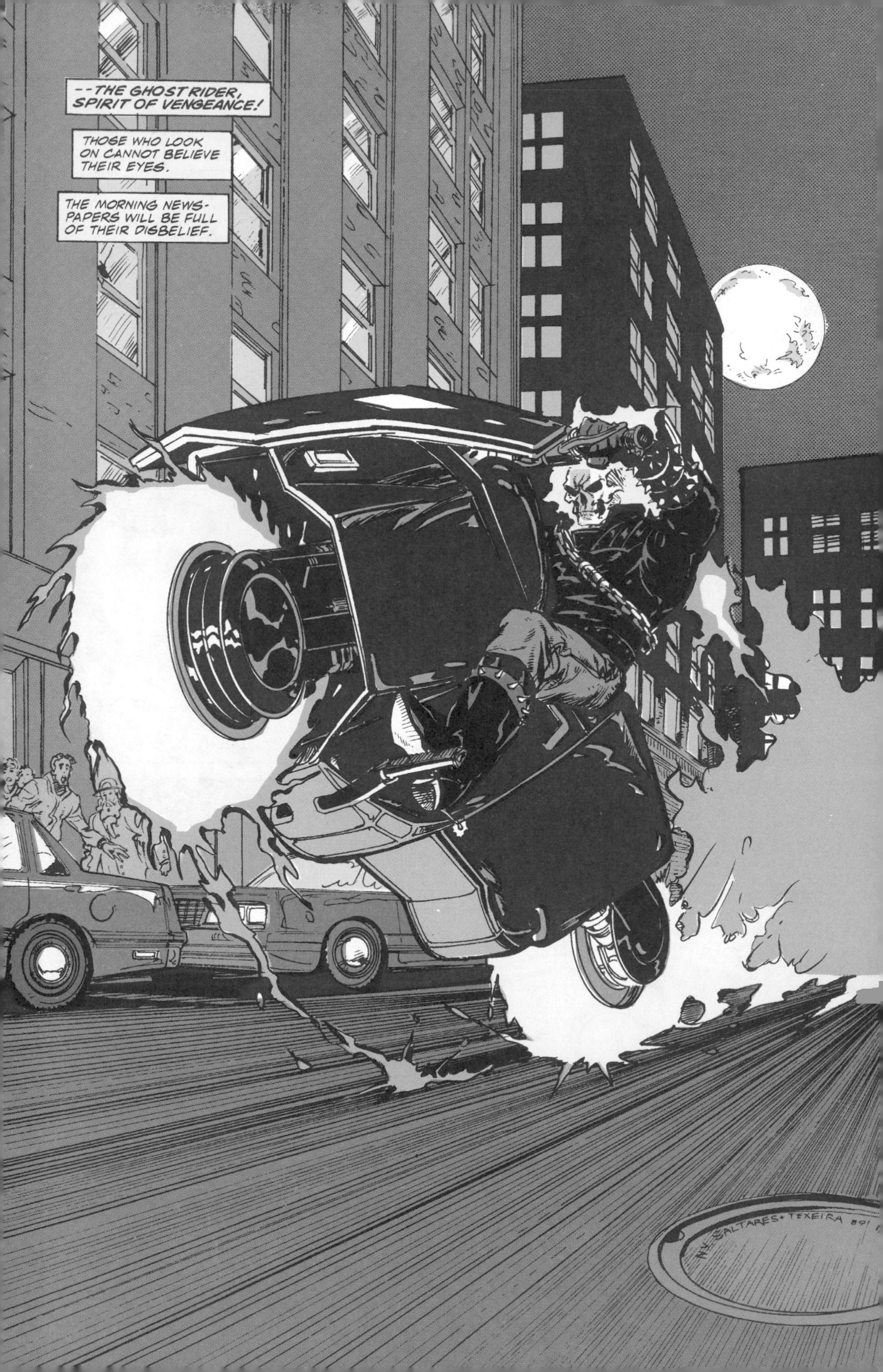
--THE GHOST RIDER, SPIRIT OF VENGEANCE!
THOSE WHO LOOK ON CANNOT BELIEVE THEIR EYES.
THE MORNING NEWS-PAPERS WILL BE FULL OF THEIR DISBELIEF.
NY SALTARES• TEXEIRA

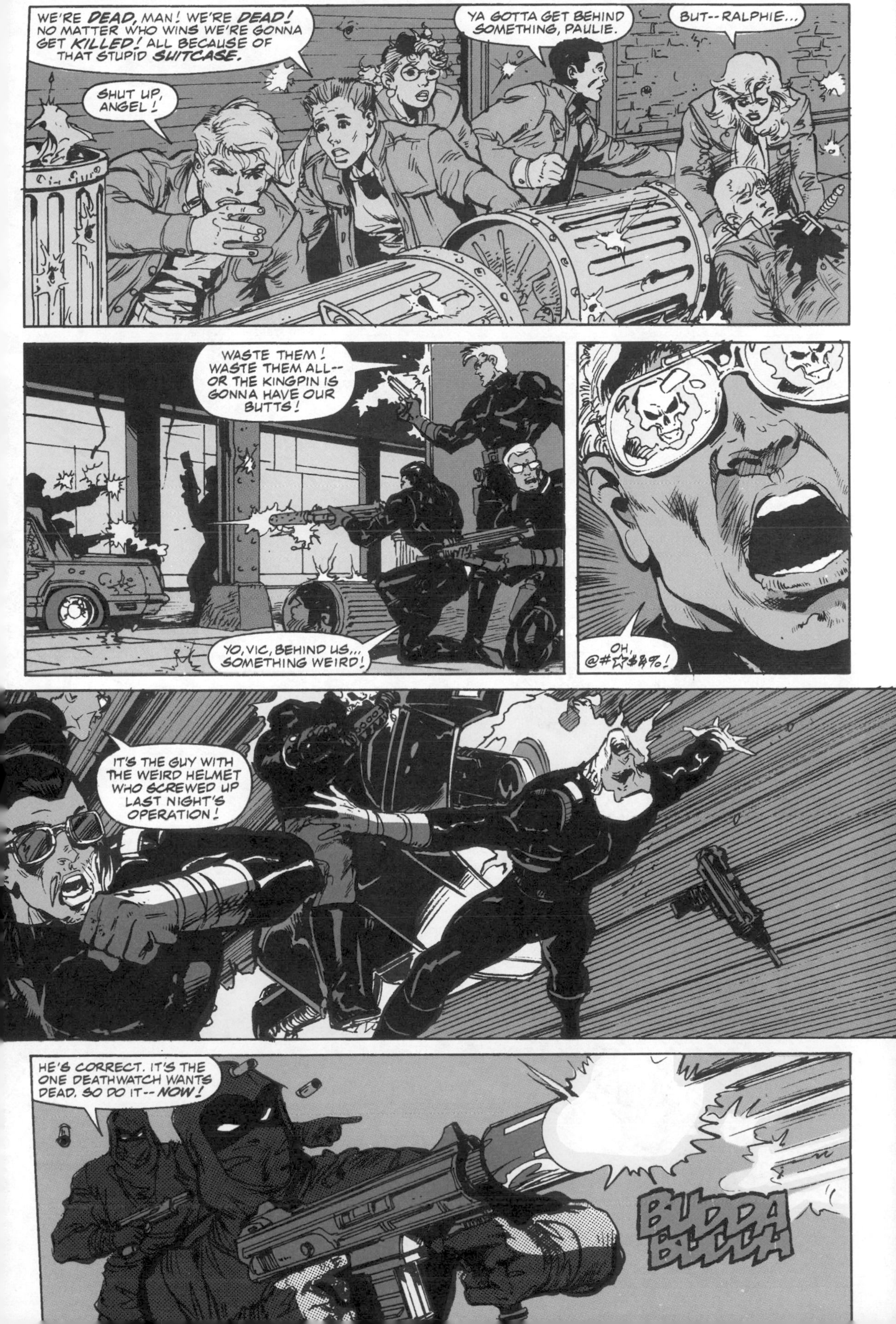
WE'RE DEAD, MAN! WE'RE DEAD! NO MATTER WHO WINS WE'RE GONNA GET KILLED! ALL BECAUSE OF THAT STUPID SUITCASE.
SHUT UP, ANGEL!
YA GOTTA GET BEHIND SOMETHING, PAULIE.
BUT--RALPHIE...
WASTE THEM! WASTE THEM ALL-- OR THE KINGPIN IS GONNA HAVE OUR BUTTS!
YO, VIC, BEHIND US... SOMETHING WEIRD!
OH, @#☆$&%!
IT'S THE GUY WITH THE WEIRD HELMET WHO SCREWED UP LAST NIGHT'S OPERATION!
HE'S CORRECT. IT'S THE ONE DEATHWATCH WANTS DEAD. SO DO IT--NOW!
BUDDA BUDDA

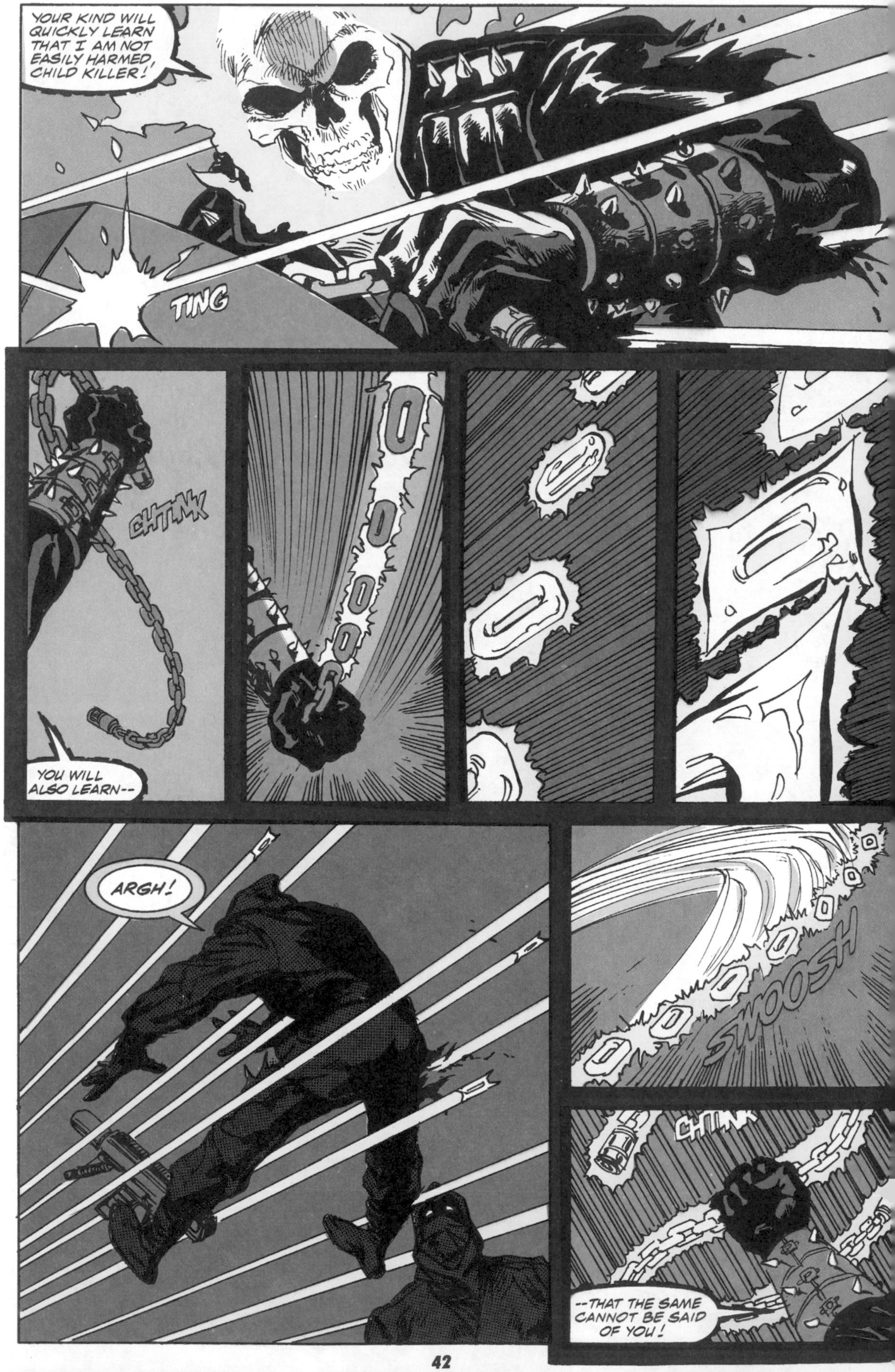
YOUR KIND WILL QUICKLY LEARN THAT I AM NOT EASILY HARMED, CHILD KILLER!
TING
CHTINK
YOU WILL ALSO LEARN--
ARGH!
SWOOSH
CHTINK
--THAT THE SAME CANNOT BE SAID OF YOU!

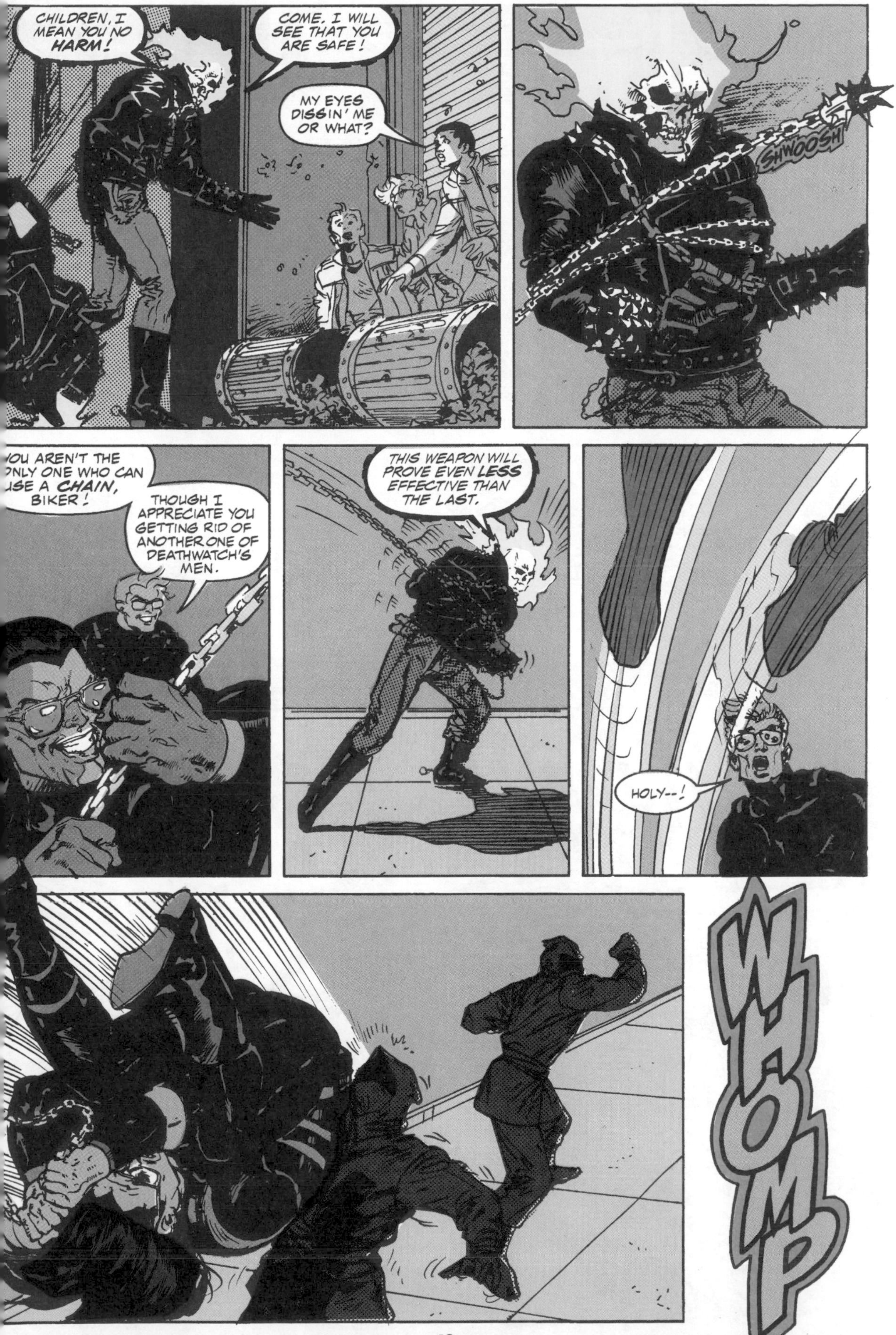
CHILDREN, I MEAN YOU NO HARM!
COME. I WILL SEE THAT YOU ARE SAFE!
MY EYES DISSIN' ME OR WHAT?
SHWOOSH
YOU AREN'T THE ONLY ONE WHO CAN USE A CHAIN, BIKER!
THOUGH I APPRECIATE YOU GETTING RID OF ANOTHER ONE OF DEATHWATCH'S MEN.
THIS WEAPON WILL PROVE EVEN LESS EFFECTIVE THAN THE LAST.
HOLY--!
WHOMP

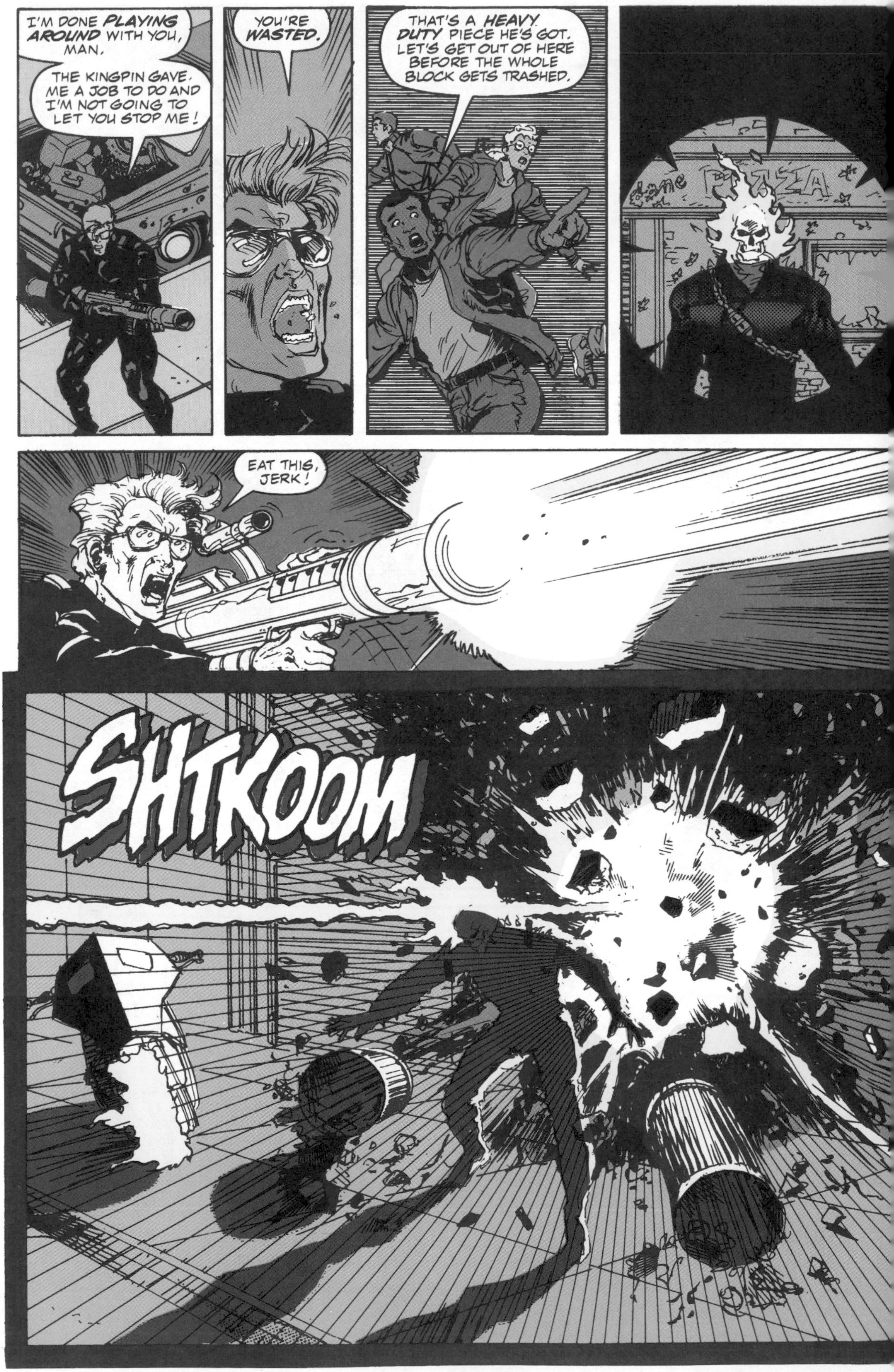
I'M DONE PLAYING AROUND WITH YOU, MAN.
THE KINGPIN GAVE ME A JOB TO DO AND I'M NOT GOING TO LET YOU STOP ME!
YOU'RE WASTED.
THAT'S A HEAVY DUTY PIECE HE'S GOT. LET'S GET OUT OF HERE BEFORE THE WHOLE BLOCK GETS TRASHED.
PIZZA
EAT THIS, JERK!
SHTKOOM

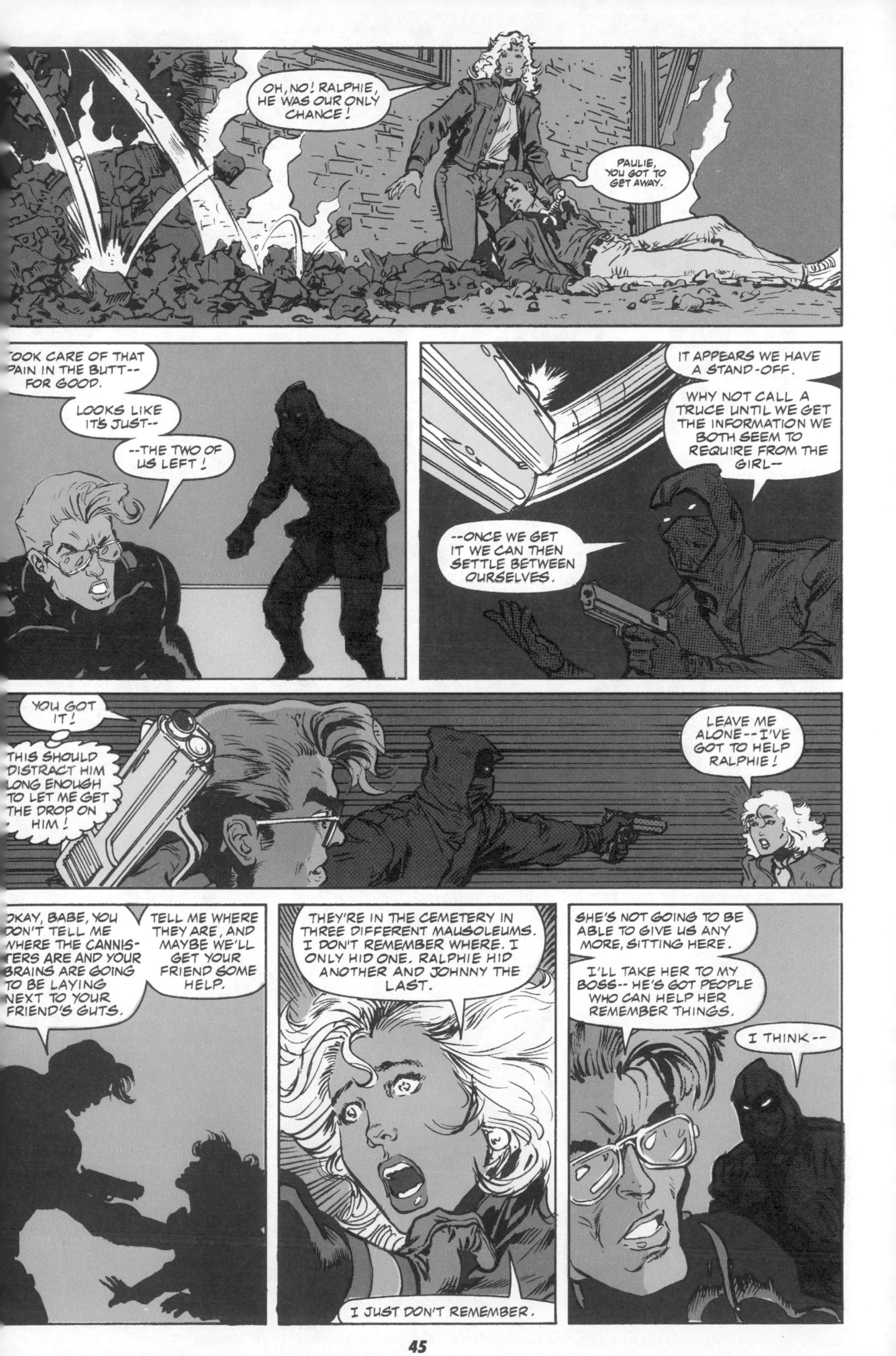

OH, NO! RALPHIE, HE WAS OUR ONLY CHANCE!
PAULIE, YOU GOT TO GET AWAY.
TOOK CARE OF THAT PAIN IN THE BUTT-- FOR GOOD.
LOOKS LIKE IT'S JUST--
--THE TWO OF US LEFT!
IT APPEARS WE HAVE A STAND-OFF.
WHY NOT CALL A TRUCE UNTIL WE GET THE INFORMATION WE BOTH SEEM TO REQUIRE FROM THE GIRL--
--ONCE WE GET IT WE CAN THEN SETTLE BETWEEN OURSELVES.
YOU GOT IT!
THIS SHOULD DISTRACT HIM LONG ENOUGH TO LET ME GET THE DROP ON HIM!
LEAVE ME ALONE--I'VE GOT TO HELP RALPHIE!
OKAY, BABE, YOU DON'T TELL ME WHERE THE CANNISTERS ARE AND YOUR BRAINS ARE GOING TO BE LAYING NEXT TO YOUR FRIEND'S GUTS.
TELL ME WHERE THEY ARE, AND MAYBE WE'LL GET YOUR FRIEND SOME HELP.
THEY'RE IN THE CEMETERY IN THREE DIFFERENT MAUSOLEUMS. I DON'T REMEMBER WHERE. I ONLY HID ONE. RALPHIE HID ANOTHER AND JOHNNY THE LAST.
I JUST DON'T REMEMBER.
SHE'S NOT GOING TO BE ABLE TO GIVE US ANY MORE, SITTING HERE.
I'LL TAKE HER TO MY BOSS-- HE'S GOT PEOPLE WHO CAN HELP HER REMEMBER THINGS.
I THINK--

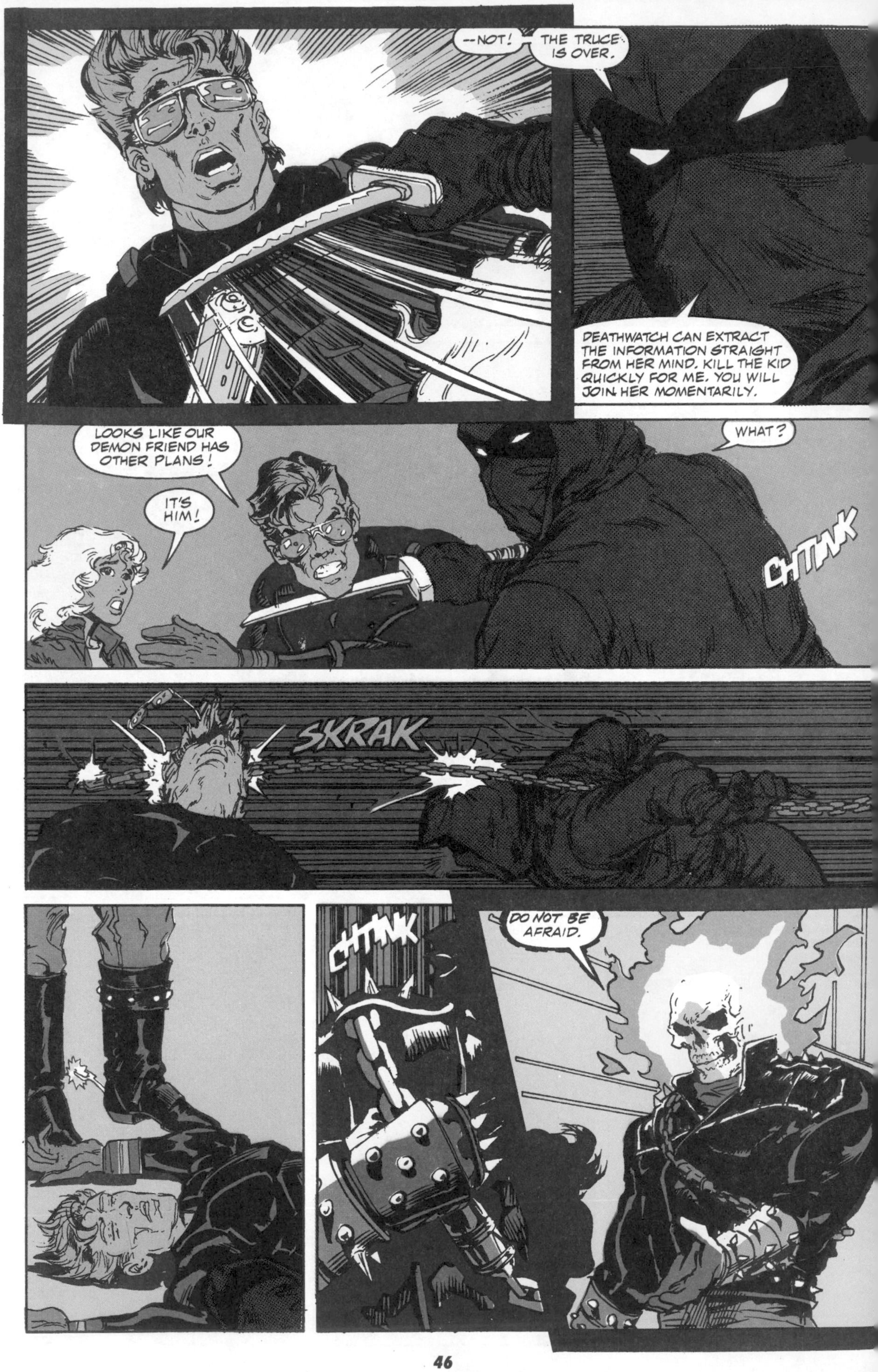
--NOT!
THE TRUCE IS OVER.
DEATHWATCH CAN EXTRACT THE INFORMATION STRAIGHT FROM HER MIND. KILL THE KID QUICKLY FOR ME. YOU WILL JOIN HER MOMENTARILY.
LOOKS LIKE OUR DEMON FRIEND HAS OTHER PLANS!
IT'S HIM!
WHAT?
CHTINK
SKRAK
CHTINK
DO NOT BE AFRAID.

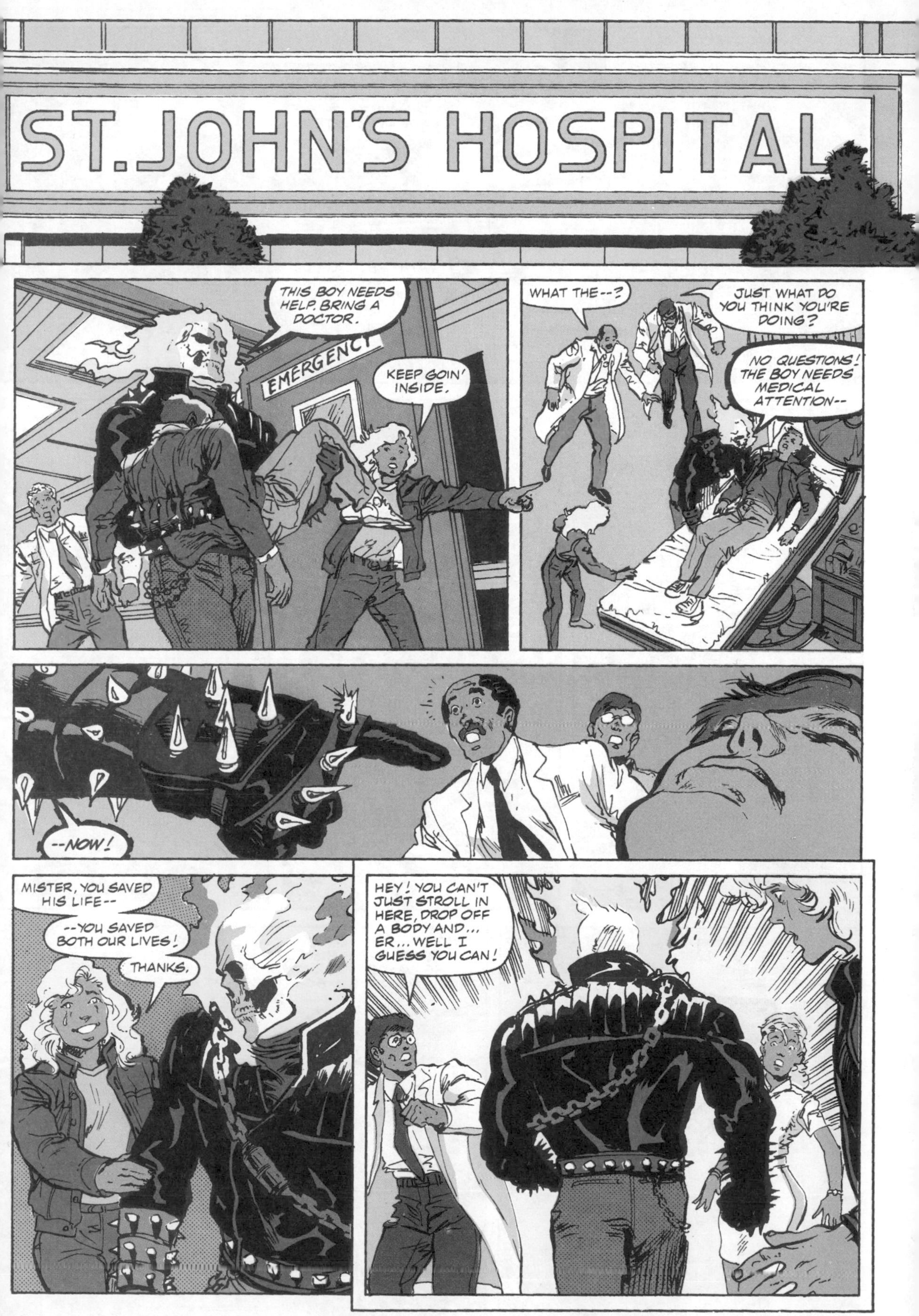
ST. JOHN'S HOSPITAL
THIS BOY NEEDS HELP. BRING A DOCTOR.
EMERGENCY
KEEP GOIN' INSIDE.
WHAT THE--?
JUST WHAT DO YOU THINK YOU'RE DOING?
NO QUESTIONS! THE BOY NEEDS MEDICAL ATTENTION--
--NOW!
MISTER, YOU SAVED HIS LIFE--
--YOU SAVED BOTH OUR LIVES!
THANKS.
HEY! YOU CAN'T JUST STROLL IN HERE, DROP OFF A BODY AND... ER... WELL I GUESS YOU CAN!

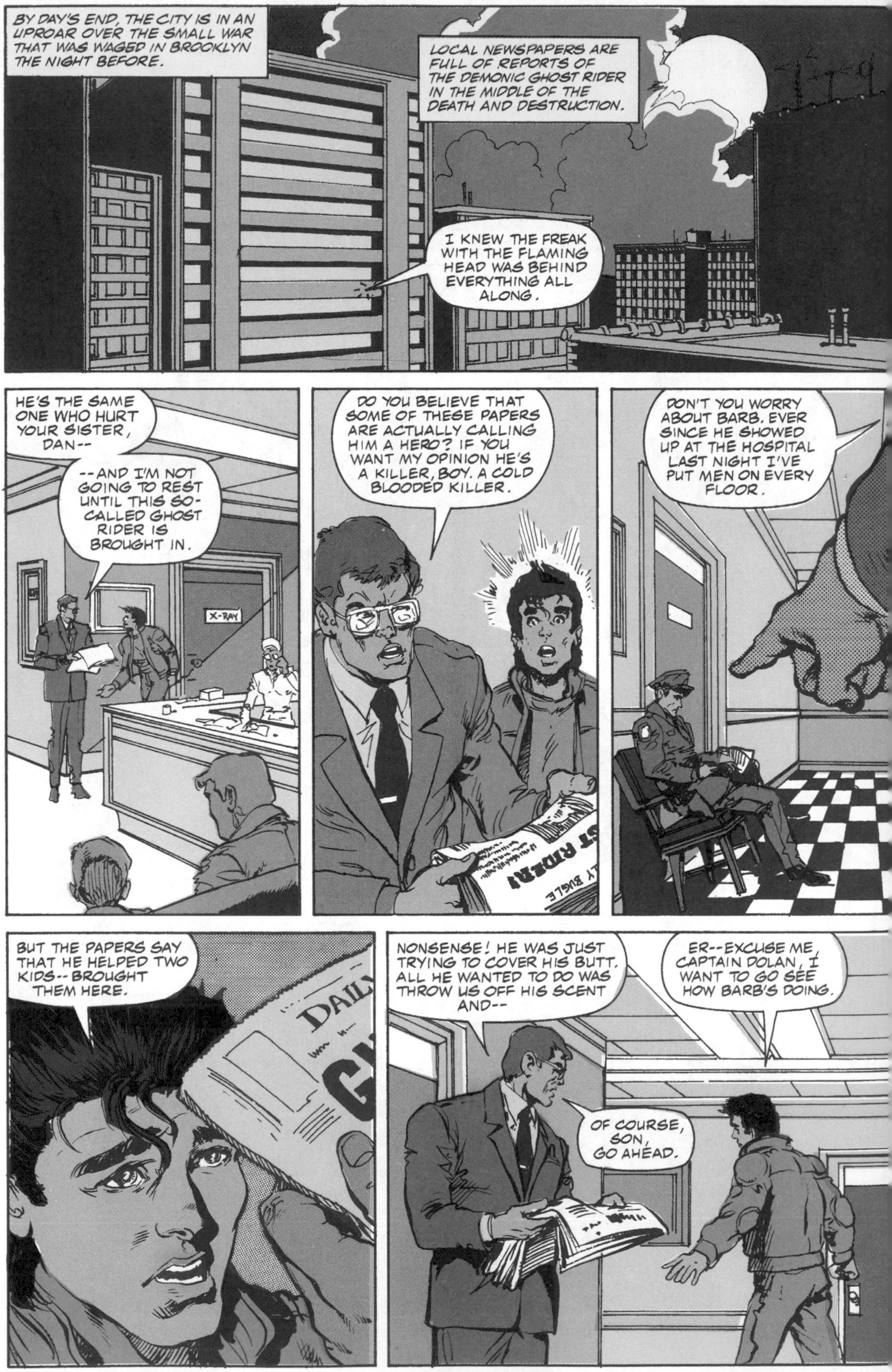
BY DAY'S END, THE CITY IS IN AN UPROAR OVER THE SMALL WAR THAT WAS WAGED IN BROOKLYN THE NIGHT BEFORE.
LOCAL NEWSPAPERS ARE FULL OF REPORTS OF THE DEMONIC GHOST RIDER IN THE MIDDLE OF THE DEATH AND DESTRUCTION.
I KNEW THE FREAK WITH THE FLAMING HEAD WAS BEHIND EVERYTHING ALL ALONG.
HE'S THE SAME ONE WHO HURT YOUR SISTER, DAN--
--AND I'M NOT GOING TO REST UNTIL THIS SO-CALLED GHOST RIDER IS BROUGHT IN.
X-RAY
DO YOU BELIEVE THAT SOME OF THESE PAPERS ARE ACTUALLY CALLING HIM A HERO? IF YOU WANT MY OPINION HE'S A KILLER, BOY. A COLD BLOODED KILLER.
ST RIDER!
DON'T YOU WORRY ABOUT BARB. EVER SINCE HE SHOWED UP AT THE HOSPITAL LAST NIGHT I'VE PUT MEN ON EVERY FLOOR.
BUT THE PAPERS SAY THAT HE HELPED TWO KIDS--BROUGHT THEM HERE.
NONSENSE! HE WAS JUST TRYING TO COVER HIS BUTT. ALL HE WANTED TO DO WAS THROW US OFF HIS SCENT AND--
ER--EXCUSE ME, CAPTAIN DOLAN, I WANT TO GO SEE HOW BARB'S DOING.
OF COURSE, SON, GO AHEAD.

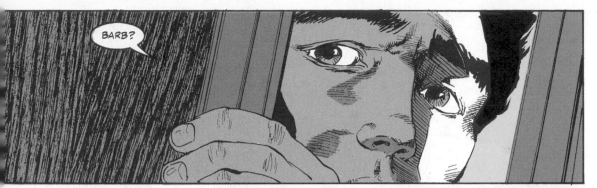

BARB?

NEED YOUR ELP AGAIN. I'M O CONFUSED.

HEN I RIDE THAT MOTORCYCLE T FEELS LIKE I'M TRANSFORMED NTO SOME SORT OF A MONSTER.

I CAN'T BELIEVE THE THINGS THAT I-- IT-- DOES. IT'S SO BRUTAL.

THIS IS ALL SO CRAZY. I DON'T WANT IT TO HAPPEN ANYMORE, BUT I CAN'T BRING MYSELF TO GET RID OF THAT BIKE.

I--UH, IT--DID SAVE TWO KIDS' LIVES TODAY. IF I AM THIS POWERFUL GHOST RIDER--

--WHY CAN'T I SAVE YOU?

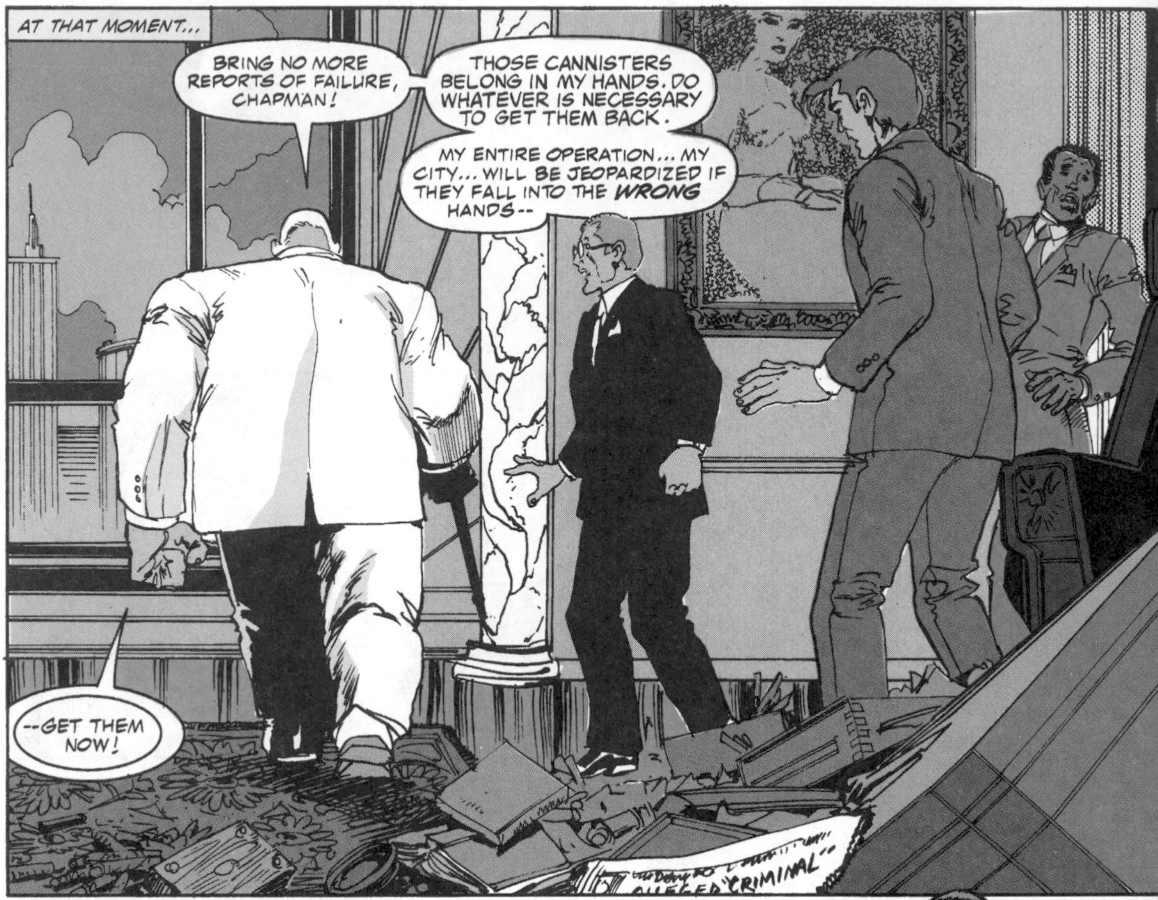
AT THAT MOMENT...
BRING NO MORE REPORTS OF FAILURE, CHAPMAN!
THOSE CANNISTERS BELONG IN MY HANDS. DO WHATEVER IS NECESSARY TO GET THEM BACK.
MY ENTIRE OPERATION... MY CITY... WILL BE JEOPARDIZED IF THEY FALL INTO THE ***WRONG*** HANDS--
--GET THEM NOW!

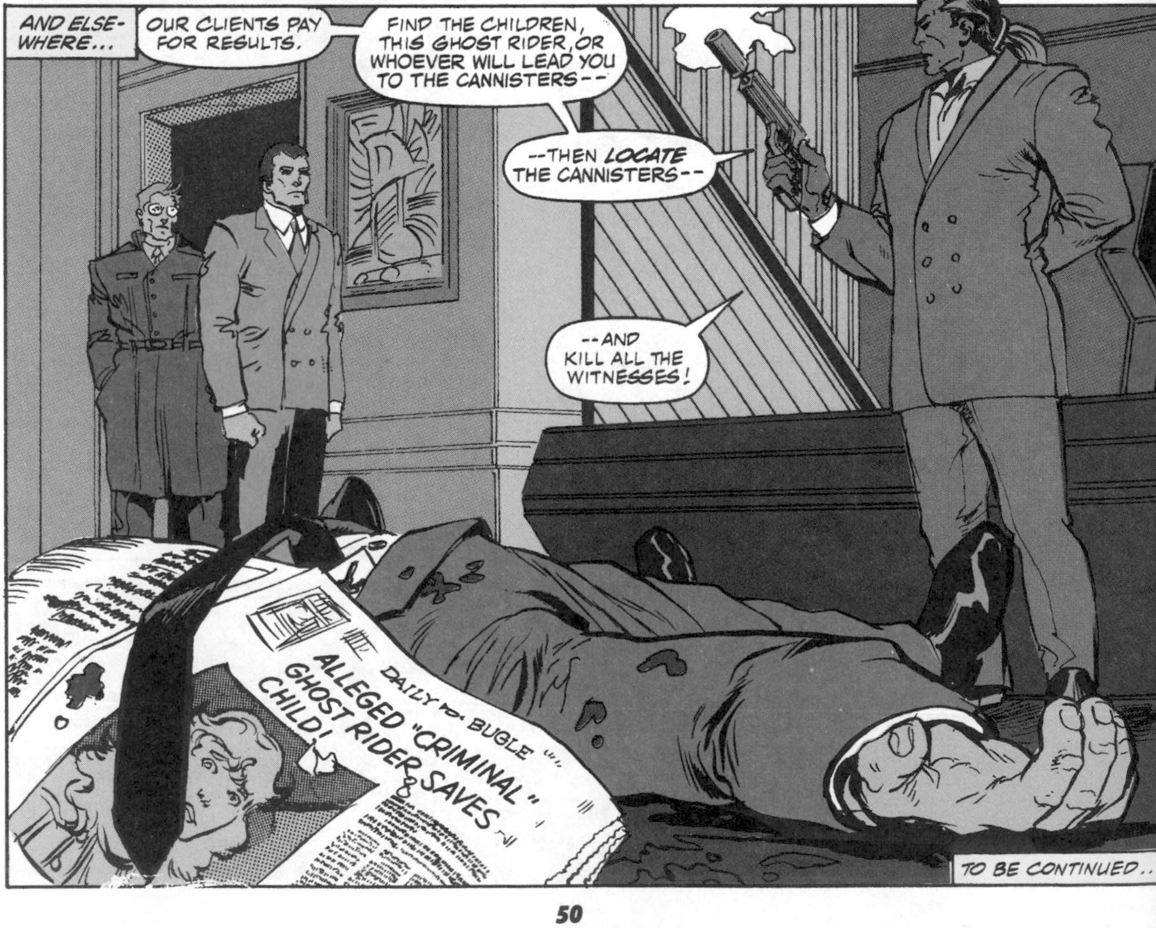
AND ELSEWHERE...
OUR CLIENTS PAY FOR RESULTS.
FIND THE CHILDREN, THIS GHOST RIDER, OR WHOEVER WILL LEAD YOU TO THE CANNISTERS--
--THEN ***LOCATE*** THE CANNISTERS--
--AND KILL ALL THE WITNESSES!
DAILY BUGLE
ALLEGED "CRIMINAL" GHOST RIDER SAVES CHILD!
TO BE CONTINUED...

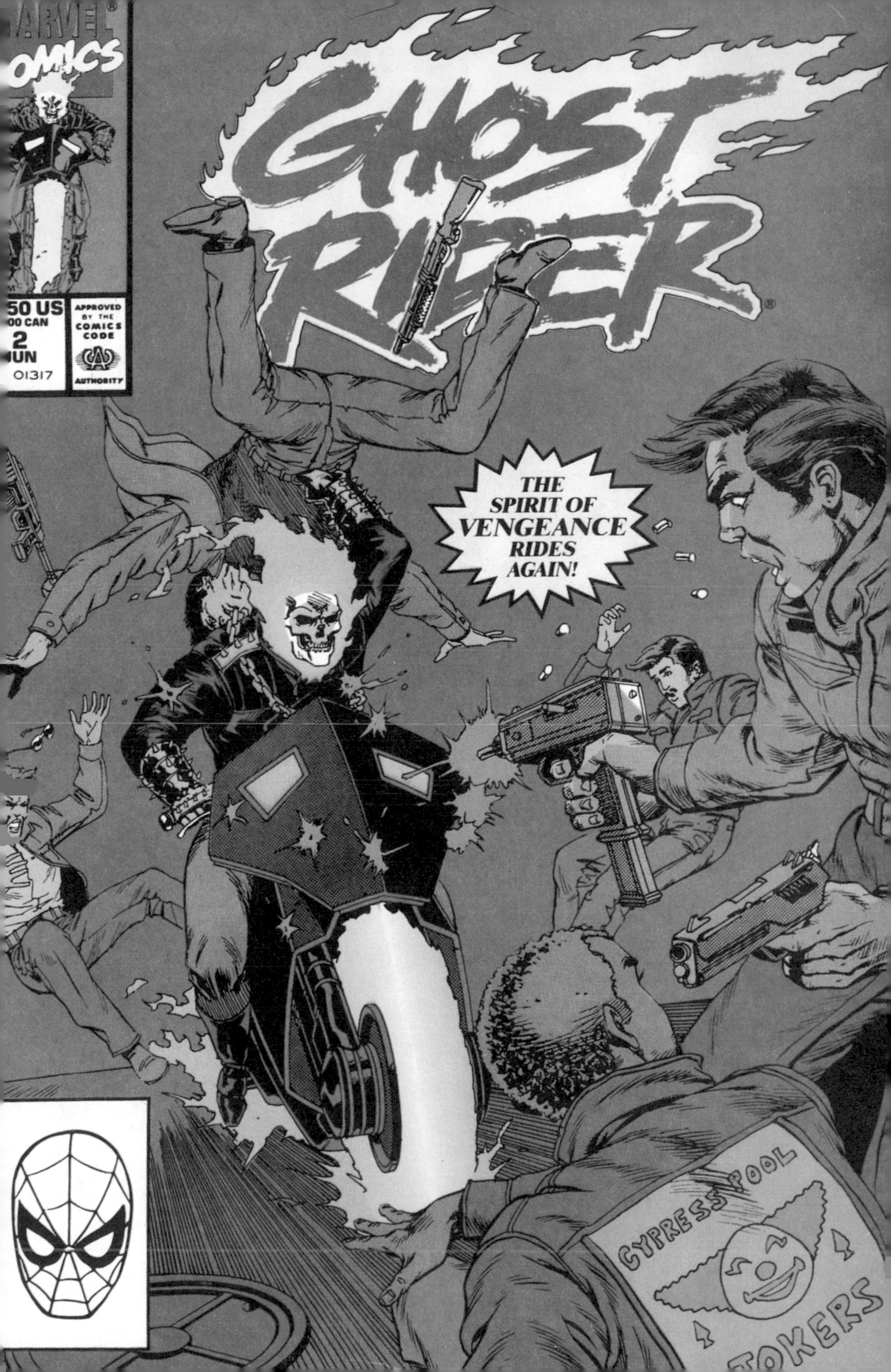

ARVEL
OMICS
GHOST RIDER
50 US
00 CAN
2
UN
01317
APPROVED BY THE COMICS CODE AUTHORITY
THE SPIRIT OF VENGEANCE RIDES AGAIN!
CYPRESS POOL

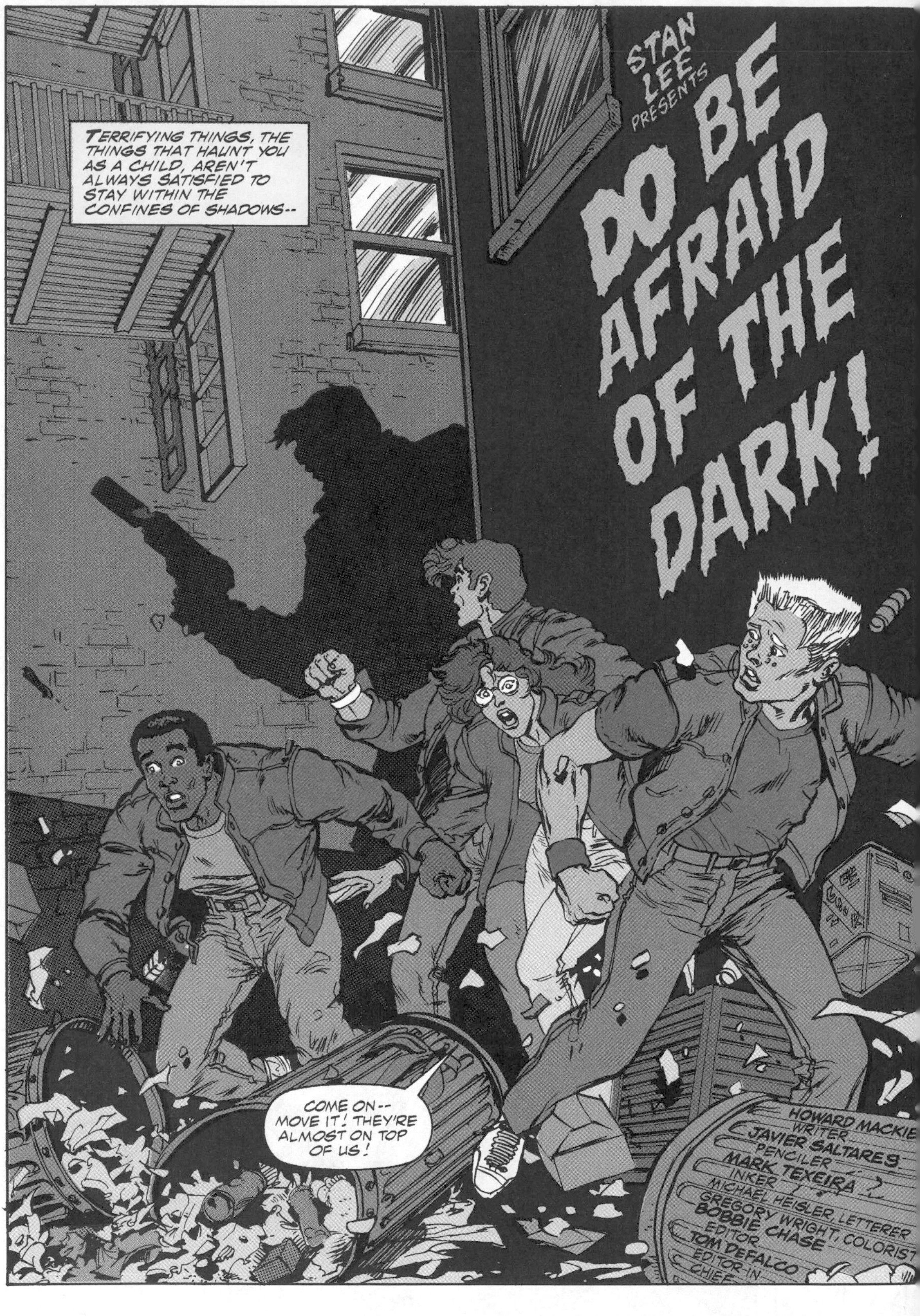
STAN LEE PRESENTS
DO BE AFRAID OF THE DARK!
TERRIFYING THINGS, THE THINGS THAT HAUNT YOU AS A CHILD, AREN'T ALWAYS SATISFIED TO STAY WITHIN THE CONFINES OF SHADOWS--
COME ON-- MOVE IT! THEY'RE ALMOST ON TOP OF US!
HOWARD MACKIE WRITER
JAVIER SALTARES PENCILER
MARK TEXEIRA INKER
MICHAEL HEISLER, LETTERER
GREGORY WRIGHT, COLORIST
BOBBIE CHASE EDITOR
TOM DEFALCO EDITOR-IN CHIEF

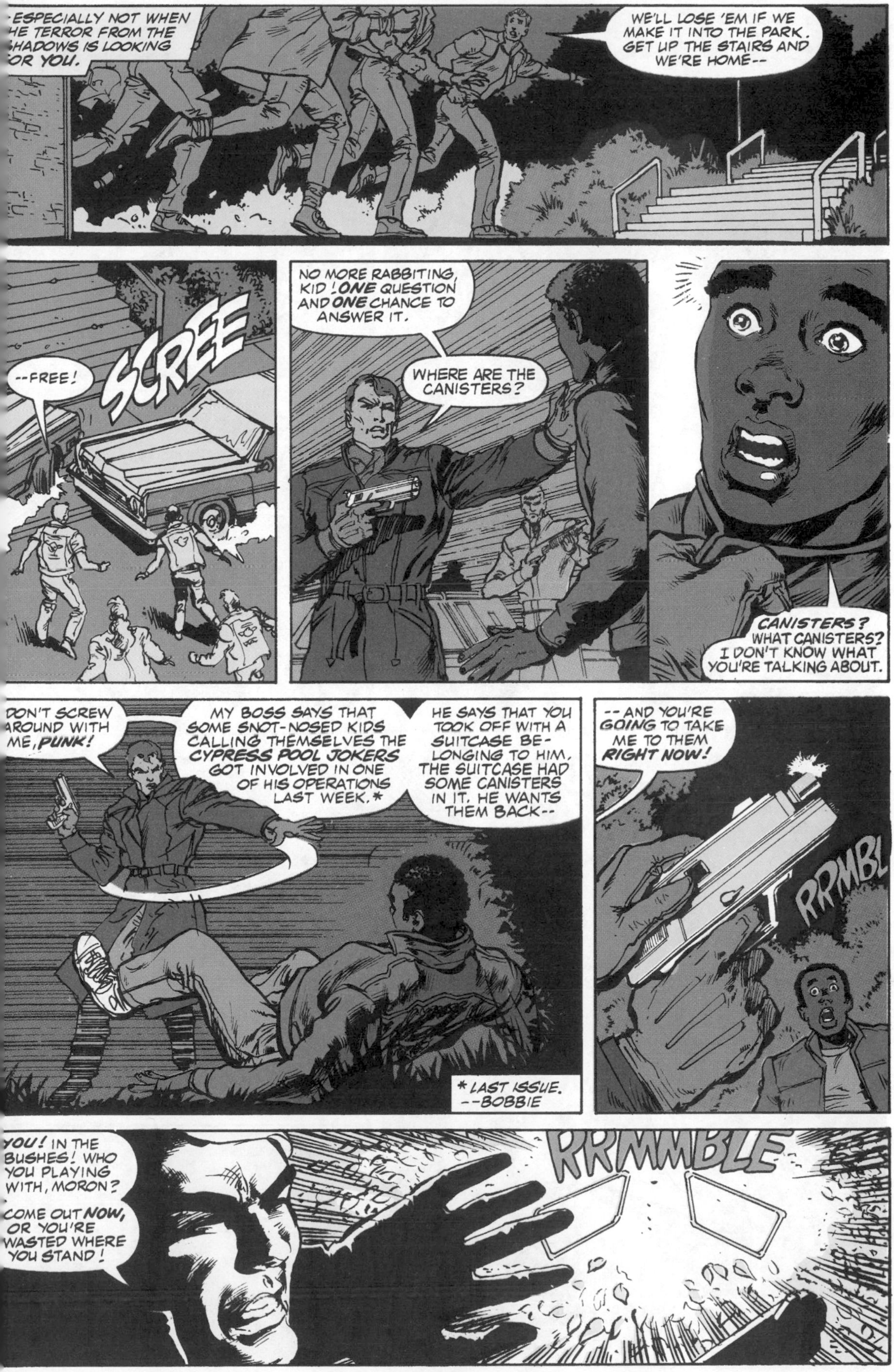

-ESPECIALLY NOT WHEN HE TERROR FROM THE SHADOWS IS LOOKING FOR YOU.
WE'LL LOSE 'EM IF WE MAKE IT INTO THE PARK. GET UP THE STAIRS AND WE'RE HOME--
SCREE
--FREE!
NO MORE RABBITING, KID! ONE QUESTION AND ONE CHANCE TO ANSWER IT.
WHERE ARE THE CANISTERS?
CANISTERS? WHAT CANISTERS? I DON'T KNOW WHAT YOU'RE TALKING ABOUT.
DON'T SCREW AROUND WITH ME, PUNK!
MY BOSS SAYS THAT SOME SNOT-NOSED KIDS CALLING THEMSELVES THE CYPRESS POOL JOKERS GOT INVOLVED IN ONE OF HIS OPERATIONS LAST WEEK.*
HE SAYS THAT YOU TOOK OFF WITH A SUITCASE BELONGING TO HIM. THE SUITCASE HAD SOME CANISTERS IN IT. HE WANTS THEM BACK--
*LAST ISSUE. --BOBBIE
--AND YOU'RE GOING TO TAKE ME TO THEM RIGHT NOW!
RRMBL
YOU! IN THE BUSHES! WHO YOU PLAYING WITH, MORON?
COME OUT NOW, OR YOU'RE WASTED WHERE YOU STAND!
RRMMBLE

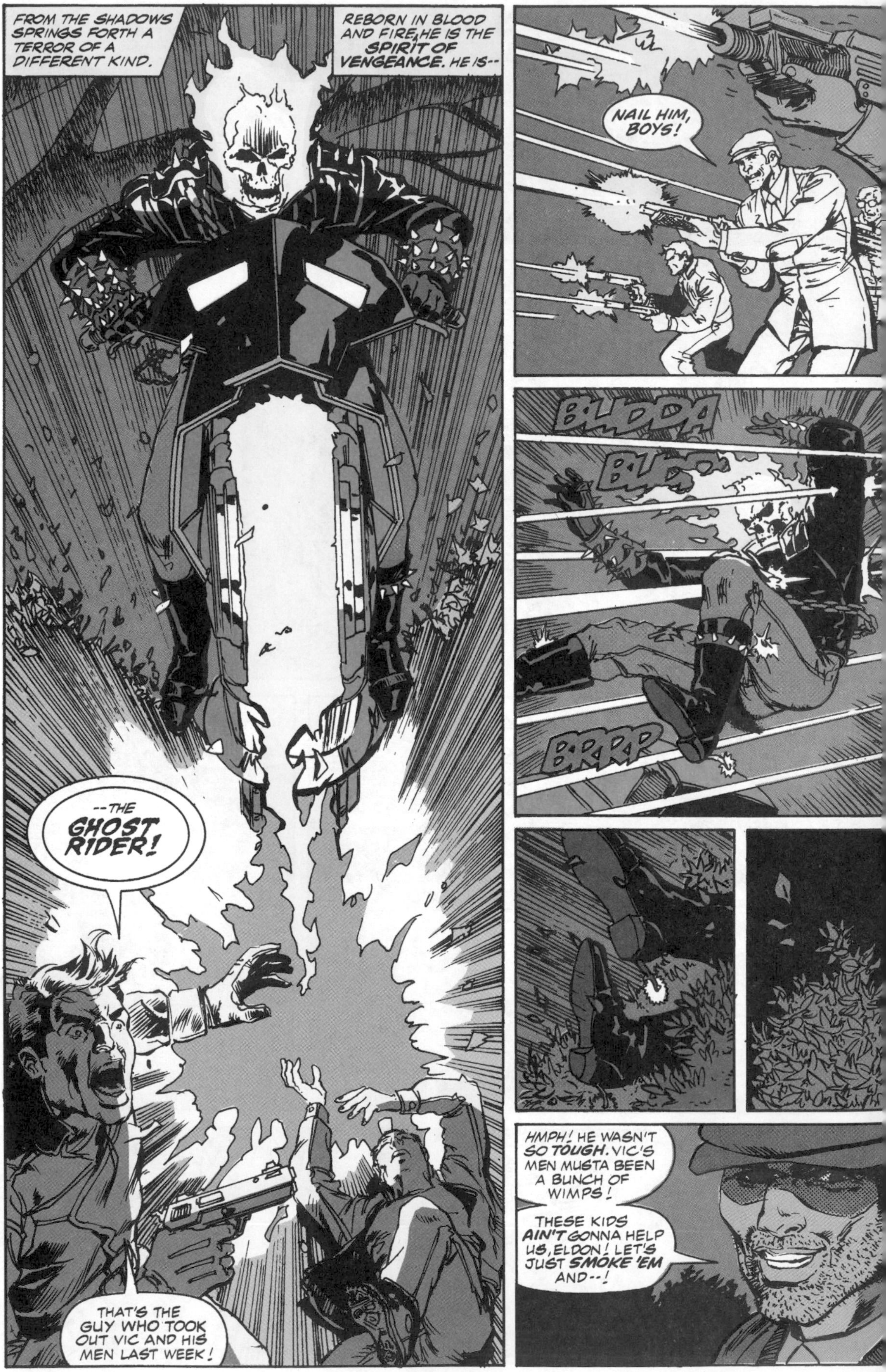
FROM THE SHADOWS SPRINGS FORTH A TERROR OF A DIFFERENT KIND.
REBORN IN BLOOD AND FIRE, HE IS THE SPIRIT OF VENGEANCE. HE IS--
--THE GHOST RIDER!
THAT'S THE GUY WHO TOOK OUT VIC AND HIS MEN LAST WEEK!
NAIL HIM, BOYS!
BUDDA
BUDD
BRRRP
HMPH! HE WASN'T SO TOUGH. VIC'S MEN MUSTA BEEN A BUNCH OF WIMPS!
THESE KIDS AIN'T GONNA HELP US, ELDON! LET'S JUST SMOKE 'EM AND--!

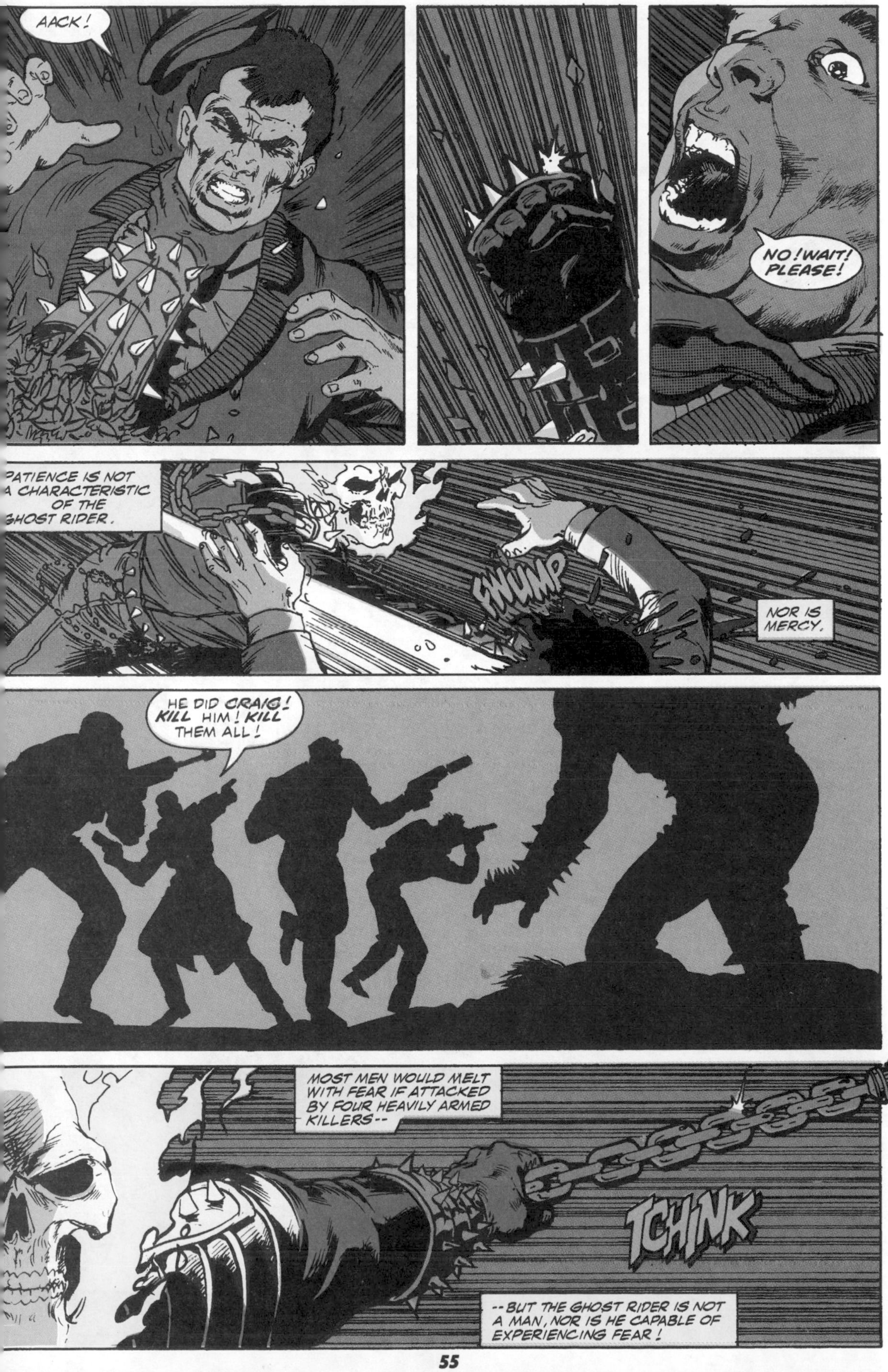

AACK!
NO! WAIT! PLEASE!
PATIENCE IS NOT A CHARACTERISTIC OF THE GHOST RIDER.
SWUMP
NOR IS MERCY.
HE DID CRAIG! KILL HIM! KILL THEM ALL!
MOST MEN WOULD MELT WITH FEAR IF ATTACKED BY FOUR HEAVILY ARMED KILLERS--
TCHINK
--BUT THE GHOST RIDER IS NOT A MAN, NOR IS HE CAPABLE OF EXPERIENCING FEAR!

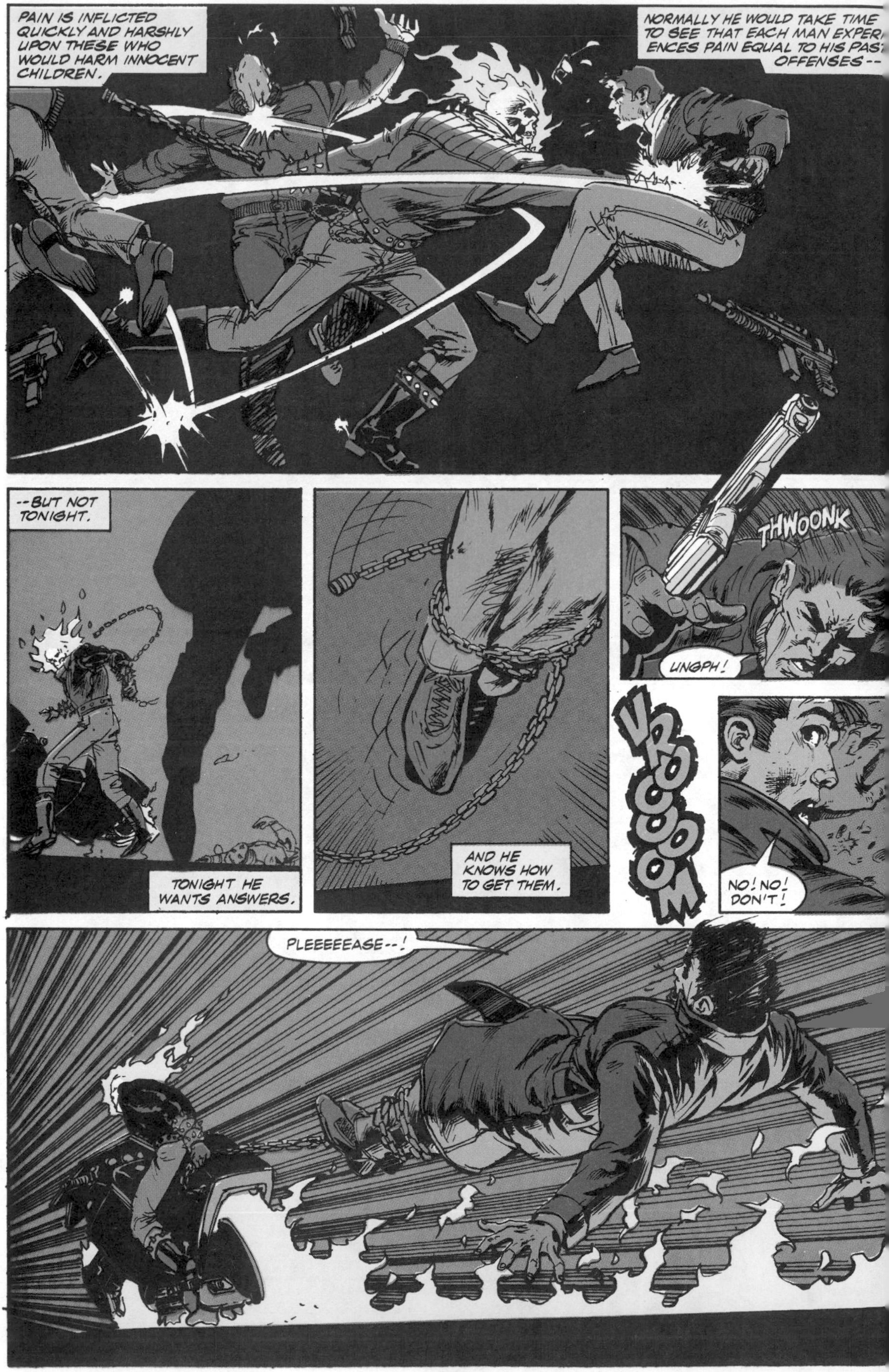
PAIN IS INFLICTED QUICKLY AND HARSHLY UPON THESE WHO WOULD HARM INNOCENT CHILDREN.
NORMALLY HE WOULD TAKE TIME TO SEE THAT EACH MAN EXPERIENCES PAIN EQUAL TO HIS PAST OFFENSES--
--BUT NOT TONIGHT.
TONIGHT HE WANTS ANSWERS.
AND HE KNOWS HOW TO GET THEM.
THWOONK
UNGPH!
VROOOOOM
NO! NO! DON'T!
PLEEEEEASE--!

ELDON'S SCREAMS ARE [A]S EFFECTIVE AS HIS BULL[E]TS WERE EARLIER.

YOU WILL NOW TELL ME WHY YOU WANTED TO HURT THOSE CHILDREN, AND FOR WHOM YOU WORK.

P-PLEASE DON'T DROP ME...

TALK.

NO, NO, NO, NO,...!

I WASN'T GONNA HURT THEM--REALLY! JUST ROUGH THEM UP. GET SOME INFORMATION.

THE WORD ON THE STREET IS THESE KIDS HAVE CANISTERS OR SOMETHING THAT THE KINGPIN WANTS.

I JUST WANTED TO MAKE THE BIG SCORE AND GET IN GOOD WITH HIM! I'M GONNA BE SICK.

WHAT ARE IN THESE CAN-ISTERS THAT MAKES THEM SO VALUABLE?

I DON'T KNOW -- I SWEAR I DON'T KNOW!

YET YOU ENDANGER THE LIVES OF INNOCENT CHILDREN TO FIND THEM.

THIS WILL NEVER HAPPEN AGAIN.

ELDON LAMBERT PEERS INTO EYES WHICH REFLECT EVERY TRANSGRESSION FROM HIS PAST--

--HE EXPERIENCES ALL THE PAIN THAT HE HAS INFLICTED ON OTHERS.

HIS MIND BURNS WITH THE MENTAL ANGUISH OF HIS VICTIMS.

ELDON WISHES THAT THE GHOST RIDER HAD DROPPED HIM AND ALLOWED HIM TO ESCAPE THIS MISERY.

N-NO, NO, NO...

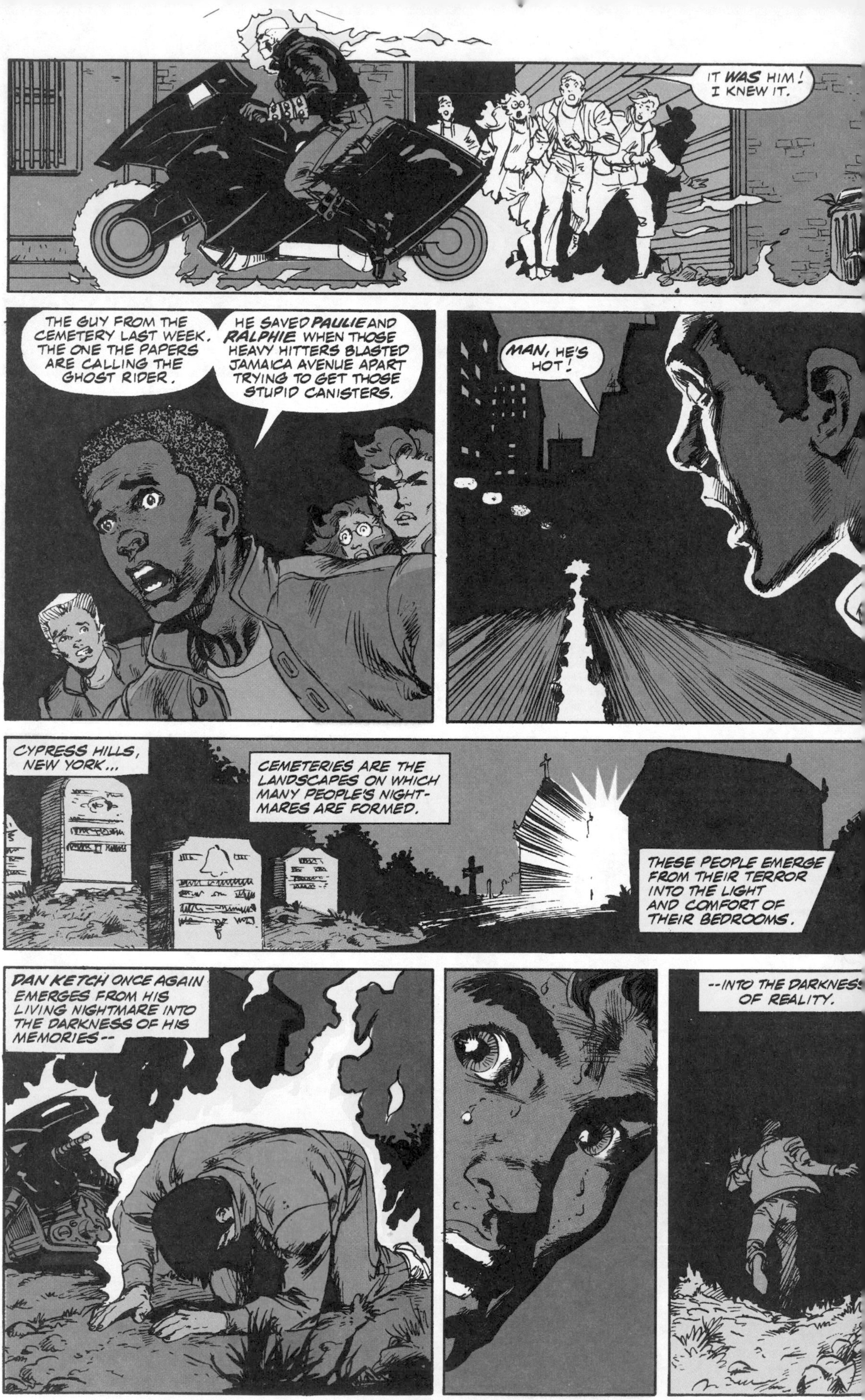
IT WAS HIM! I KNEW IT.
THE GUY FROM THE CEMETERY LAST WEEK. THE ONE THE PAPERS ARE CALLING THE GHOST RIDER.
HE SAVED PAULIE AND RALPHIE WHEN THOSE HEAVY HITTERS BLASTED JAMAICA AVENUE APART TRYING TO GET THOSE STUPID CANISTERS.
MAN, HE'S HOT!
CYPRESS HILLS, NEW YORK...
CEMETERIES ARE THE LANDSCAPES ON WHICH MANY PEOPLE'S NIGHT-MARES ARE FORMED.
THESE PEOPLE EMERGE FROM THEIR TERROR INTO THE LIGHT AND COMFORT OF THEIR BEDROOMS.
DAN KETCH ONCE AGAIN EMERGES FROM HIS LIVING NIGHTMARE INTO THE DARKNESS OF HIS MEMORIES--
--INTO THE DARKNESS OF REALITY.

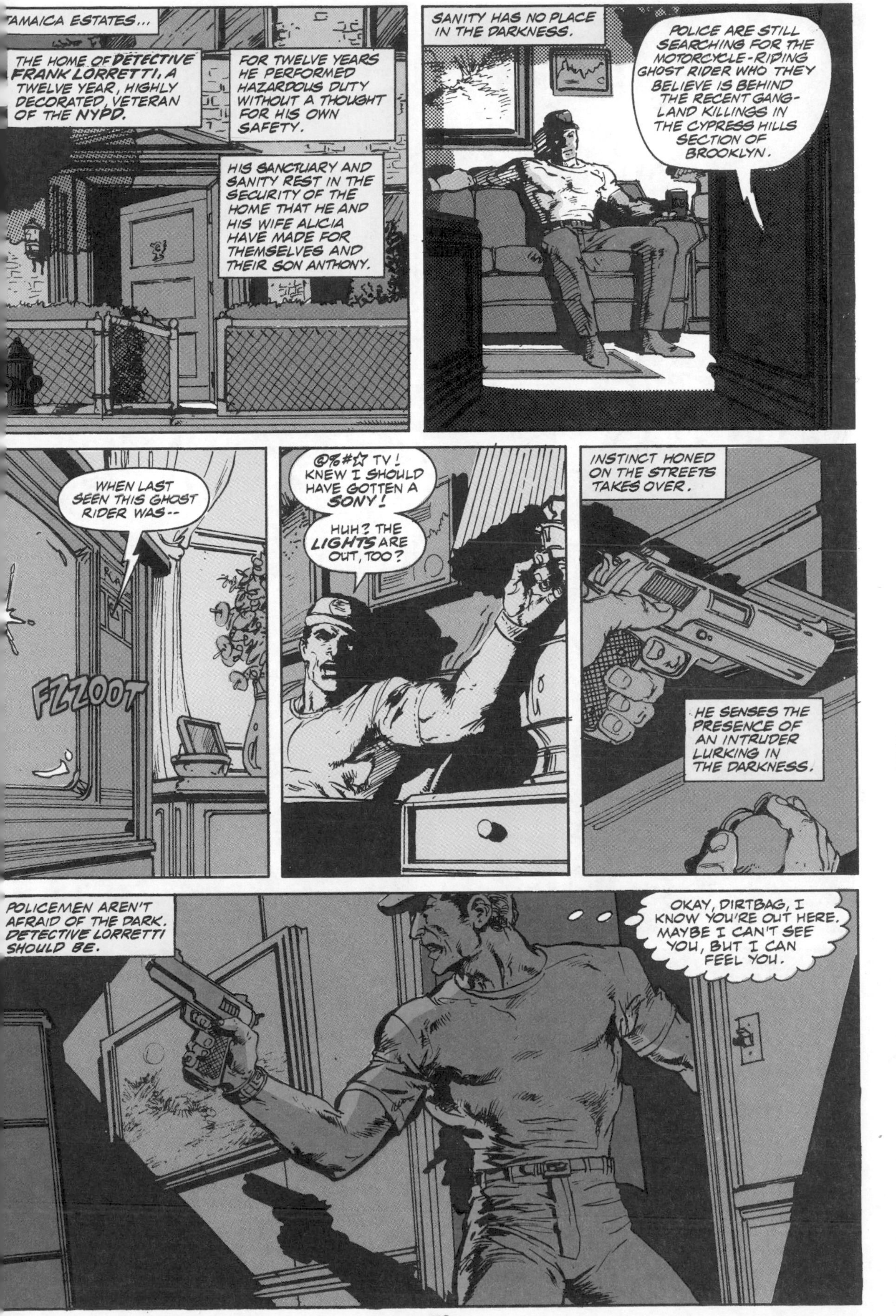

JAMAICA ESTATES...
THE HOME OF DETECTIVE FRANK LORRETTI, A TWELVE YEAR, HIGHLY DECORATED, VETERAN OF THE NYPD.
FOR TWELVE YEARS HE PERFORMED HAZARDOUS DUTY WITHOUT A THOUGHT FOR HIS OWN SAFETY.
HIS SANCTUARY AND SANITY REST IN THE SECURITY OF THE HOME THAT HE AND HIS WIFE ALICIA HAVE MADE FOR THEMSELVES AND THEIR SON ANTHONY.
SANITY HAS NO PLACE IN THE DARKNESS.
POLICE ARE STILL SEARCHING FOR THE MOTORCYCLE-RIDING GHOST RIDER WHO THEY BELIEVE IS BEHIND THE RECENT GANG-LAND KILLINGS IN THE CYPRESS HILLS SECTION OF BROOKLYN.
WHEN LAST SEEN THIS GHOST RIDER WAS--
FZZOOT
@%#☆ TV! KNEW I SHOULD HAVE GOTTEN A SONY!
HUH? THE LIGHTS ARE OUT, TOO?
INSTINCT HONED ON THE STREETS TAKES OVER.
HE SENSES THE PRESENCE OF AN INTRUDER LURKING IN THE DARKNESS.
POLICEMEN AREN'T AFRAID OF THE DARK. DETECTIVE LORRETTI SHOULD BE.
OKAY, DIRTBAG, I KNOW YOU'RE OUT HERE. MAYBE I CAN'T SEE YOU, BUT I CAN FEEL YOU.

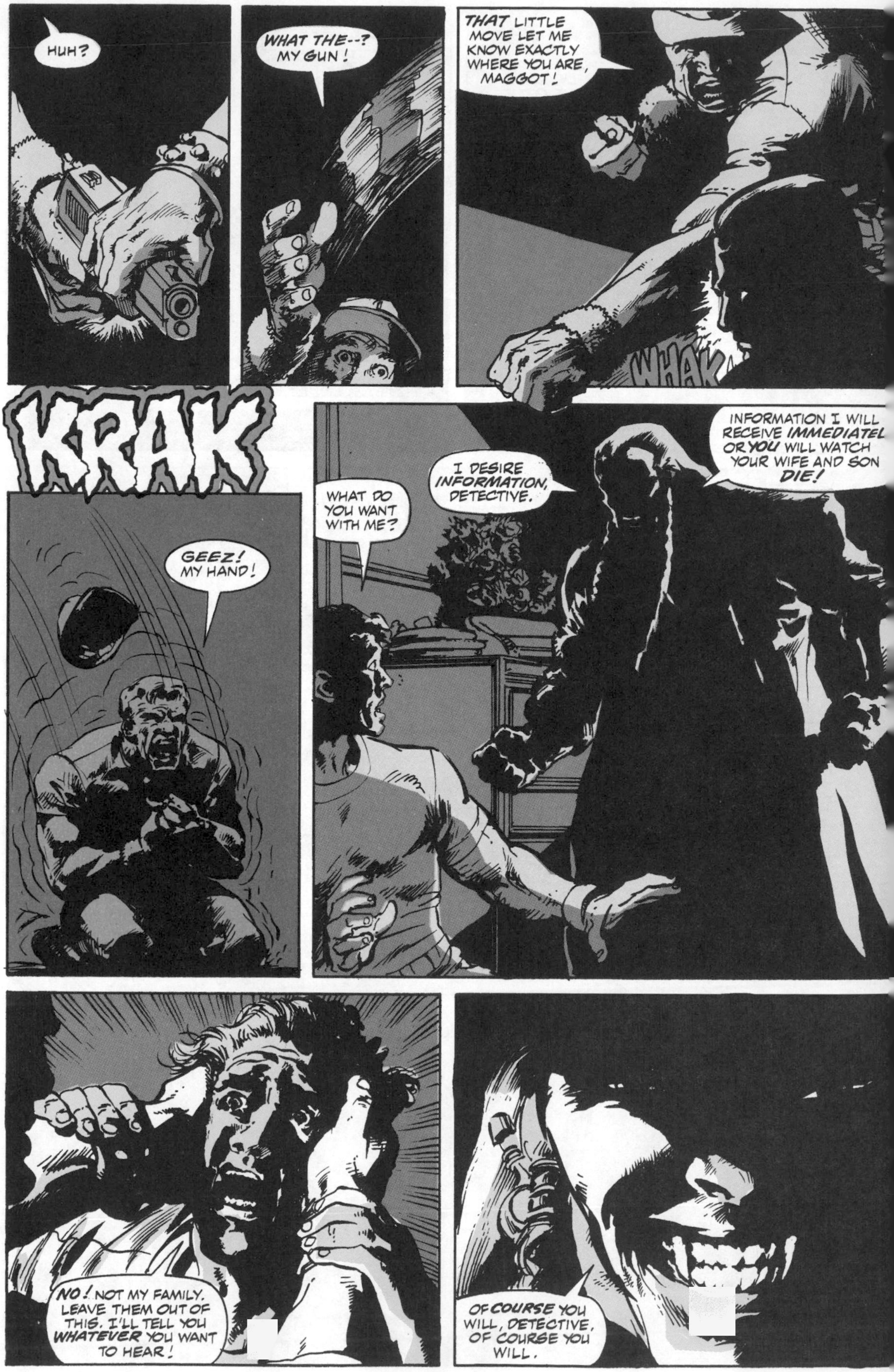

HUH?
WHAT THE--? MY GUN!
THAT LITTLE MOVE LET ME KNOW EXACTLY WHERE YOU ARE, MAGGOT!
WHAK
KRAK
GEEZ! MY HAND!
WHAT DO YOU WANT WITH ME?
I DESIRE INFORMATION, DETECTIVE.
INFORMATION I WILL RECEIVE IMMEDIATEL OR YOU WILL WATCH YOUR WIFE AND SON DIE!
NO! NOT MY FAMILY. LEAVE THEM OUT OF THIS. I'LL TELL YOU WHATEVER YOU WANT TO HEAR!
OF COURSE YOU WILL, DETECTIVE, OF COURSE YOU WILL.

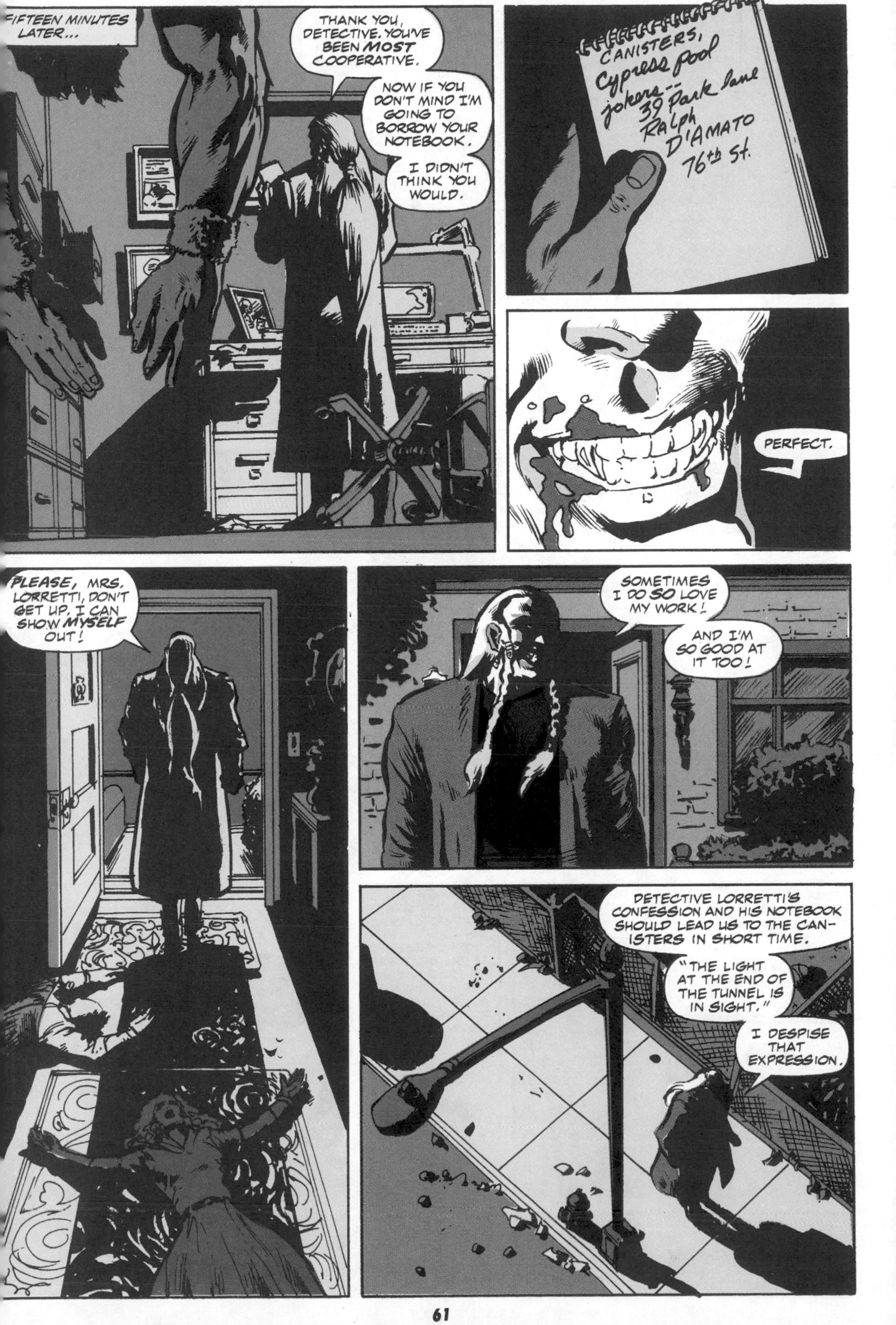
FIFTEEN MINUTES LATER...
THANK YOU, DETECTIVE. YOU'VE BEEN MOST COOPERATIVE.
NOW IF YOU DON'T MIND I'M GOING TO BORROW YOUR NOTEBOOK.
I DIDN'T THINK YOU WOULD.
CANISTERS, Cypress Pool
jokers -- 39 Park lane
Ralph D'AMATO 76th St.
PERFECT.
PLEASE, MRS. LORRETTI, DON'T GET UP. I CAN SHOW MYSELF OUT!
SOMETIMES I DO SO LOVE MY WORK!
AND I'M SO GOOD AT IT TOO!
DETECTIVE LORRETTI'S CONFESSION AND HIS NOTEBOOK SHOULD LEAD US TO THE CANISTERS IN SHORT TIME.
"THE LIGHT AT THE END OF THE TUNNEL IS IN SIGHT."
I DESPISE THAT EXPRESSION.

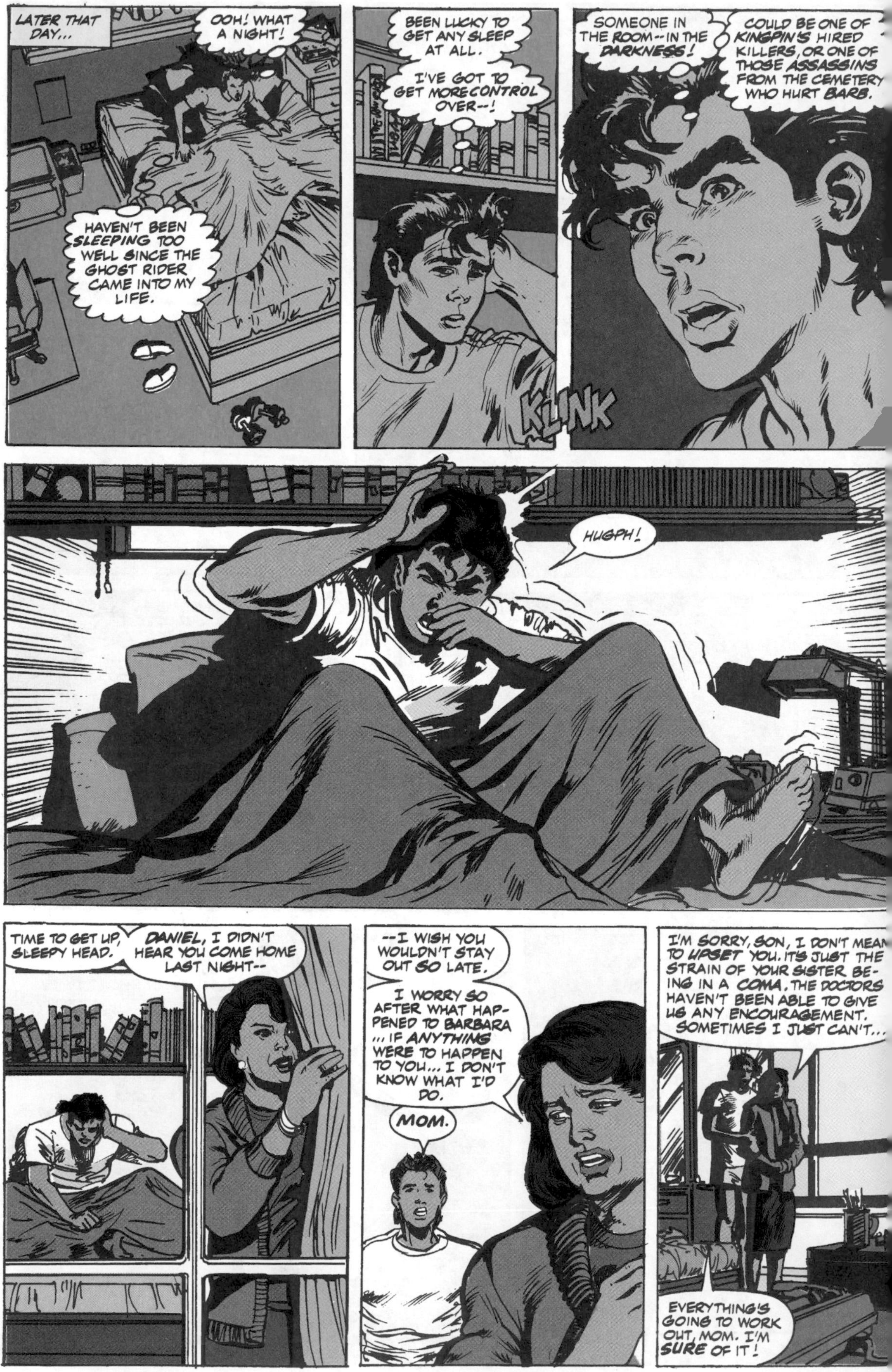
LATER THAT DAY...
OOH! WHAT A NIGHT!
HAVEN'T BEEN SLEEPING TOO WELL SINCE THE GHOST RIDER CAME INTO MY LIFE.
BEEN LUCKY TO GET ANY SLEEP AT ALL.
I'VE GOT TO GET MORE CONTROL OVER--!
KLINK
SOMEONE IN THE ROOM--IN THE DARKNESS!
COULD BE ONE OF KINGPIN'S HIRED KILLERS, OR ONE OF THOSE ASSASSINS FROM THE CEMETERY WHO HURT BARB.
HUGPH!
TIME TO GET UP, SLEEPY HEAD.
DANIEL, I DIDN'T HEAR YOU COME HOME LAST NIGHT--
--I WISH YOU WOULDN'T STAY OUT SO LATE.
I WORRY SO AFTER WHAT HAPPENED TO BARBARA ... IF ANYTHING WERE TO HAPPEN TO YOU... I DON'T KNOW WHAT I'D DO.
MOM.
I'M SORRY, SON, I DON'T MEAN TO UPSET YOU. IT'S JUST THE STRAIN OF YOUR SISTER BEING IN A COMA. THE DOCTORS HAVEN'T BEEN ABLE TO GIVE US ANY ENCOURAGEMENT. SOMETIMES I JUST CAN'T...
EVERYTHING'S GOING TO WORK OUT, MOM. I'M SURE OF IT!

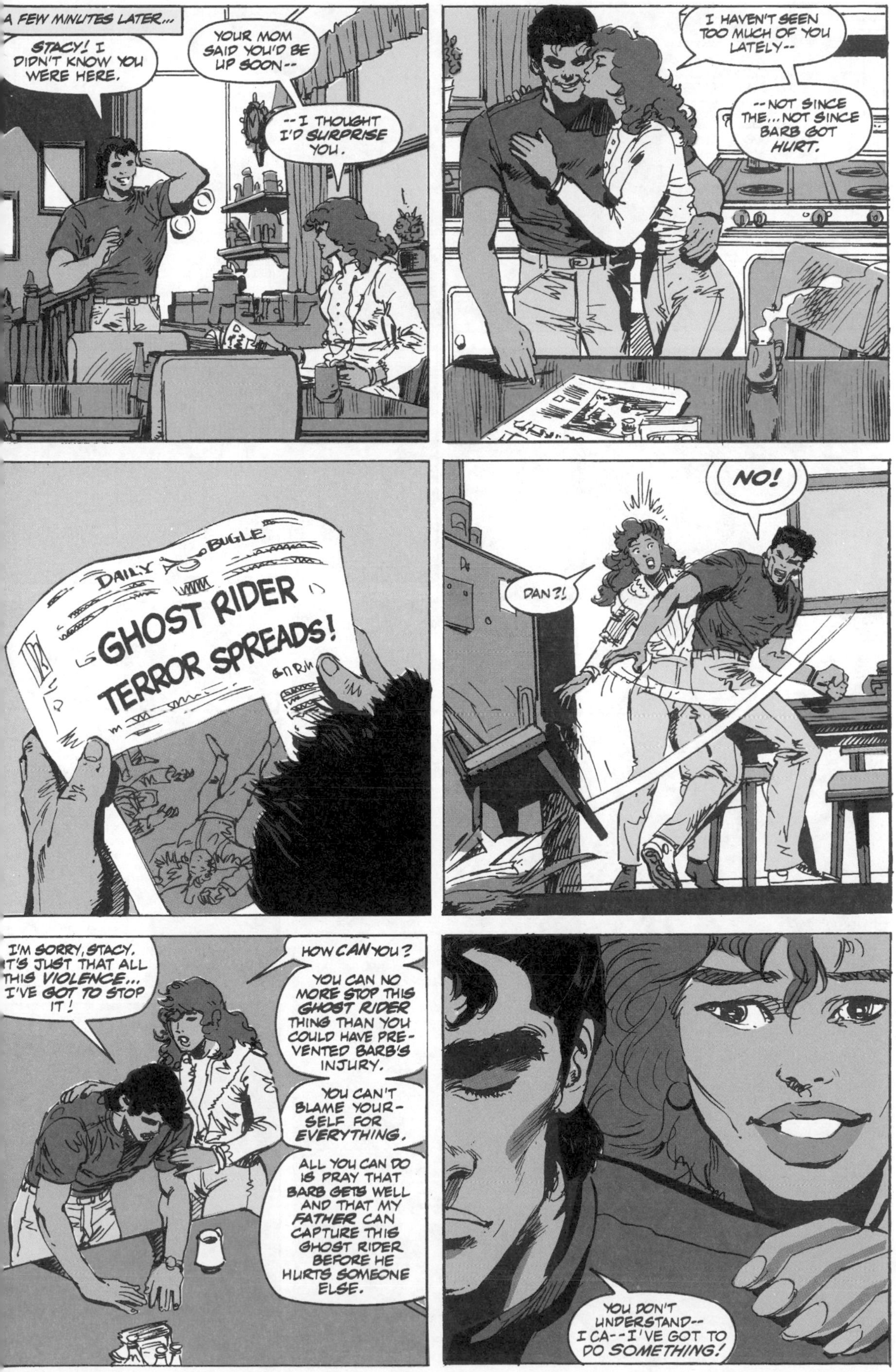
A FEW MINUTES LATER...
STACY! I DIDN'T KNOW YOU WERE HERE.
YOUR MOM SAID YOU'D BE UP SOON--
--I THOUGHT I'D SURPRISE YOU.
I HAVEN'T SEEN TOO MUCH OF YOU LATELY--
--NOT SINCE THE...NOT SINCE BARB GOT HURT.
DAILY BUGLE
GHOST RIDER TERROR SPREADS!
NO!
DAN?!
I'M SORRY, STACY. IT'S JUST THAT ALL THIS VIOLENCE... I'VE GOT TO STOP IT!
HOW CAN YOU?
YOU CAN NO MORE STOP THIS GHOST RIDER THING THAN YOU COULD HAVE PREVENTED BARB'S INJURY.
YOU CAN'T BLAME YOURSELF FOR EVERYTHING.
ALL YOU CAN DO IS PRAY THAT BARB GETS WELL AND THAT MY FATHER CAN CAPTURE THIS GHOST RIDER BEFORE HE HURTS SOMEONE ELSE.
YOU DON'T UNDERSTAND-- I CA--I'VE GOT TO DO SOMETHING!

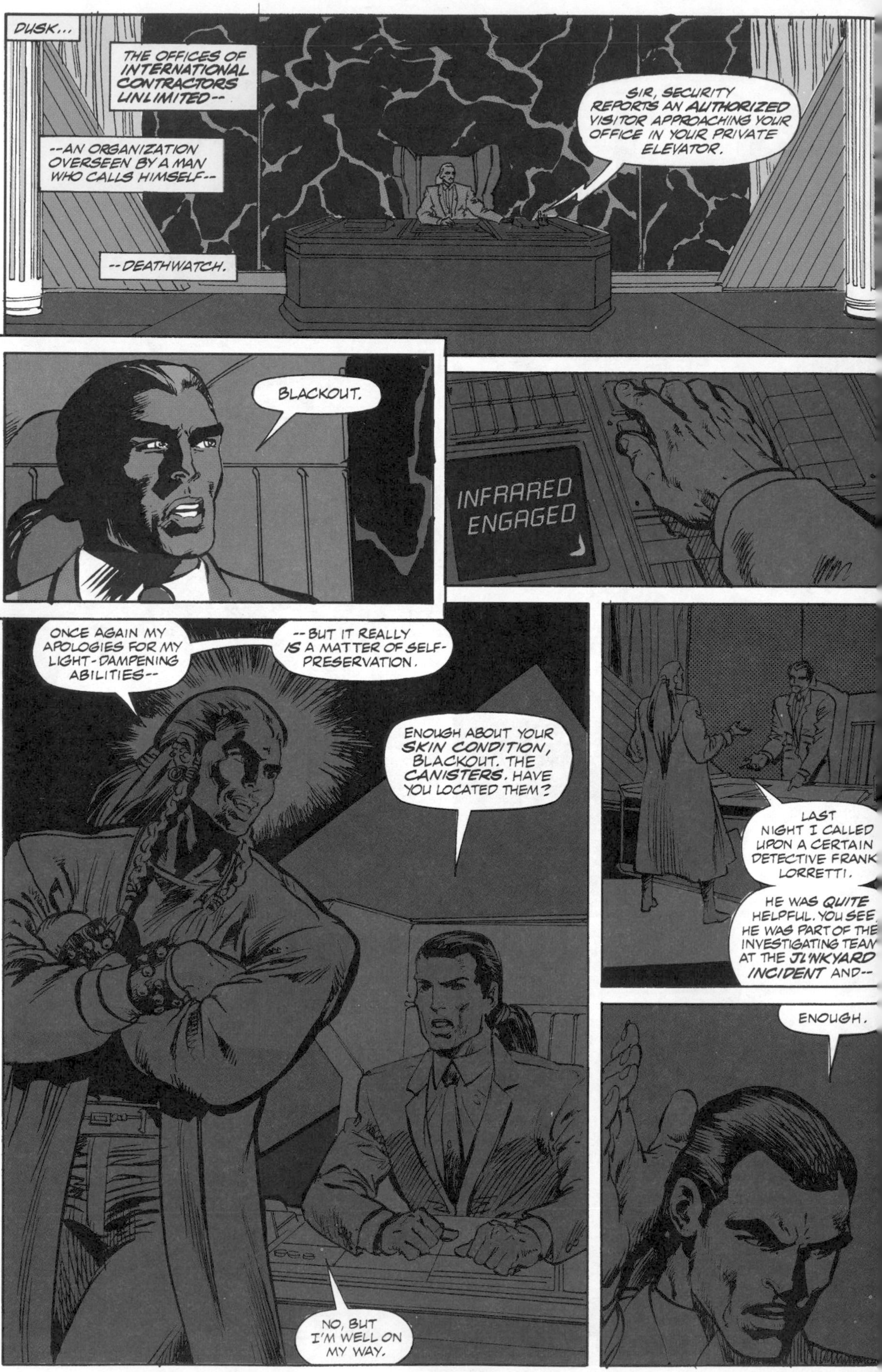
DUSK...
THE OFFICES OF INTERNATIONAL CONTRACTORS UNLIMITED--
--AN ORGANIZATION OVERSEEN BY A MAN WHO CALLS HIMSELF--
--DEATHWATCH.
SIR, SECURITY REPORTS AN AUTHORIZED VISITOR APPROACHING YOUR OFFICE IN YOUR PRIVATE ELEVATOR.
BLACKOUT.
INFRARED ENGAGED
ONCE AGAIN MY APOLOGIES FOR MY LIGHT-DAMPENING ABILITIES--
--BUT IT REALLY IS A MATTER OF SELF-PRESERVATION.
ENOUGH ABOUT YOUR SKIN CONDITION, BLACKOUT. THE CANISTERS. HAVE YOU LOCATED THEM?
NO, BUT I'M WELL ON MY WAY.
LAST NIGHT I CALLED UPON A CERTAIN DETECTIVE FRANK LORRETTI.
HE WAS QUITE HELPFUL. YOU SEE HE WAS PART OF THE INVESTIGATING TEAM AT THE JUNKYARD INCIDENT AND--
ENOUGH.

YOU KNOW THE *PROCEDURE*.

BUT OF COURSE.

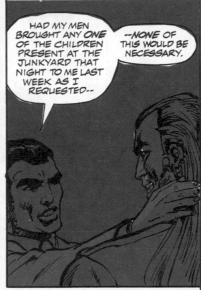

HAD MY MEN BROUGHT ANY *ONE* OF THE CHILDREN PRESENT AT THE JUNKYARD THAT NIGHT TO ME LAST WEEK AS I REQUESTED--

--NONE OF THIS WOULD BE NECESSARY.

BUT I AM *ENJOYING* MYSELF SO.

YES. LET'S SEE JUST HOW MUCH.

DEATHWATCH'S FINGERS *PSYCHICALLY* ENTER BLACKOUT'S BRAIN--

--STROKING SYNAPSES, ABSORBING THE *SHORT-TERM* MEMORIES--

--HE WITNESSES *DEATH*--

--HE EXPERIENCES *ECSTASY*.

THANK YOU. ONCE AGAIN YOU'VE PROVIDED ME WITH AN *EXQUISITE* KILL.

THOUGH IT STILL PUZZLES ME THAT YOU ARE ONE OF THE FEW WHO UNDERGO MY LITTLE BRAIN SCAN PAINLESSLY.

JUST LUCKY I GUESS.

I GUESS. NOW PLEASE *FIND* THE LAST CANISTER. I'LL TAKE CARE OF THE TWO IN *POLICE CUSTODY*.

ASIDE FROM HIS DEATH, THE GOOD DETECTIVE PROVIDED ME WITH THE MEANS TO TRACK DOWN THOSE PRESENT AT THE JUNKYARD.

PERHAPS I CAN PERSUADE THEM TO COOPERATE WITH US.

SEE THAT YOU DO. OUR *CLIENTS* ARE GETTING QUITE ANXIOUS FOR THE DELIVERY OF THOSE CANISTERS.

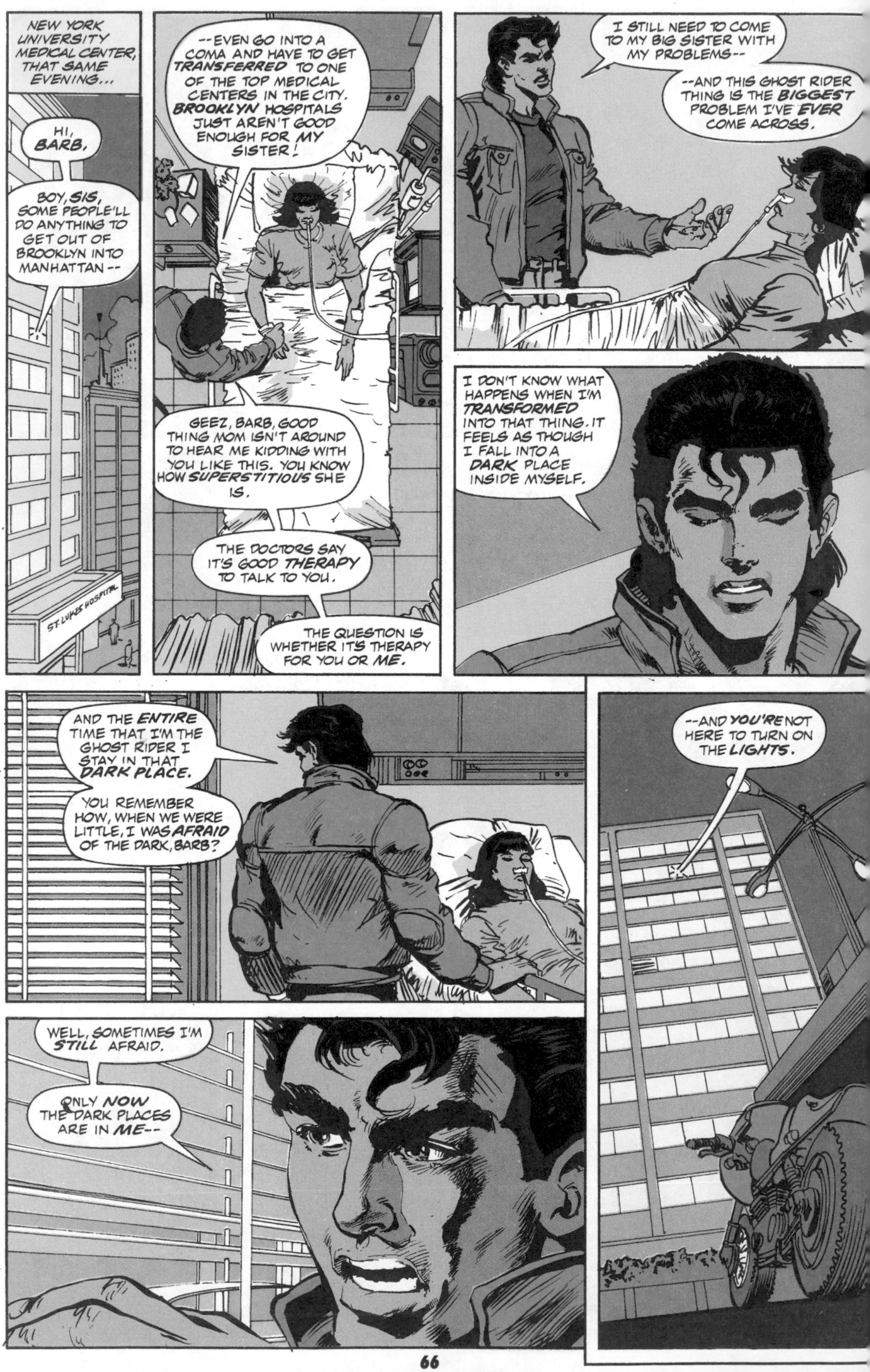
NEW YORK UNIVERSITY MEDICAL CENTER, THAT SAME EVENING...
HI, BARB.
BOY, SIS, SOME PEOPLE'LL DO ANYTHING TO GET OUT OF BROOKLYN INTO MANHATTAN --
ST. LUKES HOSPITAL
--EVEN GO INTO A COMA AND HAVE TO GET TRANSFERRED TO ONE OF THE TOP MEDICAL CENTERS IN THE CITY. BROOKLYN HOSPITALS JUST AREN'T GOOD ENOUGH FOR MY SISTER!
GEEZ, BARB, GOOD THING MOM ISN'T AROUND TO HEAR ME KIDDING WITH YOU LIKE THIS. YOU KNOW HOW SUPERSTITIOUS SHE IS.
THE DOCTORS SAY IT'S GOOD THERAPY TO TALK TO YOU.
THE QUESTION IS WHETHER IT'S THERAPY FOR YOU OR ME.
I STILL NEED TO COME TO MY BIG SISTER WITH MY PROBLEMS--
--AND THIS GHOST RIDER THING IS THE BIGGEST PROBLEM I'VE EVER COME ACROSS.
I DON'T KNOW WHAT HAPPENS WHEN I'M TRANSFORMED INTO THAT THING. IT FEELS AS THOUGH I FALL INTO A DARK PLACE INSIDE MYSELF.
AND THE ENTIRE TIME THAT I'M THE GHOST RIDER I STAY IN THAT DARK PLACE.
YOU REMEMBER HOW, WHEN WE WERE LITTLE, I WAS AFRAID OF THE DARK, BARB?
WELL, SOMETIMES I'M STILL AFRAID.
ONLY NOW THE DARK PLACES ARE IN ME--
--AND YOU'RE NOT HERE TO TURN ON THE LIGHTS.

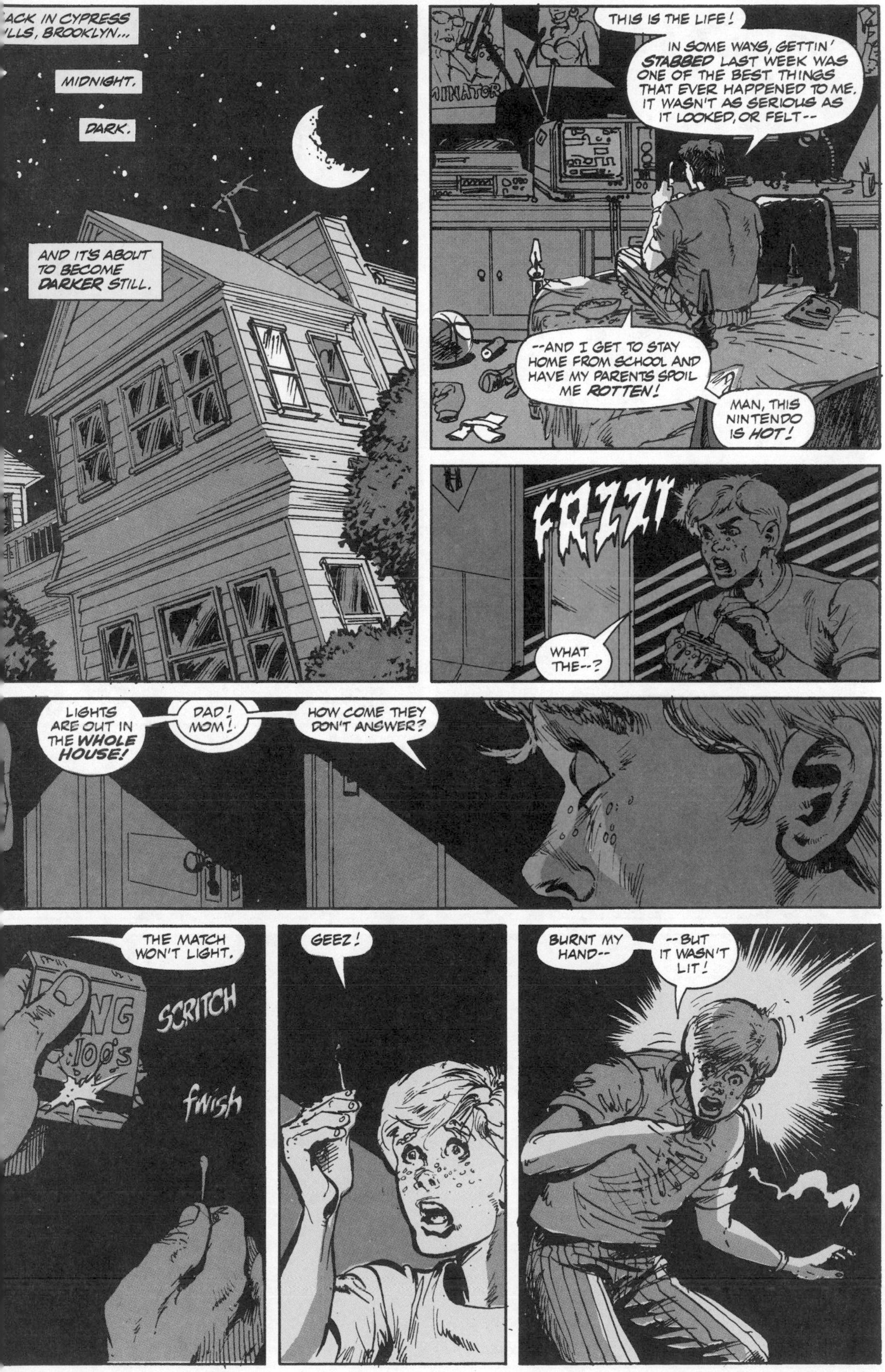

ACK IN CYPRESS
ILLS, BROOKLYN...
MIDNIGHT.
DARK.
AND IT'S ABOUT TO BECOME DARKER STILL.
THIS IS THE LIFE!
IN SOME WAYS, GETTIN' STABBED LAST WEEK WAS ONE OF THE BEST THINGS THAT EVER HAPPENED TO ME. IT WASN'T AS SERIOUS AS IT LOOKED, OR FELT--
--AND I GET TO STAY HOME FROM SCHOOL AND HAVE MY PARENTS SPOIL ME ROTTEN!
MAN, THIS NINTENDO IS HOT!
FRZZT
WHAT THE--?
LIGHTS ARE OUT IN THE WHOLE HOUSE!
DAD! MOM!
HOW COME THEY DON'T ANSWER?
THE MATCH WON'T LIGHT.
SCRITCH
fwish
GEEZ!
BURNT MY HAND--
--BUT IT WASN'T LIT!

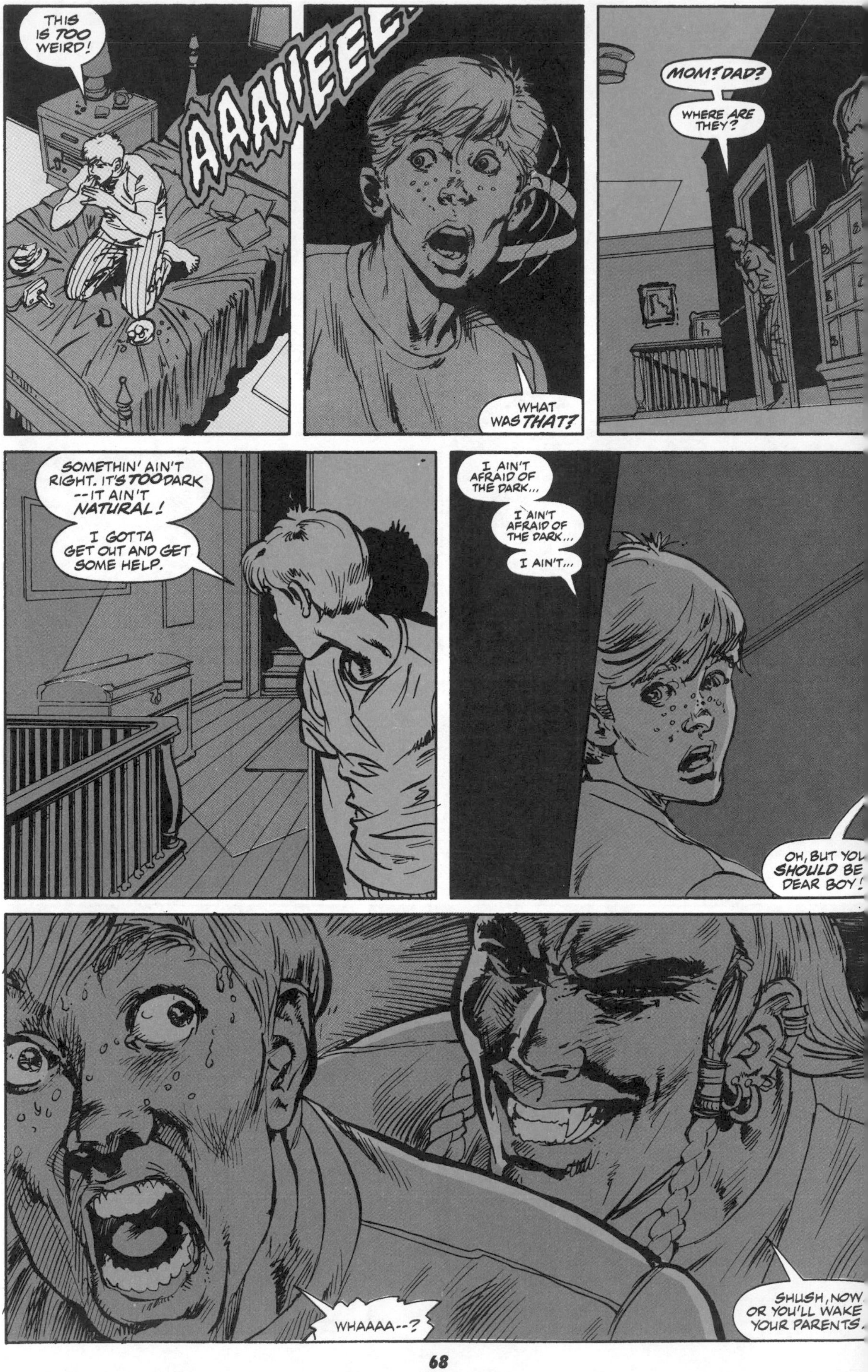
THIS IS TOO WEIRD!
AAAIIEEE!
WHAT WAS THAT?
MOM? DAD?
WHERE ARE THEY?
SOMETHIN' AIN'T RIGHT. IT'S TOO DARK --IT AIN'T NATURAL!
I GOTTA GET OUT AND GET SOME HELP.
I AIN'T AFRAID OF THE DARK...
I AIN'T AFRAID OF THE DARK...
I AIN'T...
OH, BUT YOU SHOULD BE DEAR BOY!
WHAAAA--?
SHUSH, NOW OR YOU'LL WAKE YOUR PARENTS.

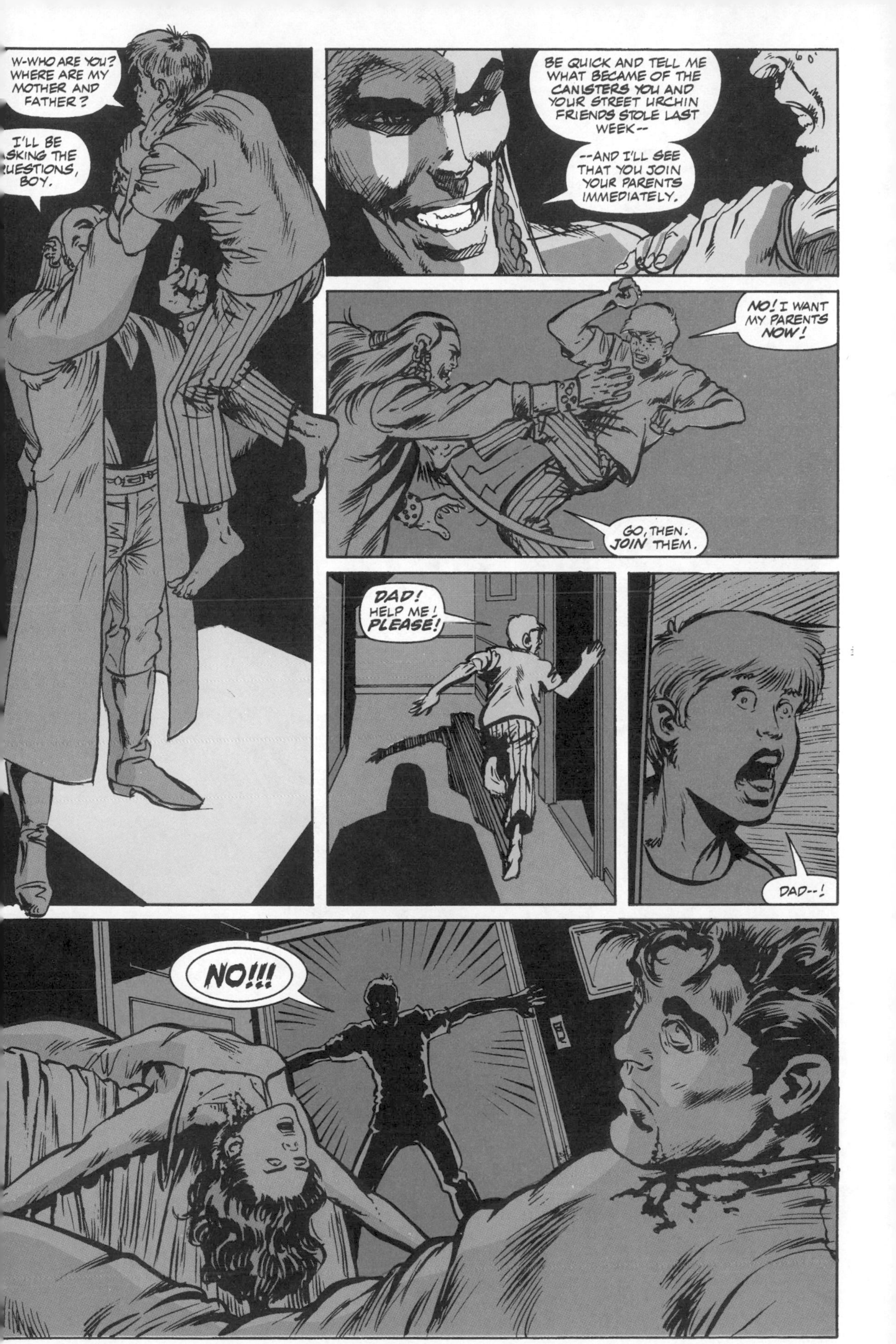
W-WHO ARE YOU? WHERE ARE MY MOTHER AND FATHER?
I'LL BE ASKING THE QUESTIONS, BOY.
BE QUICK AND TELL ME WHAT BECAME OF THE CANISTERS YOU AND YOUR STREET URCHIN FRIENDS STOLE LAST WEEK--
--AND I'LL SEE THAT YOU JOIN YOUR PARENTS IMMEDIATELY.
NO! I WANT MY PARENTS NOW!
GO, THEN. JOIN THEM.
DAD! HELP ME! PLEASE!
DAD--!
NO!!!

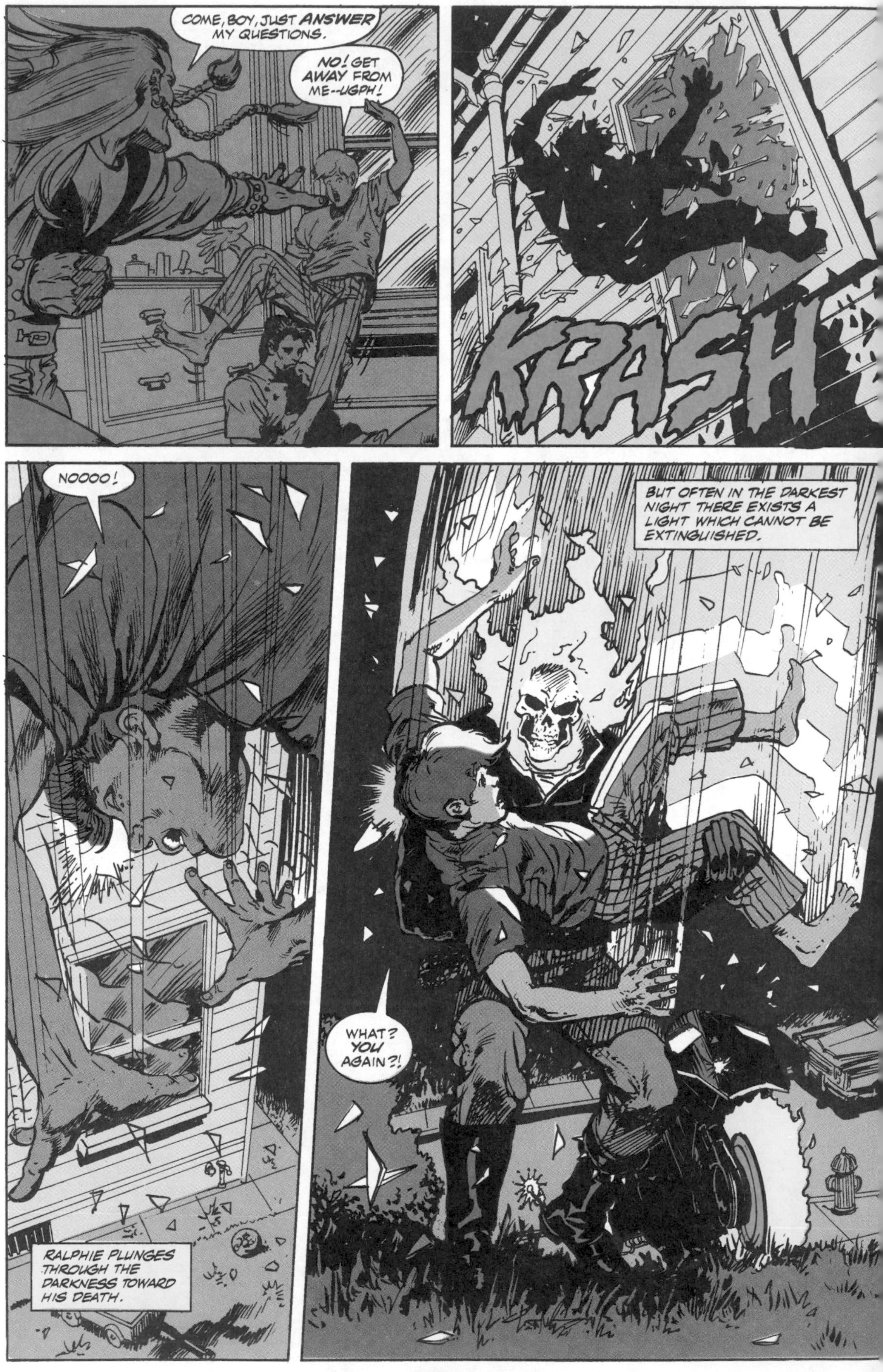
COME, BOY, JUST ANSWER MY QUESTIONS.
NO! GET AWAY FROM ME--UGPH!
KRASH
NOOOO!
RALPHIE PLUNGES THROUGH THE DARKNESS TOWARD HIS DEATH.
BUT OFTEN IN THE DARKEST NIGHT THERE EXISTS A LIGHT WHICH CANNOT BE EXTINGUISHED.
WHAT? YOU AGAIN?!

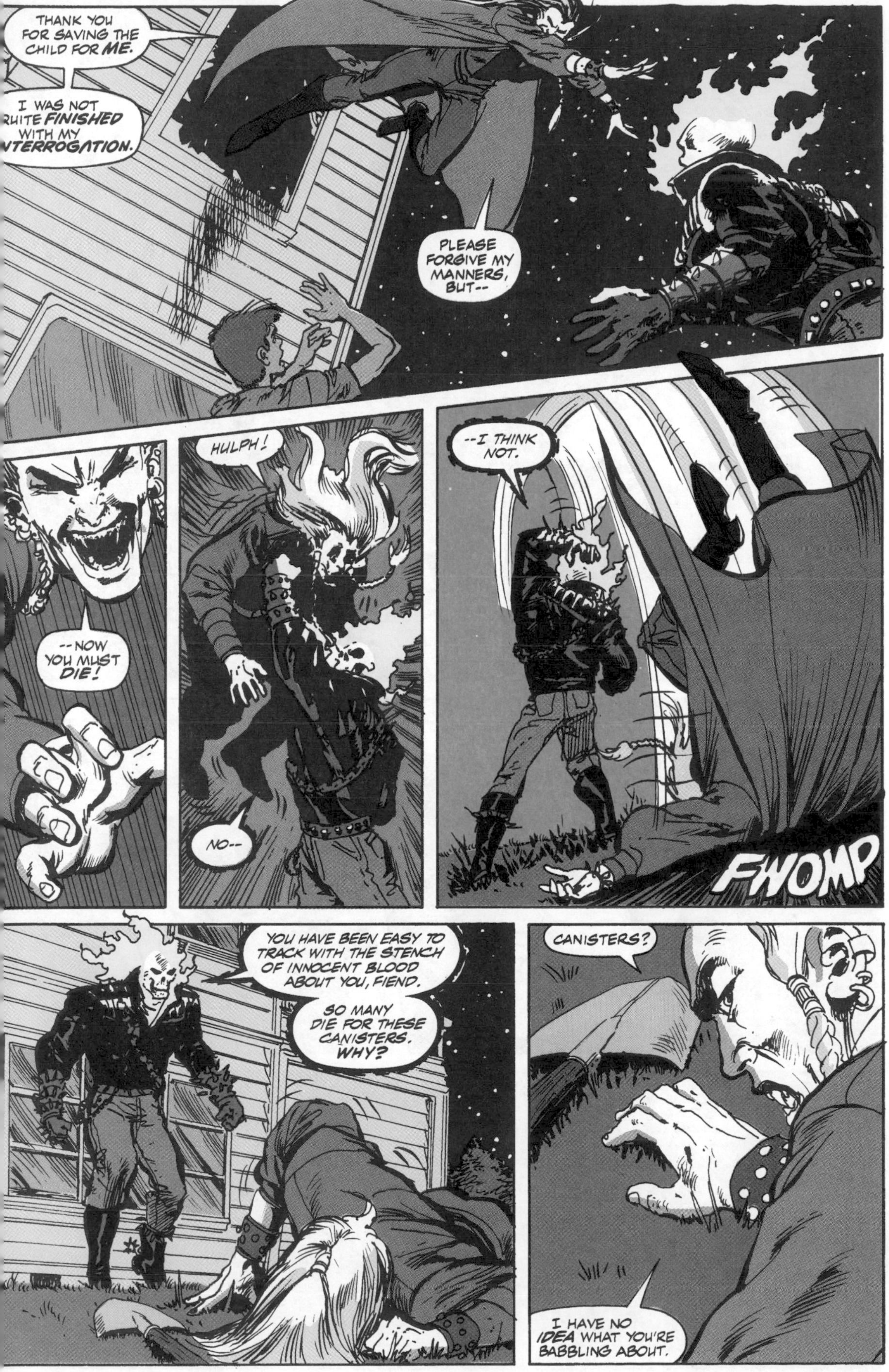
THANK YOU FOR SAVING THE CHILD FOR ME.
I WAS NOT QUITE FINISHED WITH MY INTERROGATION.
PLEASE FORGIVE MY MANNERS, BUT--
--NOW YOU MUST DIE!
HULPH!
NO--
--I THINK NOT.
FWOMP
YOU HAVE BEEN EASY TO TRACK WITH THE STENCH OF INNOCENT BLOOD ABOUT YOU, FIEND.
SO MANY DIE FOR THESE CANISTERS. WHY?
CANISTERS?
I HAVE NO IDEA WHAT YOU'RE BABBLING ABOUT.

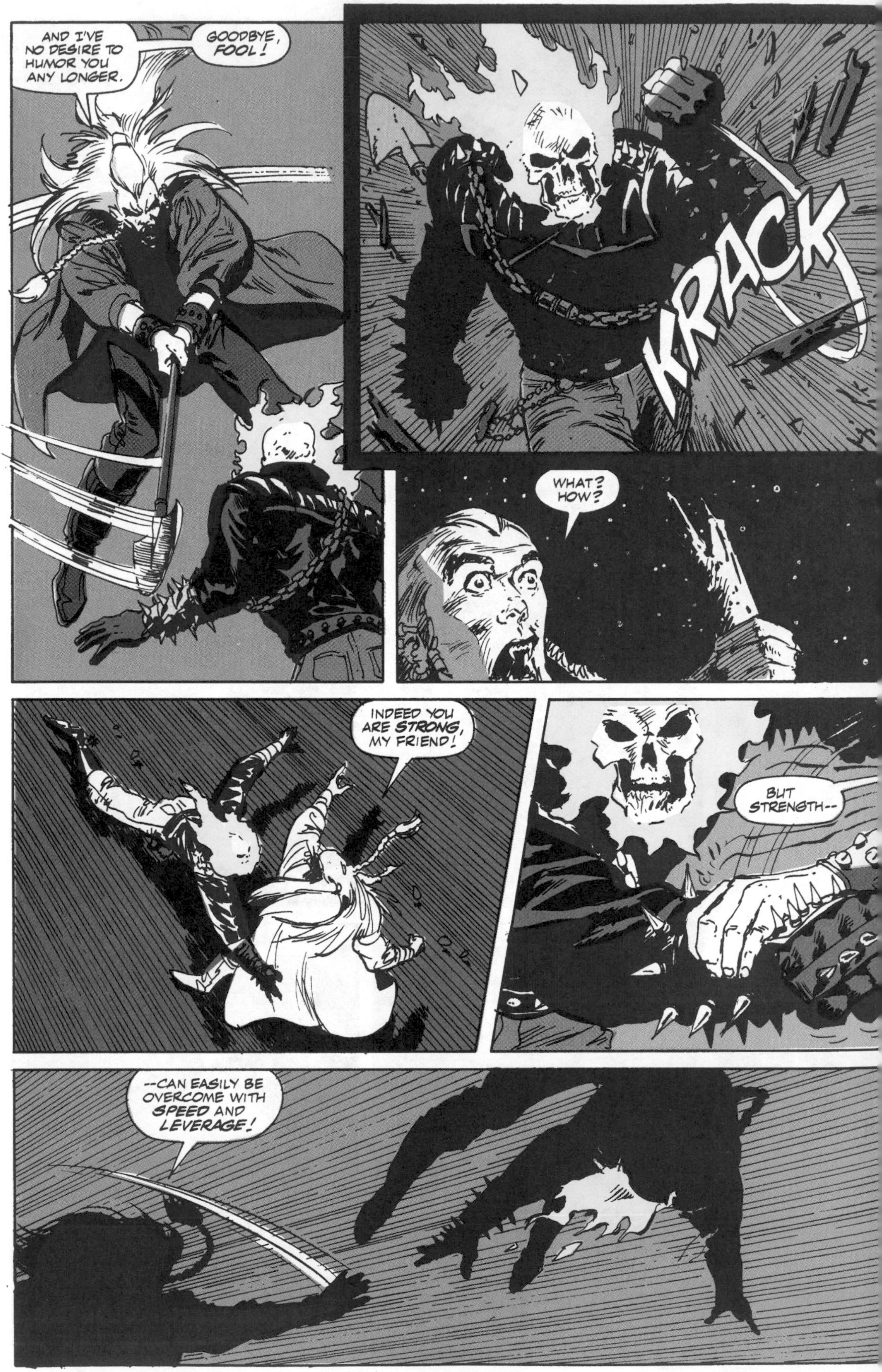
AND I'VE NO DESIRE TO HUMOR YOU ANY LONGER.
GOODBYE, FOOL!
KRACK
WHAT? HOW?
INDEED YOU ARE STRONG, MY FRIEND!
BUT STRENGTH--
--CAN EASILY BE OVERCOME WITH SPEED AND LEVERAGE!

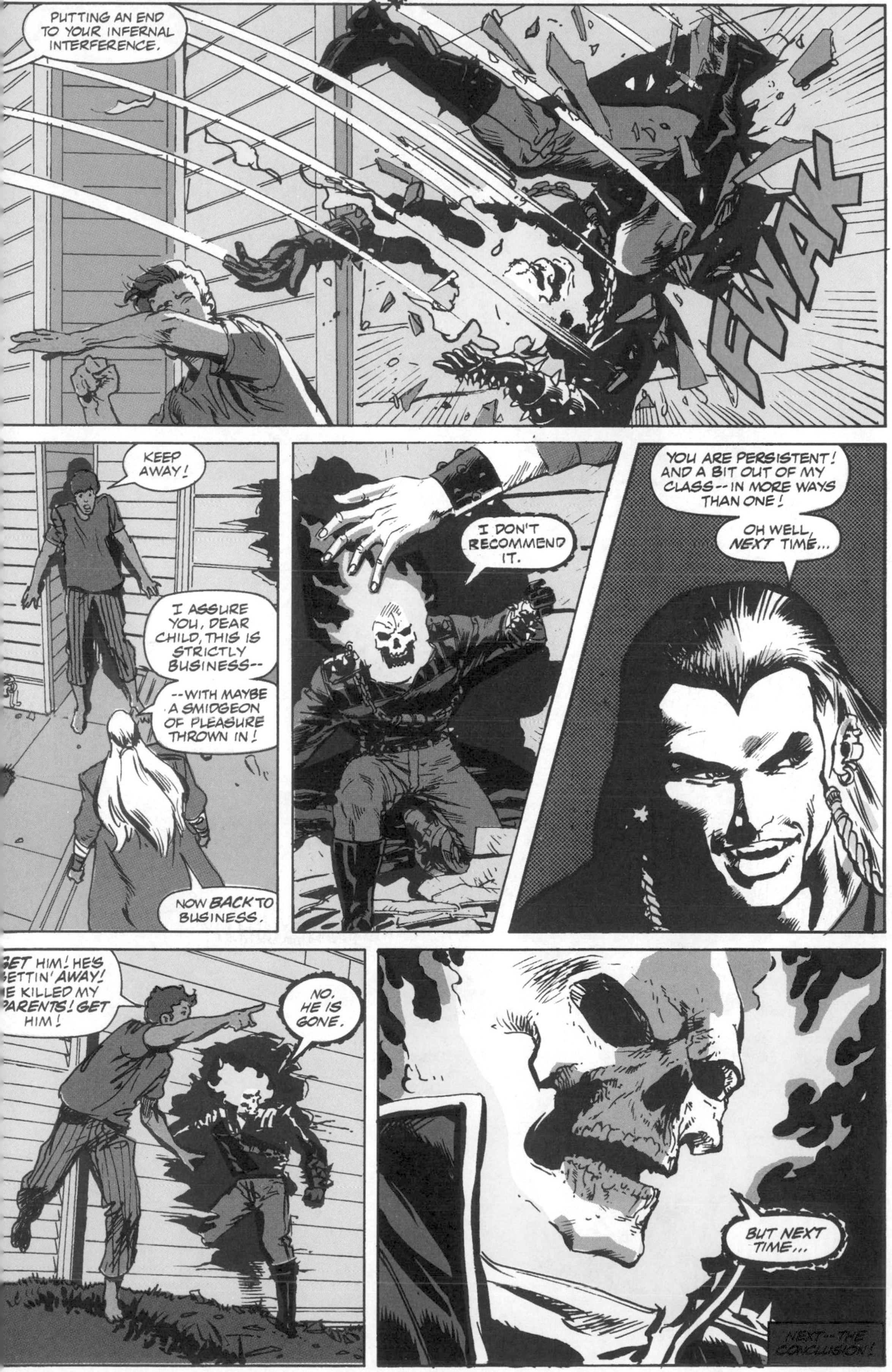
PUTTING AN END TO YOUR INFERNAL INTERFERENCE.
FWAK
KEEP AWAY!
I ASSURE YOU, DEAR CHILD, THIS IS STRICTLY BUSINESS--
--WITH MAYBE A SMIDGEON OF PLEASURE THROWN IN!
NOW BACK TO BUSINESS.
I DON'T RECOMMEND IT.
YOU ARE PERSISTENT! AND A BIT OUT OF MY CLASS--IN MORE WAYS THAN ONE!
OH WELL, NEXT TIME...
GET HIM! HE'S GETTIN' AWAY! HE KILLED MY PARENTS! GET HIM!
NO. HE IS GONE.
BUT NEXT TIME...
NEXT--THE CONCLUSION!

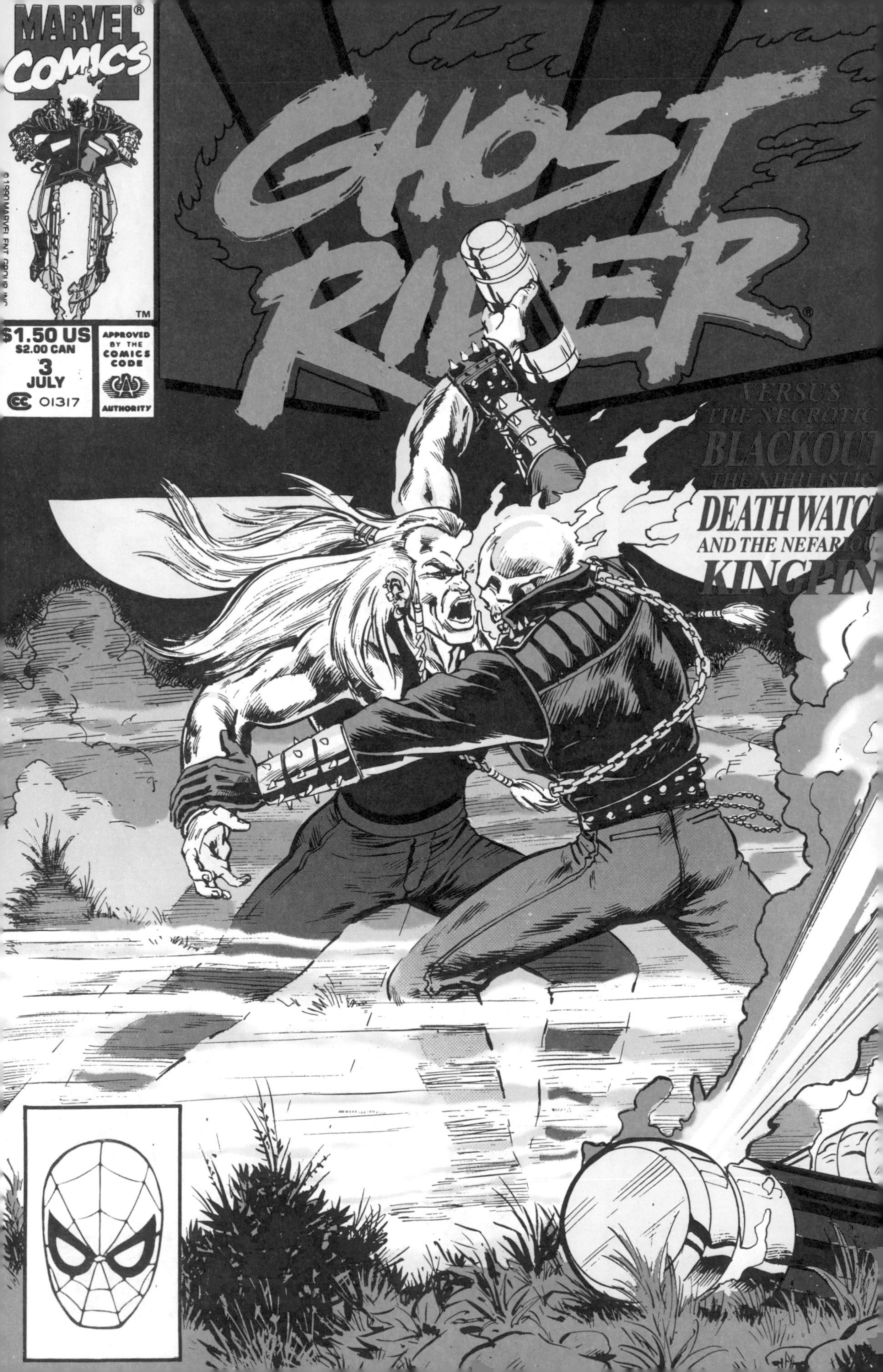

MARVEL® COMICS
GHOST RIDER®
$1.50 US
$2.00 CAN
3
JULY
01317
APPROVED BY THE COMICS CODE AUTHORITY
VERSUS
THE NECROTIC
BLACKOUT
THE NIHILISTIC
DEATHWATCH
AND THE NEFARIOUS
KINGPIN

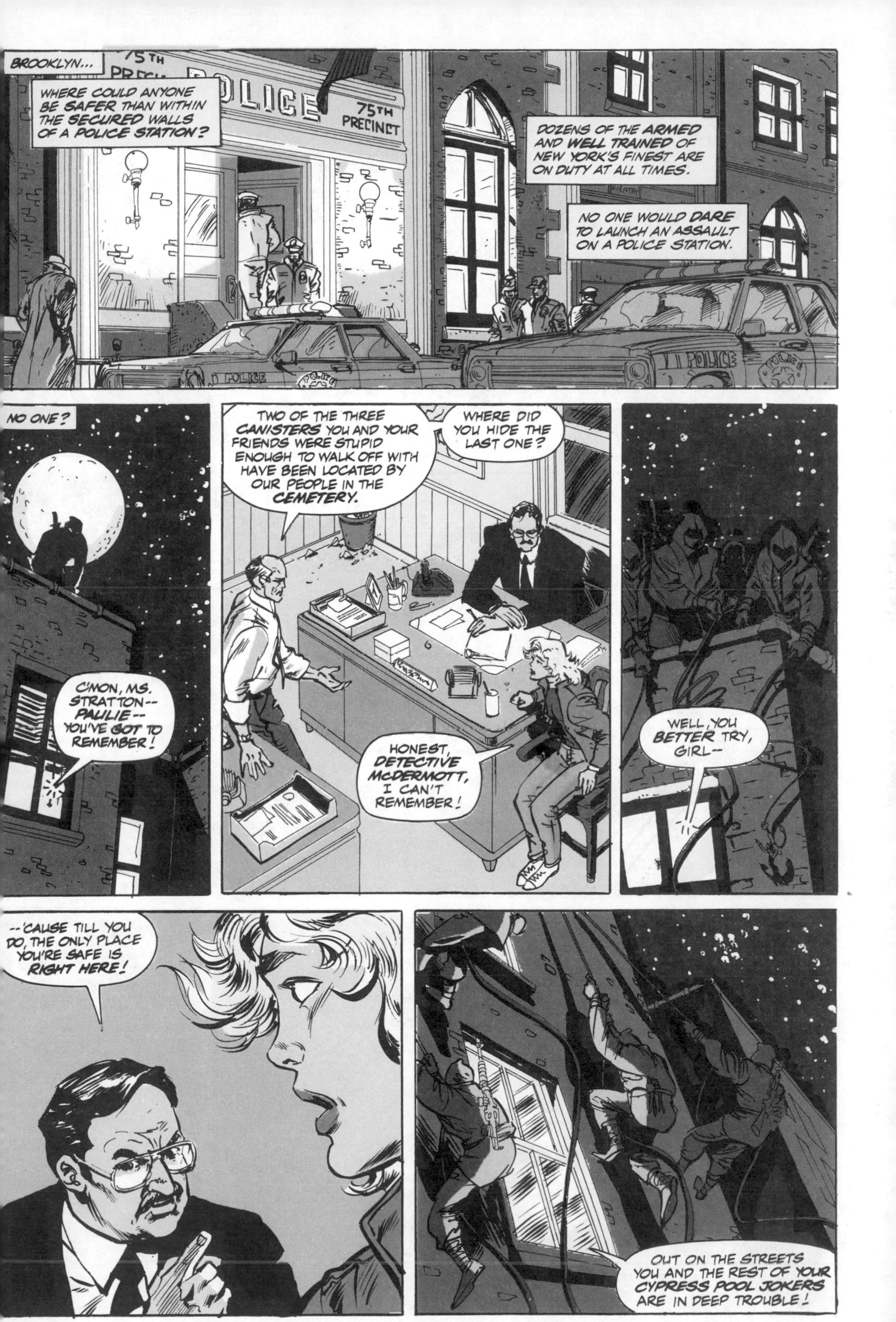

BROOKLYN...
WHERE COULD ANYONE BE SAFER THAN WITHIN THE SECURED WALLS OF A POLICE STATION?
75TH PRECINCT
POLICE
75TH PRECINCT
DOZENS OF THE ARMED AND WELL TRAINED OF NEW YORK'S FINEST ARE ON DUTY AT ALL TIMES.
NO ONE WOULD DARE TO LAUNCH AN ASSAULT ON A POLICE STATION.
POLICE
POLICE
NO ONE?
C'MON, MS. STRATTON-- PAULIE-- YOU'VE GOT TO REMEMBER!
TWO OF THE THREE CANISTERS YOU AND YOUR FRIENDS WERE STUPID ENOUGH TO WALK OFF WITH HAVE BEEN LOCATED BY OUR PEOPLE IN THE CEMETERY.
WHERE DID YOU HIDE THE LAST ONE?
HONEST, DETECTIVE McDERMOTT, I CAN'T REMEMBER!
WELL, YOU BETTER TRY, GIRL--
--'CAUSE TILL YOU DO, THE ONLY PLACE YOU'RE SAFE IS RIGHT HERE!
OUT ON THE STREETS YOU AND THE REST OF YOUR CYPRESS POOL JOKERS ARE IN DEEP TROUBLE!

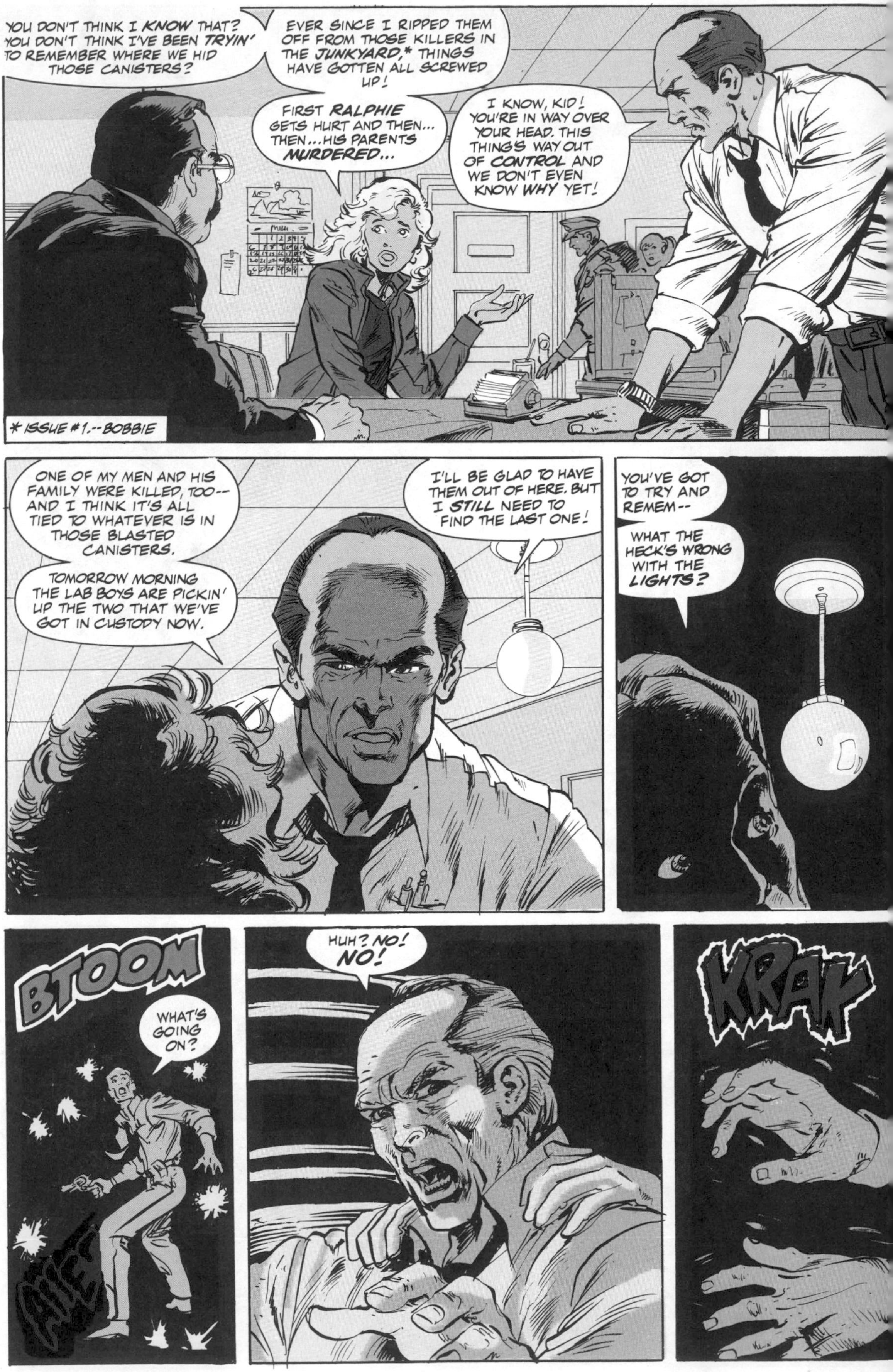
YOU DON'T THINK I KNOW THAT? YOU DON'T THINK I'VE BEEN TRYIN' TO REMEMBER WHERE WE HID THOSE CANISTERS?
EVER SINCE I RIPPED THEM OFF FROM THOSE KILLERS IN THE JUNKYARD,* THINGS HAVE GOTTEN ALL SCREWED UP!
FIRST RALPHIE GETS HURT AND THEN... THEN...HIS PARENTS MURDERED...
I KNOW, KID! YOU'RE IN WAY OVER YOUR HEAD. THIS THING'S WAY OUT OF CONTROL AND WE DON'T EVEN KNOW WHY YET!
* ISSUE #1.--BOBBIE
ONE OF MY MEN AND HIS FAMILY WERE KILLED, TOO-- AND I THINK IT'S ALL TIED TO WHATEVER IS IN THOSE BLASTED CANISTERS.
TOMORROW MORNING THE LAB BOYS ARE PICKIN' UP THE TWO THAT WE'VE GOT IN CUSTODY NOW.
I'LL BE GLAD TO HAVE THEM OUT OF HERE. BUT I STILL NEED TO FIND THE LAST ONE!
YOU'VE GOT TO TRY AND REMEM--
WHAT THE HECK'S WRONG WITH THE LIGHTS?
BTOOM
WHAT'S GOING ON?
HUH? NO! NO!
KRAK

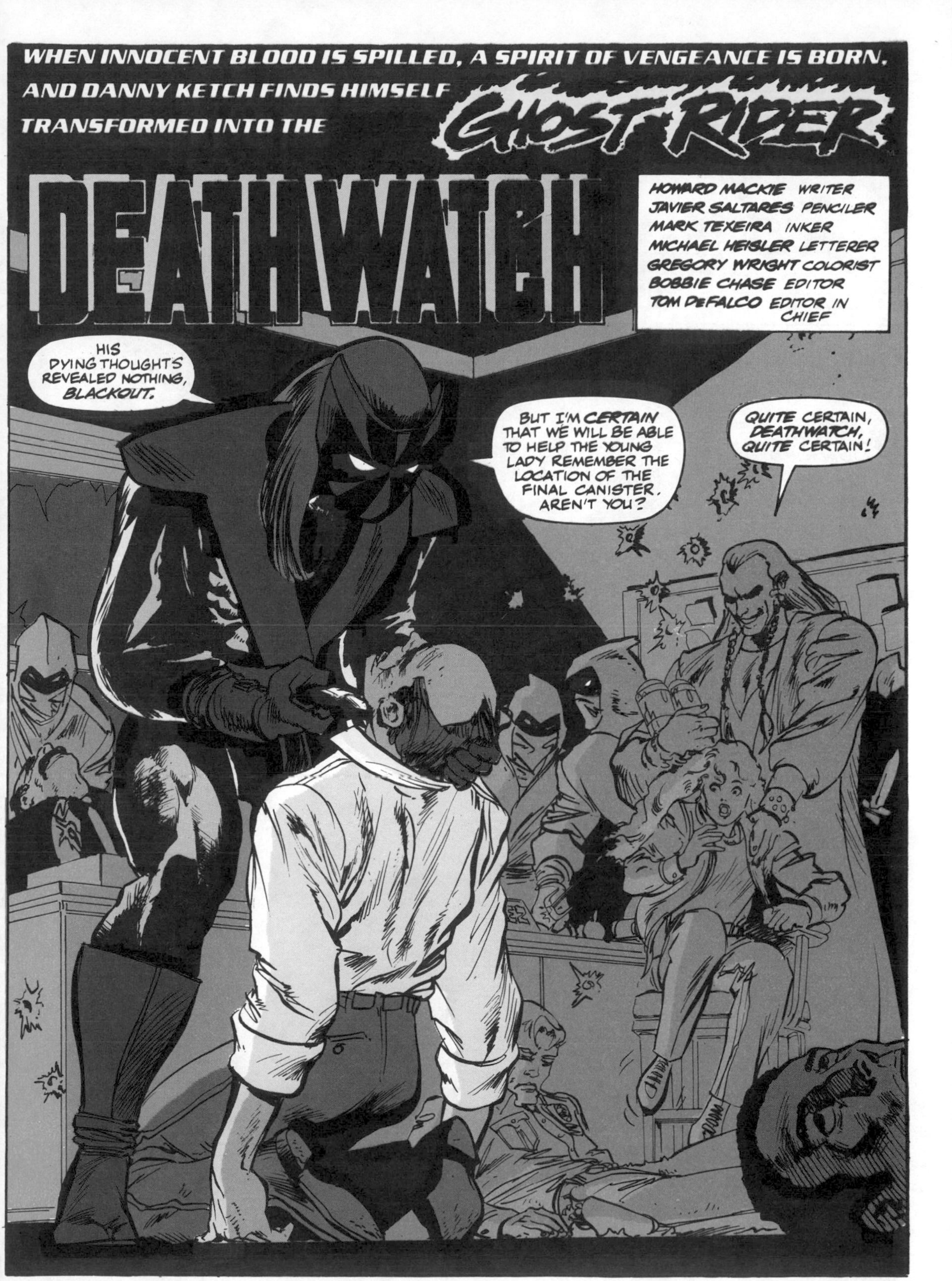

WHEN INNOCENT BLOOD IS SPILLED, A SPIRIT OF VENGEANCE IS BORN, AND DANNY KETCH FINDS HIMSELF TRANSFORMED INTO THE
GHOST RIDER
DEATHWATCH
HOWARD MACKIE WRITER
JAVIER SALTARES PENCILER
MARK TEXEIRA INKER
MICHAEL HEISLER LETTERER
GREGORY WRIGHT COLORIST
BOBBIE CHASE EDITOR
TOM DeFALCO EDITOR IN CHIEF
HIS DYING THOUGHTS REVEALED NOTHING, BLACKOUT.
BUT I'M CERTAIN THAT WE WILL BE ABLE TO HELP THE YOUNG LADY REMEMBER THE LOCATION OF THE FINAL CANISTER. AREN'T YOU?
QUITE CERTAIN, DEATHWATCH, QUITE CERTAIN!

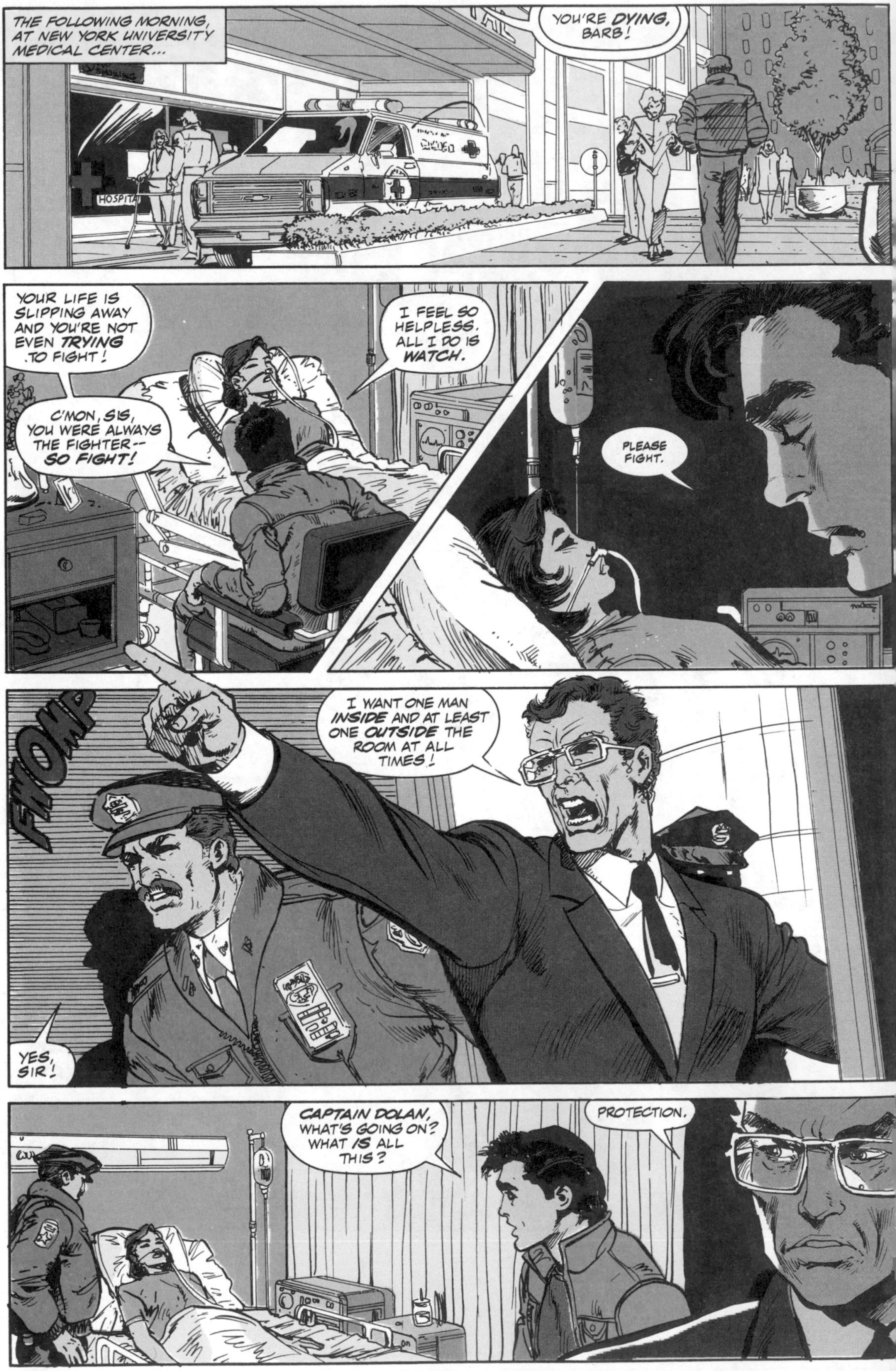
THE FOLLOWING MORNING, AT NEW YORK UNIVERSITY MEDICAL CENTER...
YOU'RE DYING, BARB!
YOUR LIFE IS SLIPPING AWAY AND YOU'RE NOT EVEN TRYING TO FIGHT!
C'MON, SIS, YOU WERE ALWAYS THE FIGHTER-- SO FIGHT!
I FEEL SO HELPLESS. ALL I DO IS WATCH.
PLEASE FIGHT.
FWOMP
I WANT ONE MAN INSIDE AND AT LEAST ONE OUTSIDE THE ROOM AT ALL TIMES!
YES, SIR!
CAPTAIN DOLAN, WHAT'S GOING ON? WHAT IS ALL THIS?
PROTECTION.

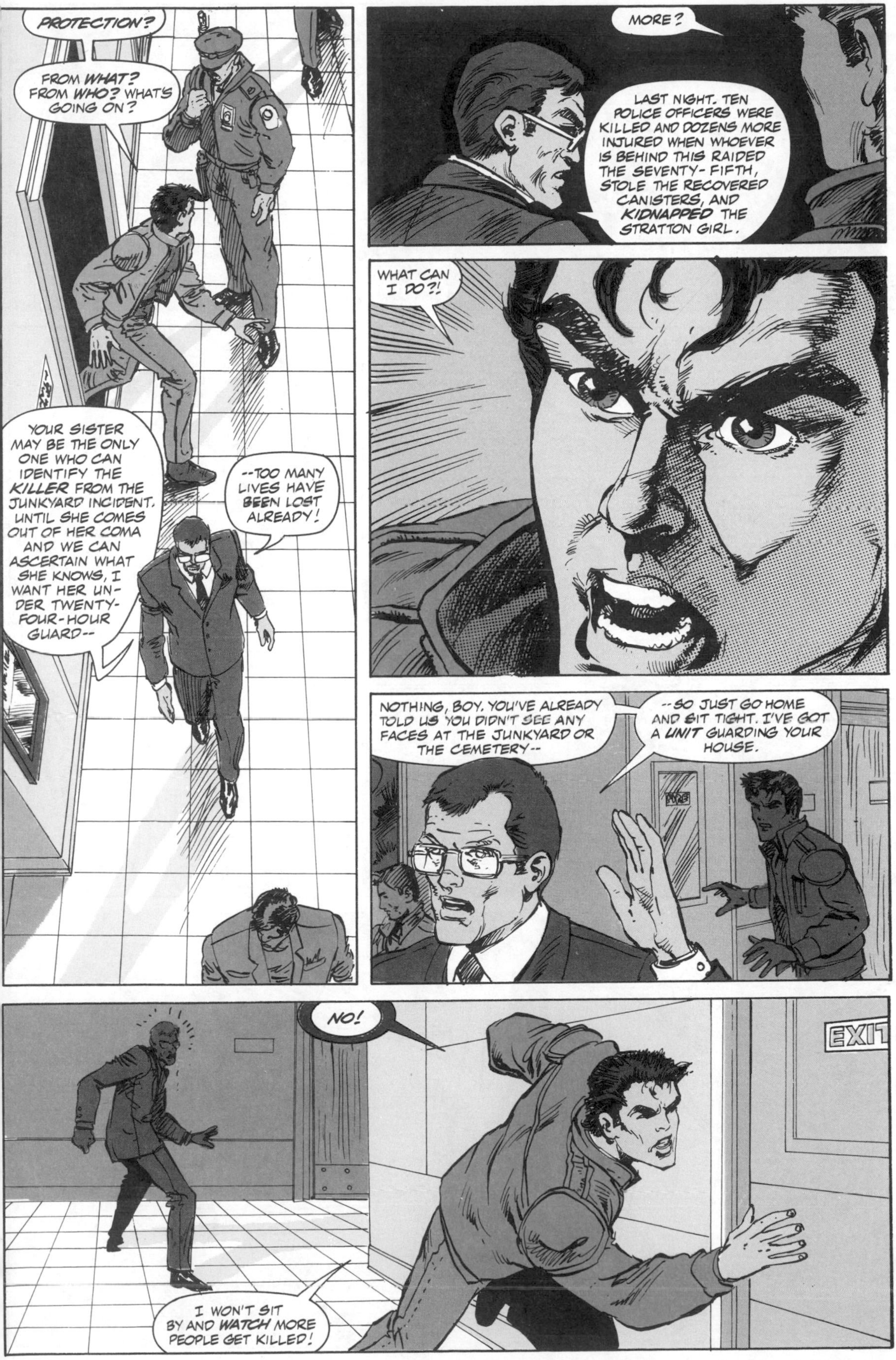

PROTECTION?
FROM WHAT? FROM WHO? WHAT'S GOING ON?
YOUR SISTER MAY BE THE ONLY ONE WHO CAN IDENTIFY THE KILLER FROM THE JUNKYARD INCIDENT. UNTIL SHE COMES OUT OF HER COMA AND WE CAN ASCERTAIN WHAT SHE KNOWS, I WANT HER UNDER TWENTY-FOUR-HOUR GUARD--
--TOO MANY LIVES HAVE BEEN LOST ALREADY!
MORE?
LAST NIGHT. TEN POLICE OFFICERS WERE KILLED AND DOZENS MORE INJURED WHEN WHOEVER IS BEHIND THIS RAIDED THE SEVENTY-FIFTH, STOLE THE RECOVERED CANISTERS, AND KIDNAPPED THE STRATTON GIRL.
WHAT CAN I DO?!
NOTHING, BOY. YOU'VE ALREADY TOLD US YOU DIDN'T SEE ANY FACES AT THE JUNKYARD OR THE CEMETERY--
--SO JUST GO HOME AND SIT TIGHT. I'VE GOT A UNIT GUARDING YOUR HOUSE.
NO!
EXIT
I WON'T SIT BY AND WATCH MORE PEOPLE GET KILLED!

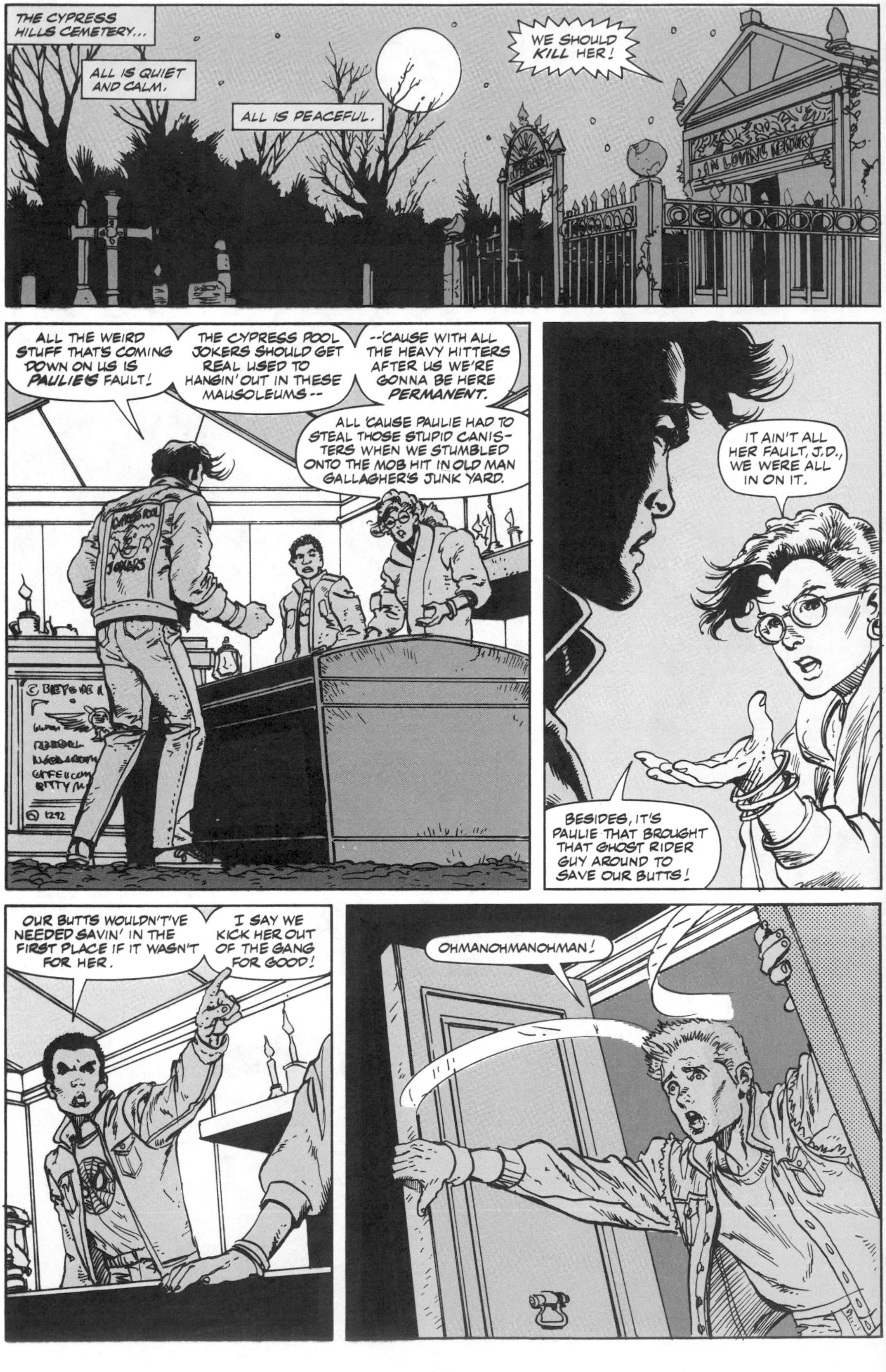
THE CYPRESS HILLS CEMETERY...
ALL IS QUIET AND CALM.
ALL IS PEACEFUL.
WE SHOULD KILL HER!
IN LOVING MEMORY
ALL THE WEIRD STUFF THAT'S COMING DOWN ON US IS PAULIE'S FAULT!
THE CYPRESS POOL JOKERS SHOULD GET REAL USED TO HANGIN' OUT IN THESE MAUSOLEUMS--
--'CAUSE WITH ALL THE HEAVY HITTERS AFTER US WE'RE GONNA BE HERE PERMANENT.
ALL 'CAUSE PAULIE HAD TO STEAL THOSE STUPID CANISTERS WHEN WE STUMBLED ONTO THE MOB HIT IN OLD MAN GALLAGHER'S JUNK YARD.
IT AIN'T ALL HER FAULT, J.D., WE WERE ALL IN ON IT.
BESIDES, IT'S PAULIE THAT BROUGHT THAT GHOST RIDER GUY AROUND TO SAVE OUR BUTTS!
OUR BUTTS WOULDN'T'VE NEEDED SAVIN' IN THE FIRST PLACE IF IT WASN'T FOR HER.
I SAY WE KICK HER OUT OF THE GANG FOR GOOD!
OHMANOHMANOHMAN!

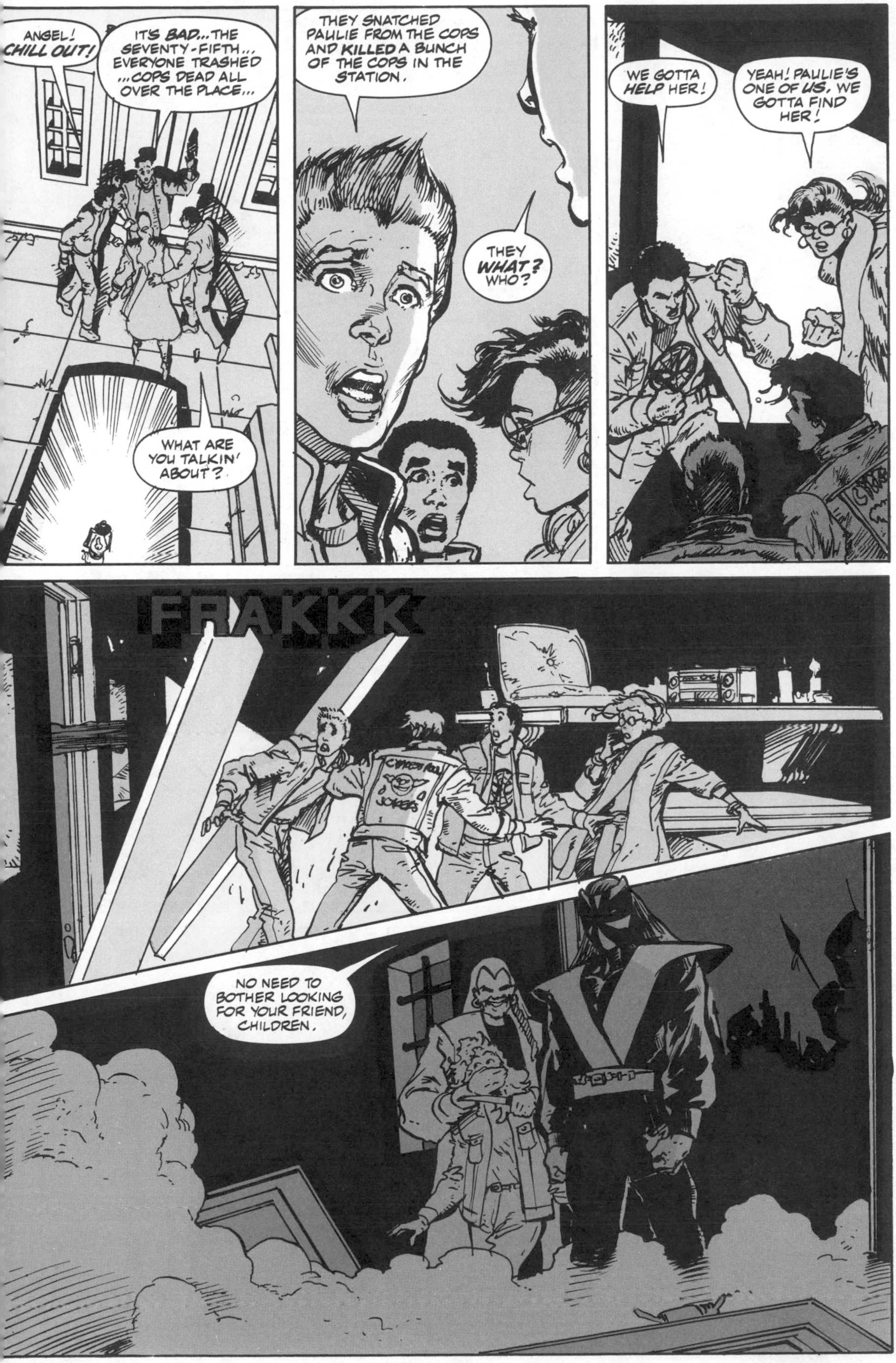
ANGEL! CHILL OUT!
IT'S BAD... THE SEVENTY-FIFTH... EVERYONE TRASHED ...COPS DEAD ALL OVER THE PLACE...
WHAT ARE YOU TALKIN' ABOUT?
THEY SNATCHED PAULIE FROM THE COPS AND KILLED A BUNCH OF THE COPS IN THE STATION.
THEY WHAT? WHO?
WE GOTTA HELP HER!
YEAH! PAULIE'S ONE OF US. WE GOTTA FIND HER!
FRAKKK
NO NEED TO BOTHER LOOKING FOR YOUR FRIEND, CHILDREN.

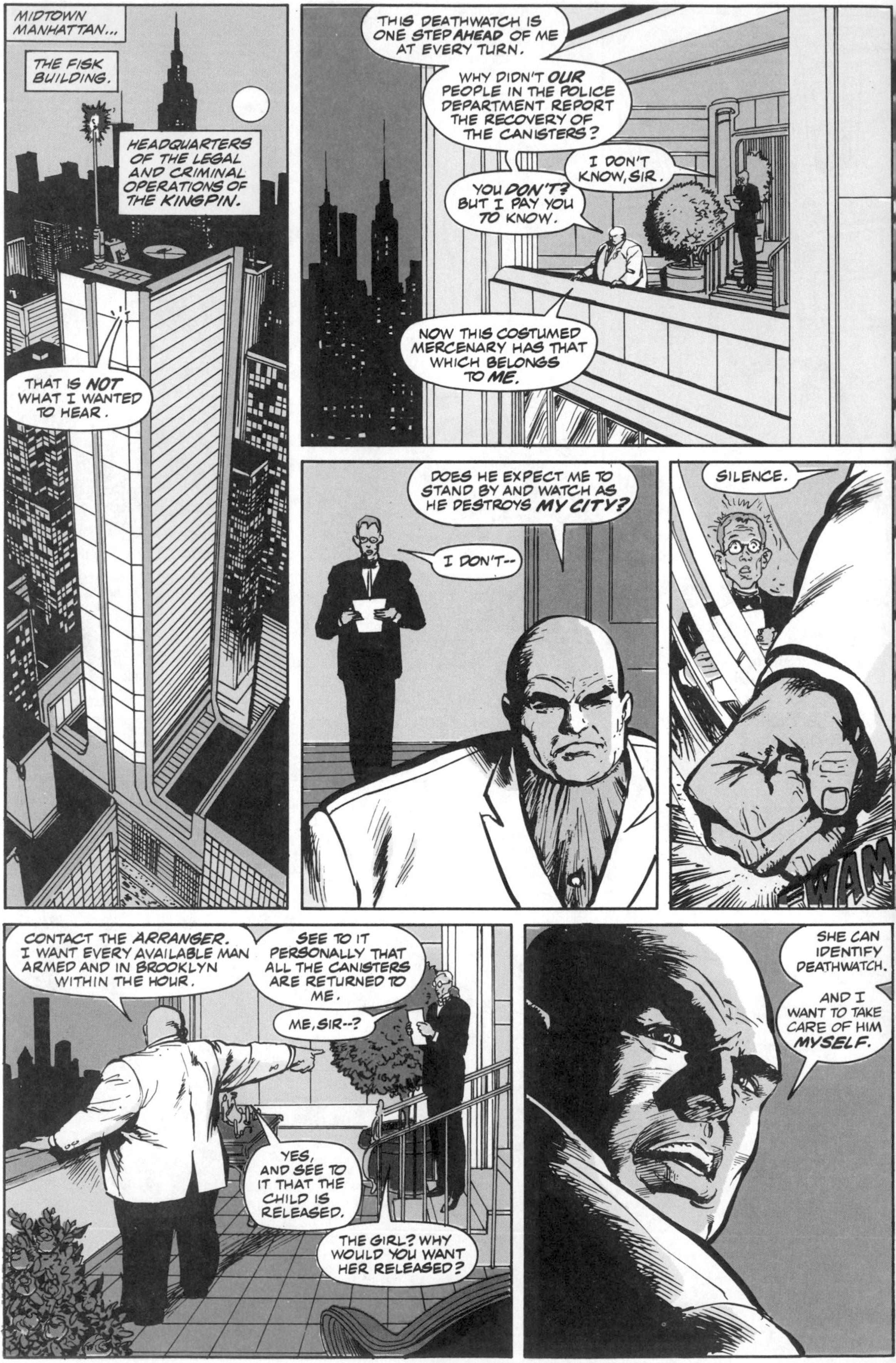
MIDTOWN MANHATTAN...
THE FISK BUILDING.
HEADQUARTERS OF THE LEGAL AND CRIMINAL OPERATIONS OF THE KINGPIN.
THAT IS NOT WHAT I WANTED TO HEAR.
THIS DEATHWATCH IS ONE STEP AHEAD OF ME AT EVERY TURN.
WHY DIDN'T OUR PEOPLE IN THE POLICE DEPARTMENT REPORT THE RECOVERY OF THE CANISTERS?
I DON'T KNOW, SIR.
YOU DON'T? BUT I PAY YOU TO KNOW.
NOW THIS COSTUMED MERCENARY HAS THAT WHICH BELONGS TO ME.
DOES HE EXPECT ME TO STAND BY AND WATCH AS HE DESTROYS MY CITY?
I DON'T--
SILENCE.
WAM
CONTACT THE ARRANGER. I WANT EVERY AVAILABLE MAN ARMED AND IN BROOKLYN WITHIN THE HOUR.
SEE TO IT PERSONALLY THAT ALL THE CANISTERS ARE RETURNED TO ME.
ME, SIR--?
YES, AND SEE TO IT THAT THE CHILD IS RELEASED.
THE GIRL? WHY WOULD YOU WANT HER RELEASED?
SHE CAN IDENTIFY DEATHWATCH.
AND I WANT TO TAKE CARE OF HIM MYSELF.

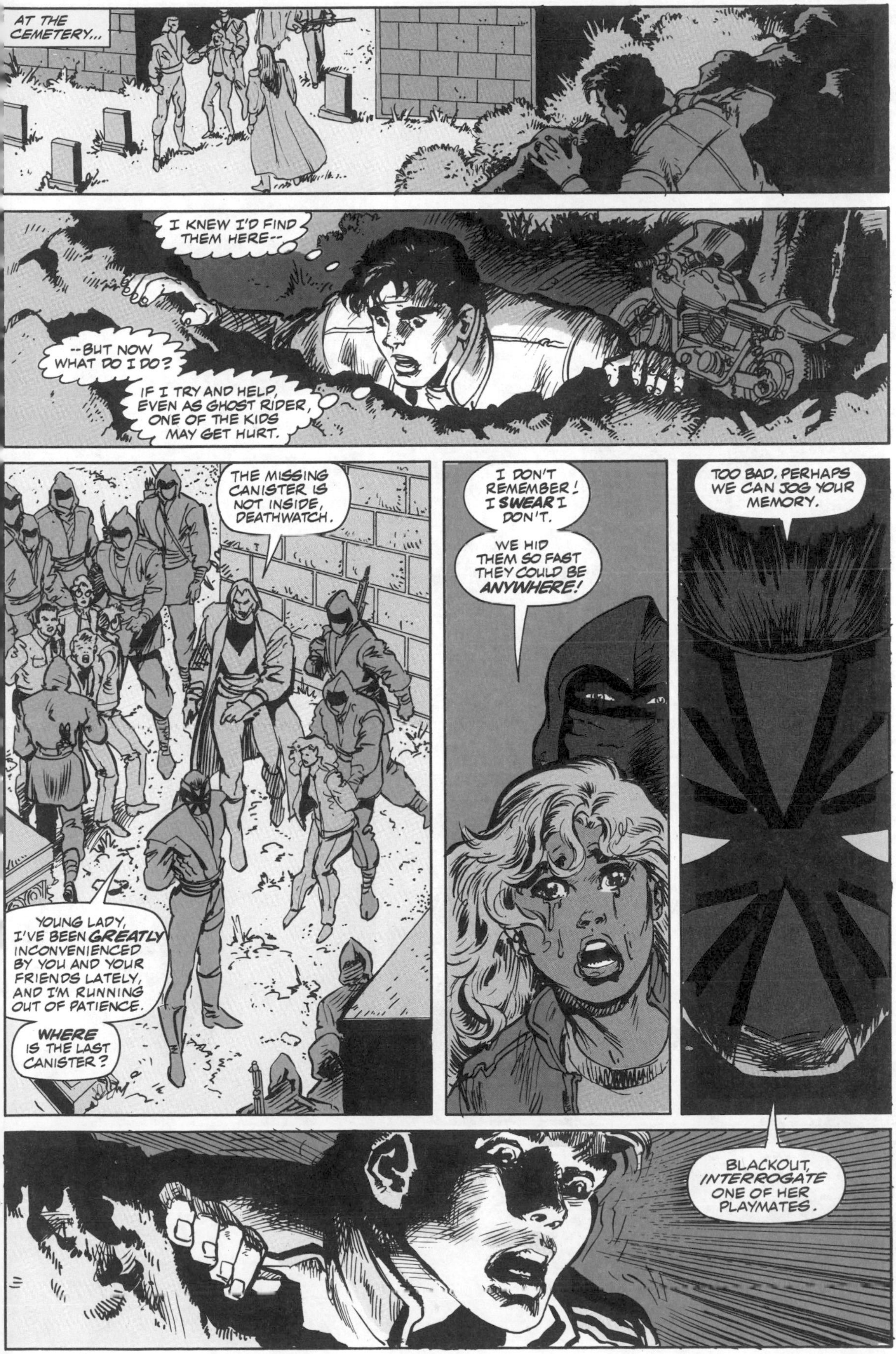
AT THE CEMETERY...
I KNEW I'D FIND THEM HERE--
--BUT NOW WHAT DO I DO?
IF I TRY AND HELP, EVEN AS GHOST RIDER, ONE OF THE KIDS MAY GET HURT.
THE MISSING CANISTER IS NOT INSIDE, DEATHWATCH.
YOUNG LADY, I'VE BEEN GREATLY INCONVENIENCED BY YOU AND YOUR FRIENDS LATELY, AND I'M RUNNING OUT OF PATIENCE.
WHERE IS THE LAST CANISTER?
I DON'T REMEMBER! I SWEAR I DON'T.
WE HID THEM SO FAST THEY COULD BE ANYWHERE!
TOO BAD. PERHAPS WE CAN JOG YOUR MEMORY.
BLACKOUT, INTERROGATE ONE OF HER PLAYMATES.

IT WILL BE MY PLEASURE, SIR.

OH, BY THE WAY, YOU MAY *KILL* HIM.

NO! ANGEL!

NO!

I'VE GOT TO *DO* SOMETHING!

YOUR FRIEND DIED BECAUSE OF YOUR *MEMORY LAPSE.*

WHO WILL BE NEXT?

I CAN'T JUST STAND BY AND WATCH HIM KILL THEM ALL. IF I EVER NEEDED THE MOTOR-CYCLE TO DO ITS THING -- I NEED IT *NOW!*

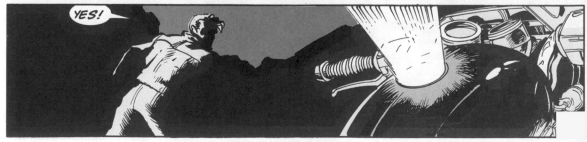

YES!

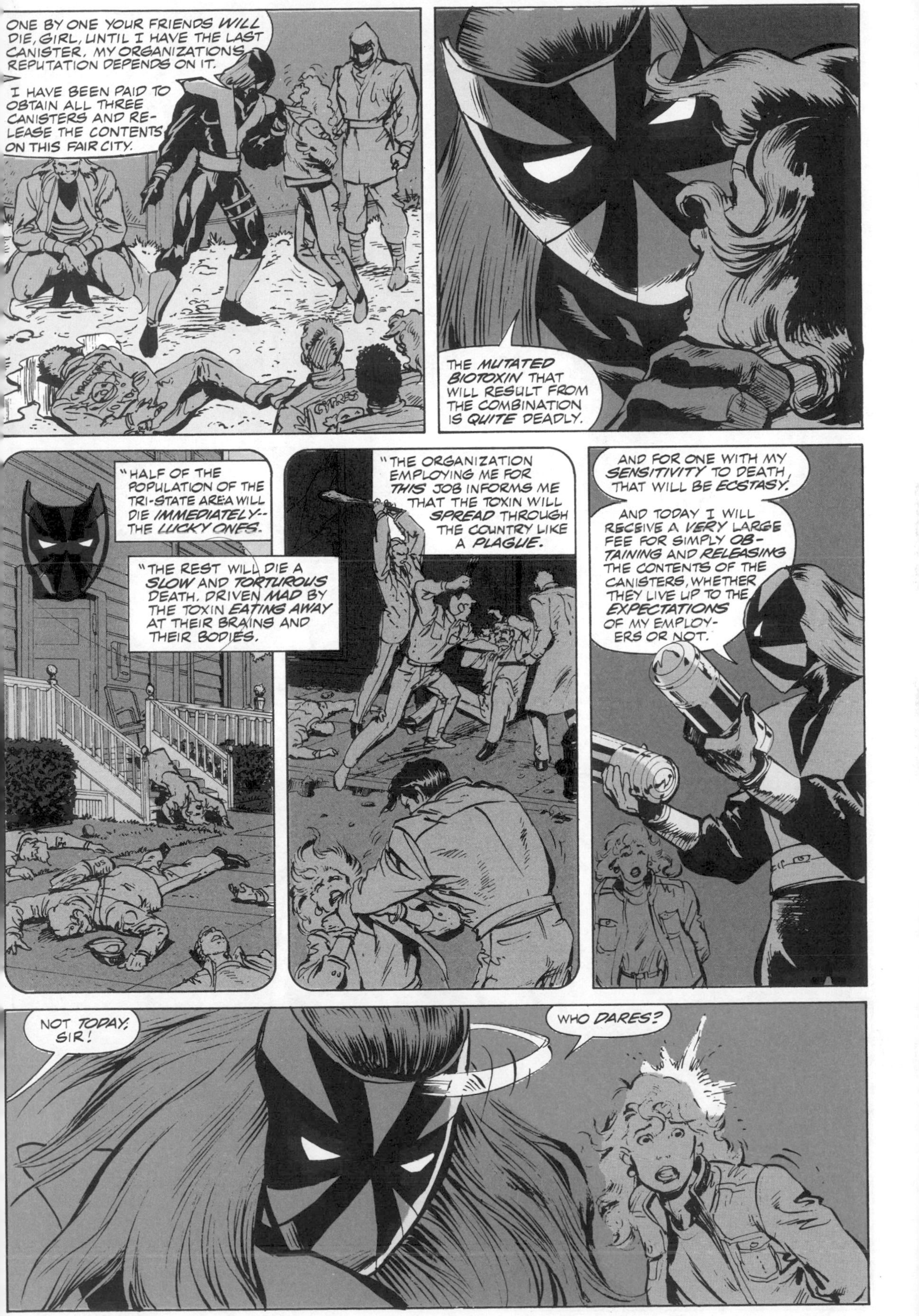
ONE BY ONE YOUR FRIENDS WILL DIE, GIRL, UNTIL I HAVE THE LAST CANISTER. MY ORGANIZATION'S REPUTATION DEPENDS ON IT.
I HAVE BEEN PAID TO OBTAIN ALL THREE CANISTERS AND RELEASE THE CONTENTS ON THIS FAIR CITY.
THE MUTATED BIOTOXIN THAT WILL RESULT FROM THE COMBINATION IS QUITE DEADLY.
"HALF OF THE POPULATION OF THE TRI-STATE AREA WILL DIE IMMEDIATELY-- THE LUCKY ONES.
"THE REST WILL DIE A SLOW AND TORTUROUS DEATH, DRIVEN MAD BY THE TOXIN EATING AWAY AT THEIR BRAINS AND THEIR BODIES.
"THE ORGANIZATION EMPLOYING ME FOR THIS JOB INFORMS ME THAT THE TOXIN WILL SPREAD THROUGH THE COUNTRY LIKE A PLAGUE.
AND FOR ONE WITH MY SENSITIVITY TO DEATH, THAT WILL BE ECSTASY.
AND TODAY I WILL RECEIVE A VERY LARGE FEE FOR SIMPLY OBTAINING AND RELEASING THE CONTENTS OF THE CANISTERS, WHETHER THEY LIVE UP TO THE EXPECTATIONS OF MY EMPLOYERS OR NOT.
NOT TODAY, SIR!
WHO DARES?

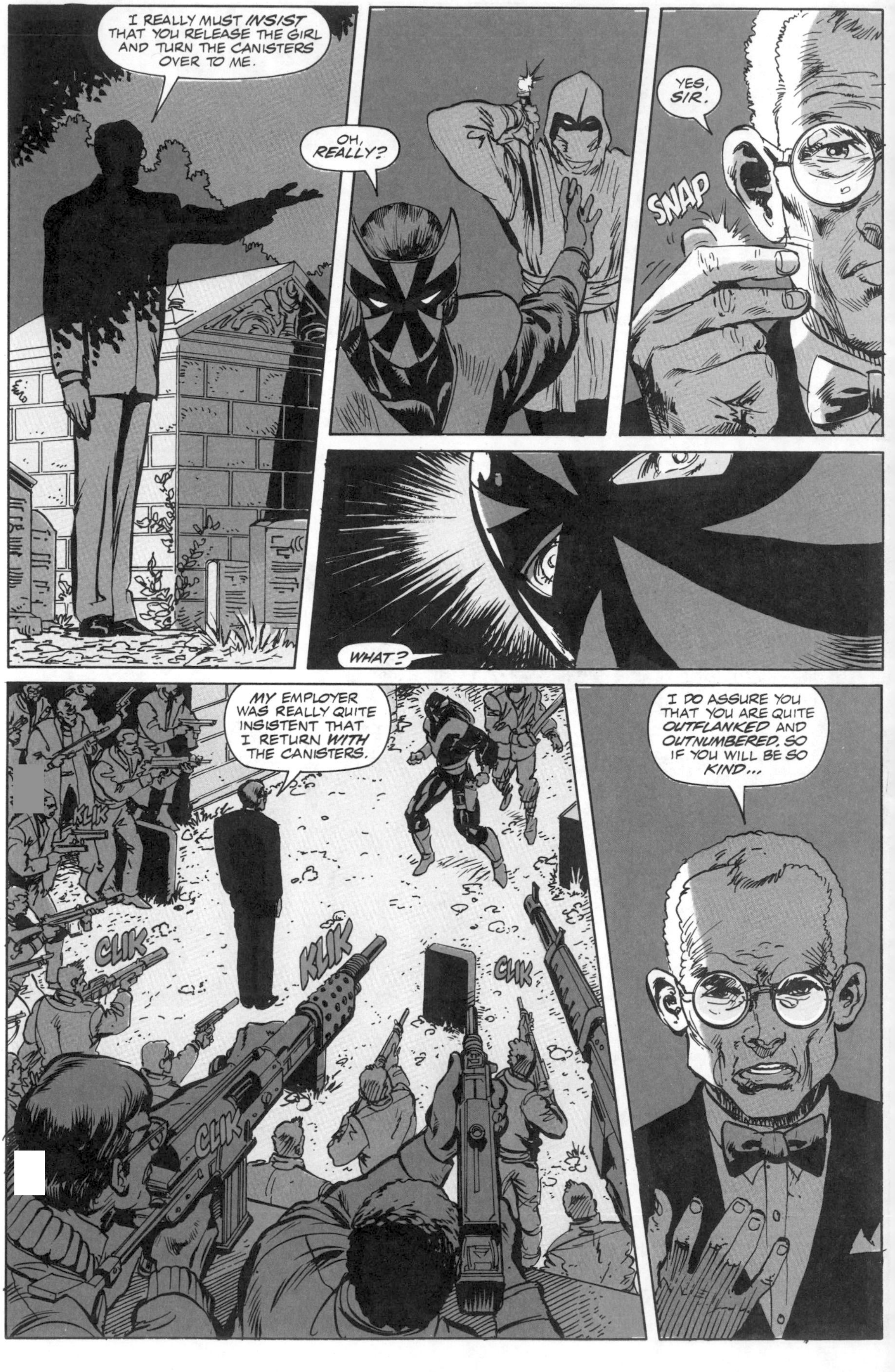
I REALLY MUST INSIST THAT YOU RELEASE THE GIRL AND TURN THE CANISTERS OVER TO ME.
OH, REALLY?
YES, SIR.
SNAP
WHAT?
MY EMPLOYER WAS REALLY QUITE INSISTENT THAT I RETURN WITH THE CANISTERS.
KLIK
CLIK
KLIK
CLIK
CLIK
I DO ASSURE YOU THAT YOU ARE QUITE OUTFLANKED AND OUTNUMBERED. SO IF YOU WILL BE SO KIND...

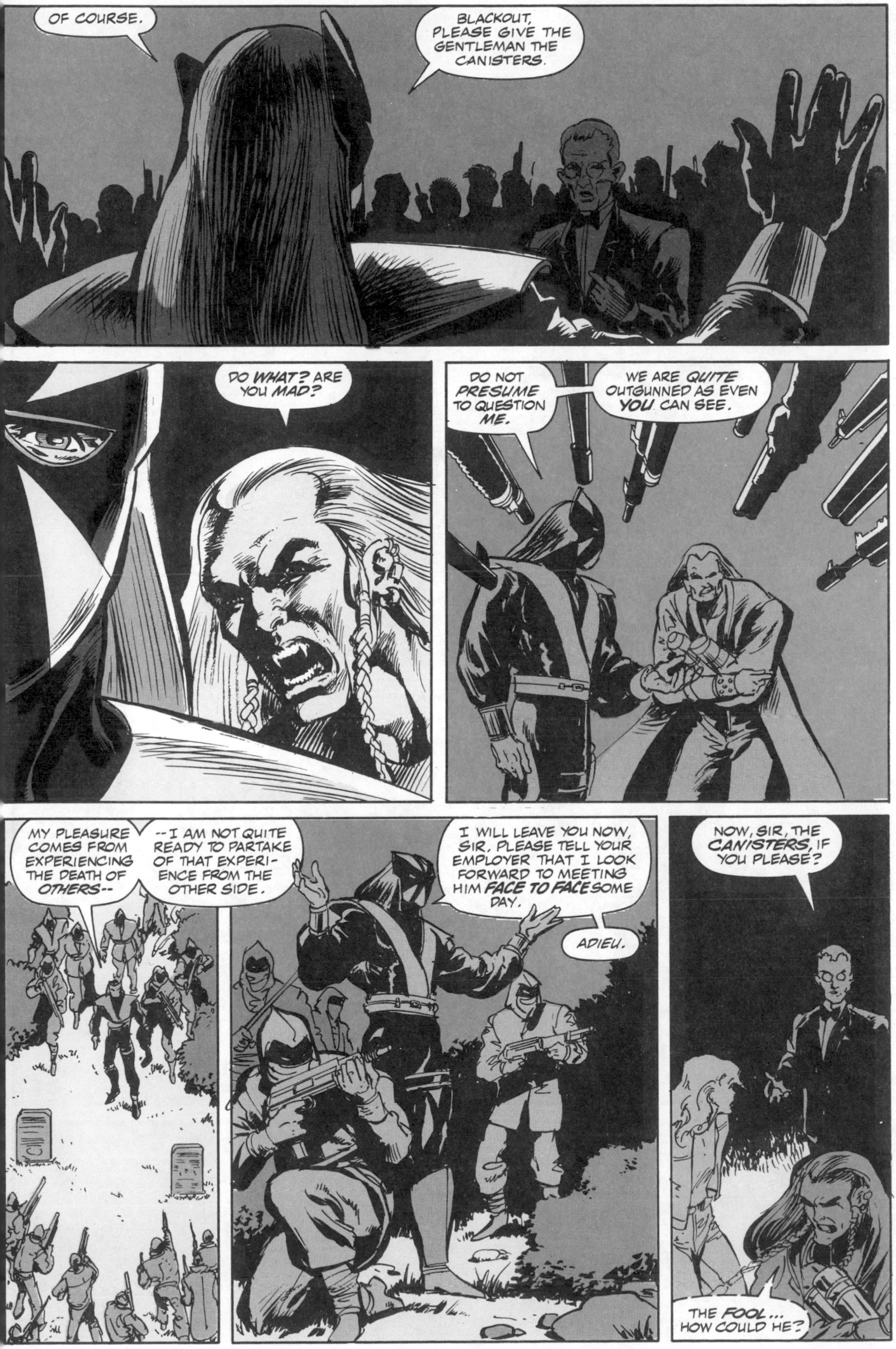
OF COURSE.
BLACKOUT, PLEASE GIVE THE GENTLEMAN THE CANISTERS.
DO WHAT? ARE YOU MAD?
DO NOT PRESUME TO QUESTION ME.
WE ARE QUITE OUTGUNNED AS EVEN YOU CAN SEE.
MY PLEASURE COMES FROM EXPERIENCING THE DEATH OF OTHERS--
--I AM NOT QUITE READY TO PARTAKE OF THAT EXPERIENCE FROM THE OTHER SIDE.
I WILL LEAVE YOU NOW, SIR. PLEASE TELL YOUR EMPLOYER THAT I LOOK FORWARD TO MEETING HIM FACE TO FACE SOME DAY.
ADIEU.
NOW, SIR, THE CANISTERS, IF YOU PLEASE?
THE FOOL... HOW COULD HE?

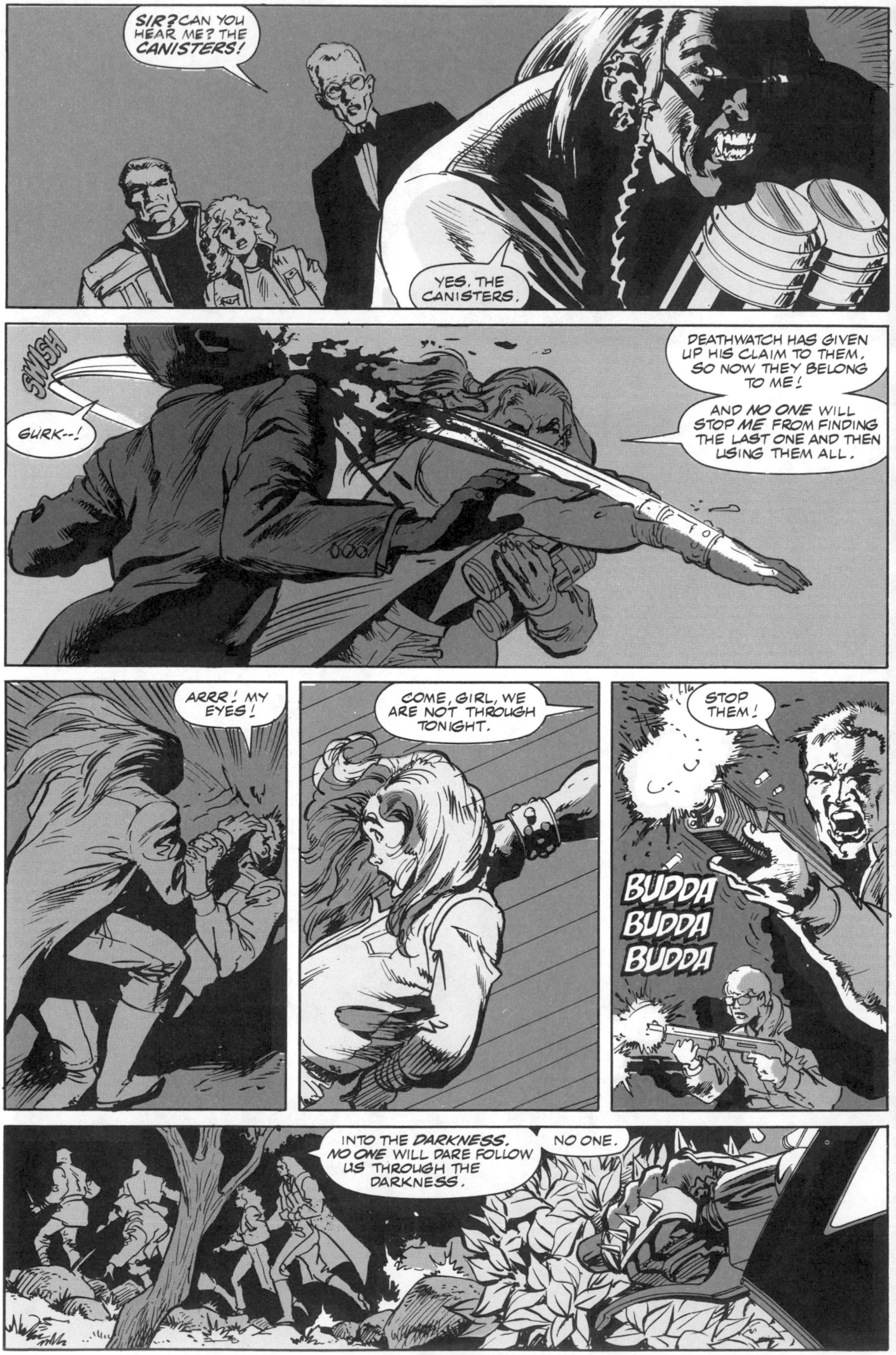
SIR? CAN YOU HEAR ME? THE CANISTERS!
YES. THE CANISTERS.
SWISH
GURK--!
DEATHWATCH HAS GIVEN UP HIS CLAIM TO THEM, SO NOW THEY BELONG TO ME!
AND NO ONE WILL STOP ME FROM FINDING THE LAST ONE AND THEN USING THEM ALL.
ARRR! MY EYES!
COME, GIRL, WE ARE NOT THROUGH TONIGHT.
STOP THEM!
BUDDA BUDDA BUDDA
INTO THE DARKNESS. NO ONE WILL DARE FOLLOW US THROUGH THE DARKNESS.
NO ONE.

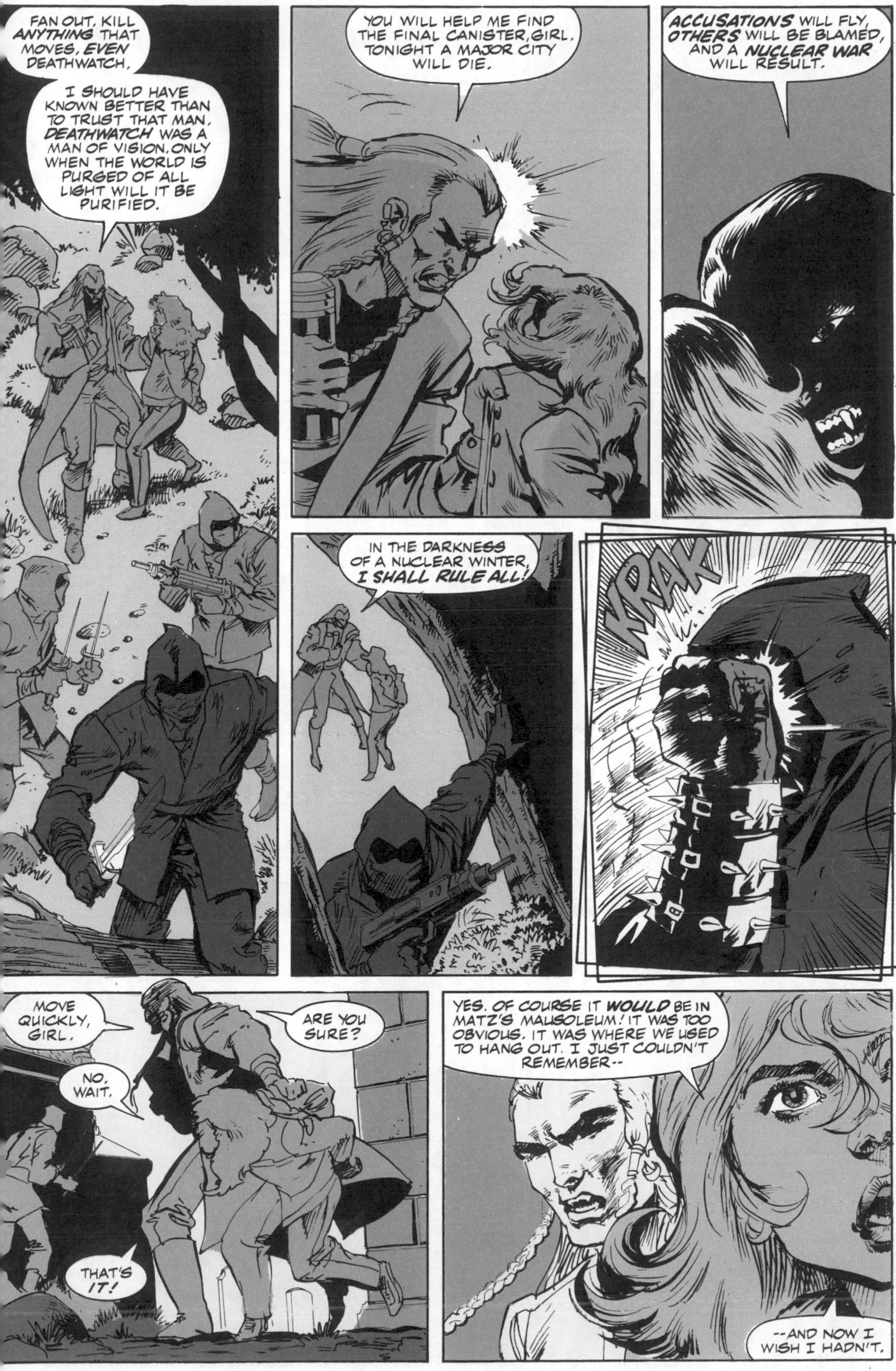

FAN OUT. KILL ANYTHING THAT MOVES, EVEN DEATHWATCH.
I SHOULD HAVE KNOWN BETTER THAN TO TRUST THAT MAN. DEATHWATCH WAS A MAN OF VISION. ONLY WHEN THE WORLD IS PURGED OF ALL LIGHT WILL IT BE PURIFIED.
YOU WILL HELP ME FIND THE FINAL CANISTER, GIRL. TONIGHT A MAJOR CITY WILL DIE.
ACCUSATIONS WILL FLY, OTHERS WILL BE BLAMED, AND A NUCLEAR WAR WILL RESULT.
IN THE DARKNESS OF A NUCLEAR WINTER, I SHALL RULE ALL!
KRAK
MOVE QUICKLY, GIRL.
ARE YOU SURE?
NO. WAIT.
THAT'S IT!
YES. OF COURSE IT WOULD BE IN MATZ'S MAUSOLEUM! IT WAS TOO OBVIOUS. IT WAS WHERE WE USED TO HANG OUT. I JUST COULDN'T REMEMBER--
--AND NOW I WISH I HADN'T.

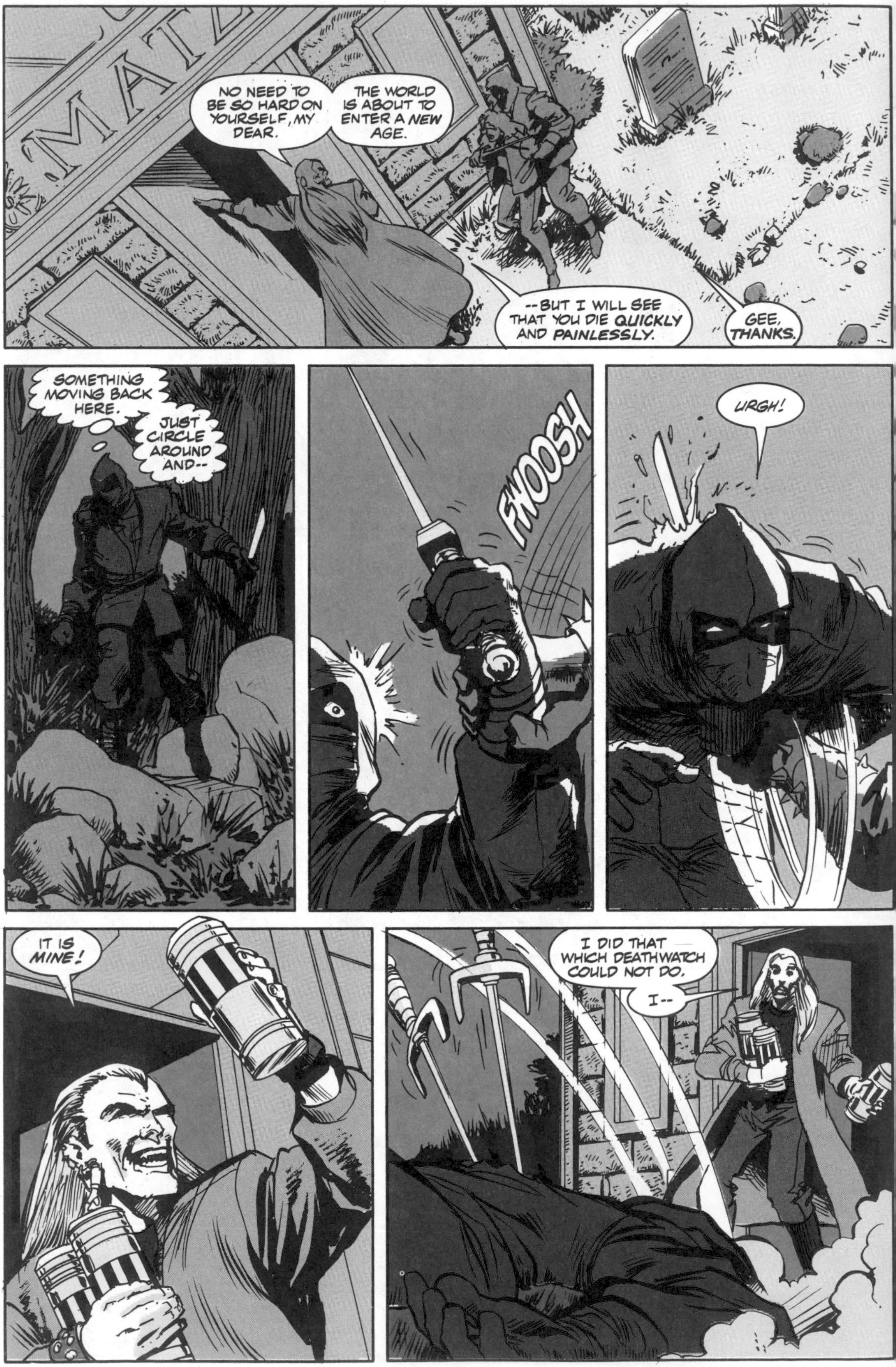
MAT
NO NEED TO BE SO HARD ON YOURSELF, MY DEAR.
THE WORLD IS ABOUT TO ENTER A NEW AGE.
--BUT I WILL SEE THAT YOU DIE QUICKLY AND PAINLESSLY.
GEE, THANKS.
SOMETHING MOVING BACK HERE.
JUST CIRCLE AROUND AND--
FWOOSH
URGH!
IT IS MINE!
I DID THAT WHICH DEATHWATCH COULD NOT DO.
I--

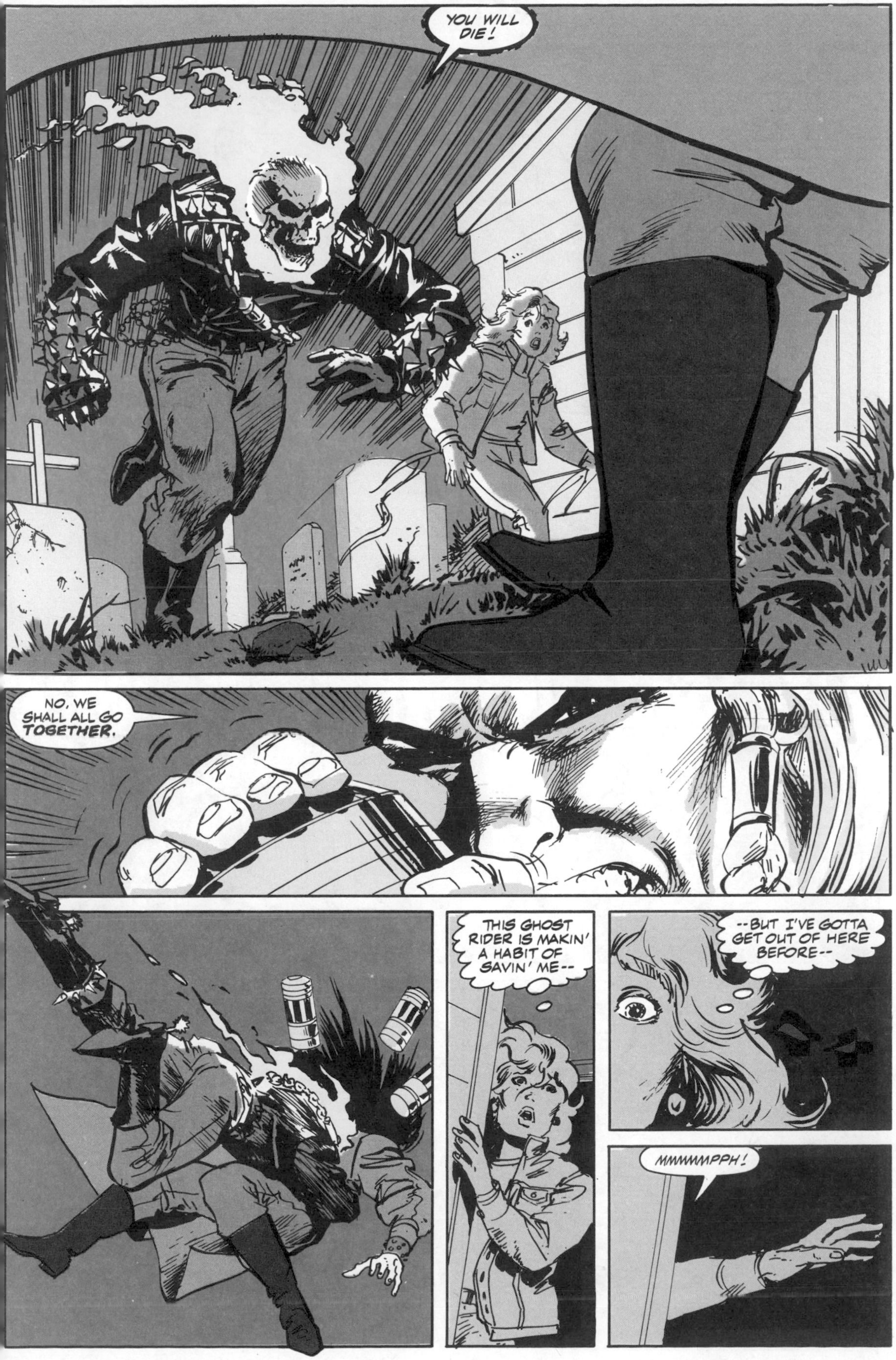
YOU WILL DIE!
NO, WE SHALL ALL GO TOGETHER.
THIS GHOST RIDER IS MAKIN' A HABIT OF SAVIN' ME--
--BUT I'VE GOTTA GET OUT OF HERE BEFORE--
MMMMMPPH!

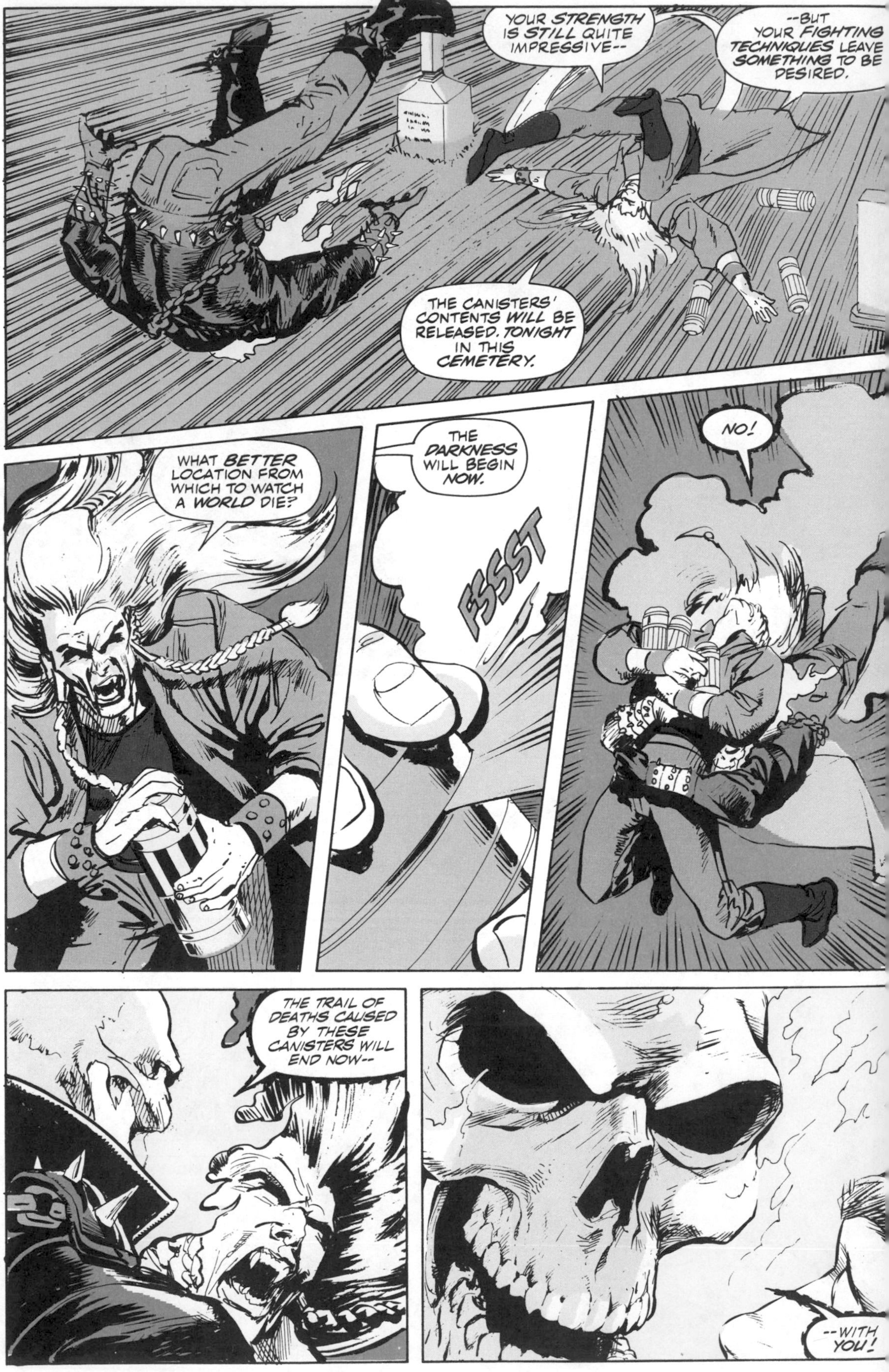
YOUR STRENGTH IS STILL QUITE IMPRESSIVE--
--BUT YOUR FIGHTING TECHNIQUES LEAVE SOMETHING TO BE DESIRED.
THE CANISTERS' CONTENTS WILL BE RELEASED. TONIGHT IN THIS CEMETERY.
WHAT BETTER LOCATION FROM WHICH TO WATCH A WORLD DIE?
THE DARKNESS WILL BEGIN NOW.
FSSST
NO!
THE TRAIL OF DEATHS CAUSED BY THESE CANISTERS WILL END NOW--
--WITH YOU!

AGAIN YOU THREATEN ME WITH YOUR PITIFUL PENANCE STARE.
YOU WISH TO BRING ME TO THE LIGHT?
ALLOW ME TO BRING YOU TO MY DARKNESS --PERMANENTLY!
ARRRRRGH!
BLACKOUT'S MECHANICAL FANGS PIERCE GHOST RIDER'S GARMENT, MAKING CONTACT WITH MYSTIC HELLFIRE. THE RESULT IS--
--AGONY.

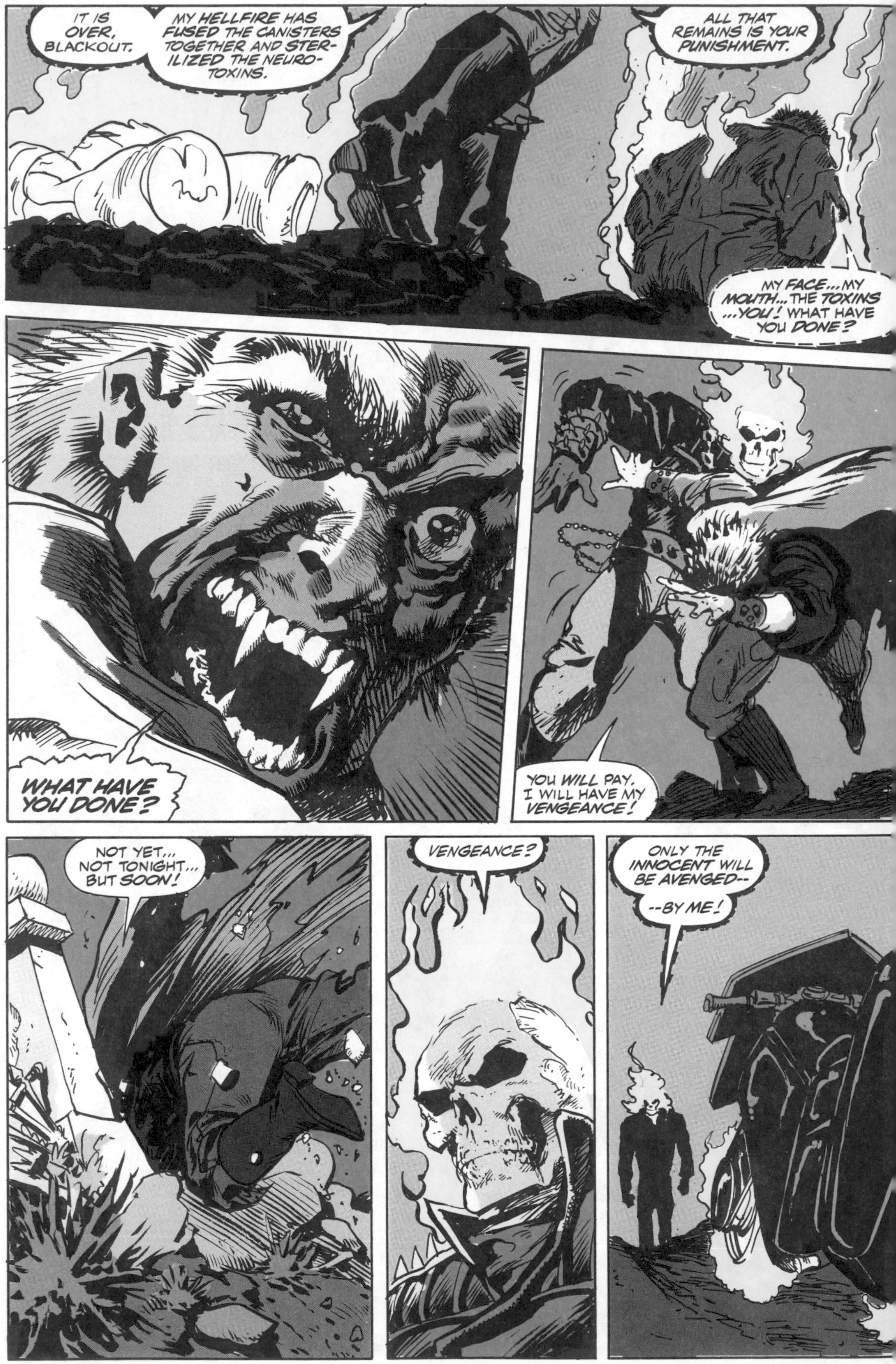

IT IS OVER, BLACKOUT.
MY HELLFIRE HAS FUSED THE CANISTERS TOGETHER AND STERILIZED THE NEURO-TOXINS.
ALL THAT REMAINS IS YOUR PUNISHMENT.
MY FACE... MY MOUTH... THE TOXINS ...YOU! WHAT HAVE YOU DONE?
WHAT HAVE YOU DONE?
YOU WILL PAY. I WILL HAVE MY VENGEANCE!
NOT YET... NOT TONIGHT... BUT SOON!
VENGEANCE?
ONLY THE INNOCENT WILL BE AVENGED--
--BY ME!

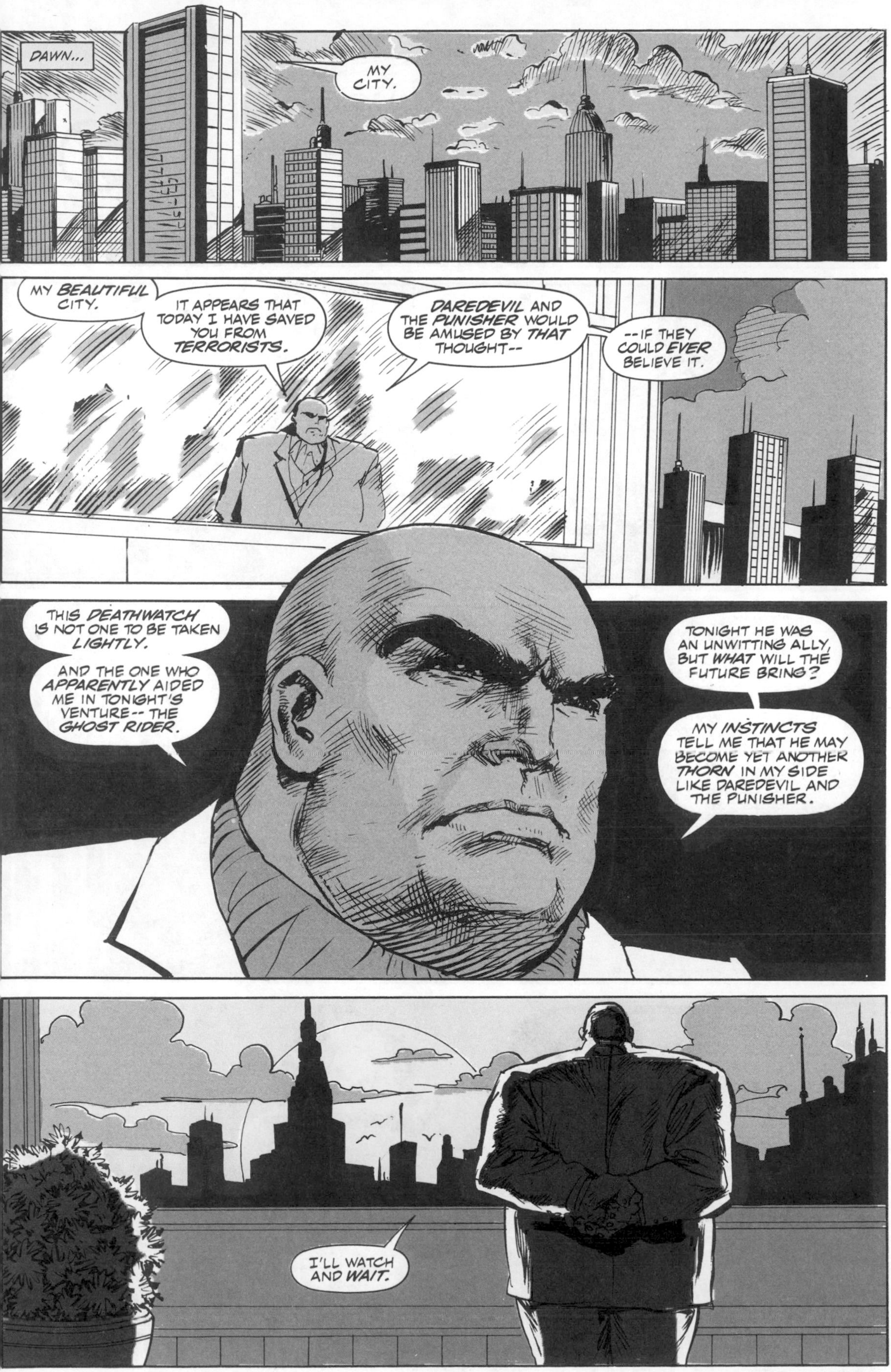
DAWN...
MY CITY.
MY BEAUTIFUL CITY.
IT APPEARS THAT TODAY I HAVE SAVED YOU FROM TERRORISTS.
DAREDEVIL AND THE PUNISHER WOULD BE AMUSED BY THAT THOUGHT--
--IF THEY COULD EVER BELIEVE IT.
THIS DEATHWATCH IS NOT ONE TO BE TAKEN LIGHTLY.
AND THE ONE WHO APPARENTLY AIDED ME IN TONIGHT'S VENTURE-- THE GHOST RIDER.
TONIGHT HE WAS AN UNWITTING ALLY, BUT WHAT WILL THE FUTURE BRING?
MY INSTINCTS TELL ME THAT HE MAY BECOME YET ANOTHER THORN IN MY SIDE LIKE DAREDEVIL AND THE PUNISHER.
I'LL WATCH AND WAIT.

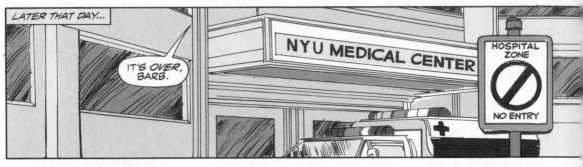

LATER THAT DAY...

NYU MEDICAL CENTER

HOSPITAL ZONE
NO ENTRY

IT'S OVER, BARB.

THE MEN WHO WANTED TO *HURT* US ARE GONE.

GHOST RIDER, THE THING THAT I BECOME, SAVED THE CITY.

MAYBE I SHOULD GET *RID* OF THE MOTOR-CYCLE NOW--

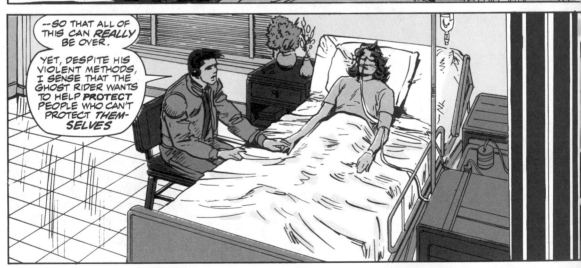

--SO THAT ALL OF THIS CAN *REALLY* BE OVER.

YET, DESPITE HIS *VIOLENT* METHODS, I SENSE THAT THE GHOST RIDER WANTS TO HELP *PROTECT* PEOPLE WHO CAN'T PROTECT *THEM-SELVES*

IS IT RIGHT FOR ME TO DEPRIVE THE INNOCENT OF A PROTECTOR?

IS IT?

THE END

NEXT ISSUE:

DAN ATTEMPTS TO SEPARATE HIMSELF FROM HIS POSSESSED MOTORCYCLE AND DISCOVERS THAT--

YOU CAN RUN, BUT YOU CAN'T HYDE!

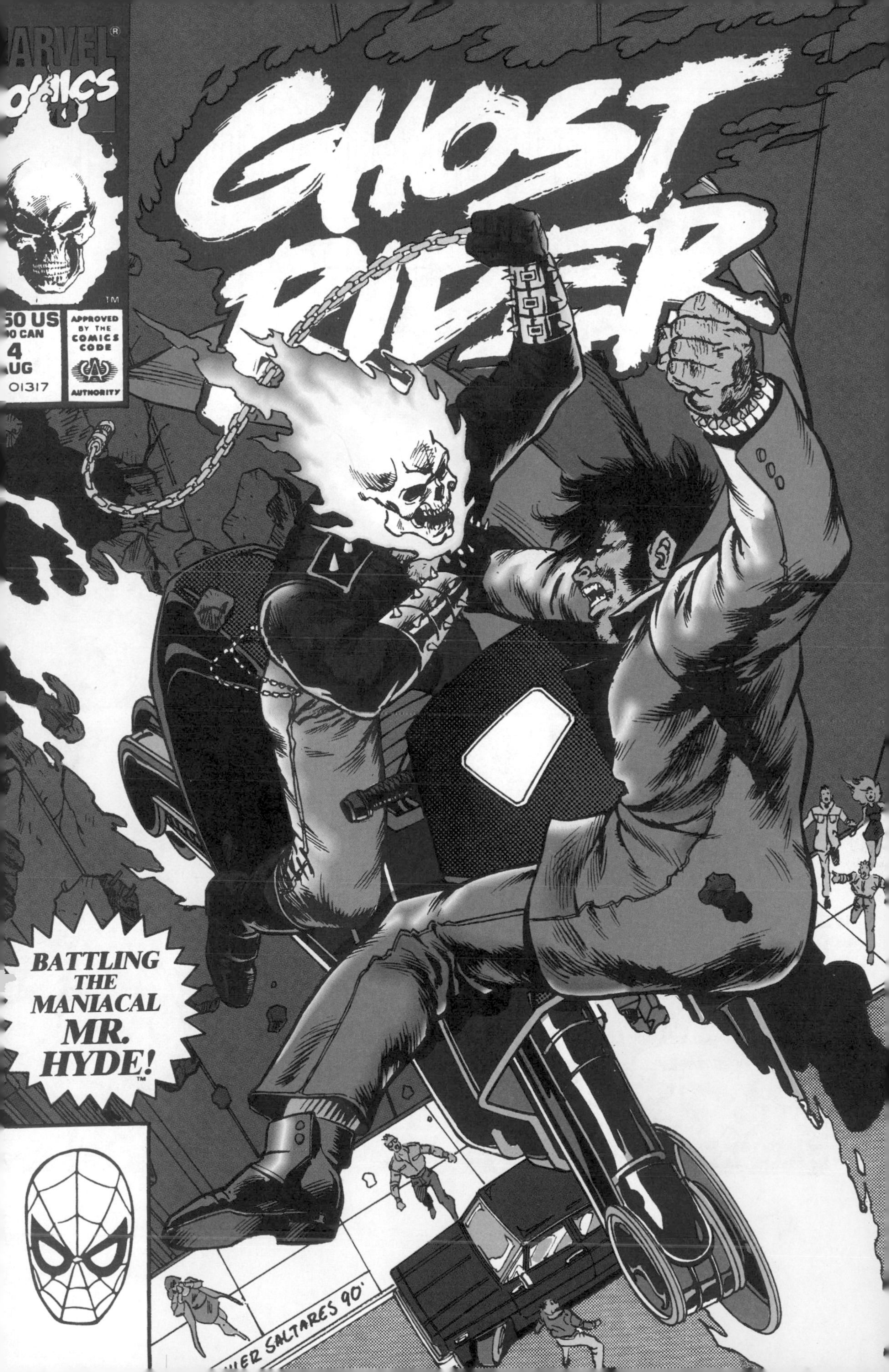
GHOST RIDER
50 US
00 CAN
4
UG
01317
APPROVED BY THE COMICS CODE AUTHORITY
BATTLING THE MANIACAL MR. HYDE!
SALTARES 90'

WHEN INNOCENT BLOOD IS SPILLED, A SPIRIT OF VENGEANCE IS BORN, AND DANNY KETCH FINDS HIMSELF TRANSFORMED. STAN LEE PRESENTS . . .

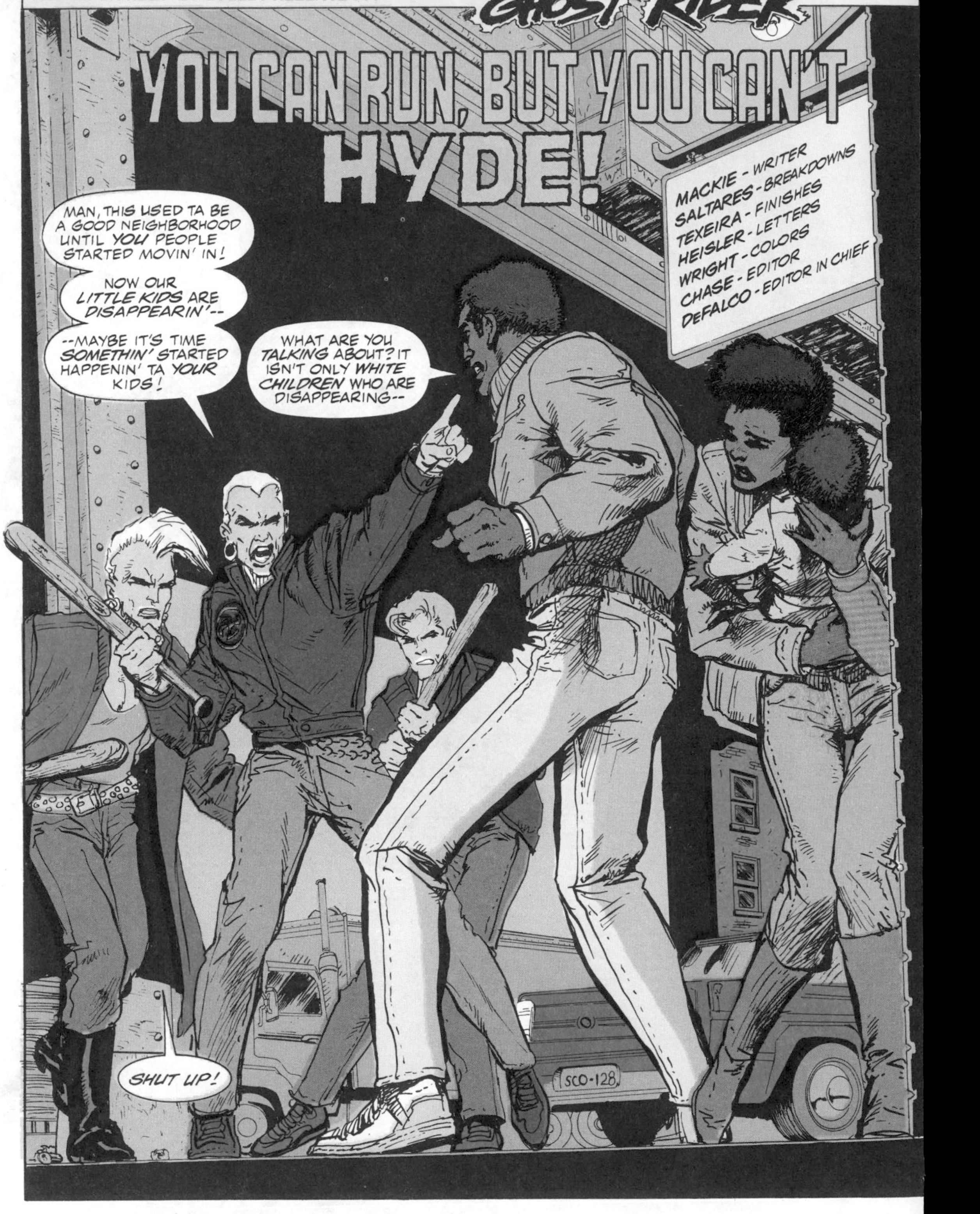
GHOST RIDER
YOU CAN RUN, BUT YOU CAN'T HYDE!
MACKIE - WRITER
SALTARES - BREAKDOWNS
TEXEIRA - FINISHES
HEISLER - LETTERS
WRIGHT - COLORS
CHASE - EDITOR
DeFALCO - EDITOR IN CHIEF
MAN, THIS USED TA BE A GOOD NEIGHBORHOOD UNTIL YOU PEOPLE STARTED MOVIN' IN!
NOW OUR LITTLE KIDS ARE DISAPPEARIN'--
--MAYBE IT'S TIME SOMETHIN' STARTED HAPPENIN' TA YOUR KIDS!
WHAT ARE YOU TALKING ABOUT? IT ISN'T ONLY WHITE CHILDREN WHO ARE DISAPPEARING--
SHUT UP!
SCO-128

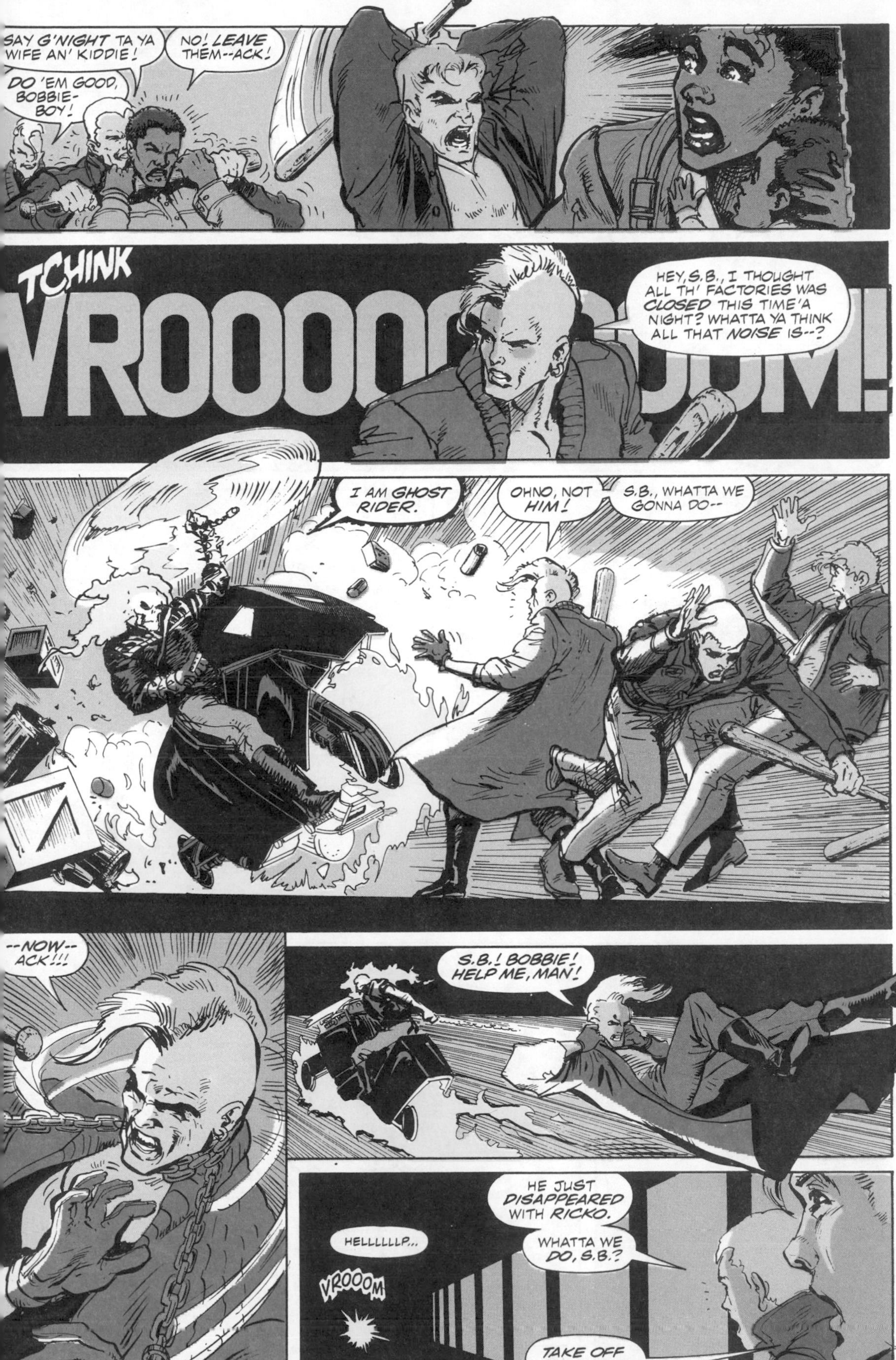
SAY G'NIGHT TA YA WIFE AN' KIDDIE!
NO! LEAVE THEM--ACK!
DO 'EM GOOD, BOBBIE-BOY!
TCHINK
VROOOOOOOOM!
HEY, S.B., I THOUGHT ALL TH' FACTORIES WAS CLOSED THIS TIME'A NIGHT? WHATTA YA THINK ALL THAT NOISE IS--?
I AM GHOST RIDER.
OHNO, NOT HIM!
S.B., WHATTA WE GONNA DO--
--NOW-- ACK!!!
S.B.! BOBBIE! HELP ME, MAN!
HE JUST DISAPPEARED WITH RICKO.
HELLLLLLP...
WHATTA WE DO, S.B.?
VROOOM
TAKE OFF BEFORE HE--

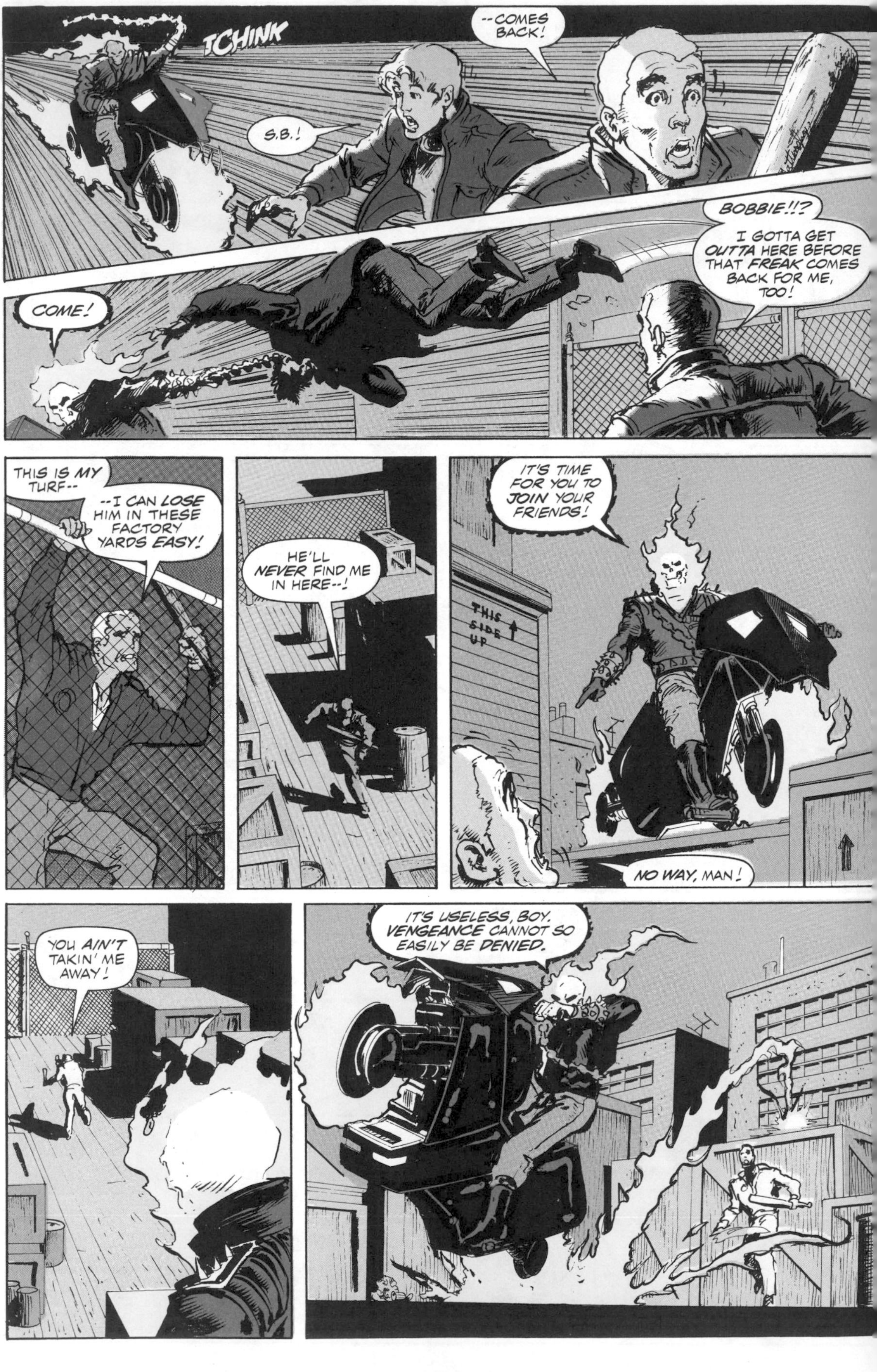
TCHINK
--COMES BACK!
S.B.!
BOBBIE!!?
I GOTTA GET OUTTA HERE BEFORE THAT FREAK COMES BACK FOR ME, TOO!
COME!
THIS IS MY TURF--
--I CAN LOSE HIM IN THESE FACTORY YARDS EASY!
HE'LL NEVER FIND ME IN HERE--!
IT'S TIME FOR YOU TO JOIN YOUR FRIENDS!
THIS SIDE UP
NO WAY, MAN!
YOU AIN'T TAKIN' ME AWAY!
IT'S USELESS, BOY. VENGEANCE CANNOT SO EASILY BE DENIED.

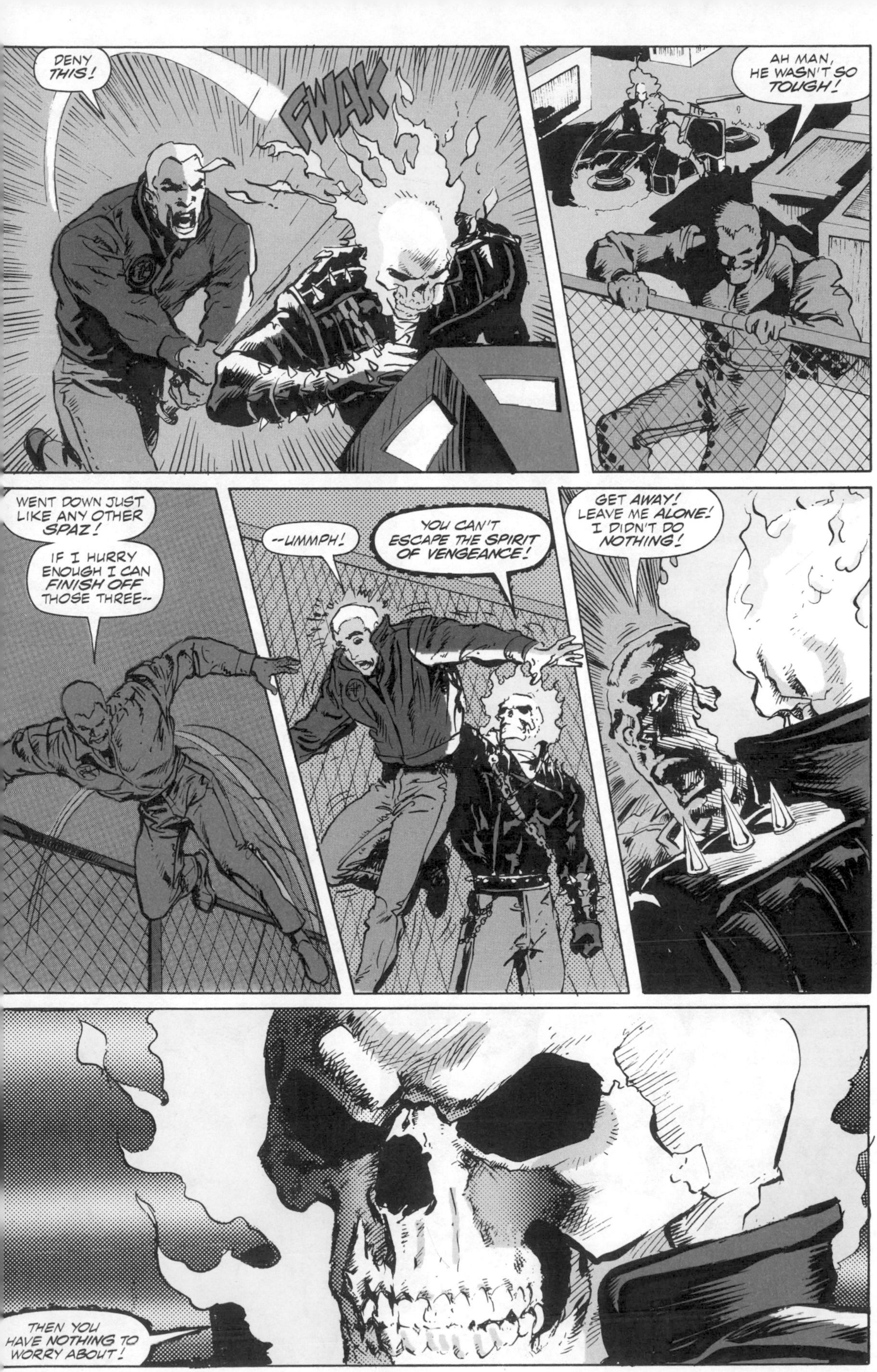
DENY THIS!
FWAK
AH MAN, HE WASN'T SO TOUGH!
WENT DOWN JUST LIKE ANY OTHER SPAZ!
IF I HURRY ENOUGH I CAN FINISH OFF THOSE THREE--
--UMMPH!
YOU CAN'T ESCAPE THE SPIRIT OF VENGEANCE!
GET AWAY! LEAVE ME ALONE! I DIDN'T DO NOTHING!
THEN YOU HAVE NOTHING TO WORRY ABOUT!

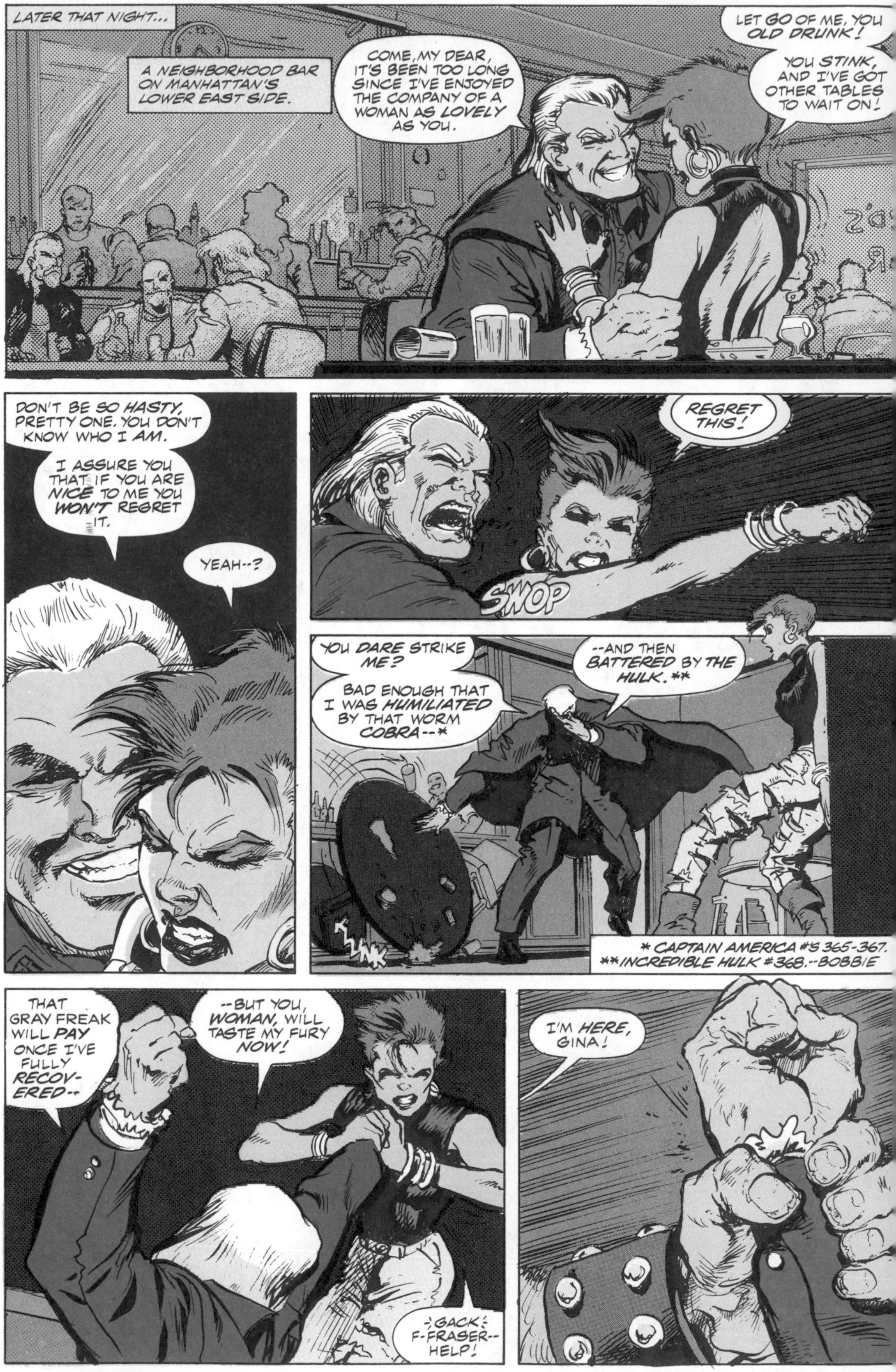

LATER THAT NIGHT...
A NEIGHBORHOOD BAR ON MANHATTAN'S LOWER EAST SIDE.
COME, MY DEAR, IT'S BEEN TOO LONG SINCE I'VE ENJOYED THE COMPANY OF A WOMAN AS LOVELY AS YOU.
LET GO OF ME, YOU OLD DRUNK!
YOU STINK, AND I'VE GOT OTHER TABLES TO WAIT ON!
DON'T BE SO HASTY, PRETTY ONE. YOU DON'T KNOW WHO I AM.
I ASSURE YOU THAT IF YOU ARE NICE TO ME YOU WON'T REGRET IT.
YEAH--?
REGRET THIS!
SWOP
YOU DARE STRIKE ME?
BAD ENOUGH THAT I WAS HUMILIATED BY THAT WORM COBRA--*
--AND THEN BATTERED BY THE HULK.**
KLUNK
* CAPTAIN AMERICA #'S 365-367.
** INCREDIBLE HULK #368.--BOBBIE
THAT GRAY FREAK WILL PAY ONCE I'VE FULLY RECOVERED--
--BUT YOU, WOMAN, WILL TASTE MY FURY NOW!
GACK F-FRASER-- HELP!
I'M HERE, GINA!

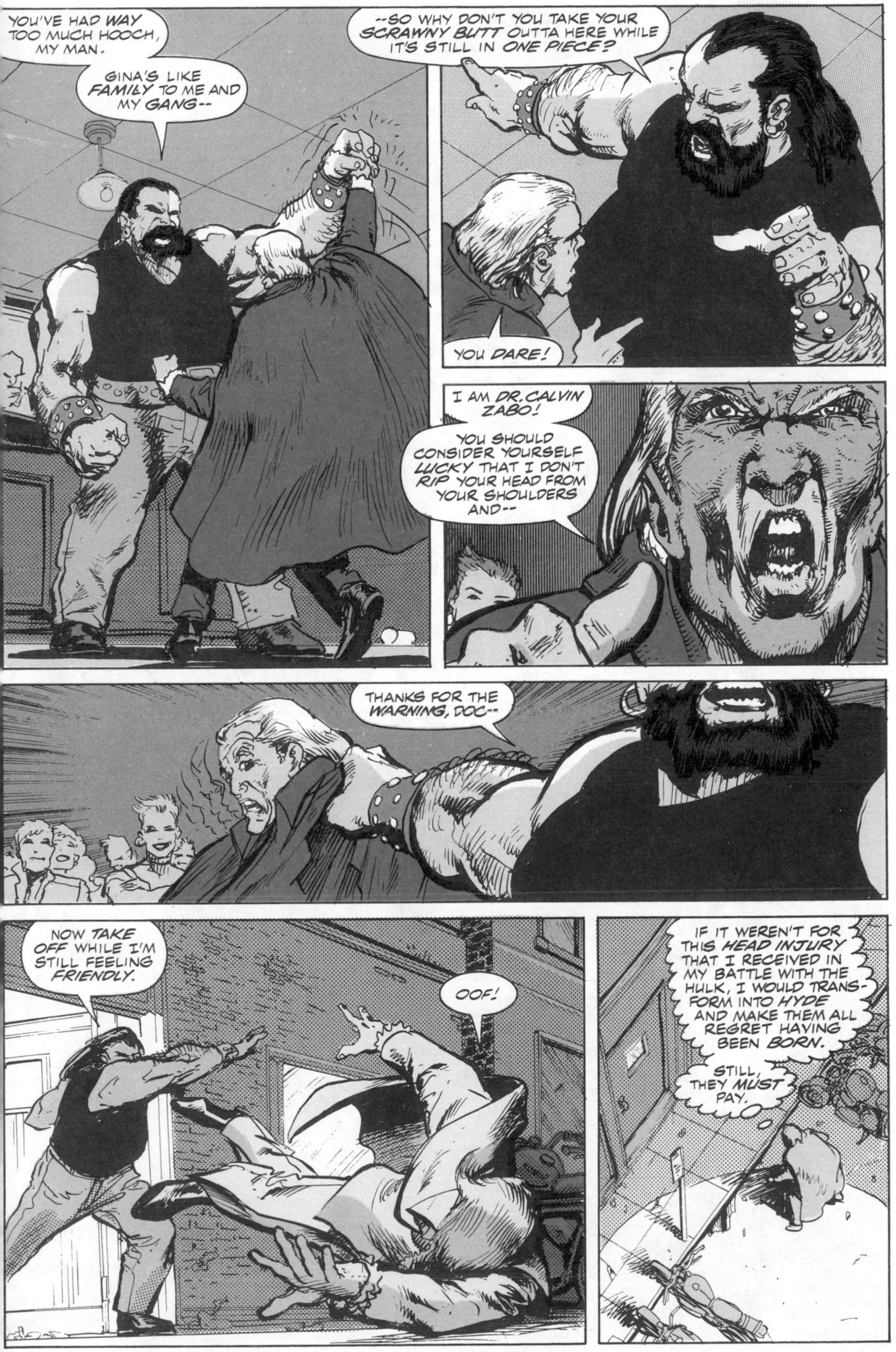
YOU'VE HAD WAY TOO MUCH HOOCH, MY MAN.
GINA'S LIKE FAMILY TO ME AND MY GANG--
--SO WHY DON'T YOU TAKE YOUR SCRAWNY BUTT OUTTA HERE WHILE IT'S STILL IN ONE PIECE?
YOU DARE!
I AM DR. CALVIN ZABO!
YOU SHOULD CONSIDER YOURSELF LUCKY THAT I DON'T RIP YOUR HEAD FROM YOUR SHOULDERS AND--
THANKS FOR THE WARNING, DOC--
NOW TAKE OFF WHILE I'M STILL FEELING FRIENDLY.
OOF!
IF IT WEREN'T FOR THIS HEAD INJURY THAT I RECEIVED IN MY BATTLE WITH THE HULK, I WOULD TRANS-FORM INTO HYDE AND MAKE THEM ALL REGRET HAVING BEEN BORN.
STILL, THEY MUST PAY.

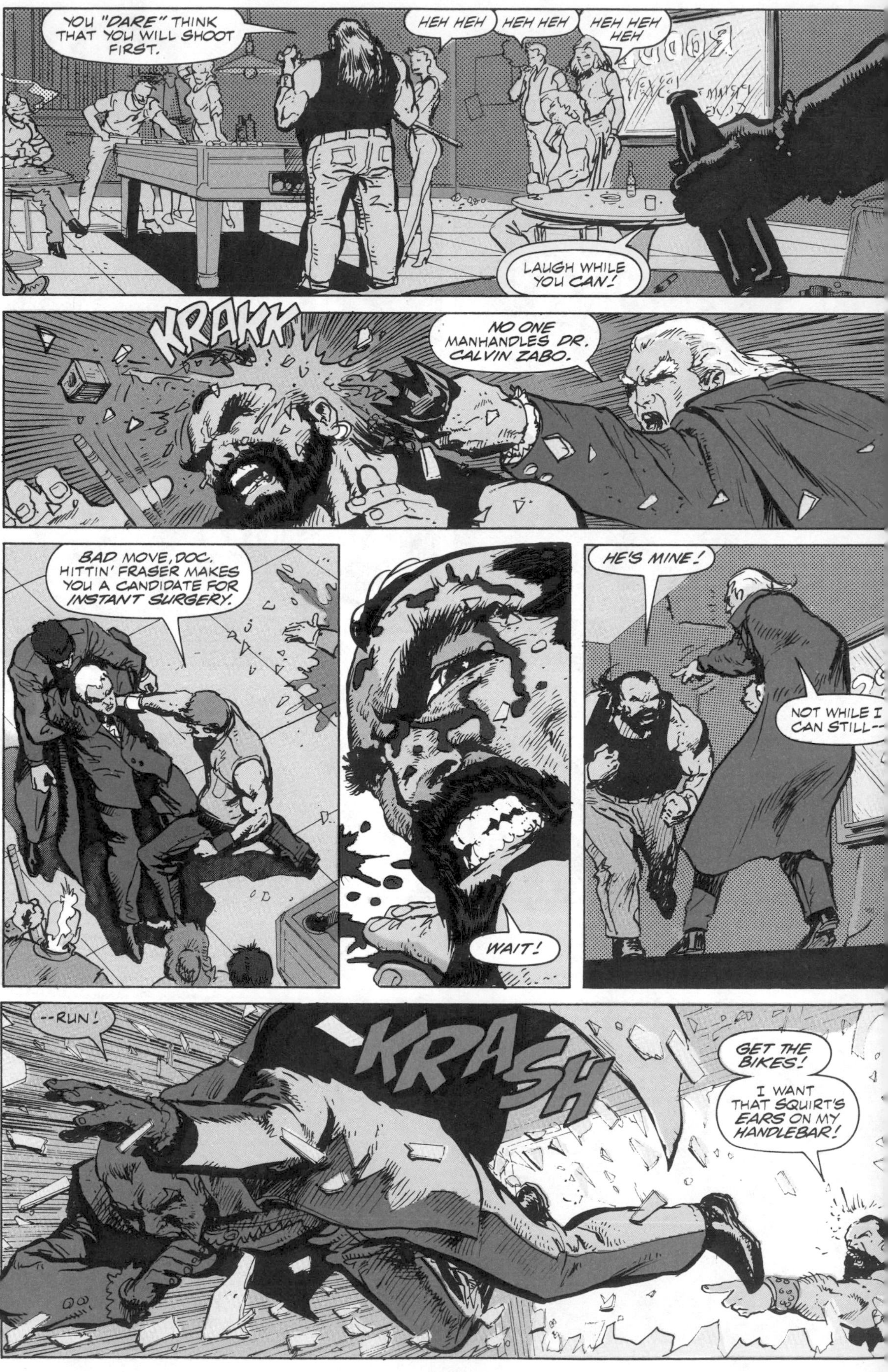
YOU "DARE" THINK THAT YOU WILL SHOOT FIRST.
HEH HEH
HEH HEH
HEH HEH HEH
LAUGH WHILE YOU CAN!
KRAKK
NO ONE MANHANDLES DR. CALVIN ZABO.
BAD MOVE, DOC. HITTIN' FRASER MAKES YOU A CANDIDATE FOR INSTANT SURGERY.
WAIT!
HE'S MINE!
NOT WHILE I CAN STILL--
--RUN!
KRASH
GET THE BIKES!
I WANT THAT SQUIRT'S EARS ON MY HANDLEBAR!

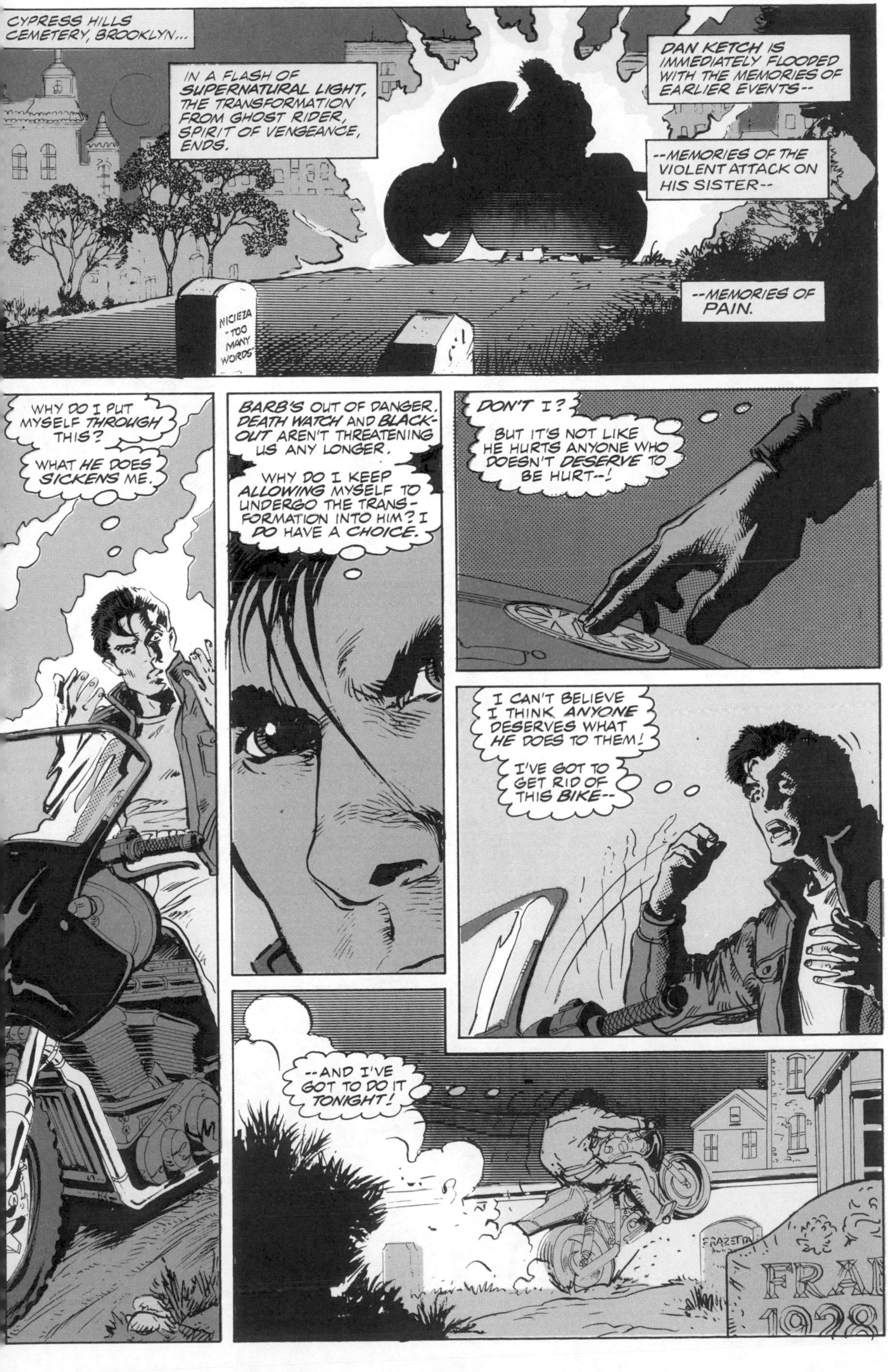
CYPRESS HILLS CEMETERY, BROOKLYN...
IN A FLASH OF SUPERNATURAL LIGHT, THE TRANSFORMATION FROM GHOST RIDER, SPIRIT OF VENGEANCE, ENDS.
DAN KETCH IS IMMEDIATELY FLOODED WITH THE MEMORIES OF EARLIER EVENTS--
--MEMORIES OF THE VIOLENT ATTACK ON HIS SISTER--
--MEMORIES OF PAIN.
NICIEZA "TOO MANY WORDS"
WHY DO I PUT MYSELF THROUGH THIS?
WHAT HE DOES SICKENS ME.
BARB'S OUT OF DANGER. DEATH WATCH AND BLACK-OUT AREN'T THREATENING US ANY LONGER.
WHY DO I KEEP ALLOWING MYSELF TO UNDERGO THE TRANS-FORMATION INTO HIM? I DO HAVE A CHOICE.
DON'T I?
BUT IT'S NOT LIKE HE HURTS ANYONE WHO DOESN'T DESERVE TO BE HURT--!
I CAN'T BELIEVE I THINK ANYONE DESERVES WHAT HE DOES TO THEM!
I'VE GOT TO GET RID OF THIS BIKE--
--AND I'VE GOT TO DO IT TONIGHT!
FRAZETTA
FRA
1928

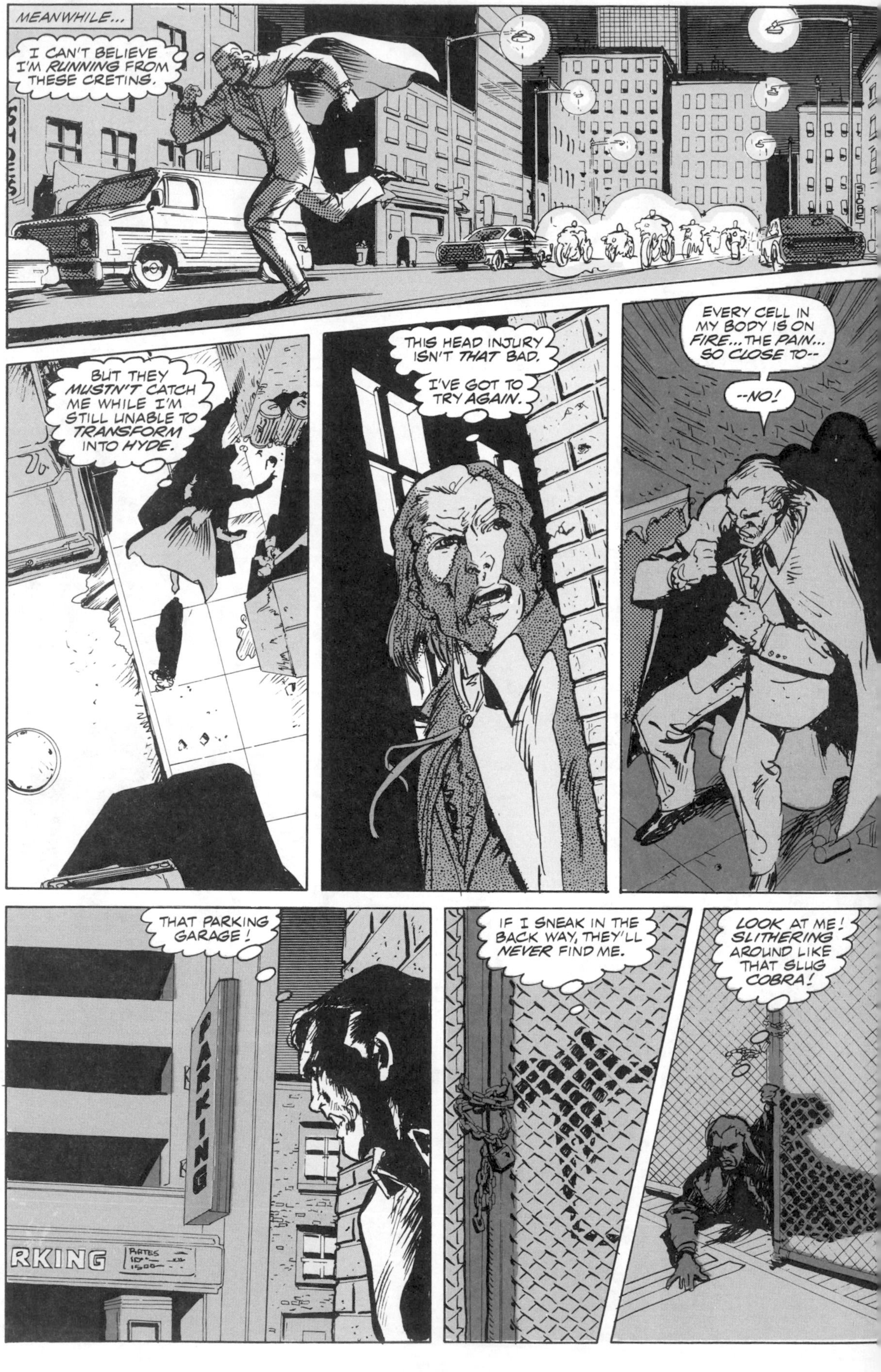
MEANWHILE...
I CAN'T BELIEVE I'M RUNNING FROM THESE CRETINS.
BUT THEY MUSTN'T CATCH ME WHILE I'M STILL UNABLE TO TRANSFORM INTO HYDE.
THIS HEAD INJURY ISN'T THAT BAD.
I'VE GOT TO TRY AGAIN.
EVERY CELL IN MY BODY IS ON FIRE... THE PAIN... SO CLOSE TO--
--NO!
THAT PARKING GARAGE!
PARKING
RKING
IF I SNEAK IN THE BACK WAY, THEY'LL NEVER FIND ME.
LOOK AT ME! SLITHERING AROUND LIKE THAT SLUG COBRA!

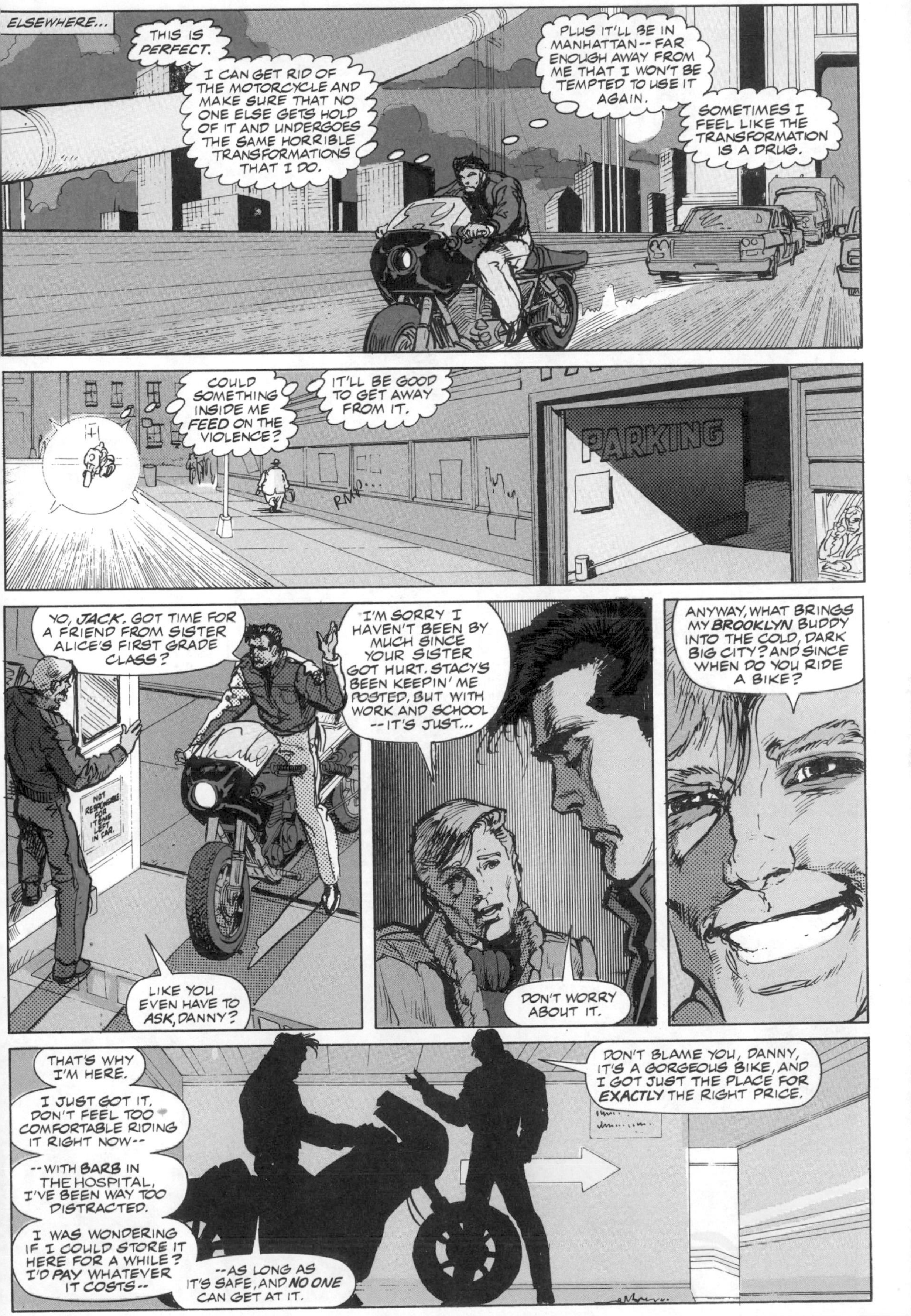
ELSEWHERE...
THIS IS PERFECT.
I CAN GET RID OF THE MOTORCYCLE AND MAKE SURE THAT NO ONE ELSE GETS HOLD OF IT AND UNDERGOES THE SAME HORRIBLE TRANSFORMATIONS THAT I DO.
PLUS IT'LL BE IN MANHATTAN-- FAR ENOUGH AWAY FROM ME THAT I WON'T BE TEMPTED TO USE IT AGAIN.
SOMETIMES I FEEL LIKE THE TRANSFORMATION IS A DRUG.
COULD SOMETHING INSIDE ME FEED ON THE VIOLENCE?
IT'LL BE GOOD TO GET AWAY FROM IT.
PARKING
RMP...
YO, JACK. GOT TIME FOR A FRIEND FROM SISTER ALICE'S FIRST GRADE CLASS?
LIKE YOU EVEN HAVE TO ASK, DANNY?
NOT RESPONSIBLE FOR ITEMS LEFT IN CAR.
I'M SORRY I HAVEN'T BEEN BY MUCH SINCE YOUR SISTER GOT HURT. STACY'S BEEN KEEPIN' ME POSTED, BUT WITH WORK AND SCHOOL --IT'S JUST...
DON'T WORRY ABOUT IT.
ANYWAY, WHAT BRINGS MY BROOKLYN BUDDY INTO THE COLD, DARK BIG CITY? AND SINCE WHEN DO YOU RIDE A BIKE?
THAT'S WHY I'M HERE.
I JUST GOT IT, DON'T FEEL TOO COMFORTABLE RIDING IT RIGHT NOW--
--WITH BARB IN THE HOSPITAL, I'VE BEEN WAY TOO DISTRACTED.
I WAS WONDERING IF I COULD STORE IT HERE FOR A WHILE? I'D PAY WHATEVER IT COSTS--
--AS LONG AS IT'S SAFE, AND NO ONE CAN GET AT IT.
DON'T BLAME YOU, DANNY, IT'S A GORGEOUS BIKE, AND I GOT JUST THE PLACE FOR EXACTLY THE RIGHT PRICE.

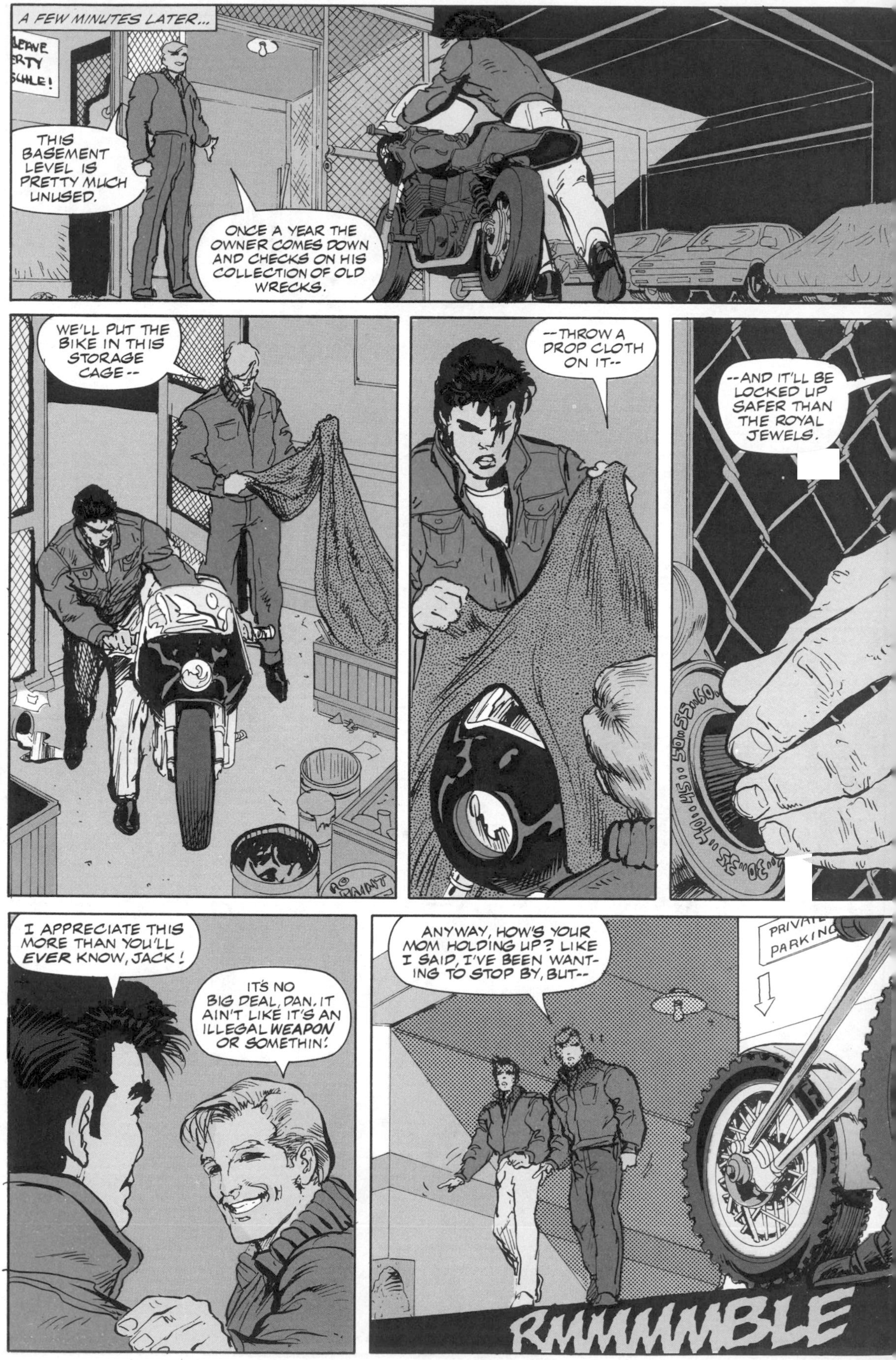
A FEW MINUTES LATER...
THIS BASEMENT LEVEL IS PRETTY MUCH UNUSED.
ONCE A YEAR THE OWNER COMES DOWN AND CHECKS ON HIS COLLECTION OF OLD WRECKS.
WE'LL PUT THE BIKE IN THIS STORAGE CAGE--
--THROW A DROP CLOTH ON IT--
--AND IT'LL BE LOCKED UP SAFER THAN THE ROYAL JEWELS.
I APPRECIATE THIS MORE THAN YOU'LL EVER KNOW, JACK!
IT'S NO BIG DEAL, DAN. IT AIN'T LIKE IT'S AN ILLEGAL WEAPON OR SOMETHIN'.
ANYWAY, HOW'S YOUR MOM HOLDING UP? LIKE I SAID, I'VE BEEN WANTING TO STOP BY, BUT--
PRIVATE PARKING
RMMMMBLE

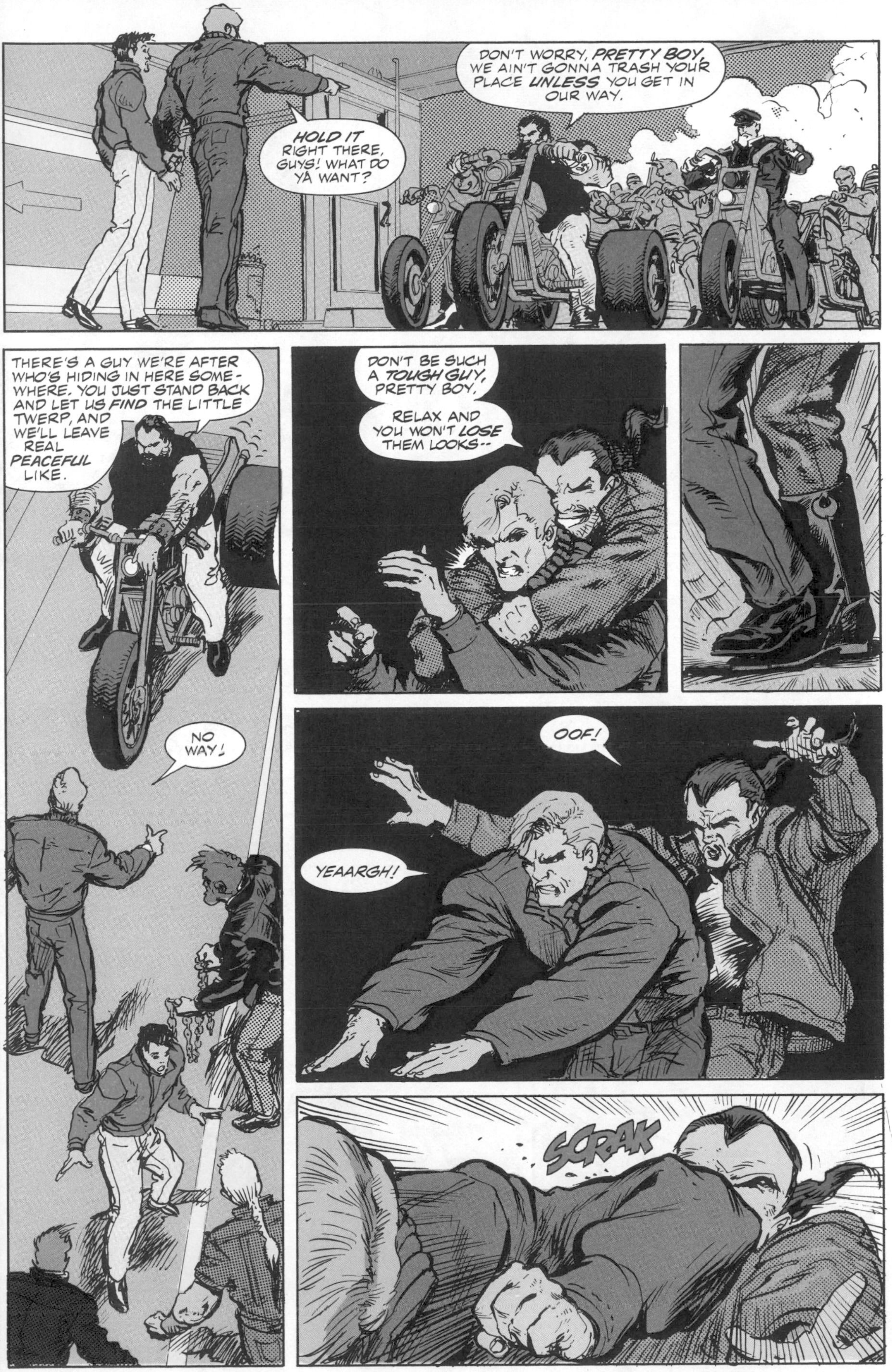
HOLD IT RIGHT THERE, GUYS! WHAT DO YA WANT?
DON'T WORRY, PRETTY BOY, WE AIN'T GONNA TRASH YOUR PLACE UNLESS YOU GET IN OUR WAY.
THERE'S A GUY WE'RE AFTER WHO'S HIDING IN HERE SOME-WHERE. YOU JUST STAND BACK AND LET US FIND THE LITTLE TWERP, AND WE'LL LEAVE REAL PEACEFUL LIKE.
NO WAY!
DON'T BE SUCH A TOUGH GUY, PRETTY BOY.
RELAX AND YOU WON'T LOSE THEM LOOKS--
OOF!
YEAARGH!
SCRAK

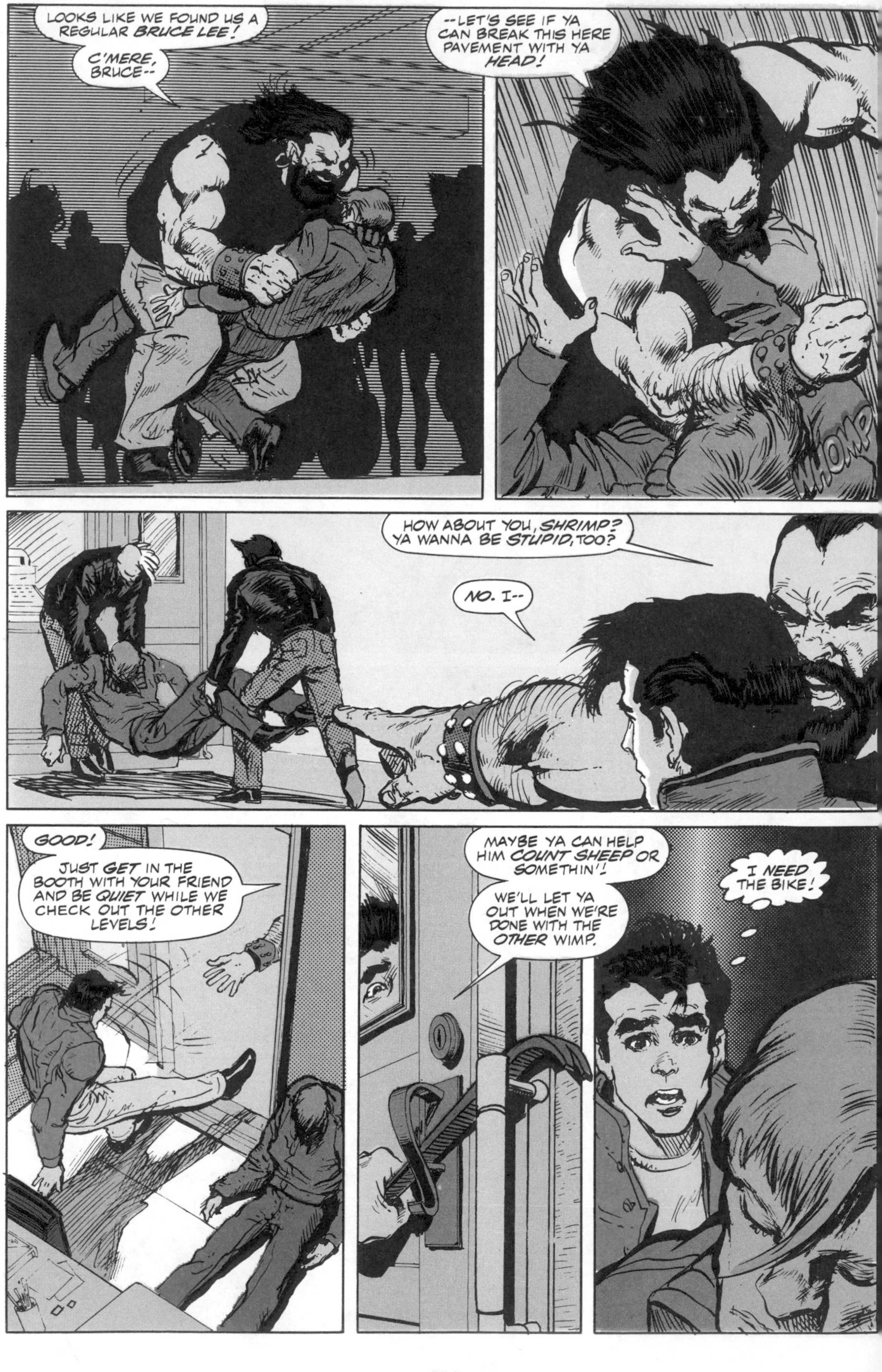
LOOKS LIKE WE FOUND US A REGULAR BRUCE LEE!
C'MERE, BRUCE--
--LET'S SEE IF YA CAN BREAK THIS HERE PAVEMENT WITH YA HEAD!
WHOMP
HOW ABOUT YOU, SHRIMP? YA WANNA BE STUPID, TOO?
NO. I--
GOOD!
JUST GET IN THE BOOTH WITH YOUR FRIEND AND BE QUIET WHILE WE CHECK OUT THE OTHER LEVELS!
MAYBE YA CAN HELP HIM COUNT SHEEP OR SOMETHIN'!
WE'LL LET YA OUT WHEN WE'RE DONE WITH THE OTHER WIMP.
I NEED THE BIKE!

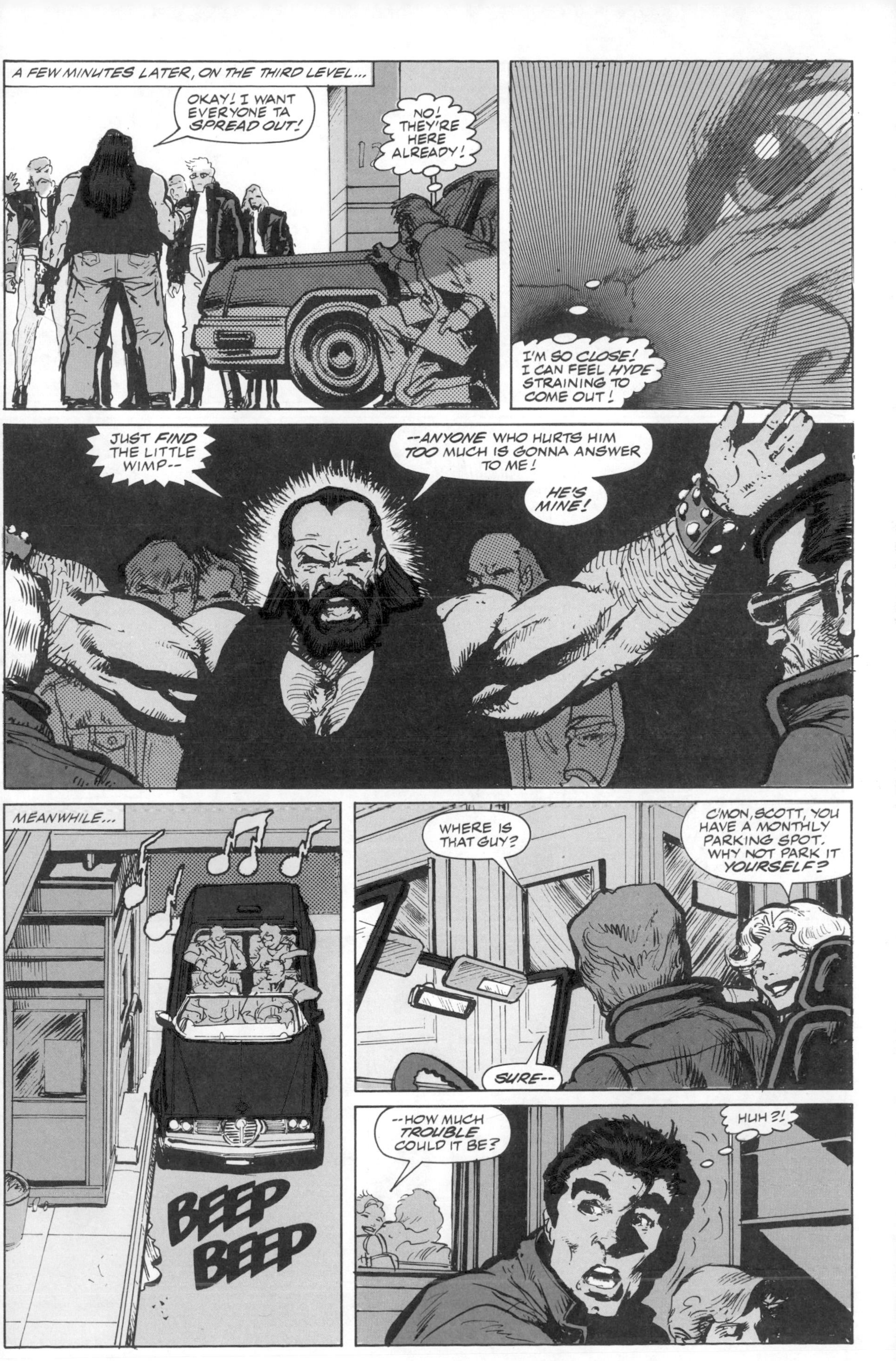
A FEW MINUTES LATER, ON THE THIRD LEVEL...
OKAY! I WANT EVERYONE TA SPREAD OUT!
NO! THEY'RE HERE ALREADY!
I'M SO CLOSE! I CAN FEEL HYDE STRAINING TO COME OUT!
JUST FIND THE LITTLE WIMP--
--ANYONE WHO HURTS HIM TOO MUCH IS GONNA ANSWER TO ME!
HE'S MINE!
MEANWHILE...
BEEP BEEP
WHERE IS THAT GUY?
C'MON, SCOTT, YOU HAVE A MONTHLY PARKING SPOT. WHY NOT PARK IT YOURSELF?
SURE--
--HOW MUCH TROUBLE COULD IT BE?
HUH?!

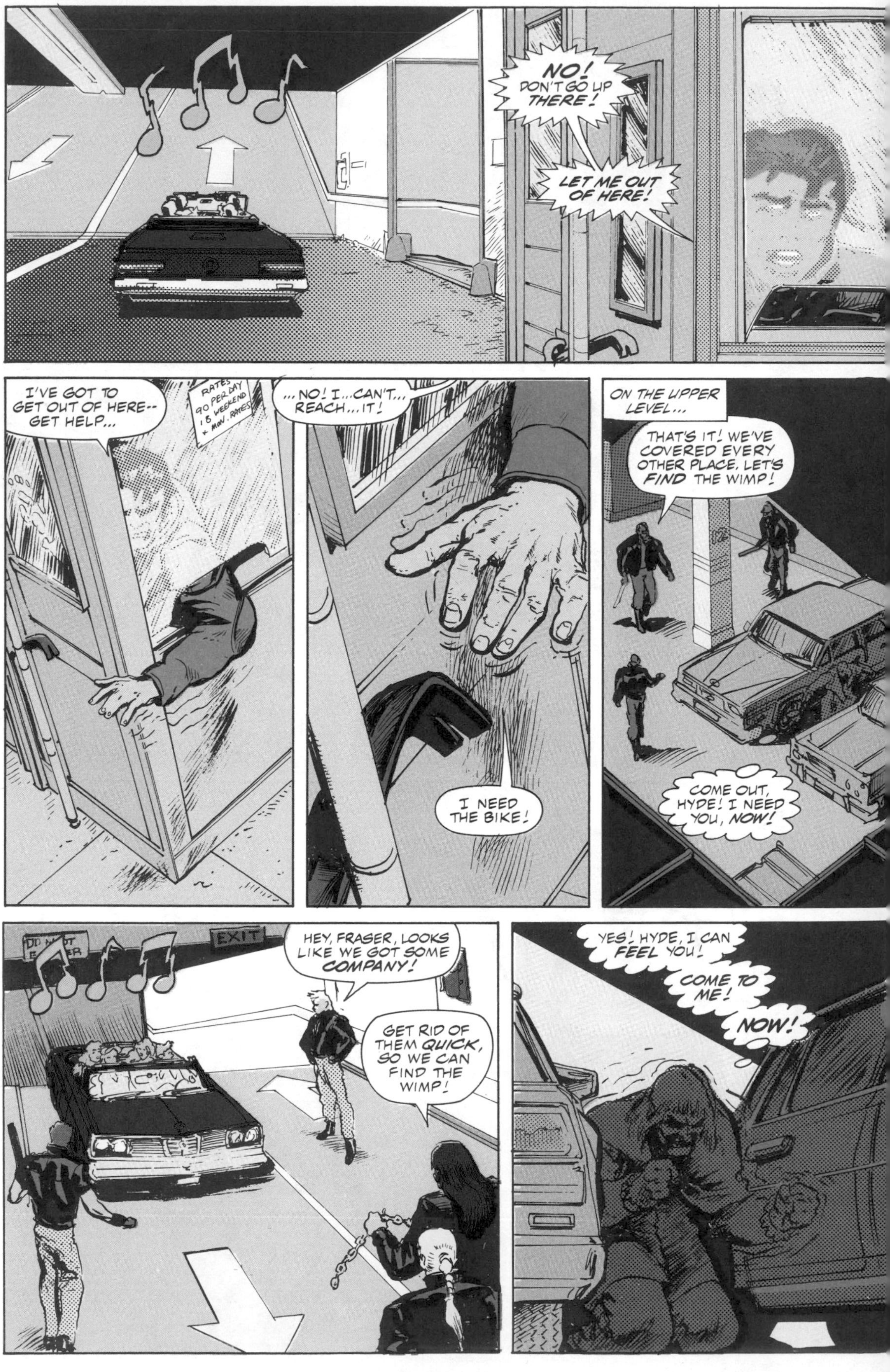
NO! DON'T GO UP THERE!
LET ME OUT OF HERE!
I'VE GOT TO GET OUT OF HERE-- GET HELP...
RATES 90 PER DAY 18 WEEKEND + MON. RATES
...NO! I...CAN'T... REACH...IT!
I NEED THE BIKE!
ON THE UPPER LEVEL...
THAT'S IT! WE'VE COVERED EVERY OTHER PLACE. LET'S FIND THE WIMP!
COME OUT, HYDE! I NEED YOU, NOW!
EXIT
HEY, FRASER, LOOKS LIKE WE GOT SOME COMPANY!
GET RID OF THEM QUICK, SO WE CAN FIND THE WIMP!
YES! HYDE, I CAN FEEL YOU!
COME TO ME!
NOW!

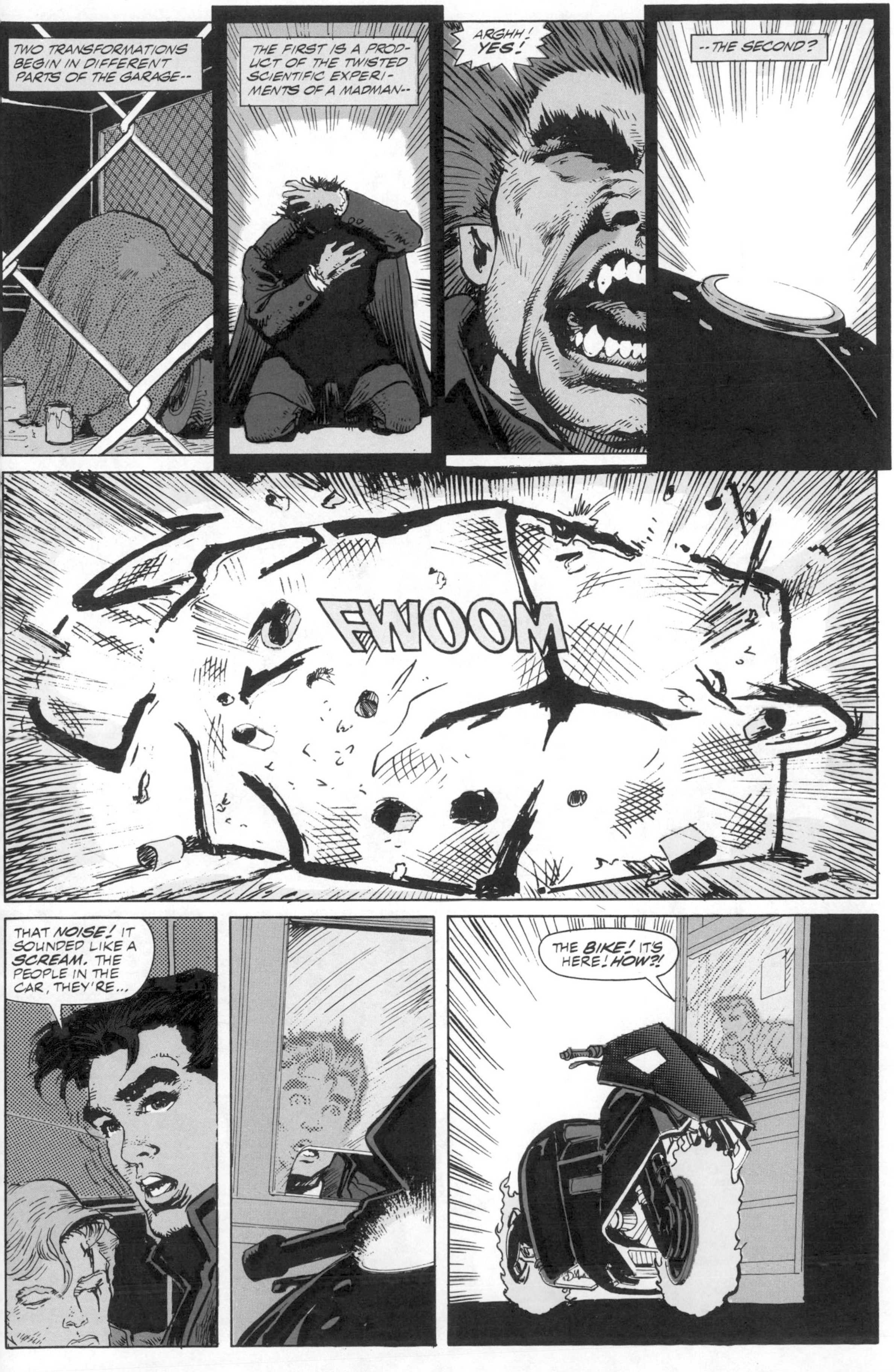
TWO TRANSFORMATIONS BEGIN IN DIFFERENT PARTS OF THE GARAGE--
THE FIRST IS A PRODUCT OF THE TWISTED SCIENTIFIC EXPERIMENTS OF A MADMAN--
ARGHH! YES!
--THE SECOND?
FWOOM
THAT NOISE! IT SOUNDED LIKE A SCREAM. THE PEOPLE IN THE CAR, THEY'RE...
THE BIKE! IT'S HERE! HOW?!

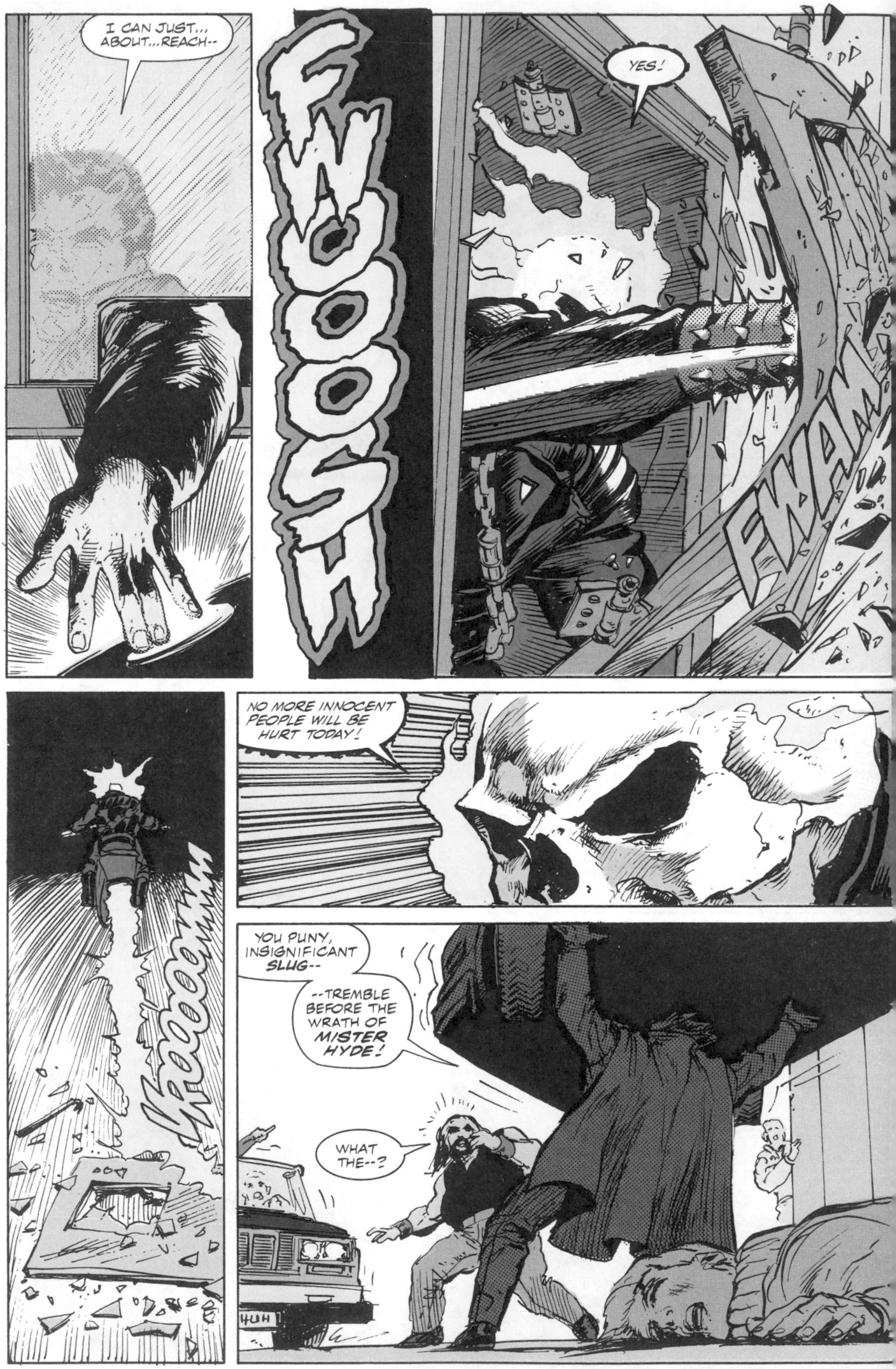

I CAN JUST... ABOUT... REACH--
FWOOOOSH
YES!
FWAM
NO MORE INNOCENT PEOPLE WILL BE HURT TODAY!
YOU PUNY, INSIGNIFICANT SLUG--
--TREMBLE BEFORE THE WRATH OF MISTER HYDE!
WHAT THE--?

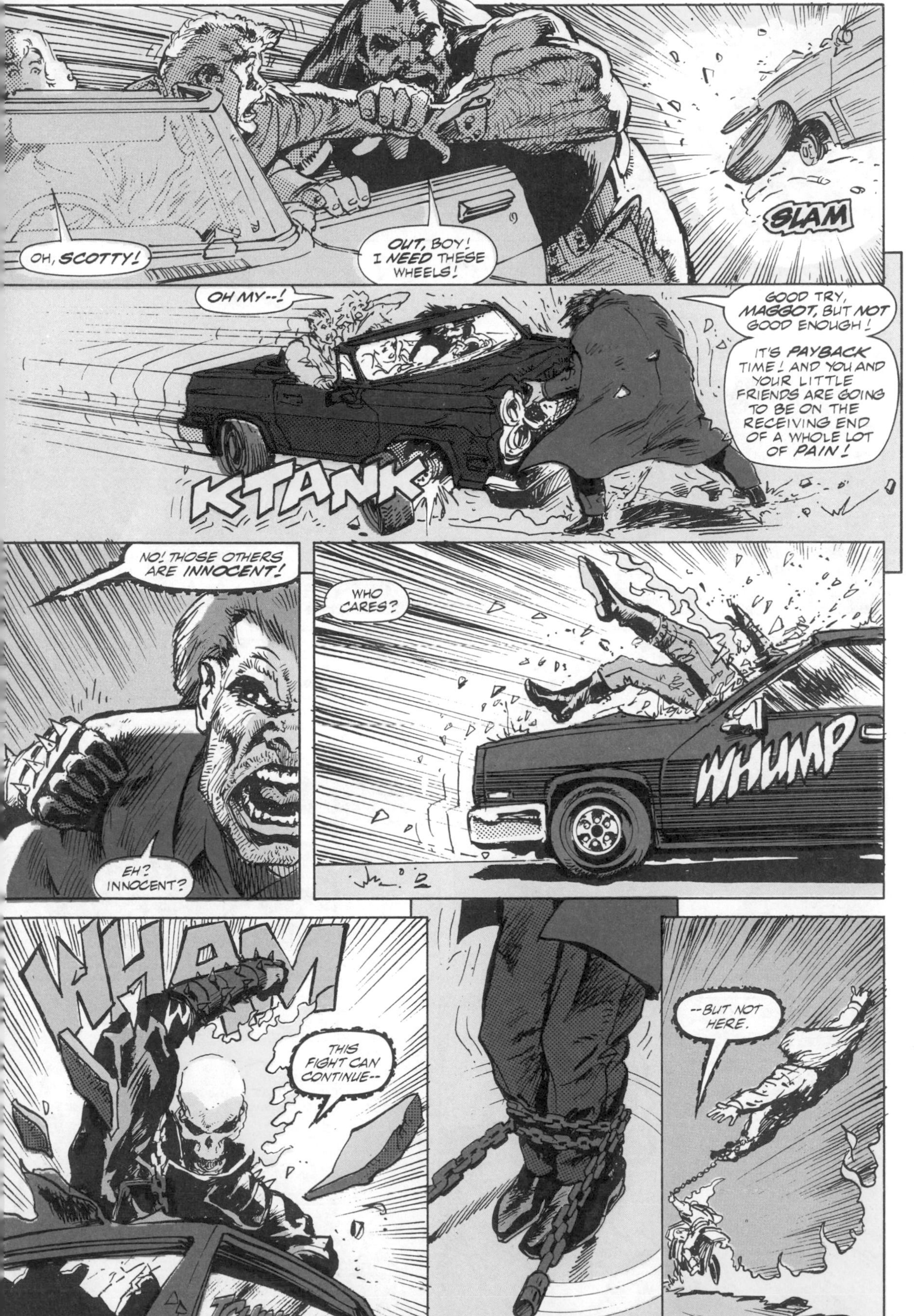
OH, SCOTTY!
OUT, BOY! I NEED THESE WHEELS!
SLAM
OH MY--!
GOOD TRY, MAGGOT, BUT NOT GOOD ENOUGH!
IT'S PAYBACK TIME! AND YOU AND YOUR LITTLE FRIENDS ARE GOING TO BE ON THE RECEIVING END OF A WHOLE LOT OF PAIN!
KTANK
NO! THOSE OTHERS ARE INNOCENT!
EH? INNOCENT?
WHO CARES?
WHUMP
WHAM
THIS FIGHT CAN CONTINUE--
TCHINK
--BUT NOT HERE.

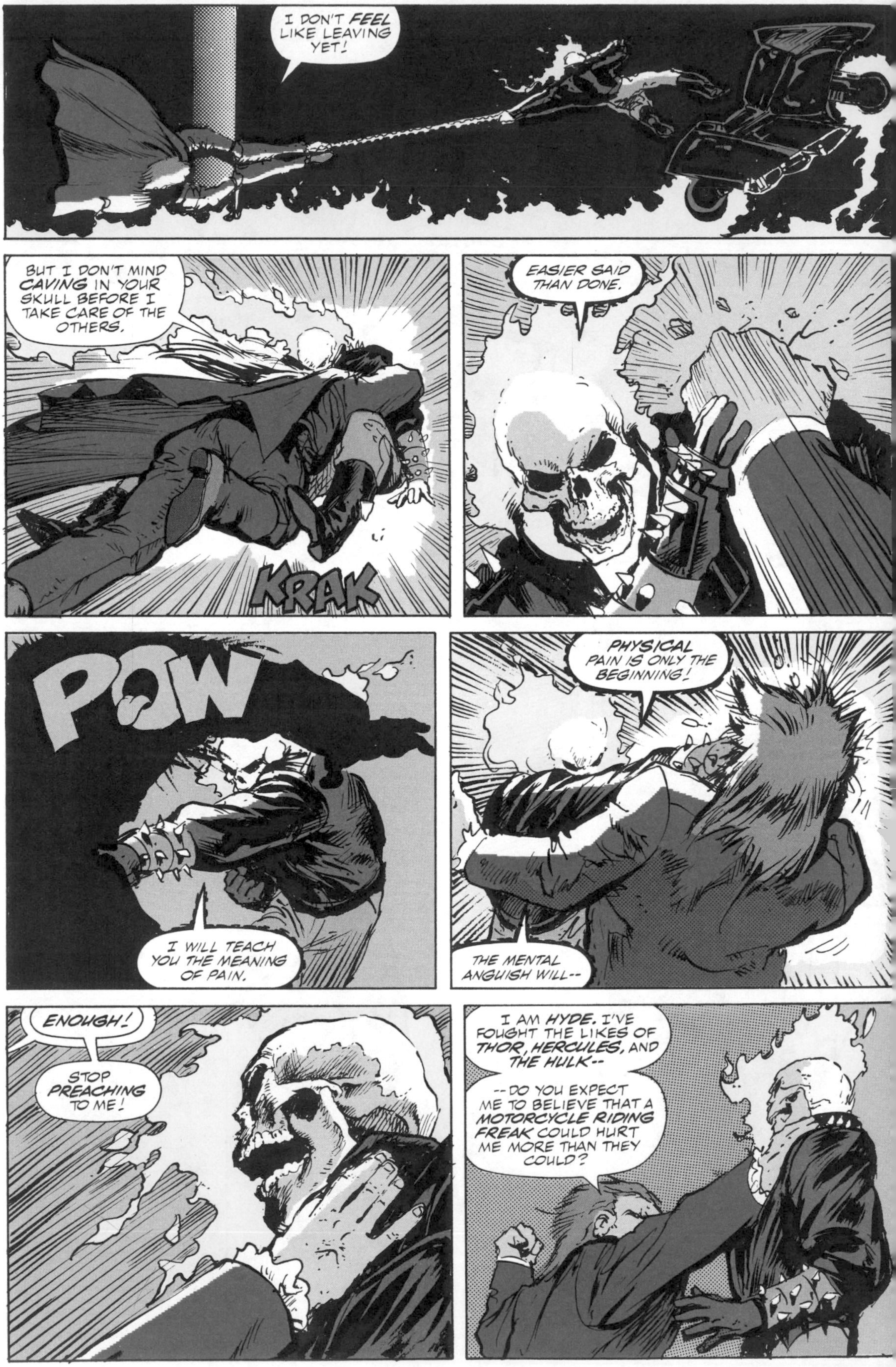

I DON'T FEEL LIKE LEAVING YET!
BUT I DON'T MIND CAVING IN YOUR SKULL BEFORE I TAKE CARE OF THE OTHERS.
KRAK
EASIER SAID THAN DONE.
POW
I WILL TEACH YOU THE MEANING OF PAIN.
PHYSICAL PAIN IS ONLY THE BEGINNING!
THE MENTAL ANGUISH WILL--
ENOUGH!
STOP PREACHING TO ME!
I AM HYDE. I'VE FOUGHT THE LIKES OF THOR, HERCULES, AND THE HULK--
--DO YOU EXPECT ME TO BELIEVE THAT A MOTORCYCLE RIDING FREAK COULD HURT ME MORE THAN THEY COULD?

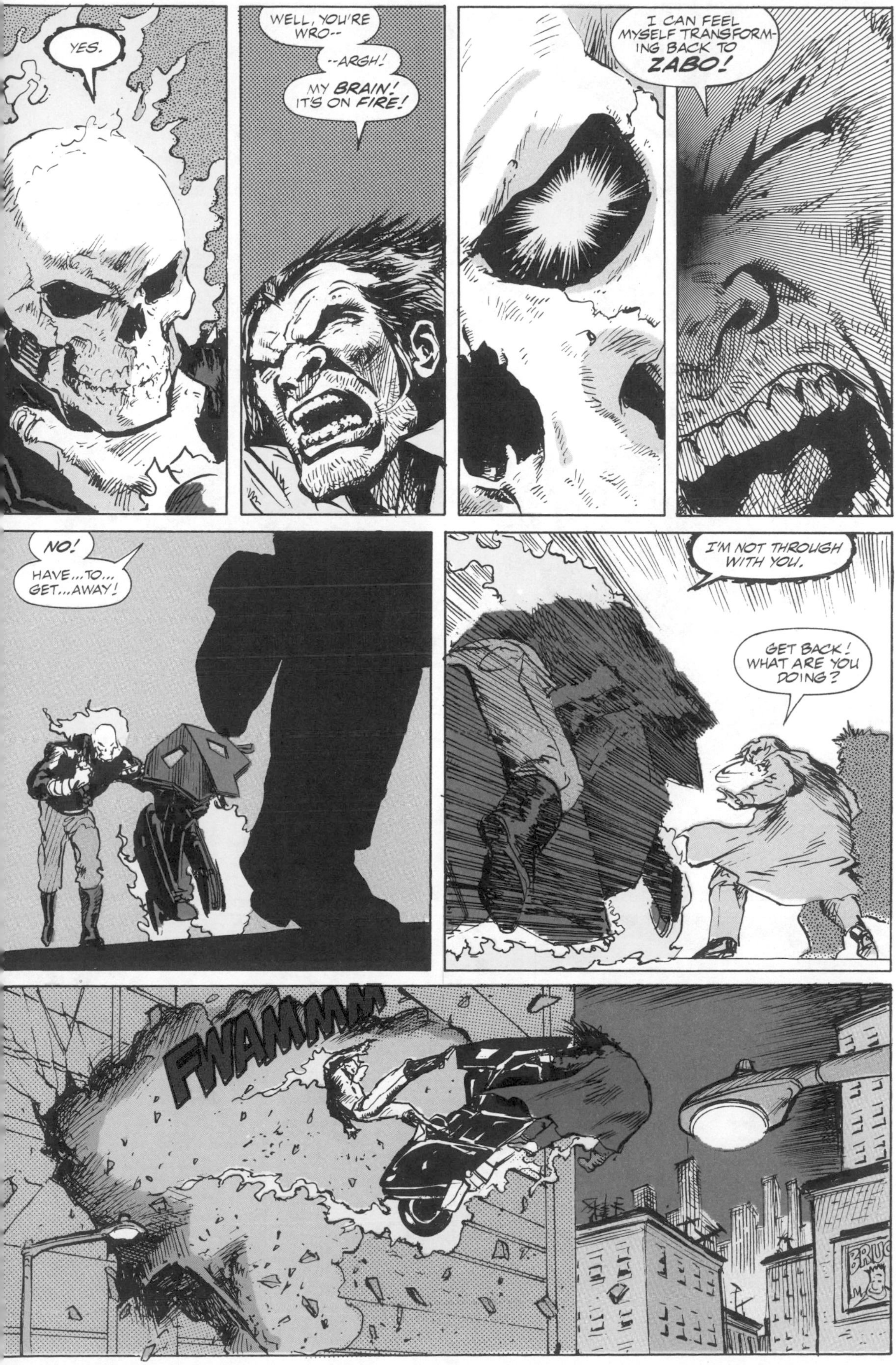
YES.
WELL, YOU'RE WRO--
--ARGH!
MY BRAIN! IT'S ON FIRE!
I CAN FEEL MYSELF TRANSFORMING BACK TO ZABO!
NO! HAVE...TO... GET...AWAY!
I'M NOT THROUGH WITH YOU.
GET BACK! WHAT ARE YOU DOING?
FWAMMM

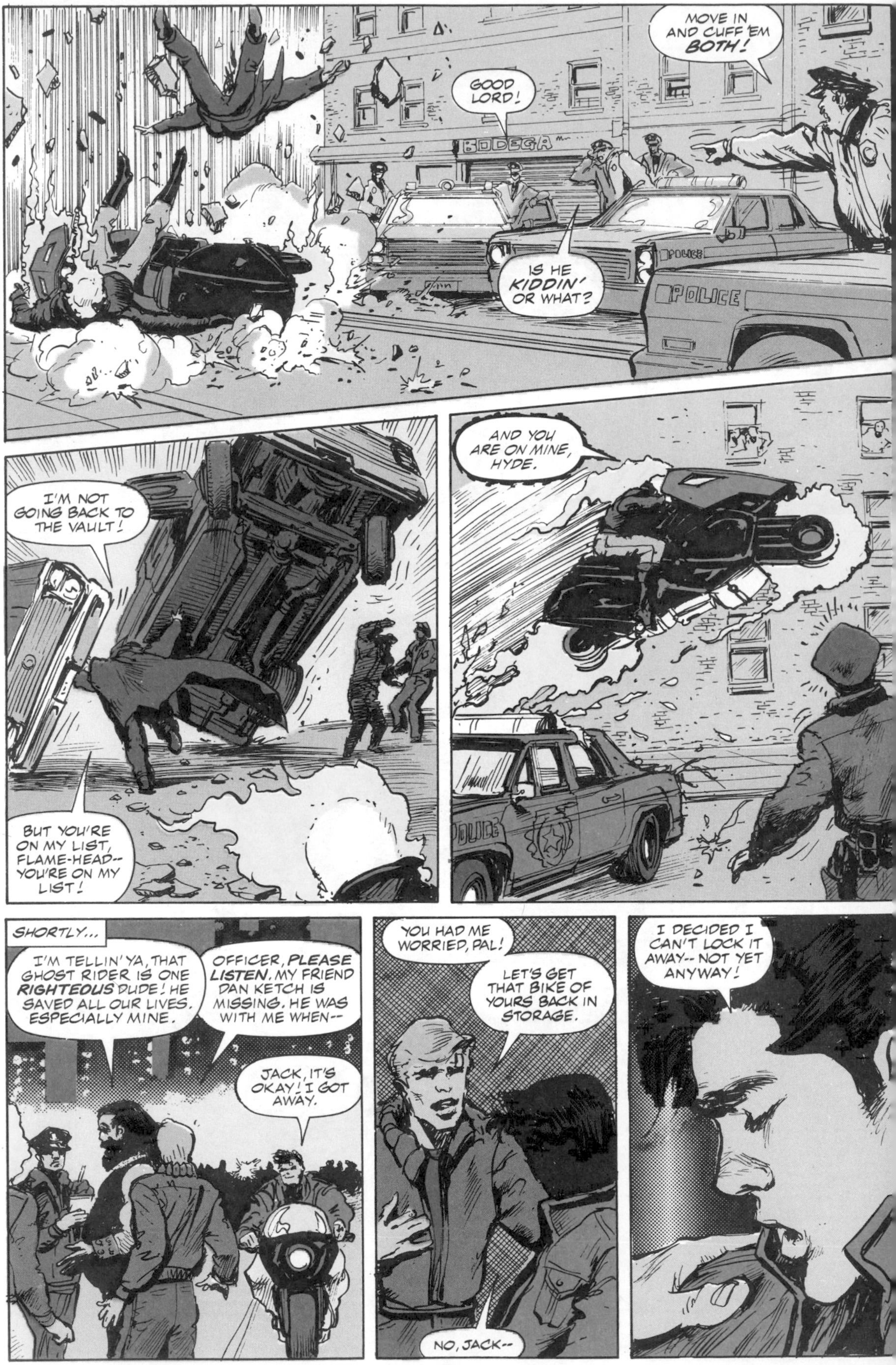
MOVE IN AND CUFF 'EM BOTH!
GOOD LORD!
BODEGA
IS HE KIDDIN' OR WHAT?
POLICE
POLICE
I'M NOT GOING BACK TO THE VAULT!
BUT YOU'RE ON MY LIST, FLAME-HEAD-- YOU'RE ON MY LIST!
AND YOU ARE ON MINE, HYDE.
POLICE
SHORTLY...
I'M TELLIN' YA, THAT GHOST RIDER IS ONE RIGHTEOUS DUDE! HE SAVED ALL OUR LIVES. ESPECIALLY MINE.
OFFICER, PLEASE LISTEN. MY FRIEND DAN KETCH IS MISSING. HE WAS WITH ME WHEN--
JACK, IT'S OKAY! I GOT AWAY.
YOU HAD ME WORRIED, PAL!
LET'S GET THAT BIKE OF YOURS BACK IN STORAGE.
NO, JACK--
I DECIDED I CAN'T LOCK IT AWAY-- NOT YET ANYWAY!

ELSEWHERE...

OKAY, JASON, WE'LL BE HOME SOON--

--I KNOW IT'S PAST YOUR BEDTIME, BUT WE HAD TO TAKE GRANDMA HER MEDICINE.

THIS STREET IS SO DARK! SO--

OH, MY--!

FWOMP

NO!

MY BABY! JASON! BRING BACK MY--

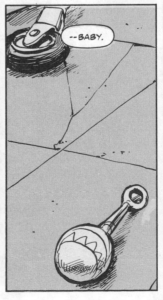

--BABY.

NEXT MONTH:

THE PUNISHER

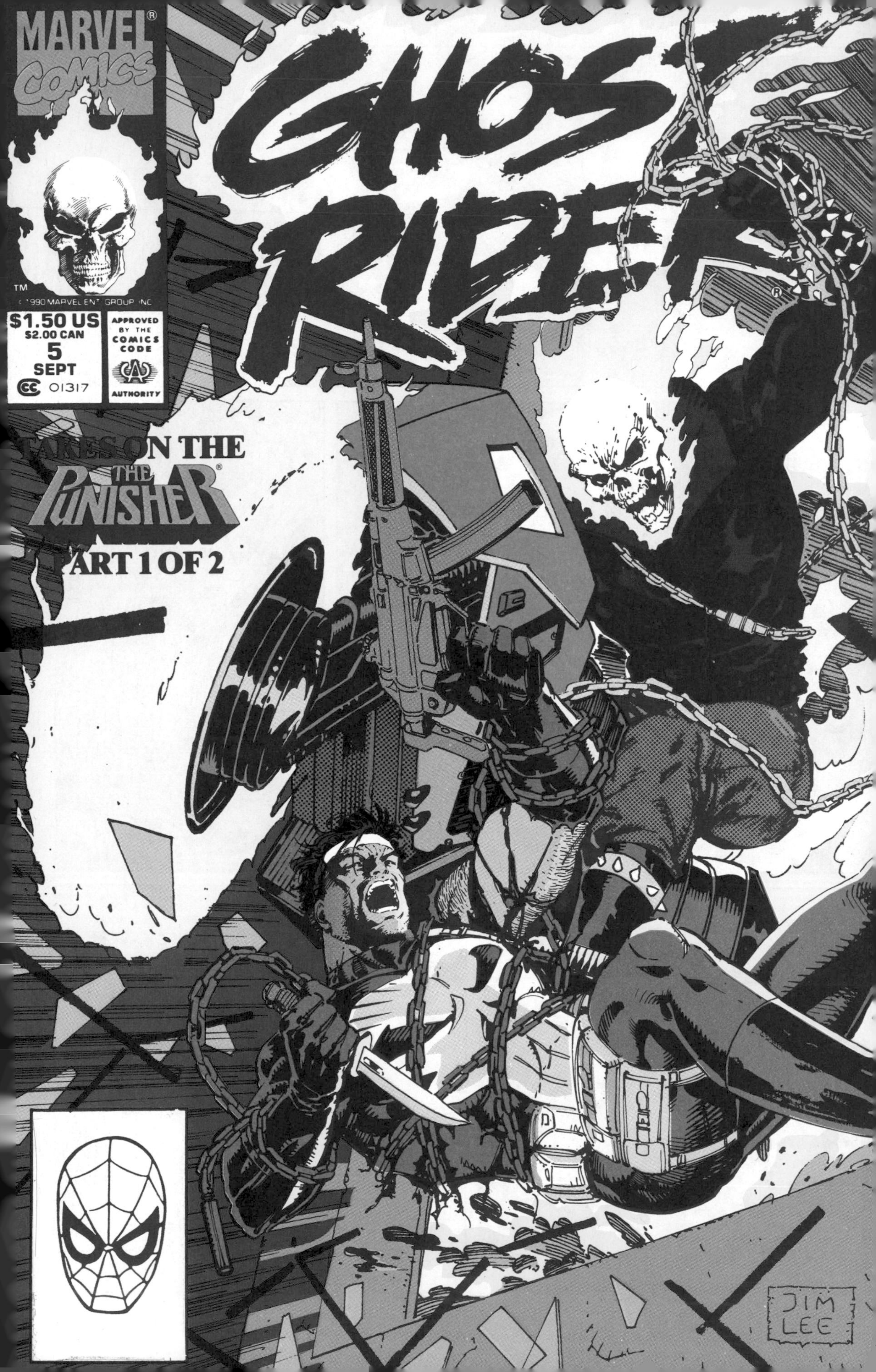
MARVEL COMICS
GHOST RIDER
TM
© 1990 MARVEL ENT. GROUP, INC.
$1.50 US
$2.00 CAN
5
SEPT
01317
APPROVED BY THE COMICS CODE AUTHORITY
TAKES ON THE
THE PUNISHER
PART 1 OF 2
JIM LEE

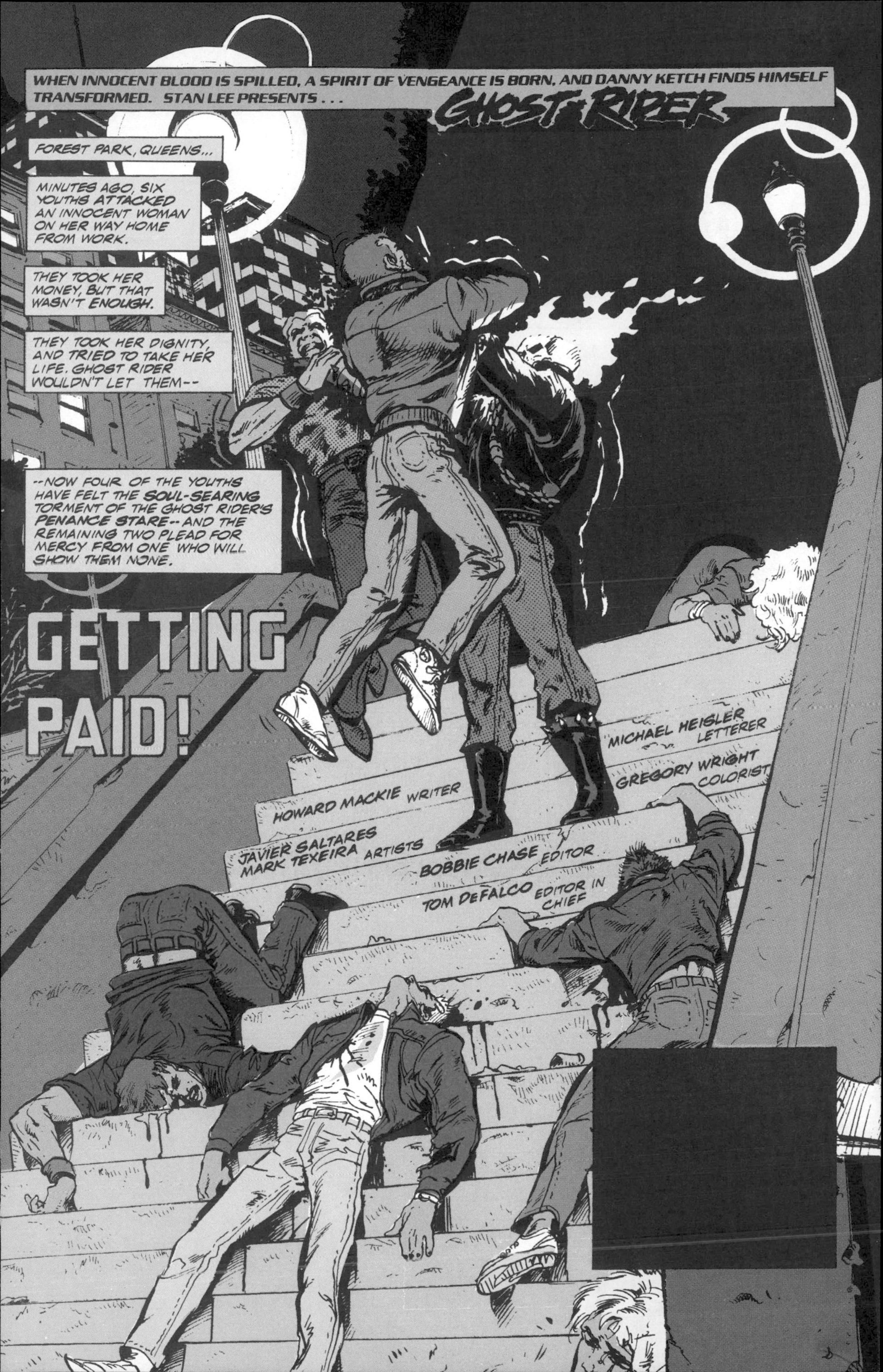
WHEN INNOCENT BLOOD IS SPILLED, A SPIRIT OF VENGEANCE IS BORN, AND DANNY KETCH FINDS HIMSELF TRANSFORMED. STAN LEE PRESENTS . . .
GHOST RIDER
FOREST PARK, QUEENS...
MINUTES AGO, SIX YOUTHS ATTACKED AN INNOCENT WOMAN ON HER WAY HOME FROM WORK.
THEY TOOK HER MONEY, BUT THAT WASN'T ENOUGH.
THEY TOOK HER DIGNITY, AND TRIED TO TAKE HER LIFE. GHOST RIDER WOULDN'T LET THEM--
--NOW FOUR OF THE YOUTHS HAVE FELT THE SOUL-SEARING TORMENT OF THE GHOST RIDER'S PENANCE STARE-- AND THE REMAINING TWO PLEAD FOR MERCY FROM ONE WHO WILL SHOW THEM NONE.
GETTING PAID!
MICHAEL HEISLER LETTERER
GREGORY WRIGHT COLORIST
HOWARD MACKIE WRITER
JAVIER SALTARES
MARK TEXEIRA ARTISTS
BOBBIE CHASE EDITOR
TOM DeFALCO EDITOR IN CHIEF

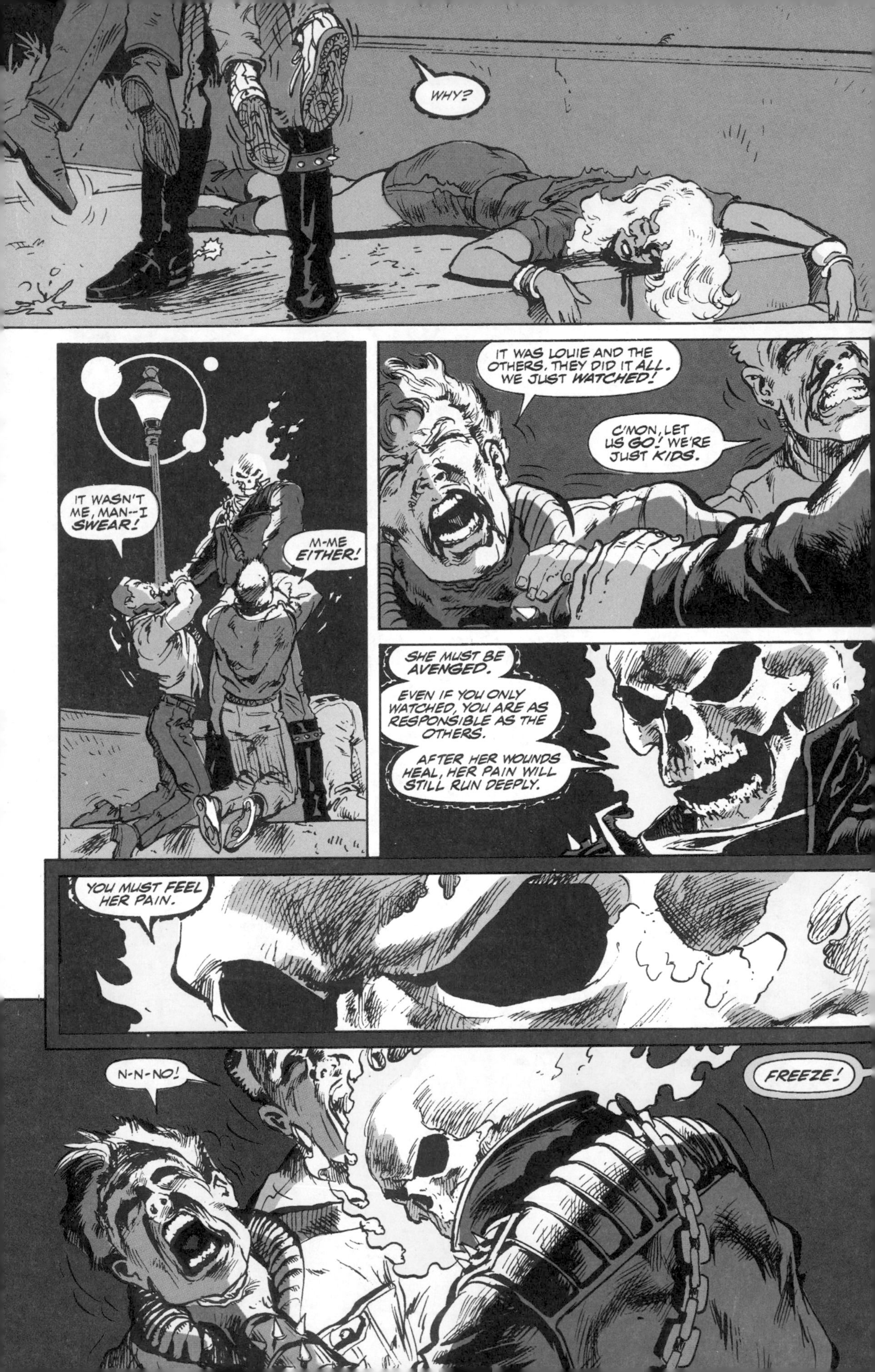
WHY?
IT WASN'T ME, MAN--I SWEAR!
M-ME EITHER!
IT WAS LOUIE AND THE OTHERS. THEY DID IT ALL. WE JUST WATCHED!
C'MON, LET US GO! WE'RE JUST KIDS.
SHE MUST BE AVENGED.
EVEN IF YOU ONLY WATCHED, YOU ARE AS RESPONSIBLE AS THE OTHERS.
AFTER HER WOUNDS HEAL, HER PAIN WILL STILL RUN DEEPLY.
YOU MUST FEEL HER PAIN.
N-N-NO!
FREEZE!

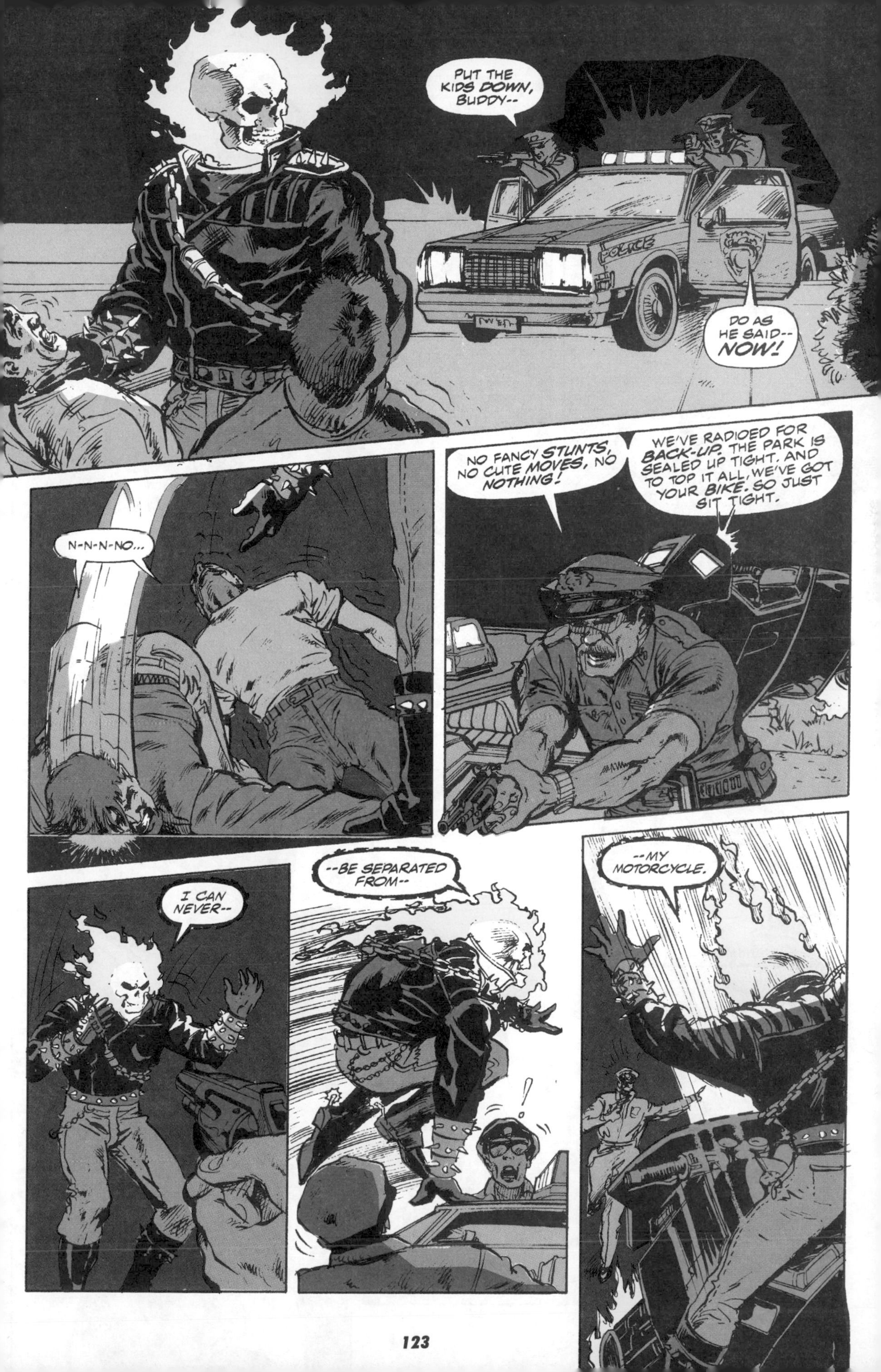
PUT THE KIDS DOWN, BUDDY--
DO AS HE SAID-- NOW!
POLICE
N-N-N-NO...
NO FANCY STUNTS, NO CUTE MOVES, NO NOTHING!
WE'VE RADIOED FOR BACK-UP. THE PARK IS SEALED UP TIGHT. AND TO TOP IT ALL, WE'VE GOT YOUR BIKE. SO JUST SIT TIGHT.
I CAN NEVER--
--BE SEPARATED FROM--
!
--MY MOTORCYCLE.

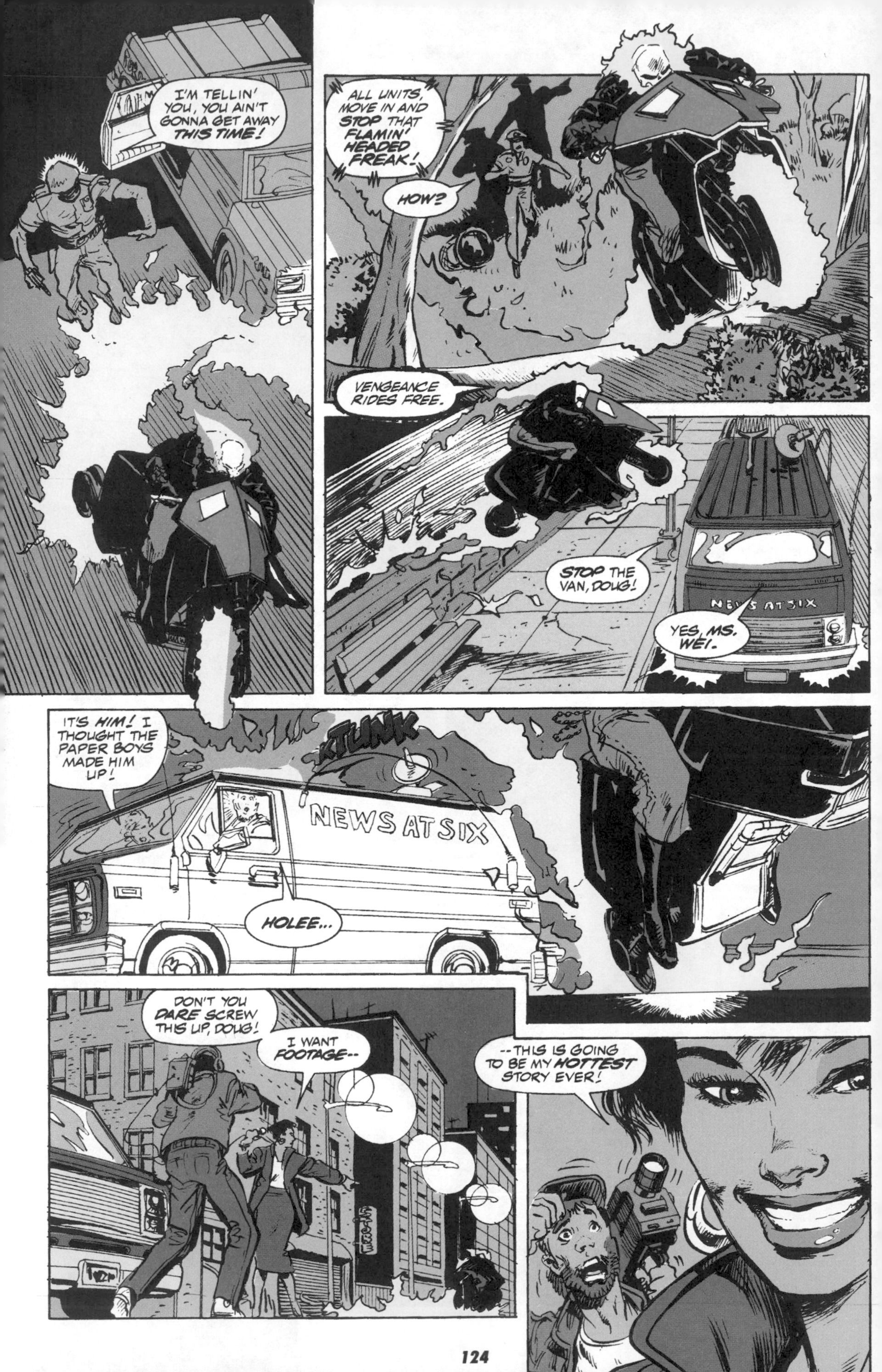
I'M TELLIN' YOU, YOU AIN'T GONNA GET AWAY THIS TIME!
ALL UNITS, MOVE IN AND STOP THAT FLAMIN' HEADED FREAK!
HOW?
VENGEANCE RIDES FREE.
STOP THE VAN, DOUG!
NEWS AT SIX
YES, MS. WEI.
IT'S HIM! I THOUGHT THE PAPER BOYS MADE HIM UP!
KTUNK
NEWS AT SIX
HOLEE...
DON'T YOU DARE SCREW THIS UP, DOUG!
I WANT FOOTAGE--
--THIS IS GOING TO BE MY HOTTEST STORY EVER!

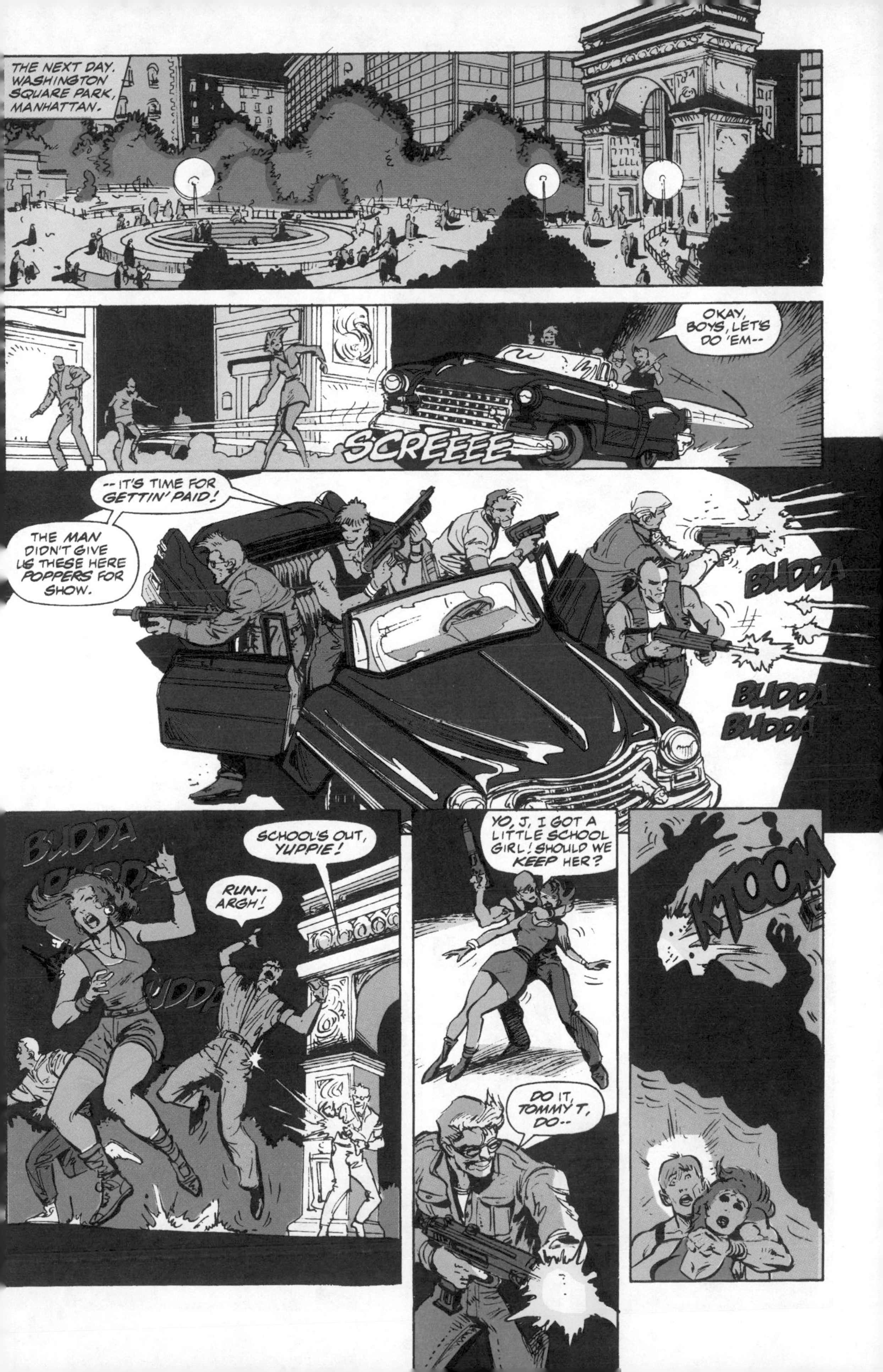
THE NEXT DAY. WASHINGTON SQUARE PARK, MANHATTAN.
OKAY, BOYS, LET'S DO 'EM--
SCREEEEE
--IT'S TIME FOR GETTIN' PAID!
THE MAN DIDN'T GIVE US THESE HERE POPPERS FOR SHOW.
BUDDA
BUDDA BUDDA
BUDDA
SCHOOL'S OUT, YUPPIE!
RUN-- ARGH!
YO, J, I GOT A LITTLE SCHOOL GIRL! SHOULD WE KEEP HER?
DO IT, TOMMY T, DO--
KTOOOM

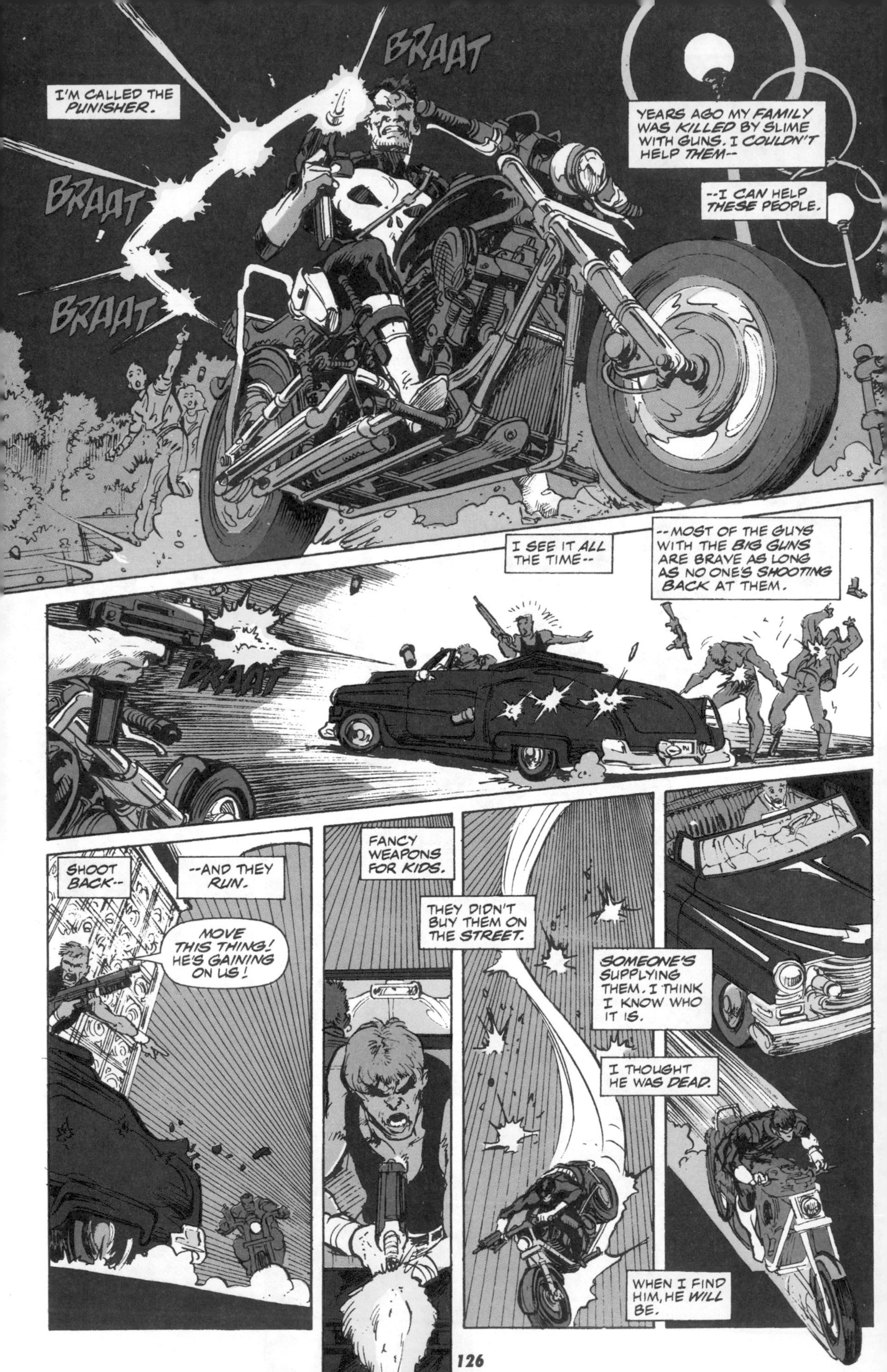
BRAAT
I'M CALLED THE PUNISHER.
BRAAT
BRAAT
YEARS AGO MY FAMILY WAS KILLED BY SLIME WITH GUNS. I COULDN'T HELP THEM--
--I CAN HELP THESE PEOPLE.
I SEE IT ALL THE TIME--
--MOST OF THE GUYS WITH THE BIG GUNS ARE BRAVE AS LONG AS NO ONE'S SHOOTING BACK AT THEM.
BRAAT
SHOOT BACK--
--AND THEY RUN.
MOVE THIS THING! HE'S GAINING ON US!
FANCY WEAPONS FOR KIDS.
THEY DIDN'T BUY THEM ON THE STREET.
SOMEONE'S SUPPLYING THEM. I THINK I KNOW WHO IT IS.
I THOUGHT HE WAS DEAD.
WHEN I FIND HIM, HE WILL BE.

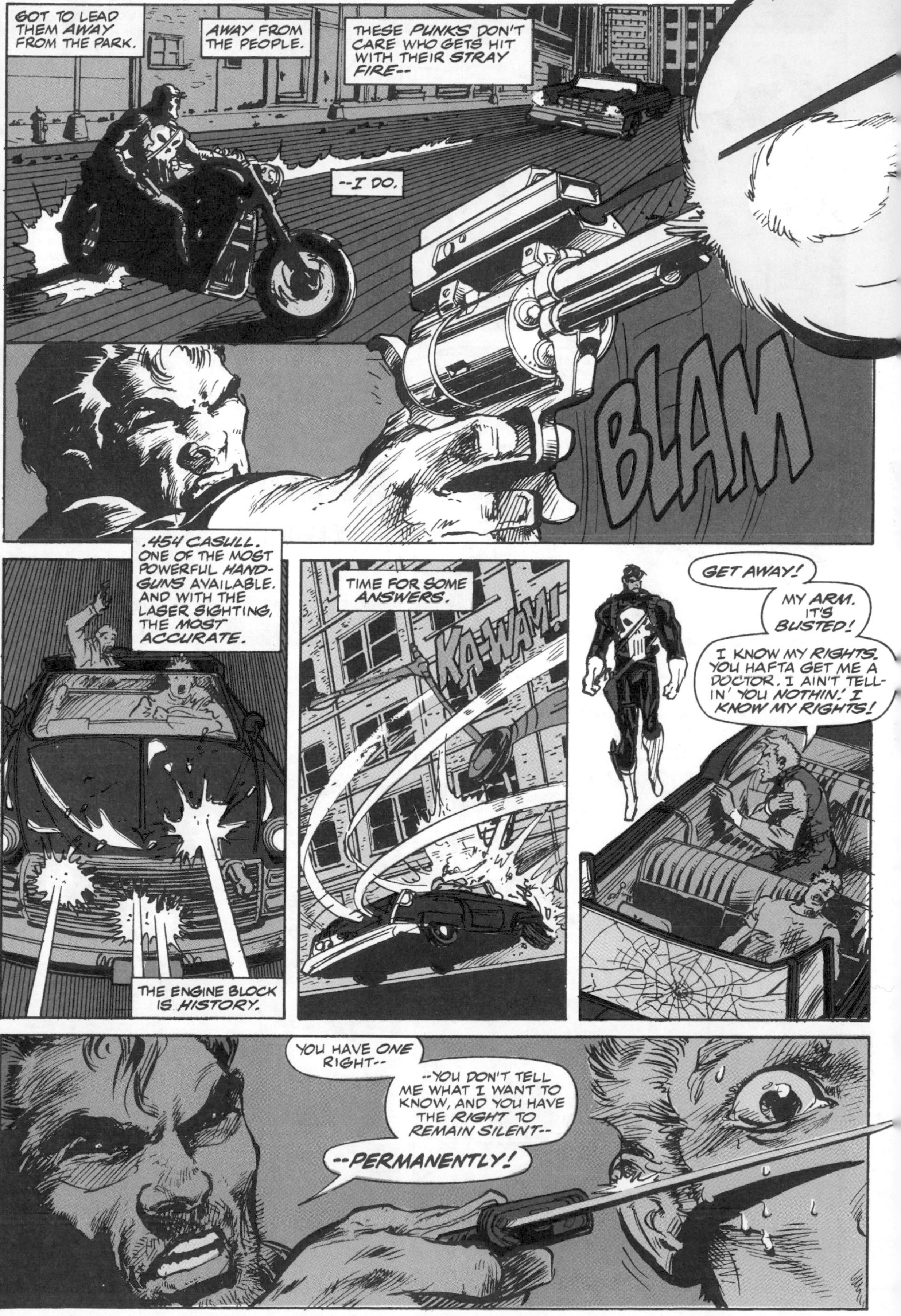

GOT TO LEAD THEM AWAY FROM THE PARK.
AWAY FROM THE PEOPLE.
THESE PUNKS DON'T CARE WHO GETS HIT WITH THEIR STRAY FIRE--
--I DO.
BLAM
.454 CASULL. ONE OF THE MOST POWERFUL HAND-GUNS AVAILABLE. AND WITH THE LASER SIGHTING, THE MOST ACCURATE.
THE ENGINE BLOCK IS HISTORY.
TIME FOR SOME ANSWERS.
KA-WAM!
GET AWAY!
MY ARM. IT'S BUSTED!
I KNOW MY RIGHTS. YOU HAFTA GET ME A DOCTOR. I AIN'T TELL-IN' YOU NOTHIN'! I KNOW MY RIGHTS!
YOU HAVE ONE RIGHT--
--YOU DON'T TELL ME WHAT I WANT TO KNOW, AND YOU HAVE THE RIGHT TO REMAIN SILENT--
--PERMANENTLY!

THE NEXT DAY IN BROOKLYN...

OH, DAN, THIS FEELS SO GOOD!

IT'S BEEN SO LONG SINCE WE'VE BEEN TOGETHER LIKE THIS.

I REALLY WISH WE COULD START GOING OUT AGAIN! IT'D BE GOOD FOR YOU--

IT'S TOO SOON, STACY. I NEED A LITTLE MORE TIME TO GET OVER WHAT HAPPENED TO BARB.

...AND NOW A SPECIAL REPORT ON THE RECENT "GETTING PAID" ACTS OF RANDOM VIOLENCE THAT HAVE BEEN PLAGUING THE CITY.

HERE WITH THAT STORY IS SPECIAL CORRESPONDENT LINDA WEI. LINDA...

THANK YOU, CHUCK.

"GETTING PAID,"

THE SLOGAN HAS BECOME A BATTLE CRY FOR THE LEGIONS OF HEAVILY ARMED YOUTHS TERRORIZING OUR CITY STREETS OVER THE PAST FEW WEEKS.

VIGILANTE ACTIVITY

"LAST NIGHT, YET ANOTHER INNOCENT VICTIM FELL PREY TO ONE OF THE ROVING BANDS OF YOUTHS.

"THE POLICE CLAIM TO BE FOLLOWING ALL LEADS, BUT ARE THEY OVERLOOKING THE OBVIOUS?

LAST NIGHT I WITNESSED THE SO-CALLED GHOST RIDER EVADE A POLICE DRAGNET AT THE SCENE OF THE CRIME, IN WHICH A YOUNG WOMAN WAS BRUTALLY ATTACKED AND SEVERAL YOUNG PEOPLE WERE HURT.

" THAT SAME NIGHT, THE PUNISHER WAS ON HAND AT WASHINGTON SQUARE DURING ANOTHER GETTING PAID INCIDENT.

ARE THE POLICE EXPLORING THE SIMILARITIES BETWEEN THE TWO ALLEGED VIGILANTES?

COULD THEY BE ONE AND THE SAME PERSON?

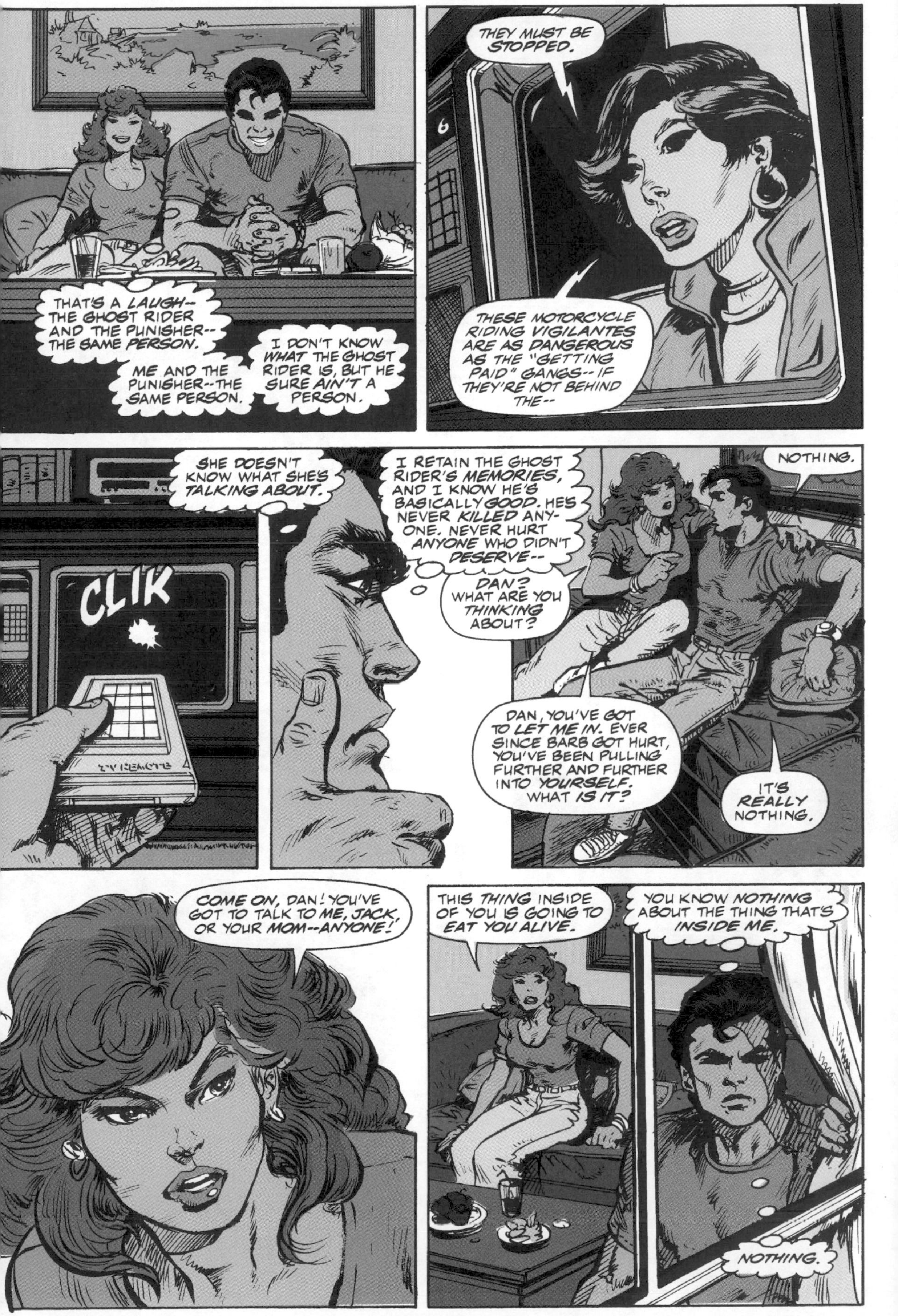

THAT'S A LAUGH-- THE GHOST RIDER AND THE PUNISHER-- THE SAME PERSON.
ME AND THE PUNISHER--THE SAME PERSON.
I DON'T KNOW WHAT THE GHOST RIDER IS, BUT HE SURE AIN'T A PERSON.
THEY MUST BE STOPPED.
6
THESE MOTORCYCLE RIDING VIGILANTES ARE AS DANGEROUS AS THE "GETTING PAID" GANGS-- IF THEY'RE NOT BEHIND THE--
CLIK
TV REMOTE
SHE DOESN'T KNOW WHAT SHE'S TALKING ABOUT.
I RETAIN THE GHOST RIDER'S MEMORIES, AND I KNOW HE'S BASICALLY GOOD. HE'S NEVER KILLED ANYONE. NEVER HURT ANYONE WHO DIDN'T DESERVE--
DAN? WHAT ARE YOU THINKING ABOUT?
NOTHING.
DAN, YOU'VE GOT TO LET ME IN. EVER SINCE BARB GOT HURT, YOU'VE BEEN PULLING FURTHER AND FURTHER INTO YOURSELF. WHAT IS IT?
IT'S REALLY NOTHING.
COME ON, DAN! YOU'VE GOT TO TALK TO ME, JACK, OR YOUR MOM--ANYONE!
THIS THING INSIDE OF YOU IS GOING TO EAT YOU ALIVE.
YOU KNOW NOTHING ABOUT THE THING THAT'S INSIDE ME.
NOTHING.

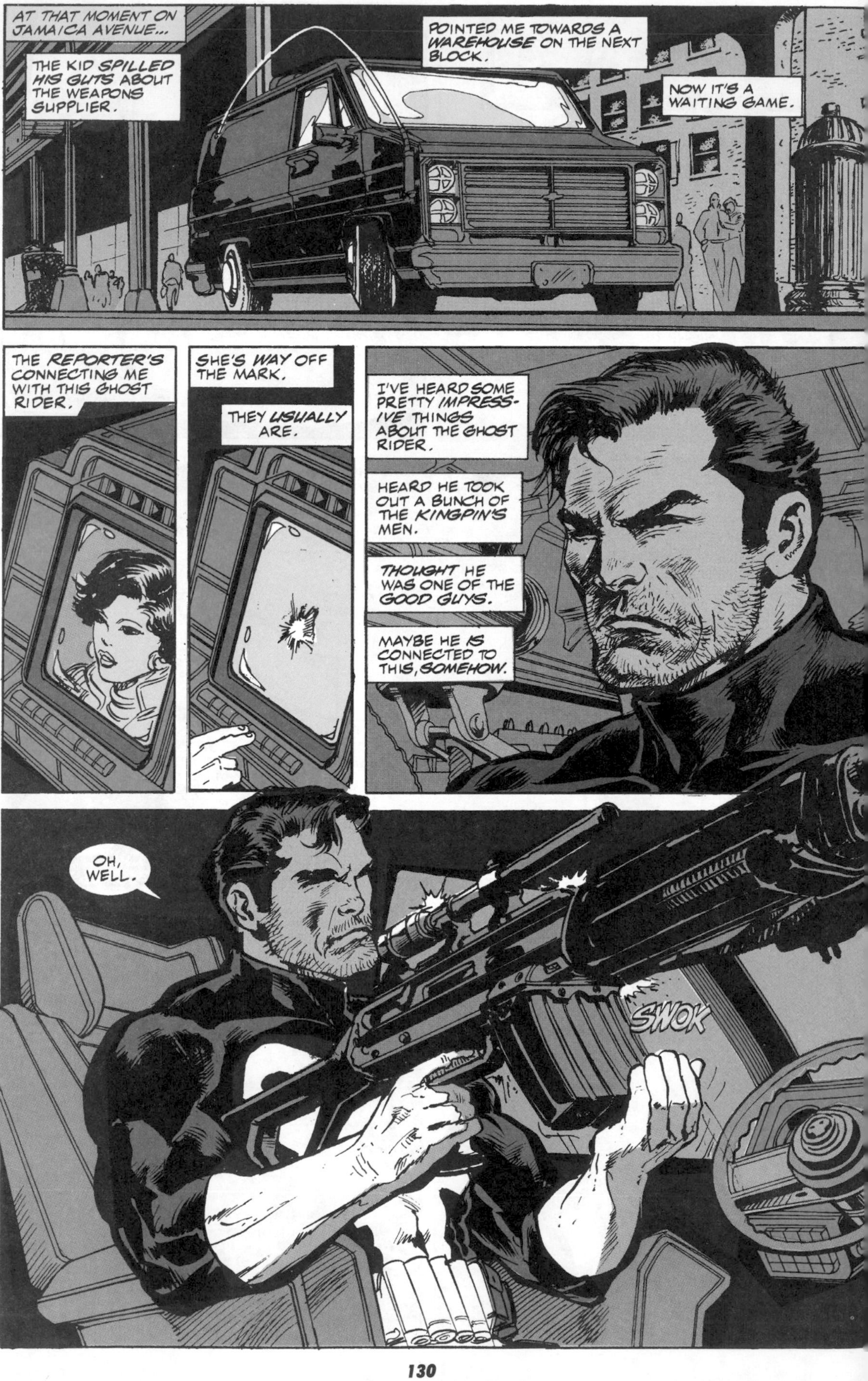
AT THAT MOMENT ON JAMAICA AVENUE...
THE KID SPILLED HIS GUTS ABOUT THE WEAPONS SUPPLIER.
POINTED ME TOWARDS A WAREHOUSE ON THE NEXT BLOCK.
NOW IT'S A WAITING GAME.
THE REPORTER'S CONNECTING ME WITH THIS GHOST RIDER.
SHE'S WAY OFF THE MARK.
THEY USUALLY ARE.
I'VE HEARD SOME PRETTY IMPRESSIVE THINGS ABOUT THE GHOST RIDER.
HEARD HE TOOK OUT A BUNCH OF THE KINGPIN'S MEN.
THOUGHT HE WAS ONE OF THE GOOD GUYS.
MAYBE HE IS CONNECTED TO THIS, SOMEHOW.
OH, WELL.
SWOK

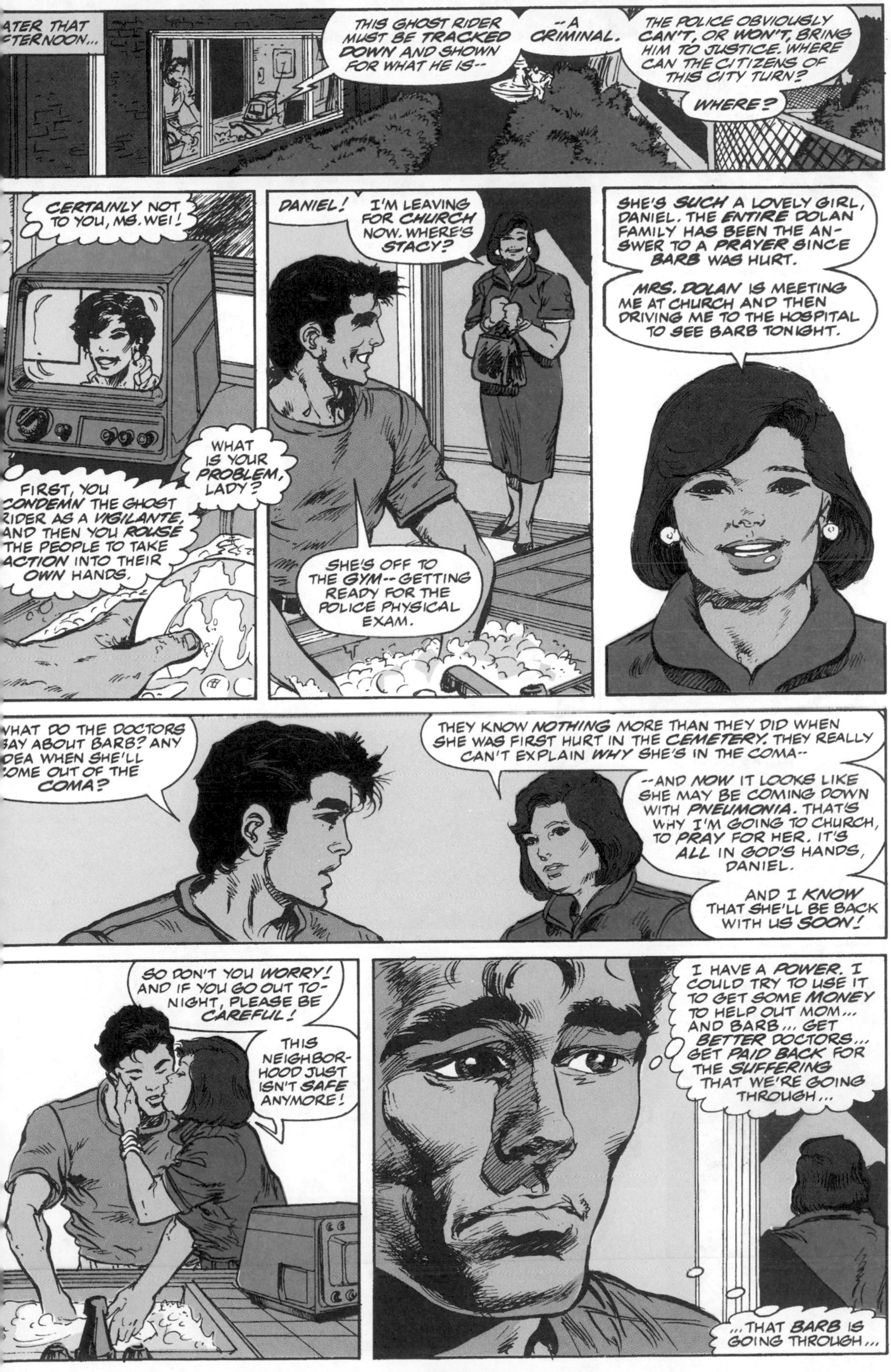

ATER THAT
TERNOON...
THIS GHOST RIDER MUST BE TRACKED DOWN AND SHOWN FOR WHAT HE IS--
--A CRIMINAL.
THE POLICE OBVIOUSLY CAN'T, OR WON'T, BRING HIM TO JUSTICE. WHERE CAN THE CITIZENS OF THIS CITY TURN?
WHERE?
CERTAINLY NOT TO YOU, MS. WEI!
WHAT IS YOUR PROBLEM, LADY?
FIRST, YOU CONDEMN THE GHOST RIDER AS A VIGILANTE, AND THEN YOU ROUSE THE PEOPLE TO TAKE ACTION INTO THEIR OWN HANDS.
DANIEL!
I'M LEAVING FOR CHURCH NOW. WHERE'S STACY?
SHE'S OFF TO THE GYM--GETTING READY FOR THE POLICE PHYSICAL EXAM.
SHE'S SUCH A LOVELY GIRL, DANIEL. THE ENTIRE DOLAN FAMILY HAS BEEN THE ANSWER TO A PRAYER SINCE BARB WAS HURT.
MRS. DOLAN IS MEETING ME AT CHURCH AND THEN DRIVING ME TO THE HOSPITAL TO SEE BARB TONIGHT.
WHAT DO THE DOCTORS SAY ABOUT BARB? ANY IDEA WHEN SHE'LL COME OUT OF THE COMA?
THEY KNOW NOTHING MORE THAN THEY DID WHEN SHE WAS FIRST HURT IN THE CEMETERY. THEY REALLY CAN'T EXPLAIN WHY SHE'S IN THE COMA--
--AND NOW IT LOOKS LIKE SHE MAY BE COMING DOWN WITH PNEUMONIA. THAT'S WHY I'M GOING TO CHURCH, TO PRAY FOR HER. IT'S ALL IN GOD'S HANDS, DANIEL.
AND I KNOW THAT SHE'LL BE BACK WITH US SOON!
SO DON'T YOU WORRY! AND IF YOU GO OUT TONIGHT, PLEASE BE CAREFUL!
THIS NEIGHBORHOOD JUST ISN'T SAFE ANYMORE!
I HAVE A POWER. I COULD TRY TO USE IT TO GET SOME MONEY TO HELP OUT MOM... AND BARB... GET BETTER DOCTORS... GET PAID BACK FOR THE SUFFERING THAT WE'RE GOING THROUGH...
...THAT BARB IS GOING THROUGH...

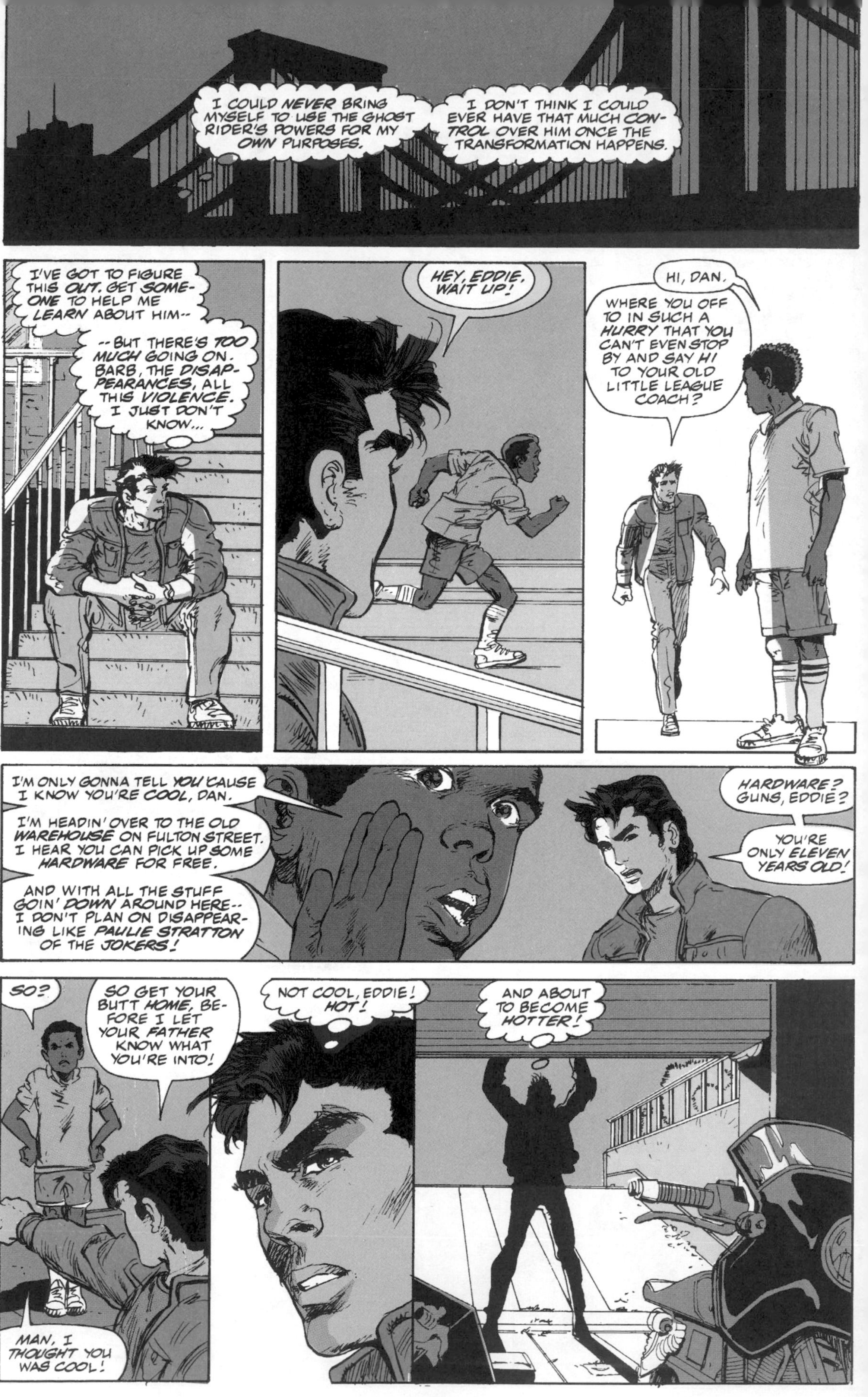

I COULD NEVER BRING MYSELF TO USE THE GHOST RIDER'S POWERS FOR MY OWN PURPOSES.
I DON'T THINK I COULD EVER HAVE THAT MUCH CONTROL OVER HIM ONCE THE TRANSFORMATION HAPPENS.
I'VE GOT TO FIGURE THIS OUT. GET SOMEONE TO HELP ME LEARN ABOUT HIM--
--BUT THERE'S TOO MUCH GOING ON. BARB, THE DISAPPEARANCES, ALL THIS VIOLENCE. I JUST DON'T KNOW...
HEY, EDDIE, WAIT UP!
HI, DAN.
WHERE YOU OFF TO IN SUCH A HURRY THAT YOU CAN'T EVEN STOP BY AND SAY HI TO YOUR OLD LITTLE LEAGUE COACH?
I'M ONLY GONNA TELL YOU 'CAUSE I KNOW YOU'RE COOL, DAN.
I'M HEADIN' OVER TO THE OLD WAREHOUSE ON FULTON STREET. I HEAR YOU CAN PICK UP SOME HARDWARE FOR FREE.
AND WITH ALL THE STUFF GOIN' DOWN AROUND HERE-- I DON'T PLAN ON DISAPPEARING LIKE PAULIE STRATTON OF THE JOKERS!
HARDWARE? GUNS, EDDIE?
YOU'RE ONLY ELEVEN YEARS OLD!
SO?
SO GET YOUR BUTT HOME, BEFORE I LET YOUR FATHER KNOW WHAT YOU'RE INTO!
MAN, I THOUGHT YOU WAS COOL!
NOT COOL, EDDIE! HOT!
AND ABOUT TO BECOME HOTTER!

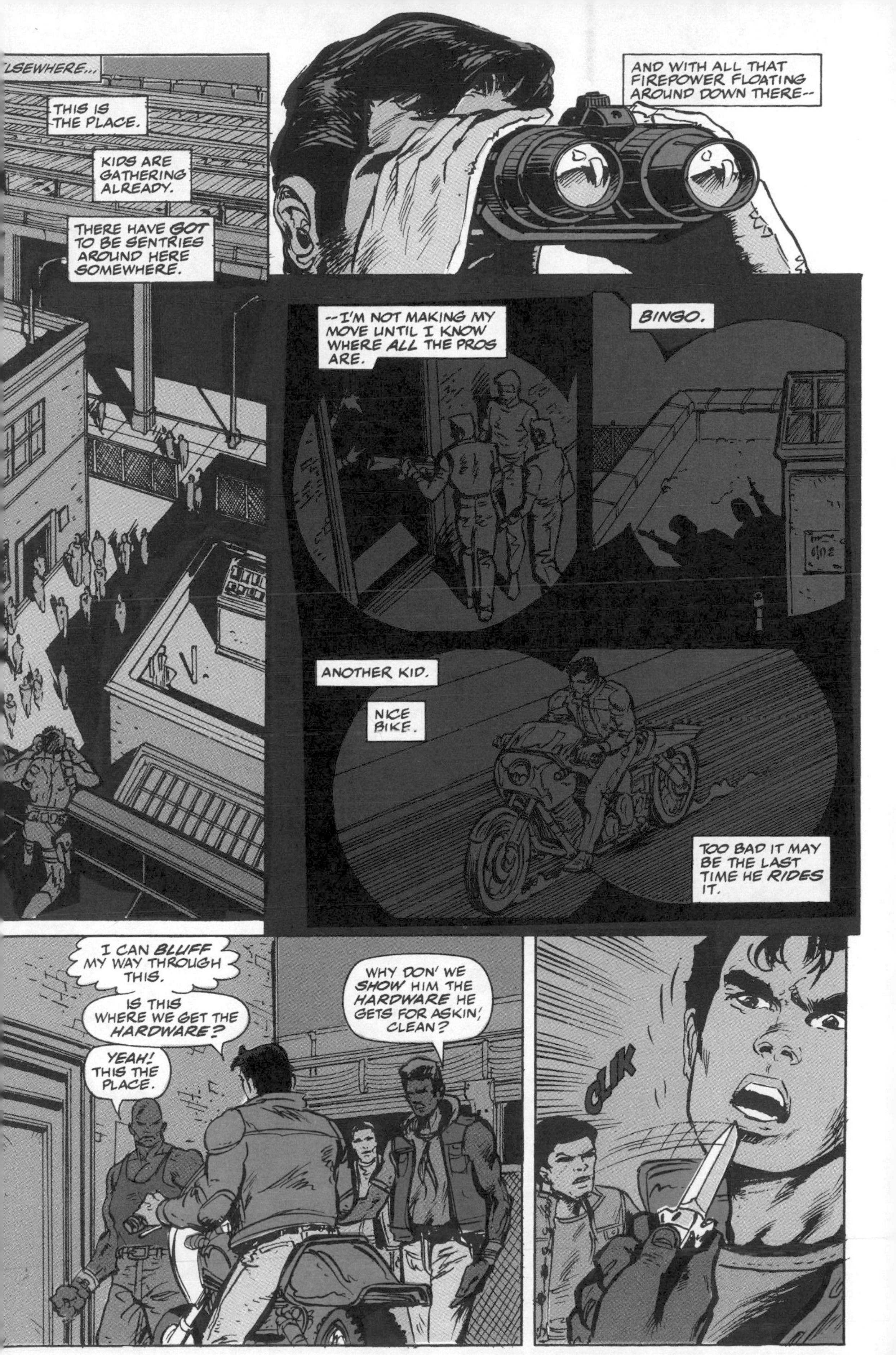
ELSEWHERE...
THIS IS THE PLACE.
KIDS ARE GATHERING ALREADY.
THERE HAVE GOT TO BE SENTRIES AROUND HERE SOMEWHERE.
AND WITH ALL THAT FIREPOWER FLOATING AROUND DOWN THERE--
--I'M NOT MAKING MY MOVE UNTIL I KNOW WHERE ALL THE PROS ARE.
BINGO.
ANOTHER KID.
NICE BIKE.
TOO BAD IT MAY BE THE LAST TIME HE RIDES IT.
I CAN BLUFF MY WAY THROUGH THIS.
IS THIS WHERE WE GET THE HARDWARE?
YEAH! THIS THE PLACE.
WHY DON' WE SHOW HIM THE HARDWARE HE GETS FOR ASKIN', CLEAN?
CLIK

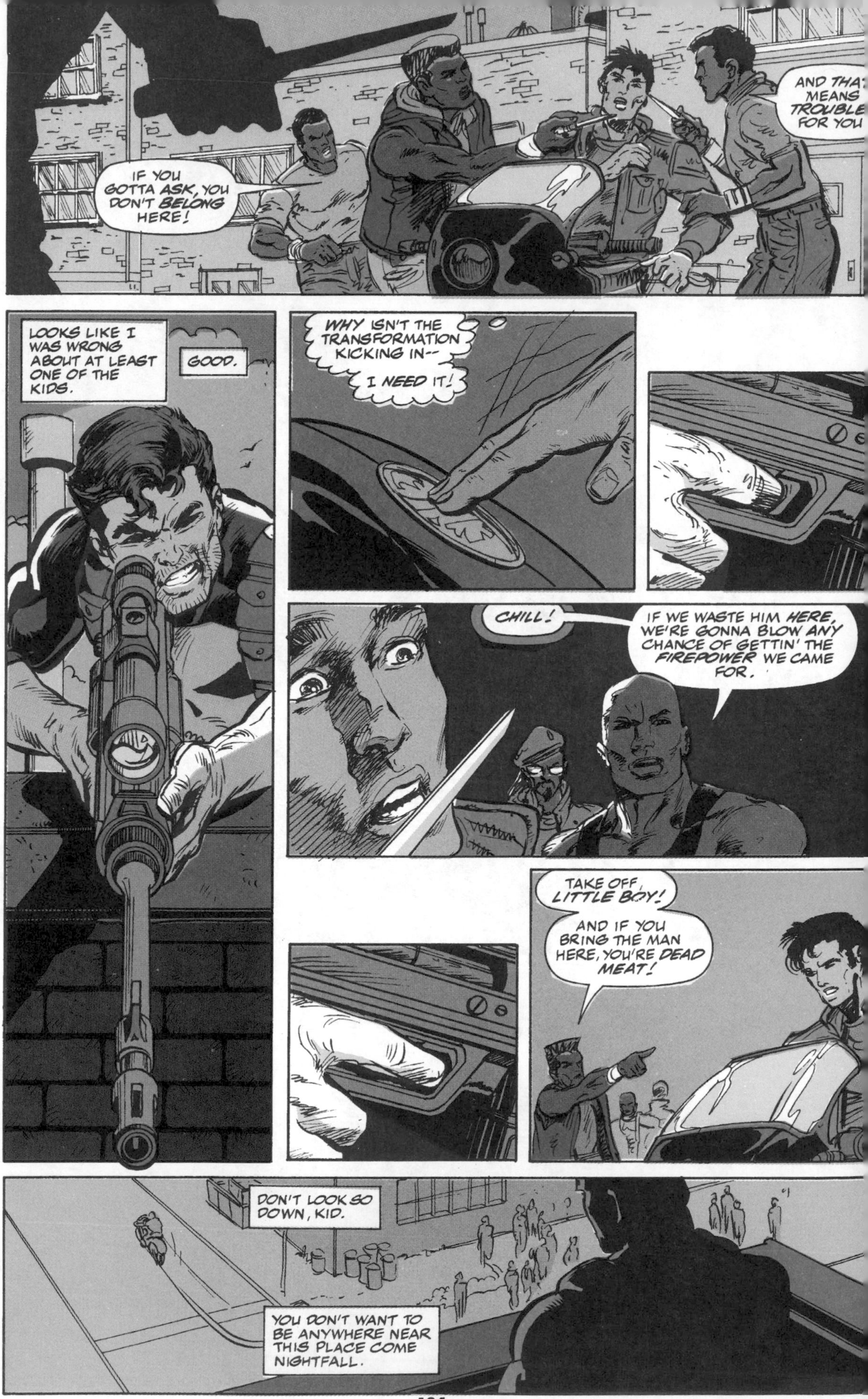
IF YOU GOTTA ASK, YOU DON'T BELONG HERE!
AND THAT MEANS TROUBLE FOR YOU
LOOKS LIKE I WAS WRONG ABOUT AT LEAST ONE OF THE KIDS.
GOOD.
WHY ISN'T THE TRANSFORMATION KICKING IN--
I NEED IT!
CHILL!
IF WE WASTE HIM HERE, WE'RE GONNA BLOW ANY CHANCE OF GETTIN' THE FIREPOWER WE CAME FOR.
TAKE OFF, LITTLE BOY!
AND IF YOU BRING THE MAN HERE, YOU'RE DEAD MEAT!
DON'T LOOK SO DOWN, KID.
YOU DON'T WANT TO BE ANYWHERE NEAR THIS PLACE COME NIGHTFALL.

SUNSET IN
FOREST PARK...

I CAN'T BELIEVE IT.

WHEN I NEEDED IT THE MOST, THIS BIKE LET ME DOWN.

GUESS I'M FINALLY *DONE* WITH THE GHOST RIDER.

I DIDN'T LIKE THE THINGS THAT HE DID, BUT THERE WAS SOME *GOOD* IN WHAT HE WAS DOING. HE *NEVER* HURT AN INNOCENT PERSON AND--

--HE WAS THE ONLY WAY I COULD GET BACK AT THE PEOPLE WHO HURT *BARB.*

NOW HE'S GONE.

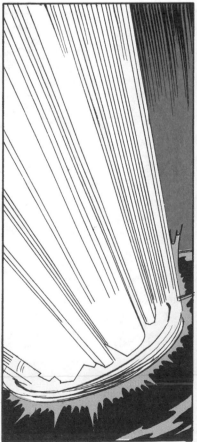

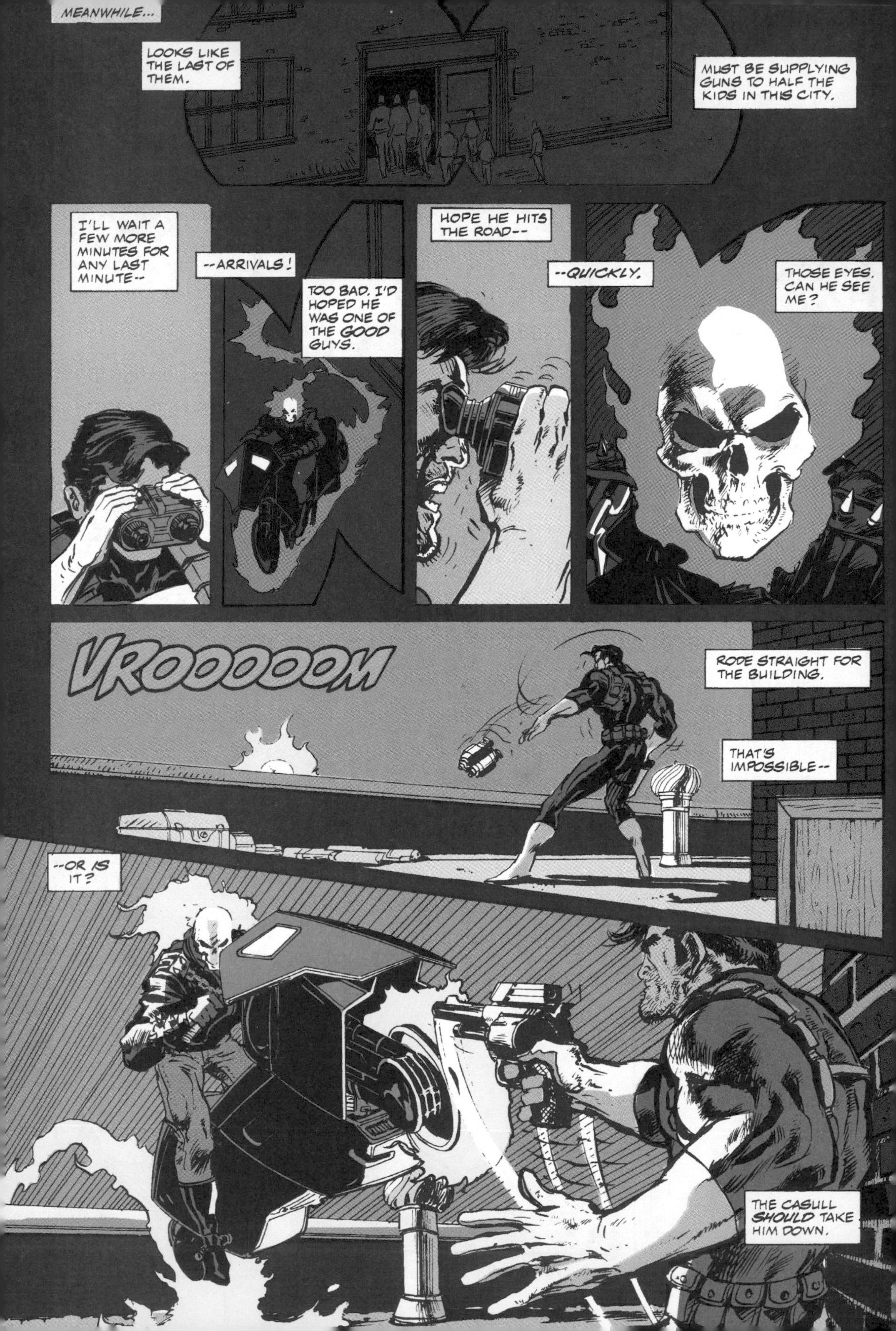

MEANWHILE...
LOOKS LIKE THE LAST OF THEM.
MUST BE SUPPLYING GUNS TO HALF THE KIDS IN THIS CITY.
I'LL WAIT A FEW MORE MINUTES FOR ANY LAST MINUTE--
--ARRIVALS!
TOO BAD. I'D HOPED HE WAS ONE OF THE GOOD GUYS.
HOPE HE HITS THE ROAD--
--QUICKLY.
THOSE EYES. CAN HE SEE ME?
VROOOOOM
RODE STRAIGHT FOR THE BUILDING.
THAT'S IMPOSSIBLE--
--OR IS IT?
THE CASULL SHOULD TAKE HIM DOWN.

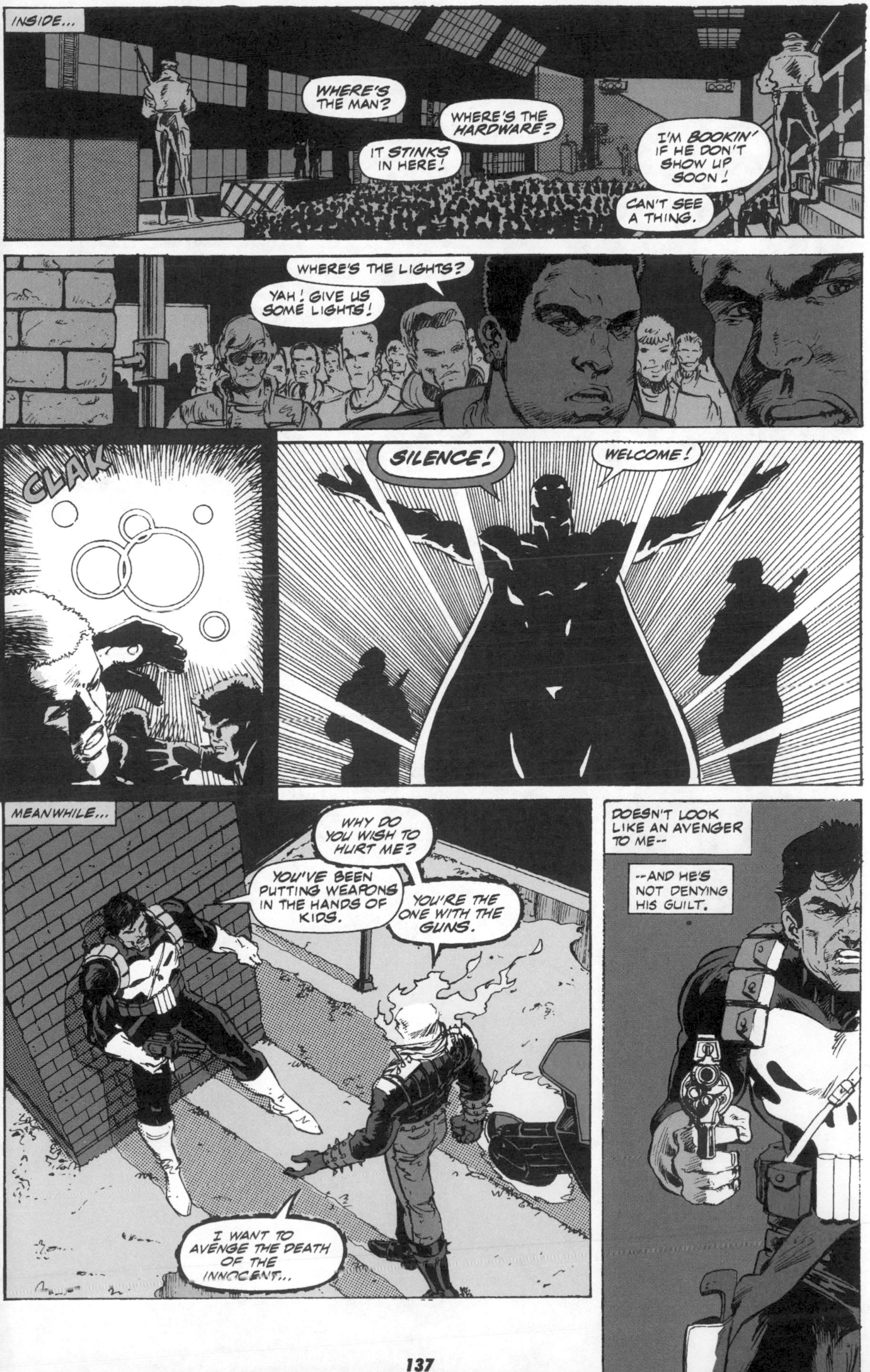
INSIDE...
WHERE'S THE MAN?
WHERE'S THE HARDWARE?
IT STINKS IN HERE!
I'M BOOKIN' IF HE DON'T SHOW UP SOON!
CAN'T SEE A THING.
WHERE'S THE LIGHTS?
YAH! GIVE US SOME LIGHTS!
CLAK
SILENCE!
WELCOME!
MEANWHILE...
WHY DO YOU WISH TO HURT ME?
YOU'VE BEEN PUTTING WEAPONS IN THE HANDS OF KIDS.
YOU'RE THE ONE WITH THE GUNS.
I WANT TO AVENGE THE DEATH OF THE INNOCENT...
DOESN'T LOOK LIKE AN AVENGER TO ME--
--AND HE'S NOT DENYING HIS GUILT.

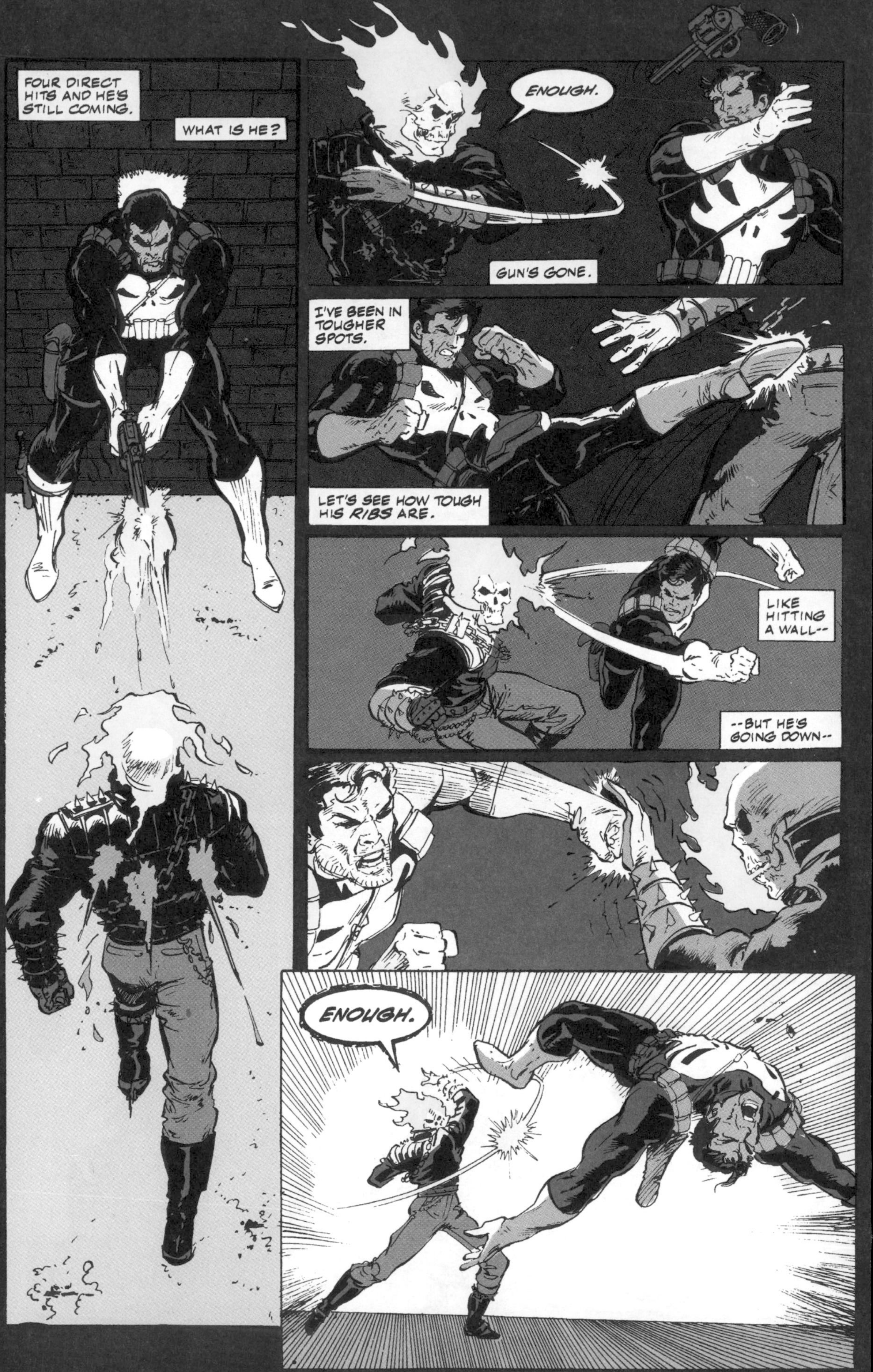
FOUR DIRECT HITS AND HE'S STILL COMING.
WHAT IS HE?
ENOUGH.
GUN'S GONE.
I'VE BEEN IN TOUGHER SPOTS.
LET'S SEE HOW TOUGH HIS RIBS ARE.
LIKE HITTING A WALL--
--BUT HE'S GOING DOWN--
ENOUGH.

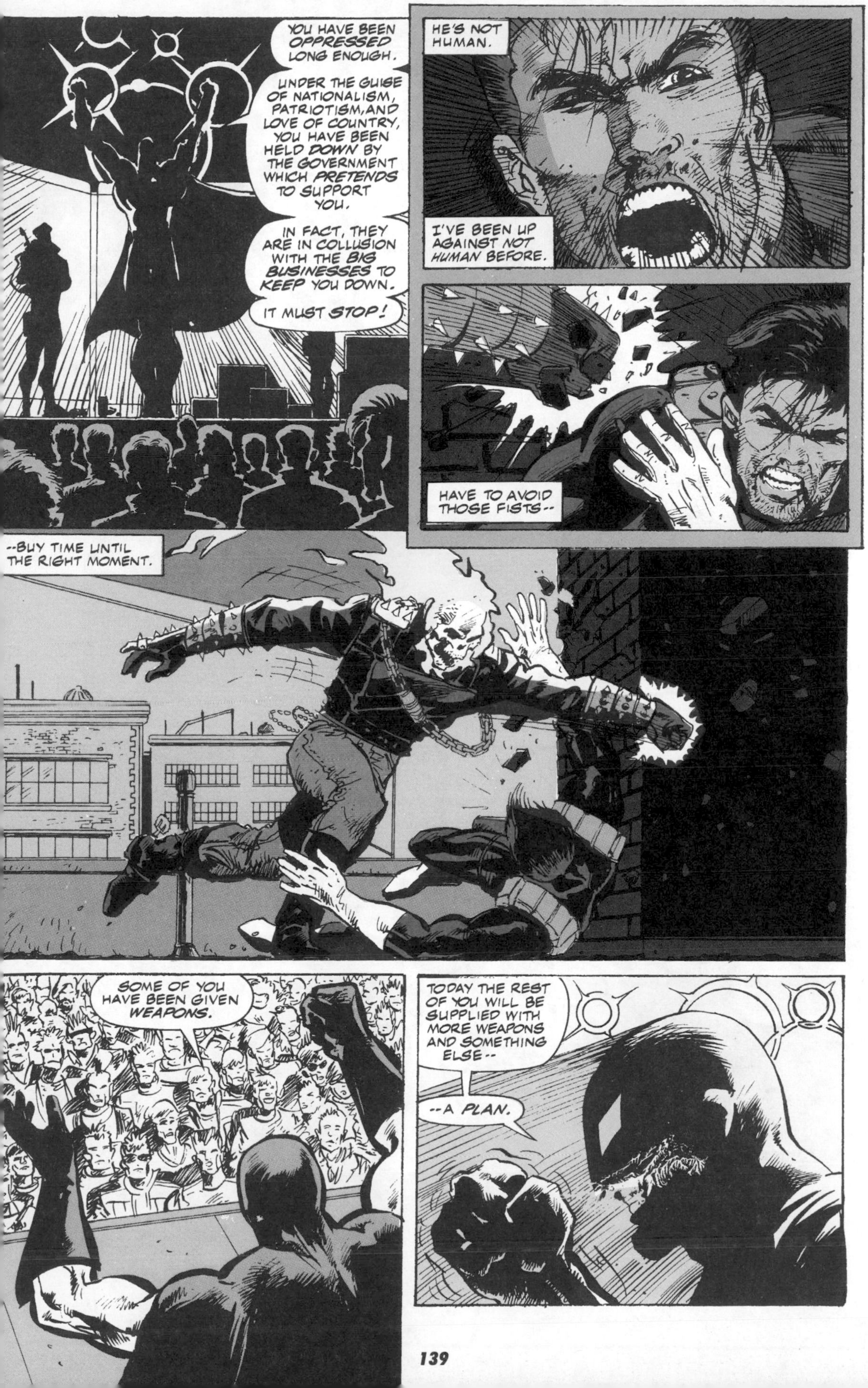

YOU HAVE BEEN OPPRESSED LONG ENOUGH.
UNDER THE GUISE OF NATIONALISM, PATRIOTISM, AND LOVE OF COUNTRY, YOU HAVE BEEN HELD DOWN BY THE GOVERNMENT WHICH PRETENDS TO SUPPORT YOU.
IN FACT, THEY ARE IN COLLUSION WITH THE BIG BUSINESSES TO KEEP YOU DOWN.
IT MUST STOP!
HE'S NOT HUMAN.
I'VE BEEN UP AGAINST NOT HUMAN BEFORE.
HAVE TO AVOID THOSE FISTS--
--BUY TIME UNTIL THE RIGHT MOMENT.
SOME OF YOU HAVE BEEN GIVEN WEAPONS.
TODAY THE REST OF YOU WILL BE SUPPLIED WITH MORE WEAPONS AND SOMETHING ELSE--
--A PLAN.

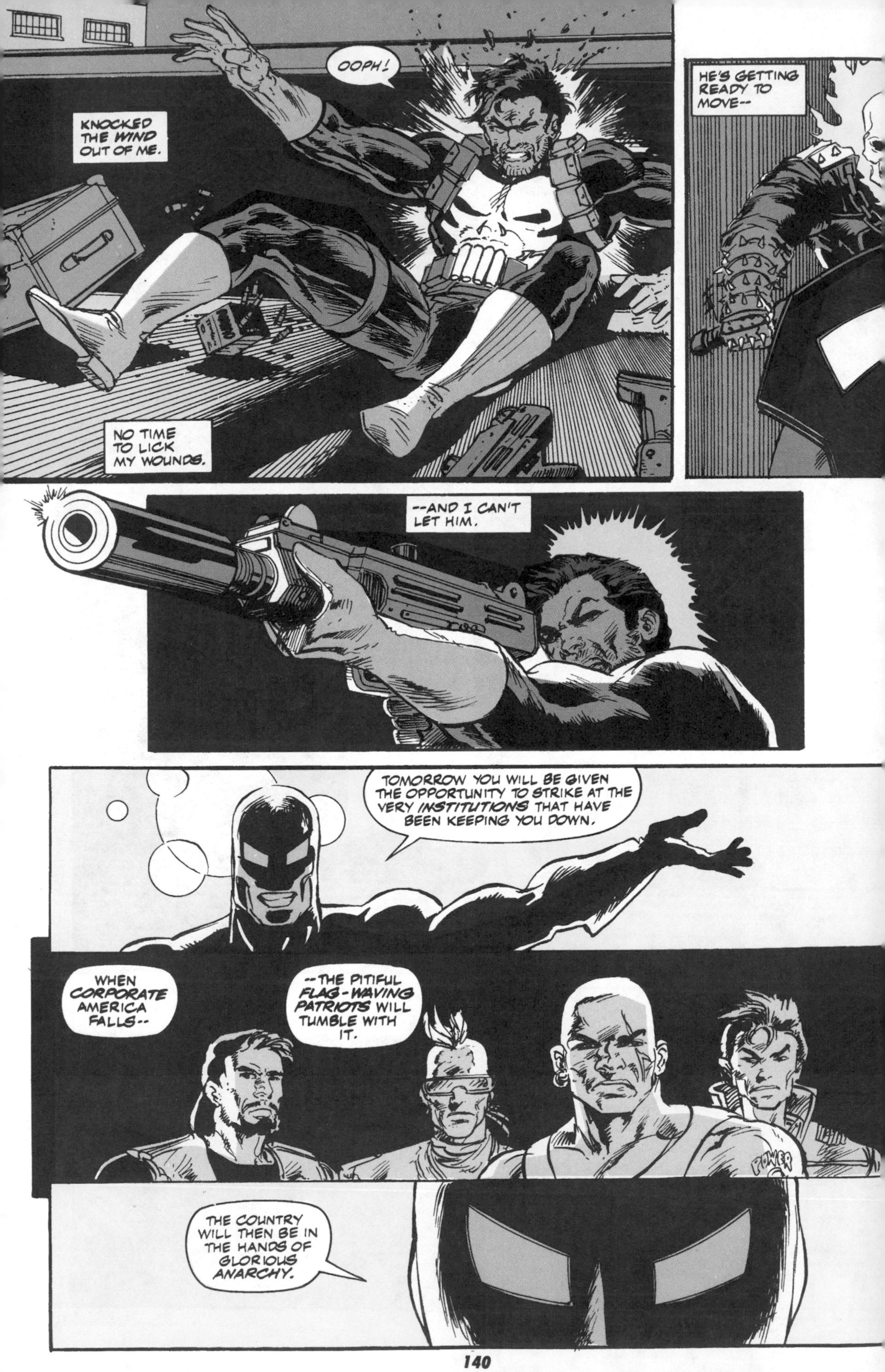
OOPH!
KNOCKED THE WIND OUT OF ME.
NO TIME TO LICK MY WOUNDS.
HE'S GETTING READY TO MOVE--
--AND I CAN'T LET HIM.
TOMORROW YOU WILL BE GIVEN THE OPPORTUNITY TO STRIKE AT THE VERY INSTITUTIONS THAT HAVE BEEN KEEPING YOU DOWN.
WHEN CORPORATE AMERICA FALLS--
--THE PITIFUL FLAG-WAVING PATRIOTS WILL TUMBLE WITH IT.
POWER
THE COUNTRY WILL THEN BE IN THE HANDS OF GLORIOUS ANARCHY.

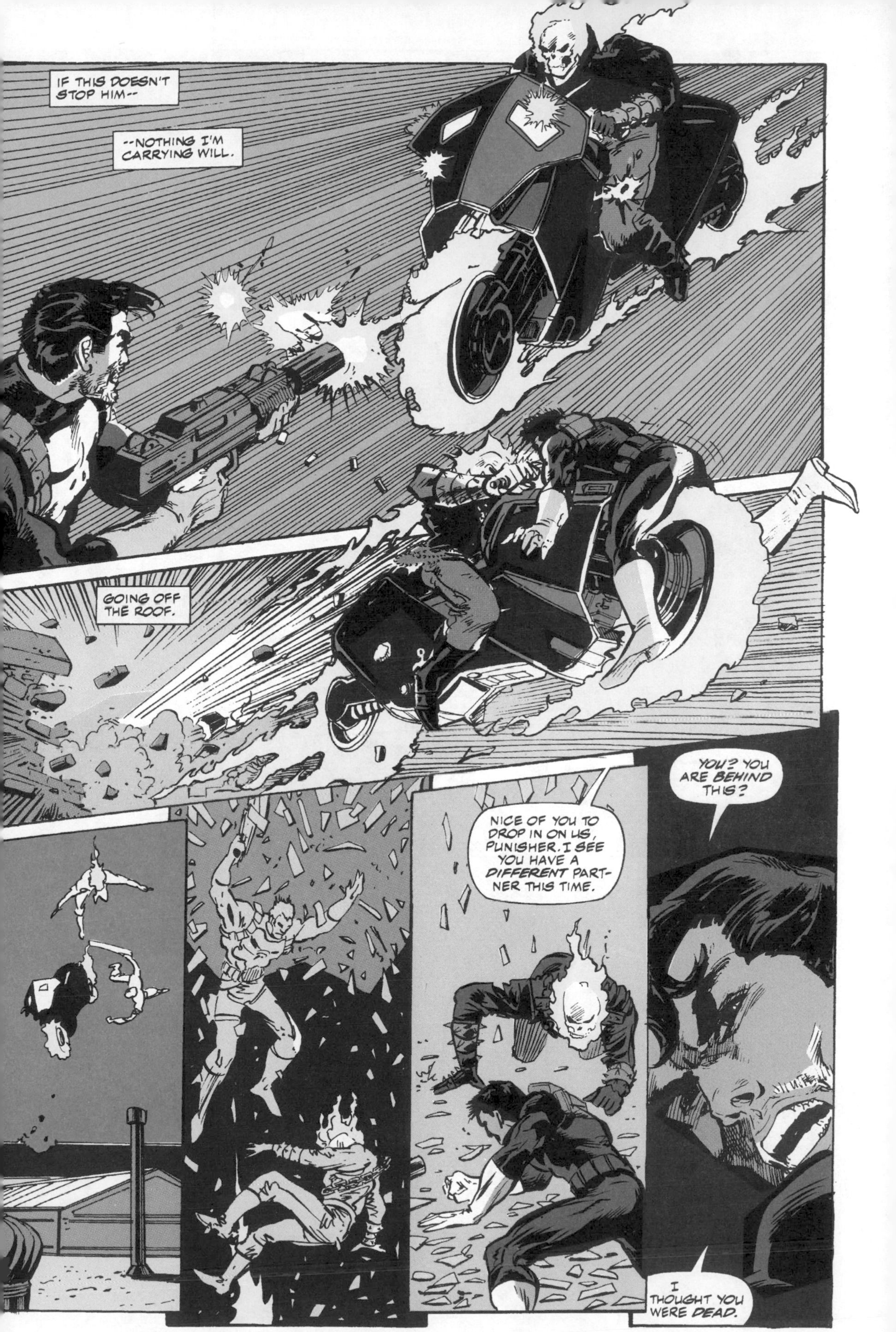
IF THIS DOESN'T STOP HIM--
--NOTHING I'M CARRYING WILL.
GOING OFF THE ROOF.
NICE OF YOU TO DROP IN ON US, PUNISHER. I SEE YOU HAVE A DIFFERENT PARTNER THIS TIME.
YOU? YOU ARE BEHIND THIS?
I THOUGHT YOU WERE DEAD.

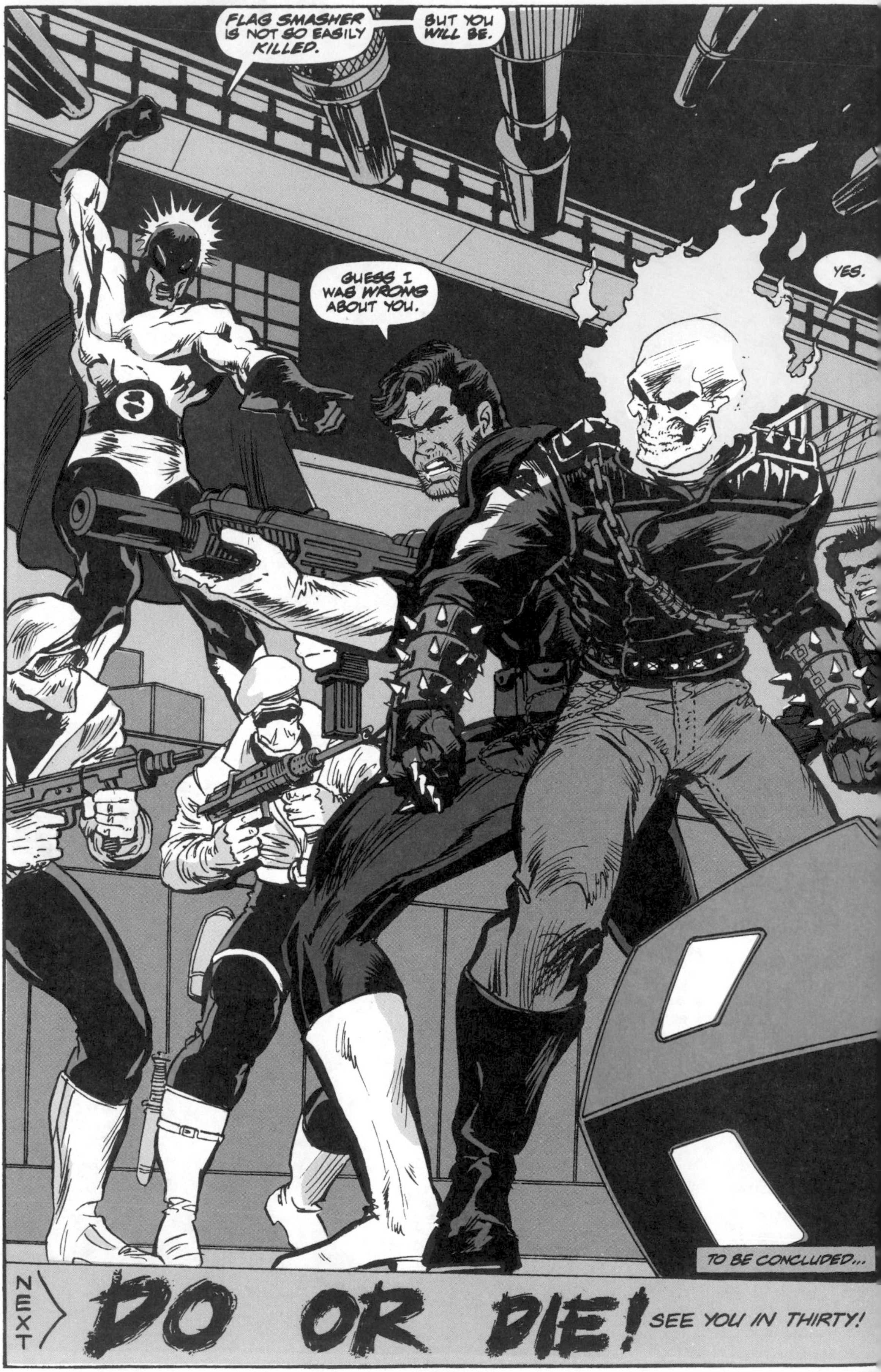
FLAG SMASHER IS NOT SO EASILY KILLED.
BUT YOU WILL BE.
GUESS I WAS WRONG ABOUT YOU.
YES.
TO BE CONCLUDED...
NEXT
DO OR DIE!
SEE YOU IN THIRTY!

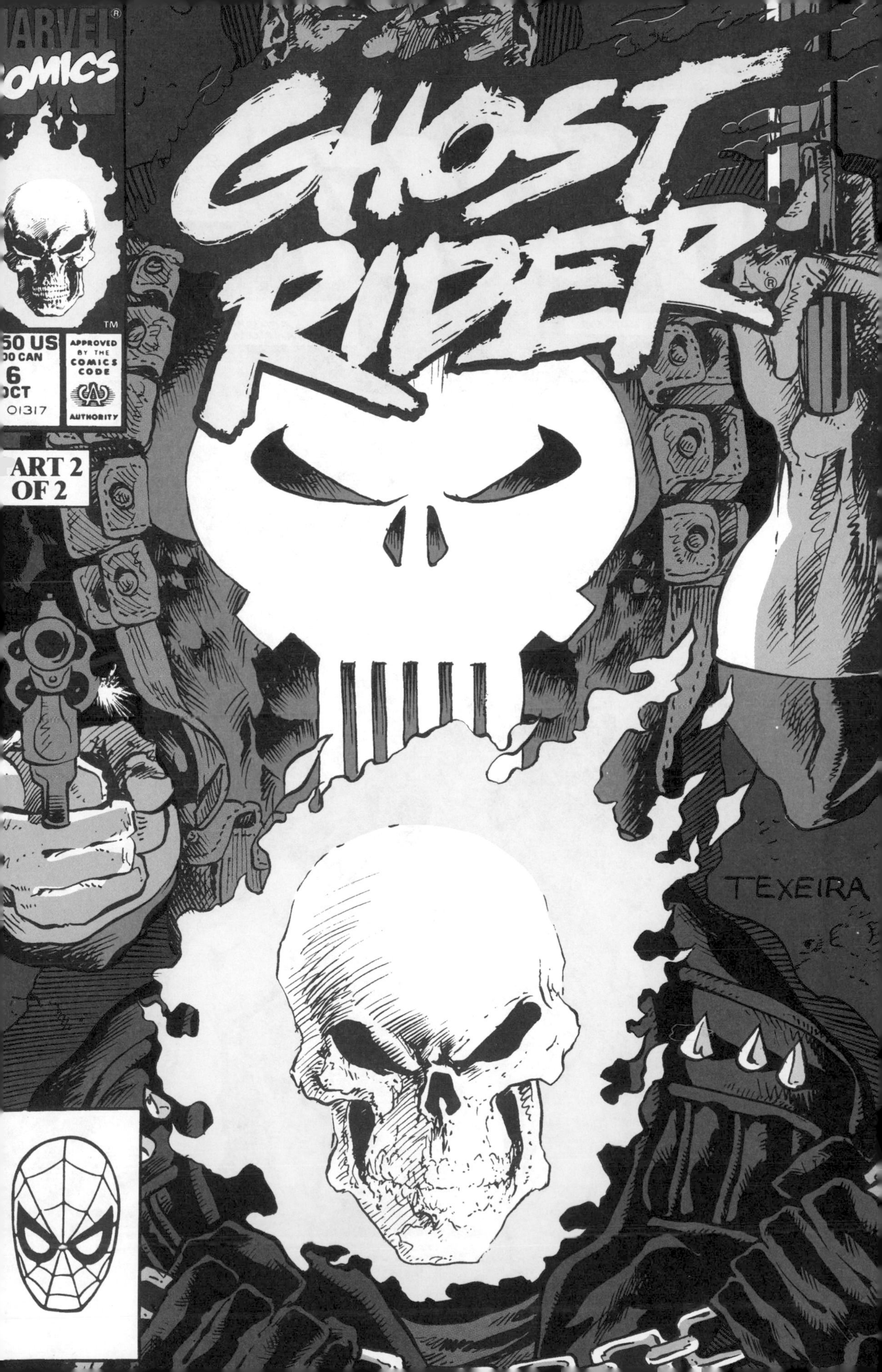
MARVEL COMICS
GHOST RIDER
50 US
00 CAN
6
OCT
01317
APPROVED BY THE COMICS CODE AUTHORITY
ART 2 OF 2
TEXEIRA

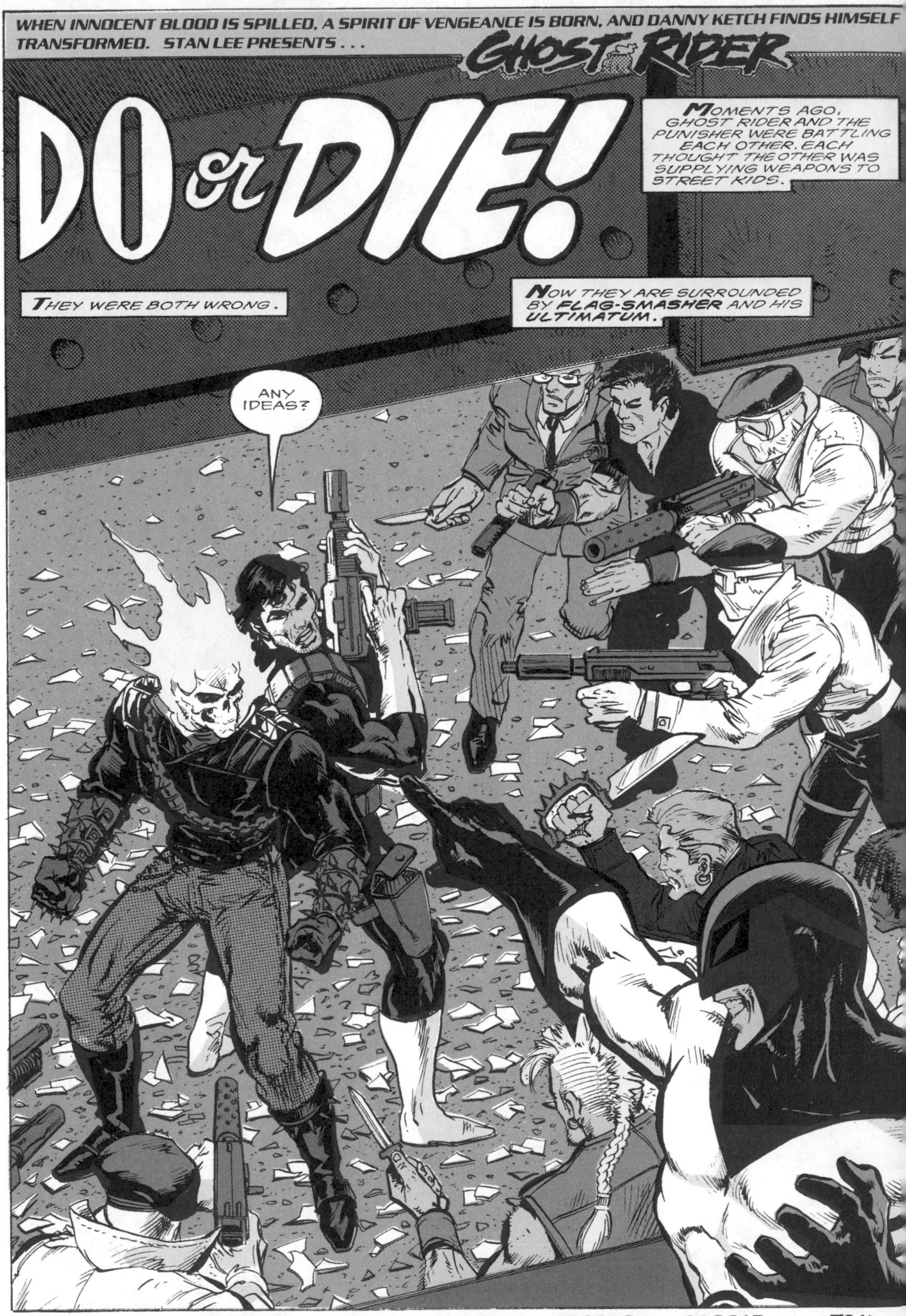
WHEN INNOCENT BLOOD IS SPILLED, A SPIRIT OF VENGEANCE IS BORN, AND DANNY KETCH FINDS HIMSELF TRANSFORMED. STAN LEE PRESENTS . . .
GHOST RIDER
DO or DIE!
MOMENTS AGO, GHOST RIDER AND THE PUNISHER WERE BATTLING EACH OTHER. EACH THOUGHT THE OTHER WAS SUPPLYING WEAPONS TO STREET KIDS.
THEY WERE BOTH WRONG.
NOW THEY ARE SURROUNDED BY FLAG-SMASHER AND HIS ULTIMATUM.
ANY IDEAS?
HOWARD MACKIE WRITER • JAVIER SALTARES PENCILER • MARK TEXEIRA INKER • JANICE CHIANG LETTERER • GREGORY WRIGHT COLORIST • BOBBIE CHASE EDITOR • TOM DeFALCO EDITOR IN CHIE

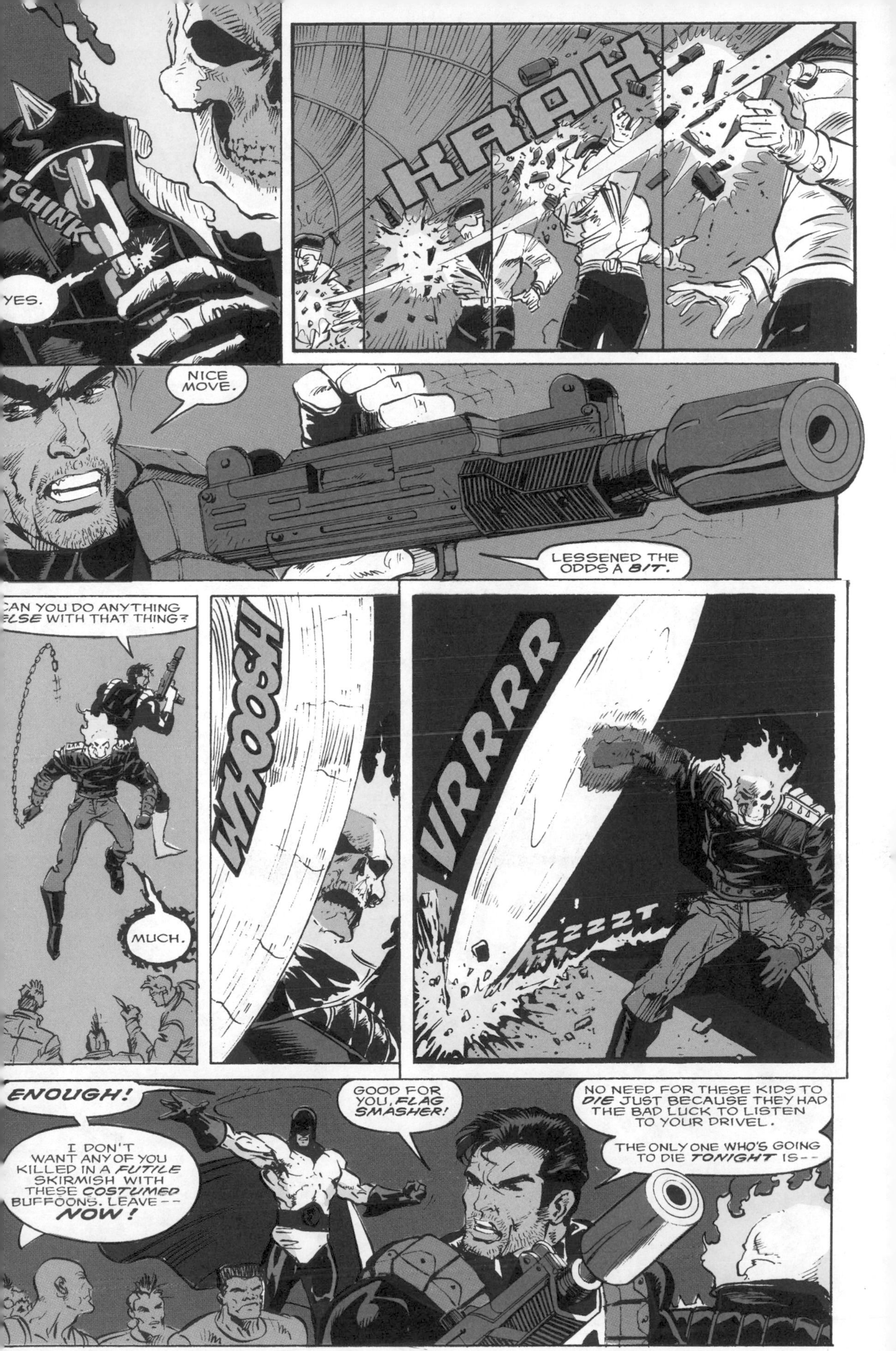
TCHINK
YES.
KRAAK
NICE MOVE.
LESSENED THE ODDS A BIT.
CAN YOU DO ANYTHING ELSE WITH THAT THING?
MUCH.
WHOOSH
VRRRR
ZZZZZT
ENOUGH!
I DON'T WANT ANY OF YOU KILLED IN A FUTILE SKIRMISH WITH THESE COSTUMED BUFFOONS. LEAVE-- NOW!
GOOD FOR YOU, FLAG SMASHER!
NO NEED FOR THESE KIDS TO DIE JUST BECAUSE THEY HAD THE BAD LUCK TO LISTEN TO YOUR DRIVEL.
THE ONLY ONE WHO'S GOING TO DIE TONIGHT IS--

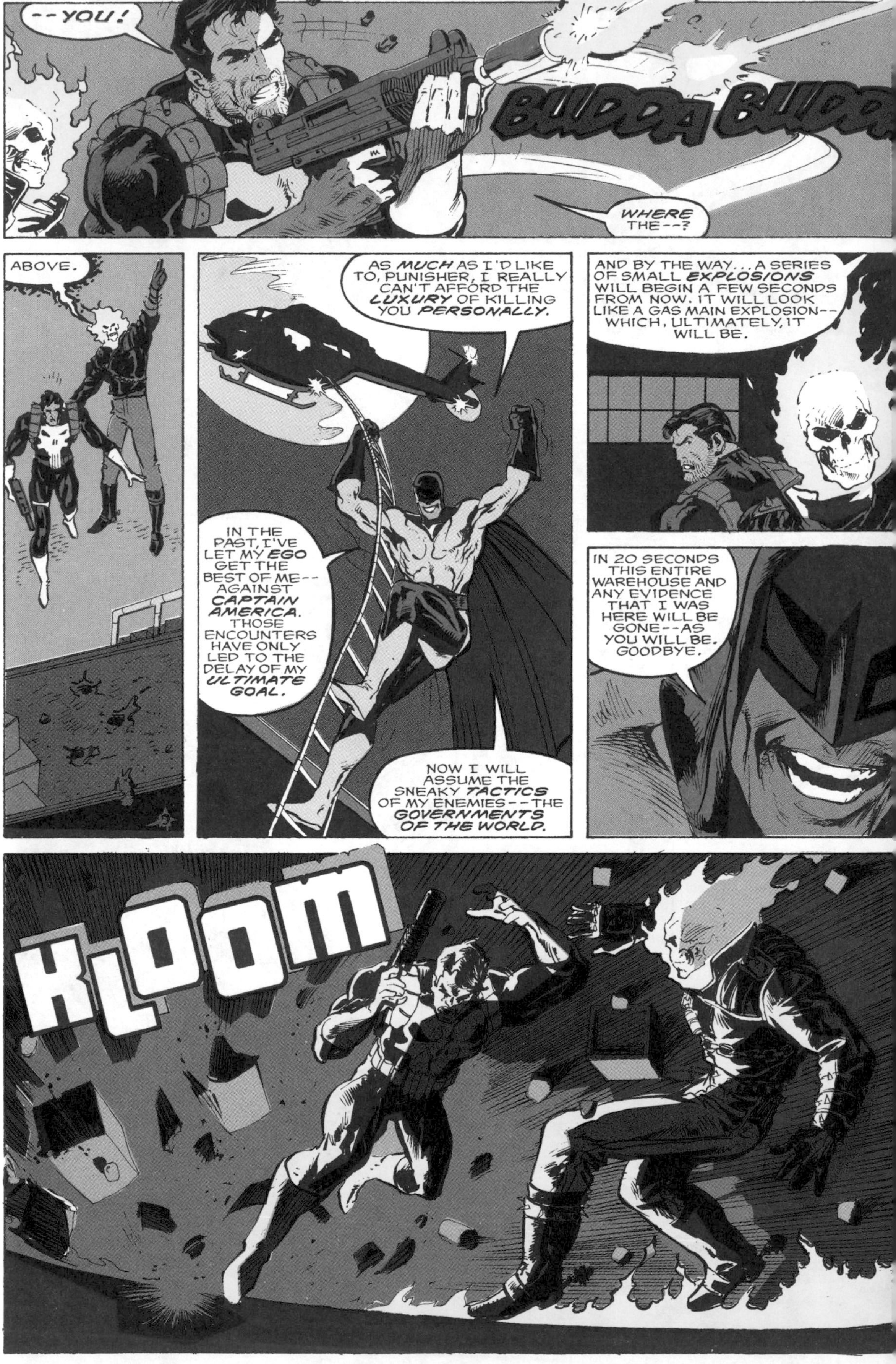
--YOU!
BUDDA BUDDA
WHERE THE--?
ABOVE.
AS MUCH AS I'D LIKE TO, PUNISHER, I REALLY CAN'T AFFORD THE LUXURY OF KILLING YOU PERSONALLY.
IN THE PAST, I'VE LET MY EGO GET THE BEST OF ME--AGAINST CAPTAIN AMERICA. THOSE ENCOUNTERS HAVE ONLY LED TO THE DELAY OF MY ULTIMATE GOAL.
NOW I WILL ASSUME THE SNEAKY TACTICS OF MY ENEMIES--THE GOVERNMENTS OF THE WORLD.
AND BY THE WAY... A SERIES OF SMALL EXPLOSIONS WILL BEGIN A FEW SECONDS FROM NOW. IT WILL LOOK LIKE A GAS MAIN EXPLOSION--WHICH, ULTIMATELY, IT WILL BE.
IN 20 SECONDS THIS ENTIRE WAREHOUSE AND ANY EVIDENCE THAT I WAS HERE WILL BE GONE--AS YOU WILL BE. GOODBYE.
KLOOM

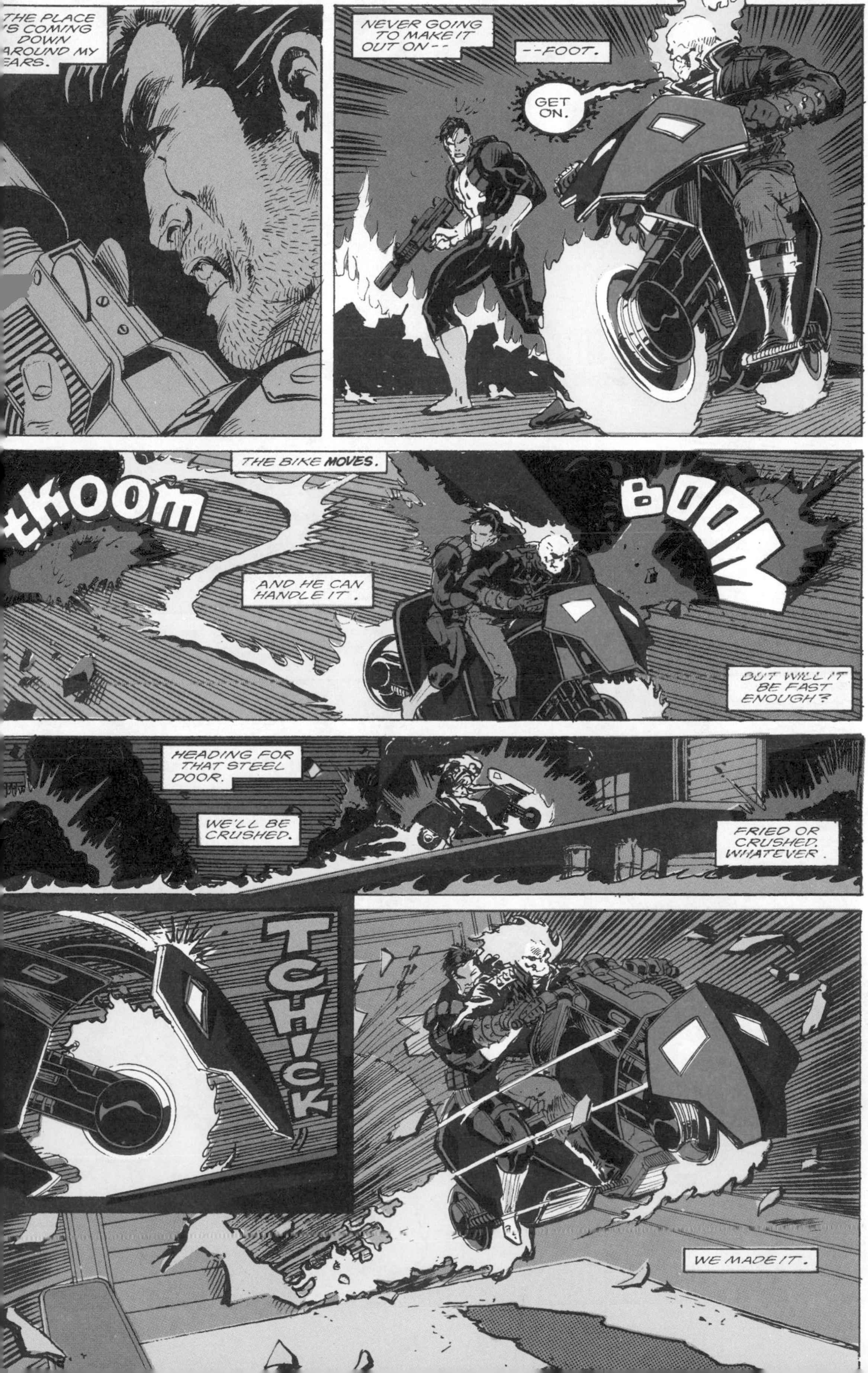
THE PLACE 'S COMING DOWN AROUND MY EARS.
NEVER GOING TO MAKE IT OUT ON--
--FOOT.
GET ON.
THE BIKE MOVES.
tkOOM
BOOM
AND HE CAN HANDLE IT.
BUT WILL IT BE FAST ENOUGH?
HEADING FOR THAT STEEL DOOR.
WE'LL BE CRUSHED.
FRIED OR CRUSHED. WHATEVER.
TCHICK
WE MADE IT.

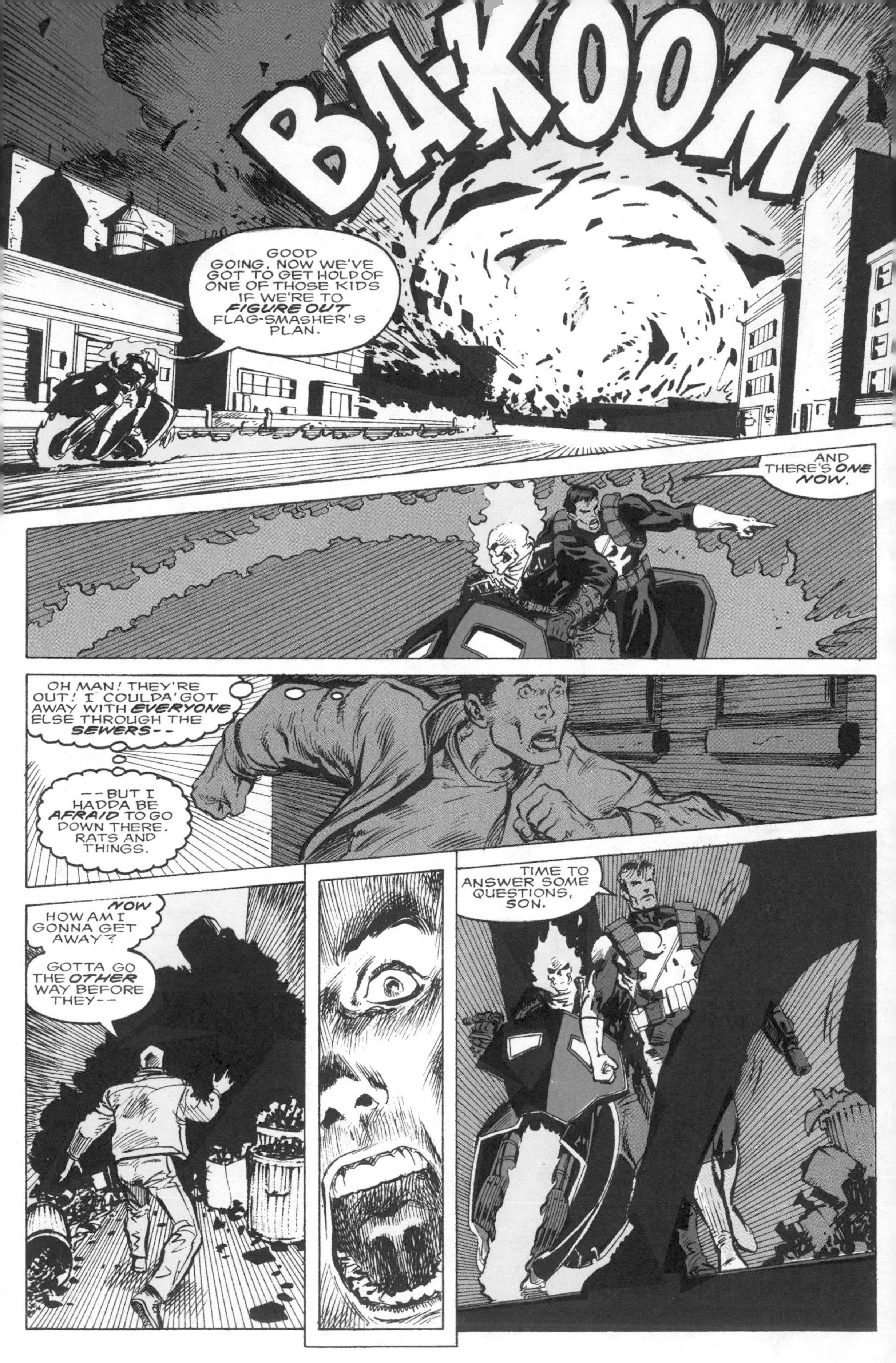
BA-KOOM
GOOD GOING. NOW WE'VE GOT TO GET HOLD OF ONE OF THOSE KIDS IF WE'RE TO FIGURE OUT FLAG-SMASHER'S PLAN.
AND THERE'S ONE NOW.
OH MAN! THEY'RE OUT! I COULDA' GOT AWAY WITH EVERYONE ELSE THROUGH THE SEWERS--
--BUT I HADDA BE AFRAID TO GO DOWN THERE. RATS AND THINGS.
NOW HOW AM I GONNA GET AWAY?
GOTTA GO THE OTHER WAY BEFORE THEY--
TIME TO ANSWER SOME QUESTIONS, SON.

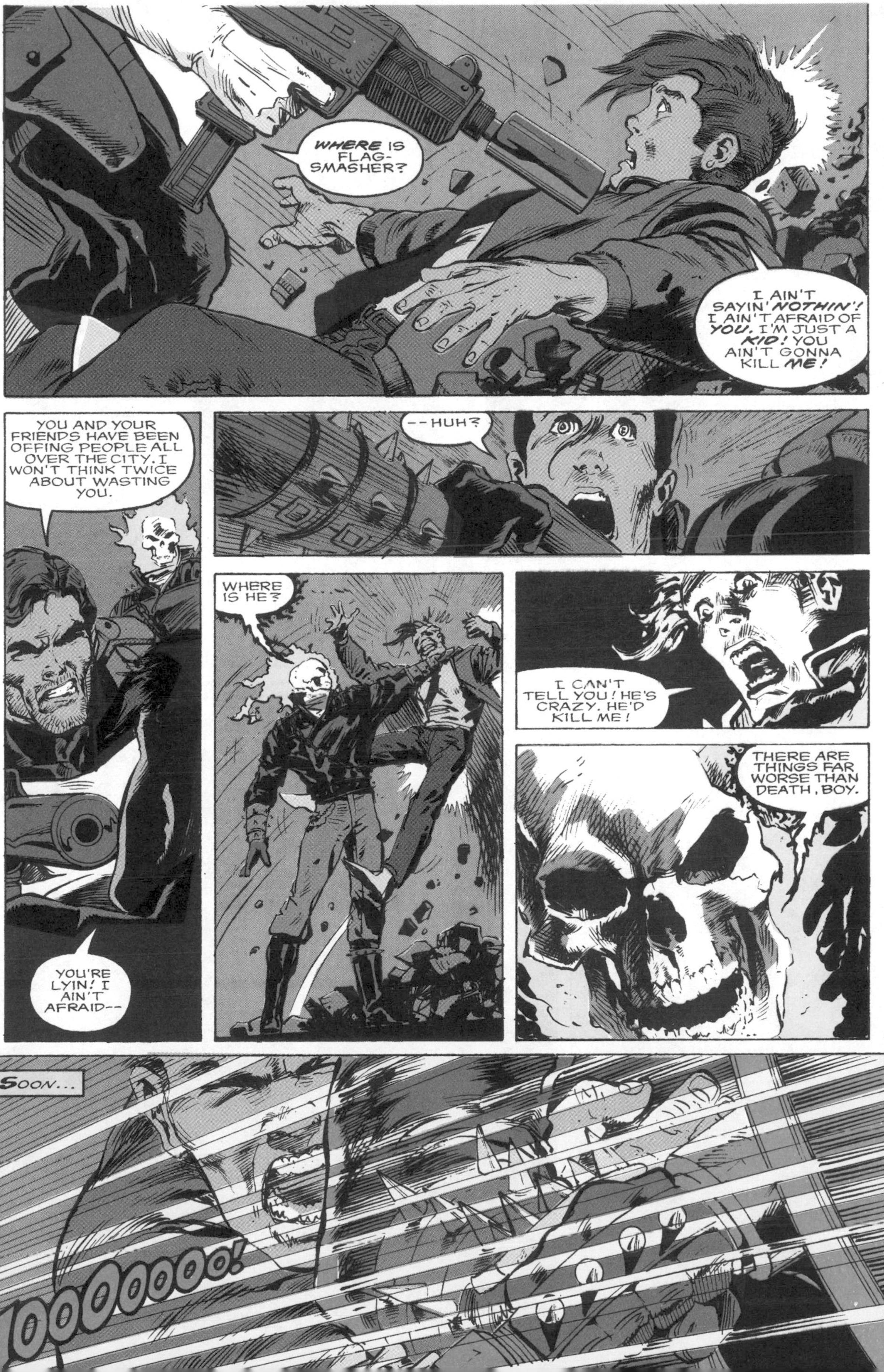
WHERE IS FLAG-SMASHER?
I AIN'T SAYIN' NOTHIN'! I AIN'T AFRAID OF YOU. I'M JUST A KID! YOU AIN'T GONNA KILL ME!
YOU AND YOUR FRIENDS HAVE BEEN OFFING PEOPLE ALL OVER THE CITY. I WON'T THINK TWICE ABOUT WASTING YOU.
YOU'RE LYIN'! I AIN'T AFRAID--
--HUH?
WHERE IS HE?
I CAN'T TELL YOU! HE'S CRAZY. HE'D KILL ME!
THERE ARE THINGS FAR WORSE THAN DEATH, BOY.
SOON...
VOOOOOOOO!

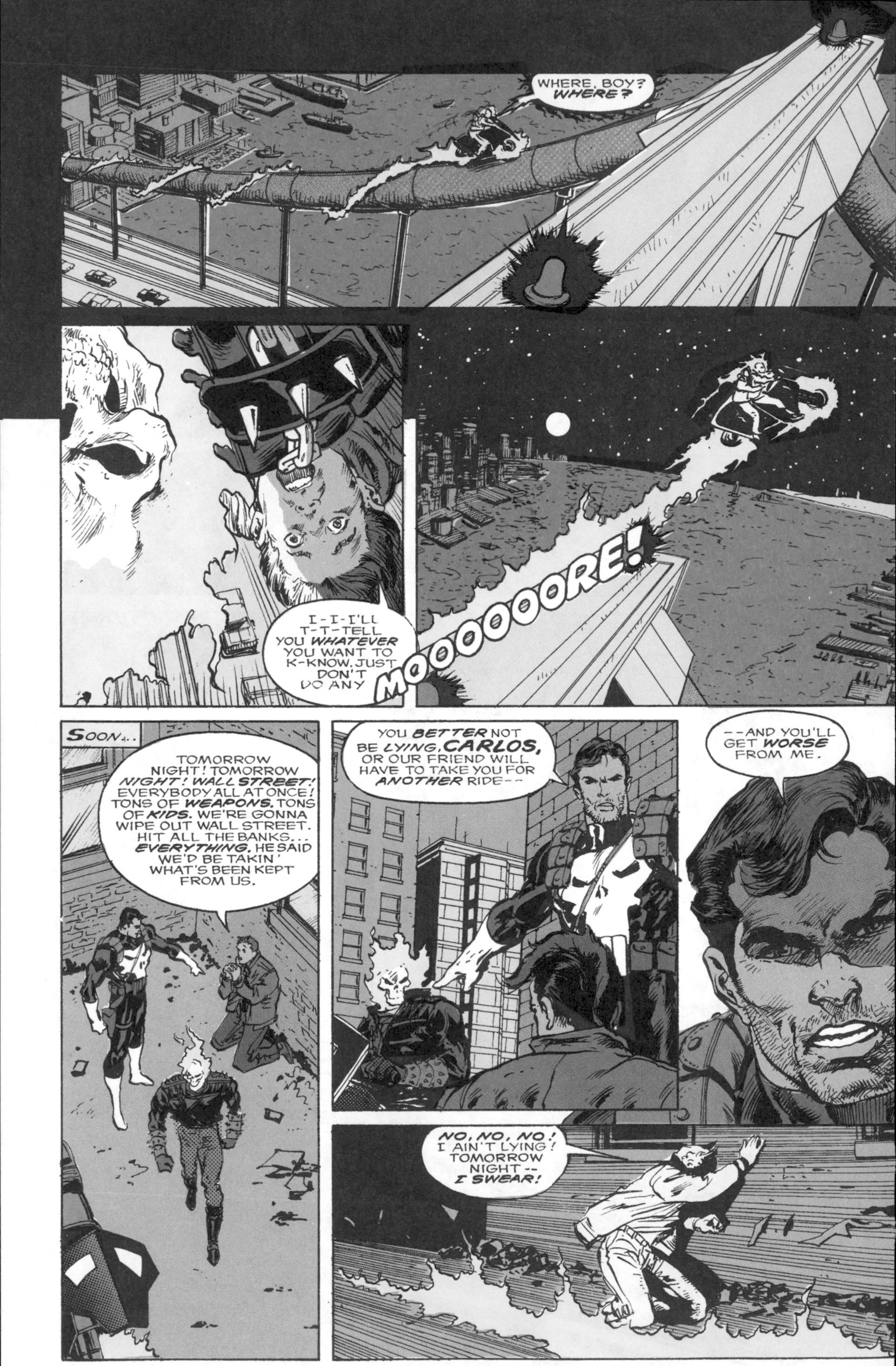
WHERE, BOY? WHERE?
I-I-I'LL T-T-TELL YOU WHATEVER YOU WANT TO K-KNOW. JUST DON'T DO ANY
MOOOOOOORE!
SOON...
TOMORROW NIGHT! TOMORROW NIGHT! WALL STREET! EVERYBODY ALL AT ONCE! TONS OF WEAPONS. TONS OF KIDS. WE'RE GONNA WIPE OUT WALL STREET. HIT ALL THE BANKS... EVERYTHING. HE SAID WE'D BE TAKIN' WHAT'S BEEN KEPT FROM US.
YOU BETTER NOT BE LYING, CARLOS, OR OUR FRIEND WILL HAVE TO TAKE YOU FOR ANOTHER RIDE--
--AND YOU'LL GET WORSE FROM ME.
NO, NO, NO! I AIN'T LYING! TOMORROW NIGHT-- I SWEAR!

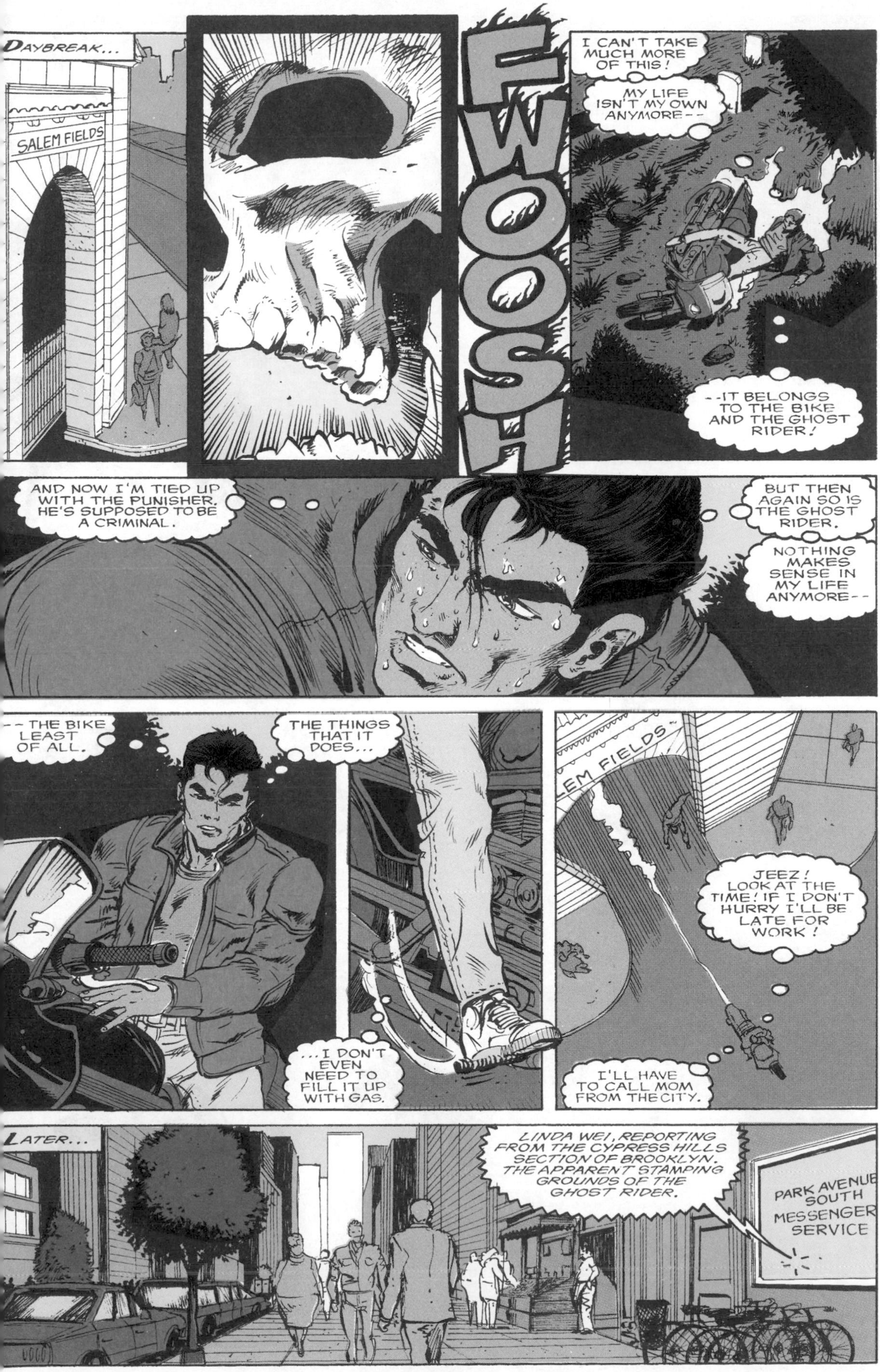
DAYBREAK...
SALEM FIELDS
FWOOSH!
I CAN'T TAKE MUCH MORE OF THIS!
MY LIFE ISN'T MY OWN ANYMORE--
--IT BELONGS TO THE BIKE AND THE GHOST RIDER!
AND NOW I'M TIED UP WITH THE PUNISHER. HE'S SUPPOSED TO BE A CRIMINAL.
BUT THEN AGAIN SO IS THE GHOST RIDER.
NOTHING MAKES SENSE IN MY LIFE ANYMORE--
--THE BIKE LEAST OF ALL.
THE THINGS THAT IT DOES...
...I DON'T EVEN NEED TO FILL IT UP WITH GAS.
LEM FIELDS
JEEZ! LOOK AT THE TIME! IF I DON'T HURRY I'LL BE LATE FOR WORK!
I'LL HAVE TO CALL MOM FROM THE CITY.
LATER...
LINDA WEI, REPORTING FROM THE CYPRESS HILLS SECTION OF BROOKLYN. THE APPARENT STAMPING GROUNDS OF THE GHOST RIDER.
PARK AVENUE SOUTH MESSENGER SERVICE

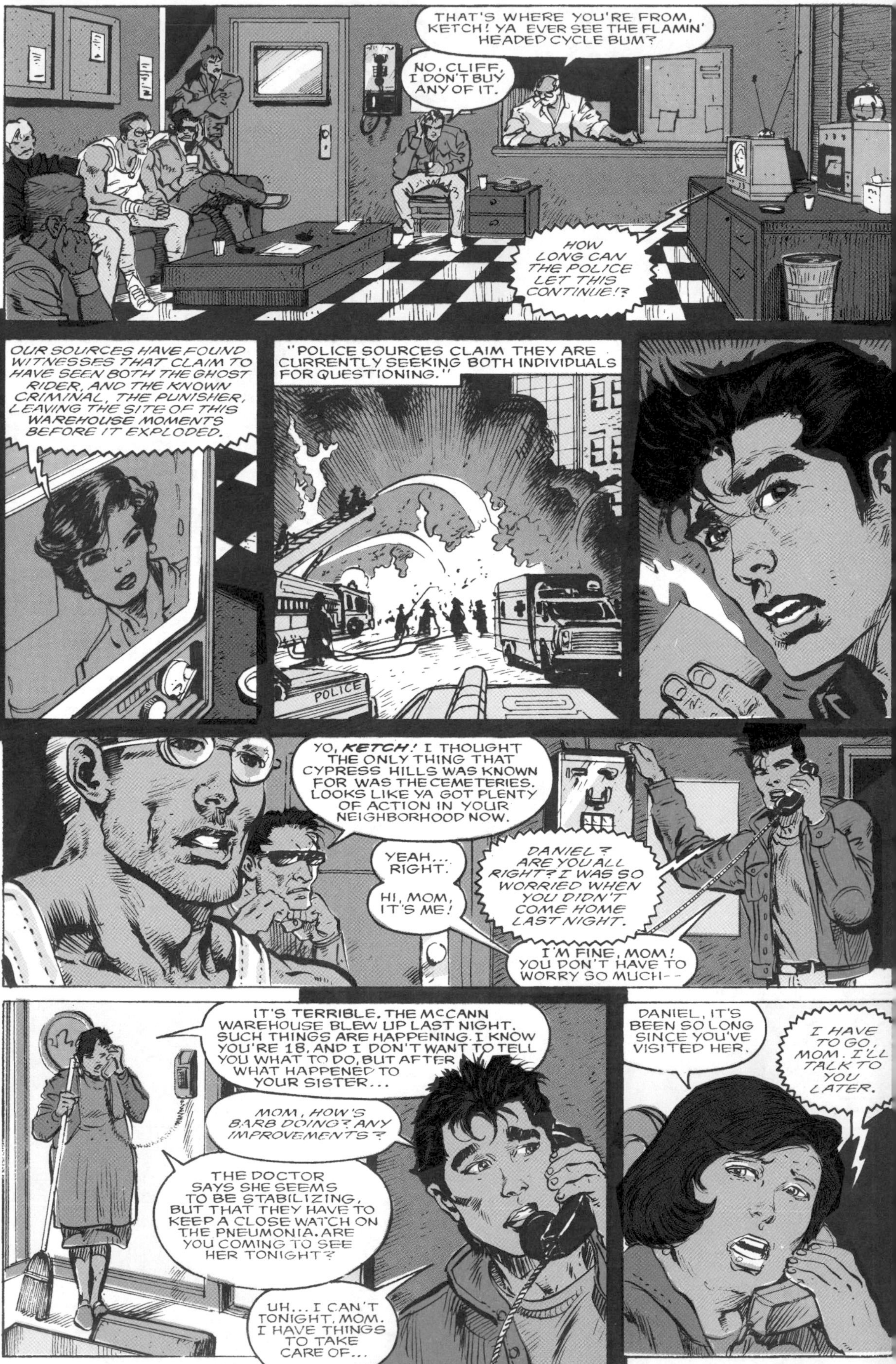

THAT'S WHERE YOU'RE FROM, KETCH! YA EVER SEE THE FLAMIN' HEADED CYCLE BUM?
NO, CLIFF, I DON'T BUY ANY OF IT.
HOW LONG CAN THE POLICE LET THIS CONTINUE!?
OUR SOURCES HAVE FOUND WITNESSES THAT CLAIM TO HAVE SEEN BOTH THE GHOST RIDER, AND THE KNOWN CRIMINAL, THE PUNISHER, LEAVING THE SITE OF THIS WAREHOUSE MOMENTS BEFORE IT EXPLODED.
"POLICE SOURCES CLAIM THEY ARE CURRENTLY SEEKING BOTH INDIVIDUALS FOR QUESTIONING."
POLICE
YO, KETCH! I THOUGHT THE ONLY THING THAT CYPRESS HILLS WAS KNOWN FOR WAS THE CEMETERIES. LOOKS LIKE YA GOT PLENTY OF ACTION IN YOUR NEIGHBORHOOD NOW.
YEAH... RIGHT.
HI, MOM, IT'S ME!
DANIEL? ARE YOU ALL RIGHT? I WAS SO WORRIED WHEN YOU DIDN'T COME HOME LAST NIGHT.
I'M FINE, MOM! YOU DON'T HAVE TO WORRY SO MUCH--
IT'S TERRIBLE. THE McCANN WAREHOUSE BLEW UP LAST NIGHT. SUCH THINGS ARE HAPPENING. I KNOW YOU'RE 18, AND I DON'T WANT TO TELL YOU WHAT TO DO, BUT AFTER WHAT HAPPENED TO YOUR SISTER...
MOM, HOW'S BARB DOING? ANY IMPROVEMENTS?
THE DOCTOR SAYS SHE SEEMS TO BE STABILIZING, BUT THAT THEY HAVE TO KEEP A CLOSE WATCH ON THE PNEUMONIA. ARE YOU COMING TO SEE HER TONIGHT?
UH... I CAN'T TONIGHT, MOM. I HAVE THINGS TO TAKE CARE OF...
DANIEL, IT'S BEEN SO LONG SINCE YOU'VE VISITED HER.
I HAVE TO GO, MOM. I'LL TALK TO YOU LATER.

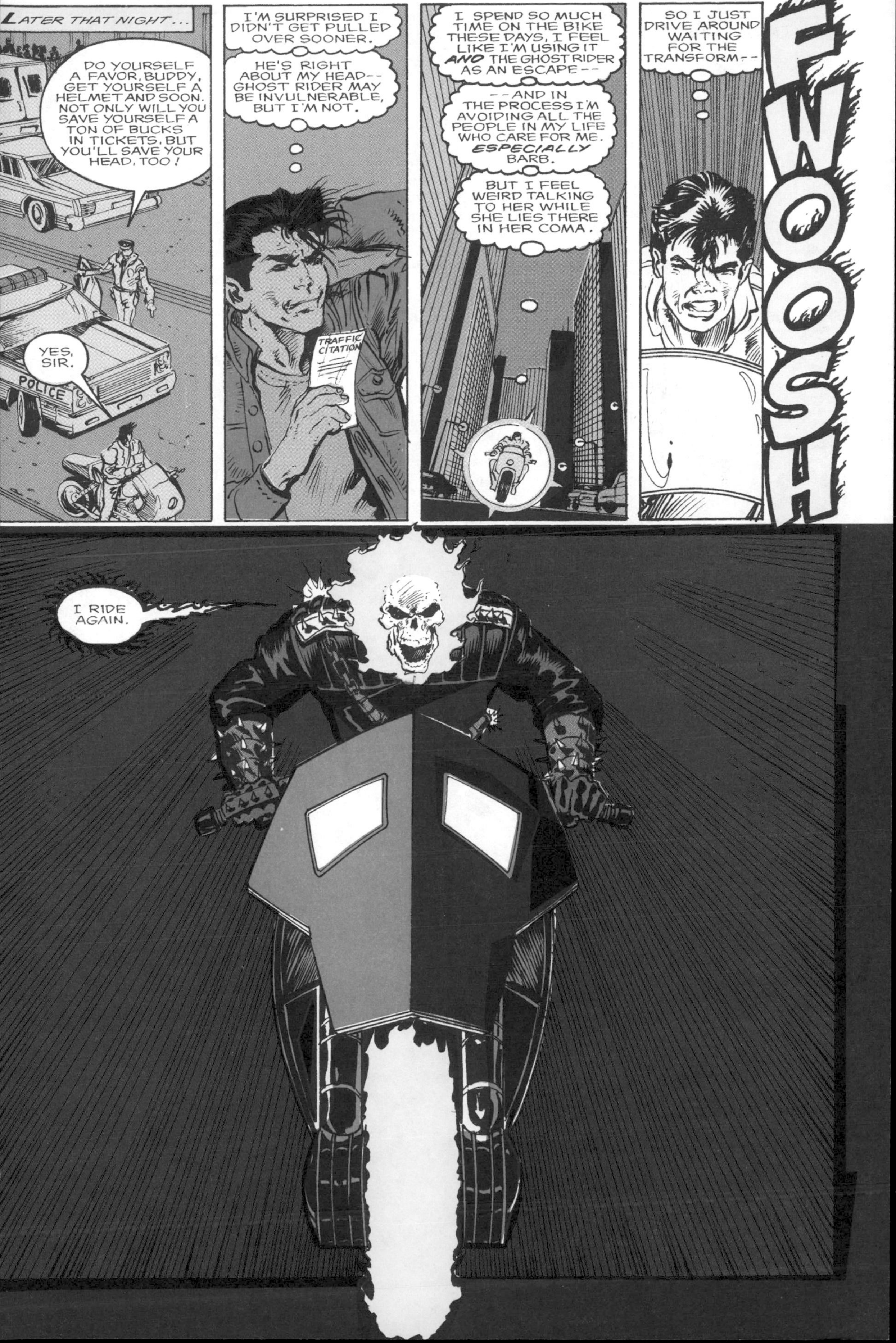
LATER THAT NIGHT...
DO YOURSELF A FAVOR, BUDDY, GET YOURSELF A HELMET AND SOON. NOT ONLY WILL YOU SAVE YOURSELF A TON OF BUCKS IN TICKETS, BUT YOU'LL SAVE YOUR HEAD, TOO!
YES, SIR.
POLICE
I'M SURPRISED I DIDN'T GET PULLED OVER SOONER.
HE'S RIGHT ABOUT MY HEAD-- GHOST RIDER MAY BE INVULNERABLE, BUT I'M NOT.
TRAFFIC CITATION
I SPEND SO MUCH TIME ON THE BIKE THESE DAYS, I FEEL LIKE I'M USING IT AND THE GHOST RIDER AS AN ESCAPE--
--AND IN THE PROCESS I'M AVOIDING ALL THE PEOPLE IN MY LIFE WHO CARE FOR ME. ESPECIALLY BARB.
BUT I FEEL WEIRD TALKING TO HER WHILE SHE LIES THERE IN HER COMA.
SO I JUST DRIVE AROUND WAITING FOR THE TRANSFORM--
FWOOSH
I RIDE AGAIN.

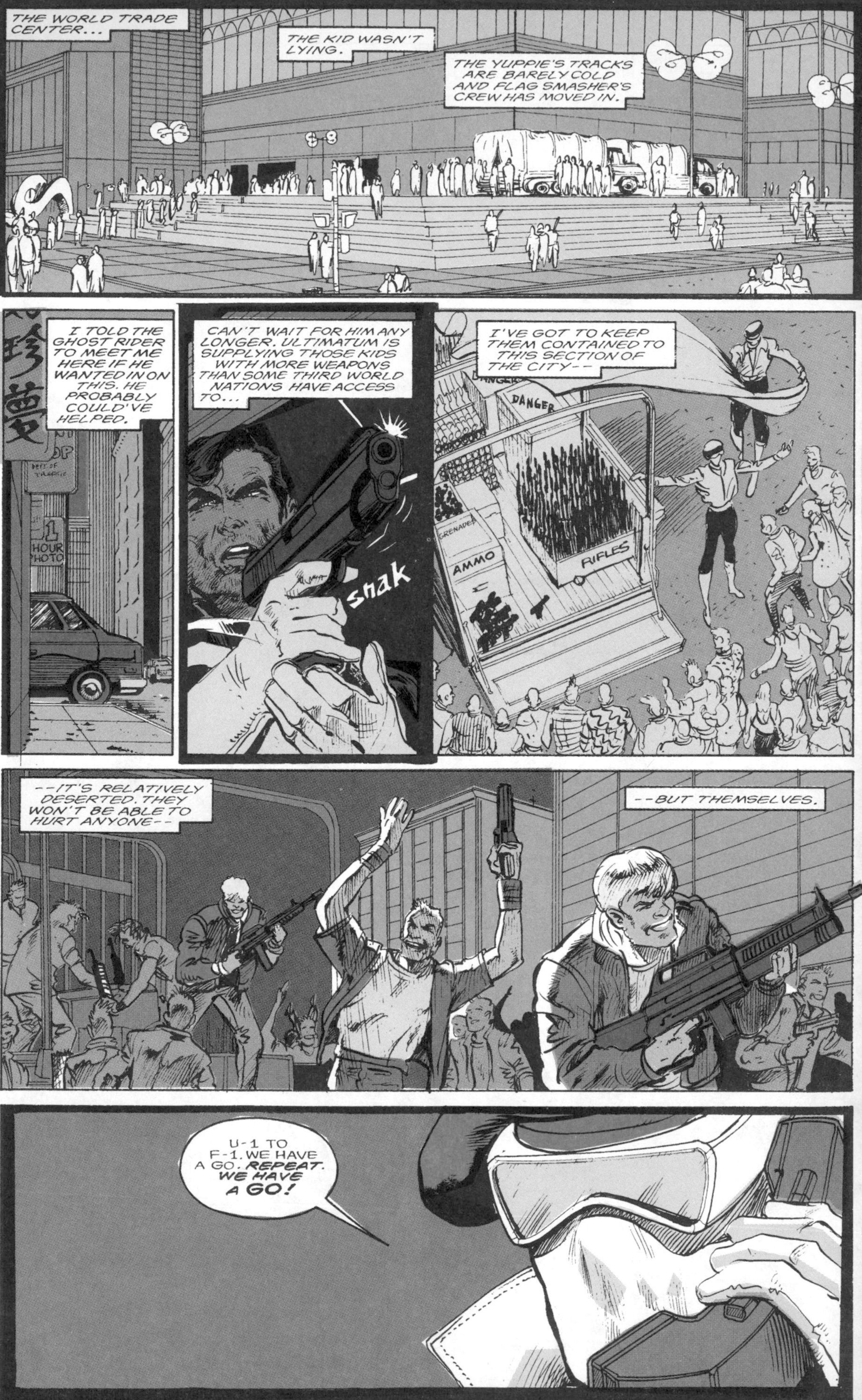
THE WORLD TRADE CENTER...
THE KID WASN'T LYING.
THE YUPPIE'S TRACKS ARE BARELY COLD AND FLAG SMASHER'S CREW HAS MOVED IN.
I TOLD THE GHOST RIDER TO MEET ME HERE IF HE WANTED IN ON THIS. HE PROBABLY COULD'VE HELPED.
1 HOUR PHOTO
CAN'T WAIT FOR HIM ANY LONGER. ULTIMATUM IS SUPPLYING THOSE KIDS WITH MORE WEAPONS THAN SOME THIRD WORLD NATIONS HAVE ACCESS TO...
SNAK
I'VE GOT TO KEEP THEM CONTAINED TO THIS SECTION OF THE CITY--
DANGER
DANGER
GRENADES
AMMO
RIFLES
--IT'S RELATIVELY DESERTED. THEY WON'T BE ABLE TO HURT ANYONE--
--BUT THEMSELVES.
U-1 TO F-1. WE HAVE A GO. REPEAT. WE HAVE A GO!

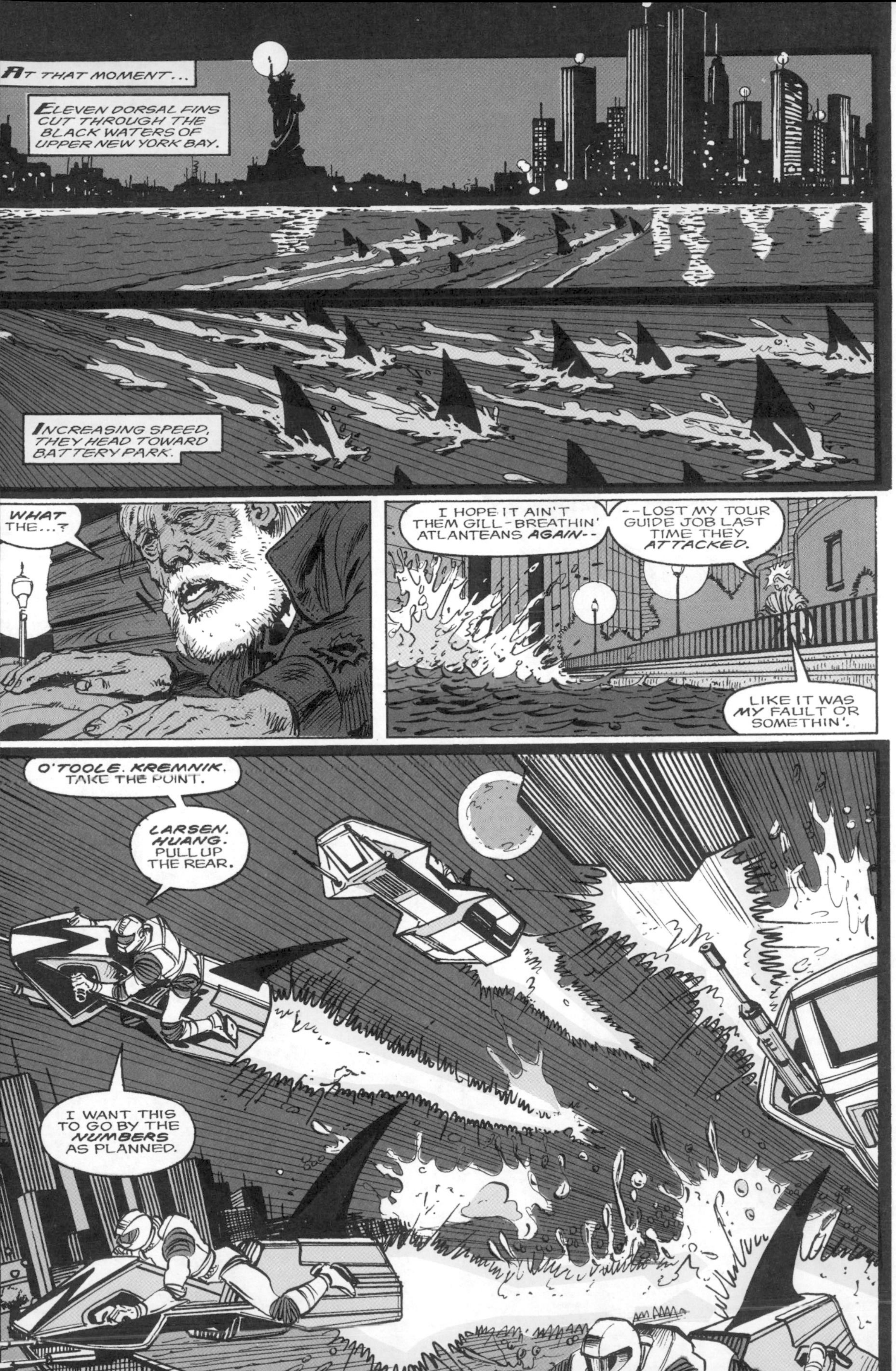
AT THAT MOMENT...
ELEVEN DORSAL FINS CUT THROUGH THE BLACK WATERS OF UPPER NEW YORK BAY.
INCREASING SPEED, THEY HEAD TOWARD BATTERY PARK.
WHAT THE...?
I HOPE IT AIN'T THEM GILL-BREATHIN' ATLANTEANS AGAIN--
--LOST MY TOUR GUIDE JOB LAST TIME THEY ATTACKED.
LIKE IT WAS MY FAULT OR SOMETHIN'.
O'TOOLE. KREMNIK. TAKE THE POINT.
LARSEN. HUANG. PULL UP THE REAR.
I WANT THIS TO GO BY THE NUMBERS AS PLANNED.

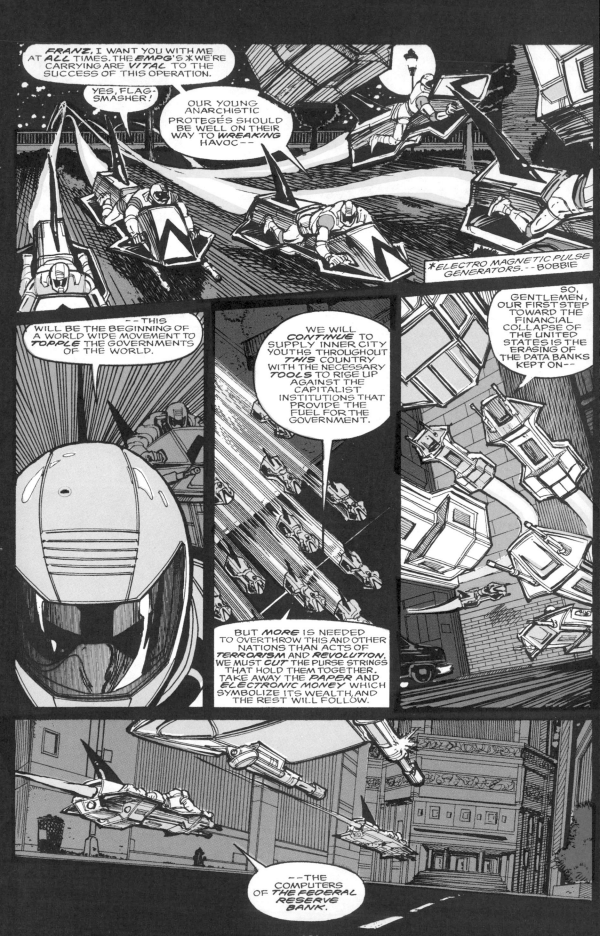

FRANZ, I WANT YOU WITH ME AT *ALL* TIMES. THE *EMPG'S* ✱ WE'RE CARRYING ARE *VITAL* TO THE SUCCESS OF THIS OPERATION.

YES, FLAG-SMASHER!

OUR YOUNG ANARCHISTIC PROTEGÉS SHOULD BE WELL ON THEIR WAY TO *WREAKING* HAVOC--

✱ELECTRO MAGNETIC PULSE GENERATORS. --BOBBIE

--THIS WILL BE THE BEGINNING OF A WORLD WIDE MOVEMENT TO *TOPPLE* THE GOVERNMENTS OF THE WORLD.

WE WILL *CONTINUE* TO SUPPLY INNER CITY YOUTHS THROUGHOUT *THIS* COUNTRY WITH THE NECESSARY *TOOLS* TO RISE UP AGAINST THE CAPITALIST INSTITUTIONS THAT PROVIDE THE FUEL FOR THE GOVERNMENT.

SO, GENTLEMEN, OUR FIRST STEP TOWARD THE FINANCIAL COLLAPSE OF THE UNITED STATES IS THE ERASING OF THE DATA BANKS KEPT ON--

BUT *MORE* IS NEEDED TO OVERTHROW THIS AND OTHER NATIONS THAN ACTS OF *TERRORISM* AND *REVOLUTION*. WE MUST *CUT* THE PURSE STRINGS THAT HOLD THEM TOGETHER. TAKE AWAY THE *PAPER* AND *ELECTRONIC MONEY* WHICH SYMBOLIZE ITS WEALTH, AND THE REST WILL FOLLOW.

--THE COMPUTERS OF *THE FEDERAL RESERVE BANK*.

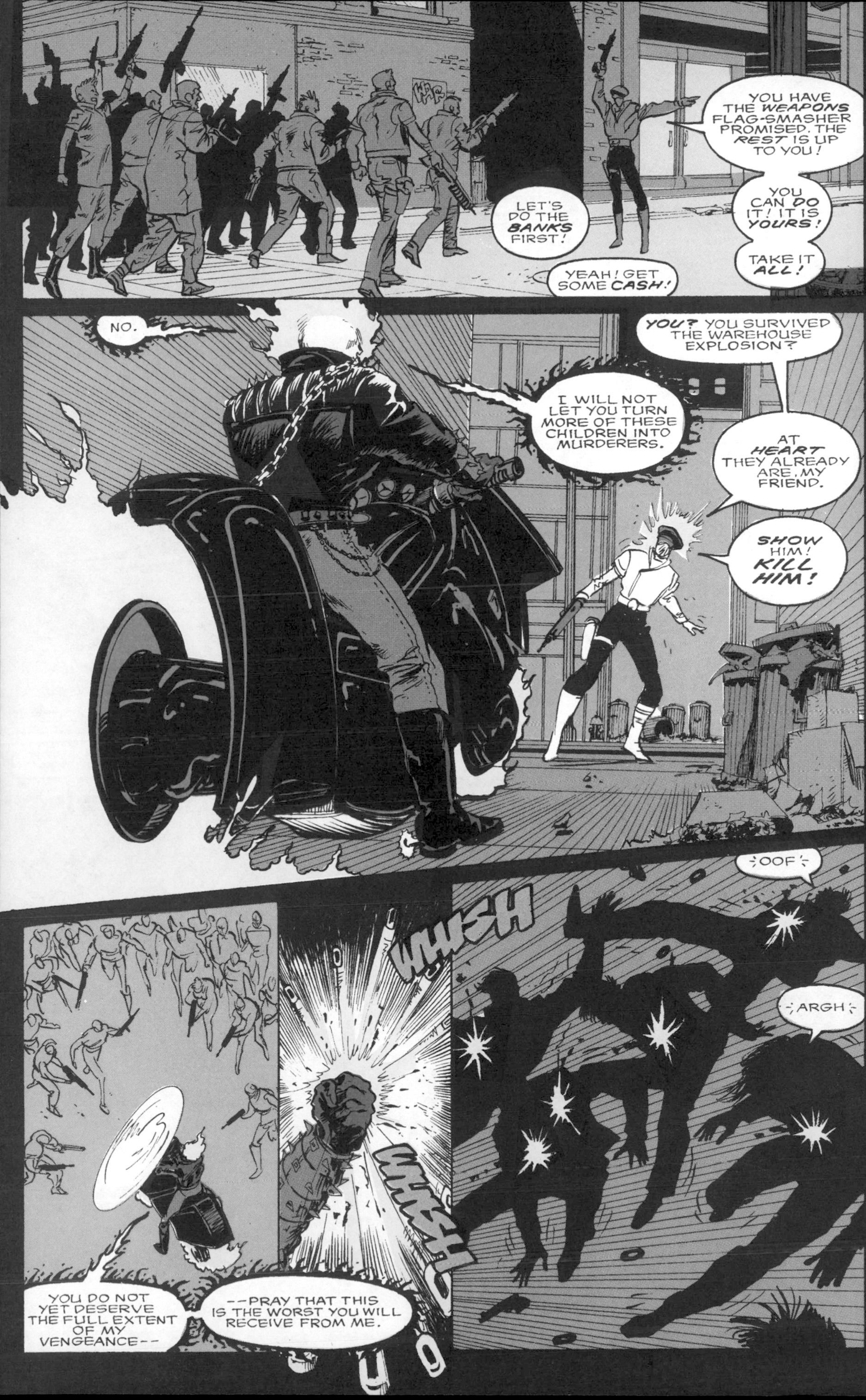
YOU HAVE THE WEAPONS FLAG-SMASHER PROMISED. THE REST IS UP TO YOU!
YOU CAN DO IT! IT IS YOURS!
TAKE IT ALL!
LET'S DO THE BANKS FIRST!
YEAH! GET SOME CASH!
NO.
I WILL NOT LET YOU TURN MORE OF THESE CHILDREN INTO MURDERERS.
YOU? YOU SURVIVED THE WAREHOUSE EXPLOSION?
AT HEART THEY ALREADY ARE, MY FRIEND.
SHOW HIM! KILL HIM!
WHUSH
WHUSH
YOU DO NOT YET DESERVE THE FULL EXTENT OF MY VENGEANCE--
--PRAY THAT THIS IS THE WORST YOU WILL RECEIVE FROM ME.
OOF
ARGH

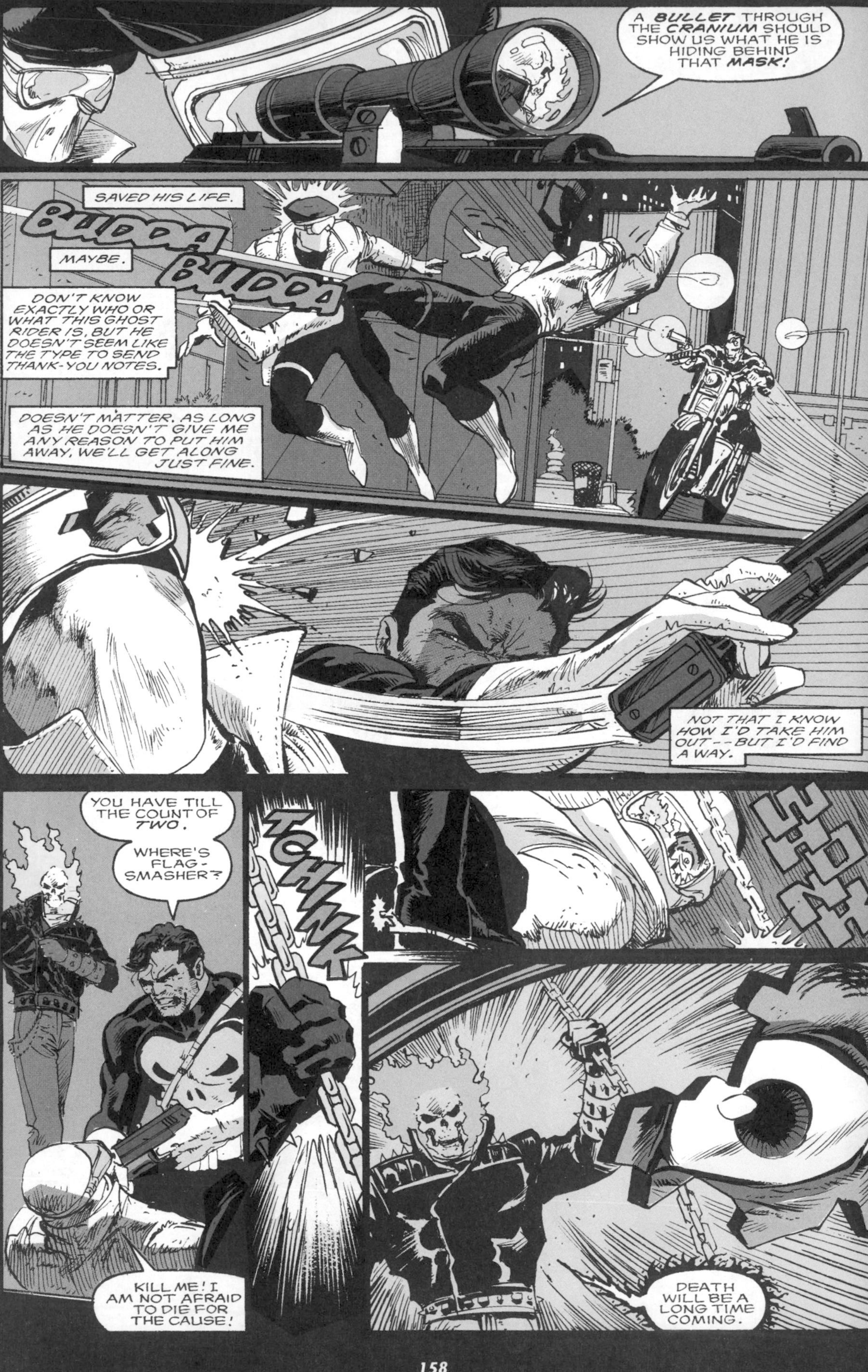
A BULLET THROUGH THE CRANIUM SHOULD SHOW US WHAT HE IS HIDING BEHIND THAT MASK!
SAVED HIS LIFE.
BUDDA
MAYBE.
BUDDA
DON'T KNOW EXACTLY WHO OR WHAT THIS GHOST RIDER IS, BUT HE DOESN'T SEEM LIKE THE TYPE TO SEND THANK-YOU NOTES.
DOESN'T MATTER. AS LONG AS HE DOESN'T GIVE ME ANY REASON TO PUT HIM AWAY, WE'LL GET ALONG JUST FINE.
NOT THAT I KNOW HOW I'D TAKE HIM OUT-- BUT I'D FIND A WAY.
YOU HAVE TILL THE COUNT OF TWO.
WHERE'S FLAG-SMASHER?
TCHINK
SHOCK
KILL ME! I AM NOT AFRAID TO DIE FOR THE CAUSE!
DEATH WILL BE A LONG TIME COMING.

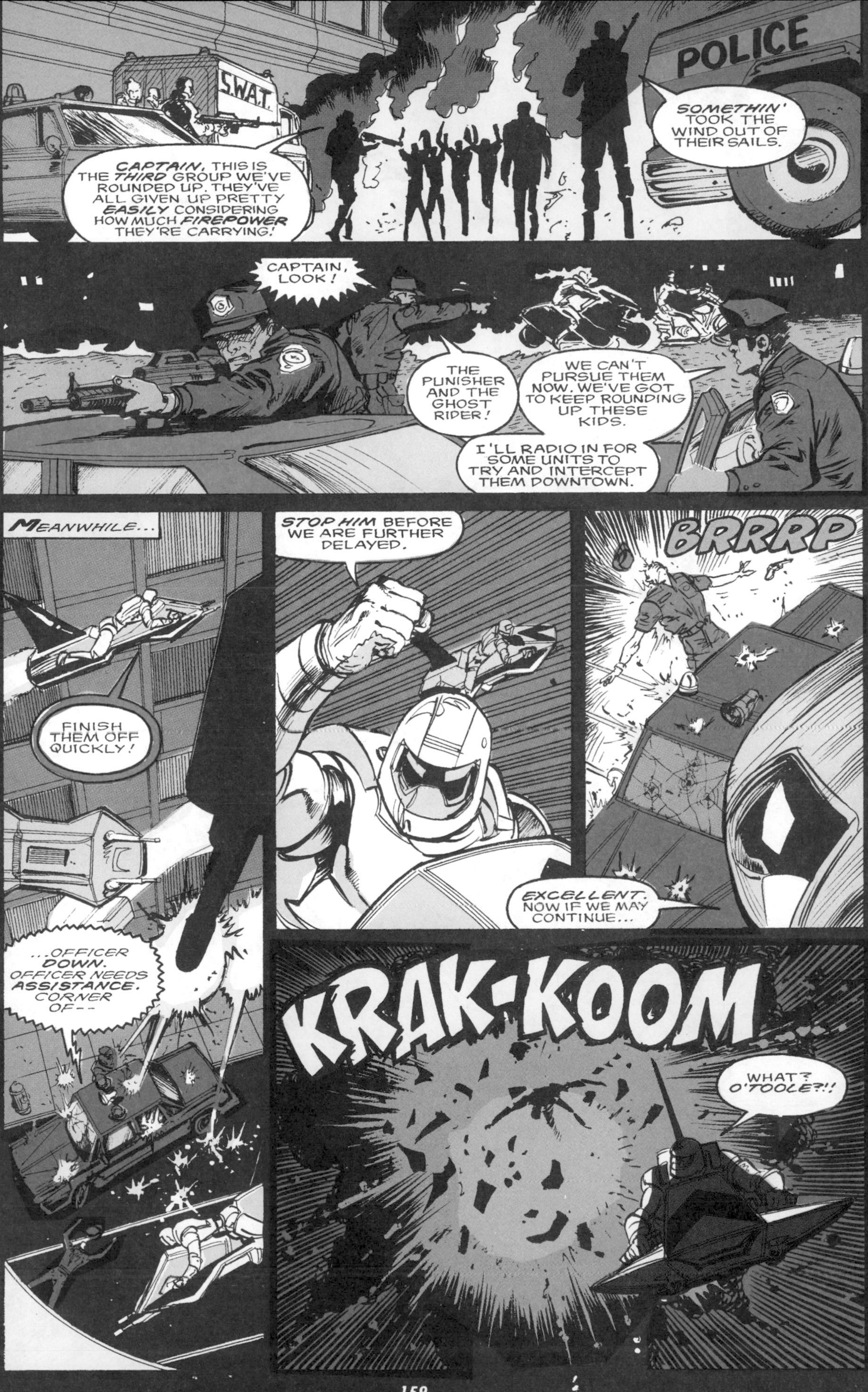
POLICE
S.W.A.T.
CAPTAIN, THIS IS THE THIRD GROUP WE'VE ROUNDED UP. THEY'VE ALL GIVEN UP PRETTY EASILY CONSIDERING HOW MUCH FIREPOWER THEY'RE CARRYING!
SOMETHIN' TOOK THE WIND OUT OF THEIR SAILS.
CAPTAIN, LOOK!
THE PUNISHER AND THE GHOST RIDER!
WE CAN'T PURSUE THEM NOW. WE'VE GOT TO KEEP ROUNDING UP THESE KIDS.
I'LL RADIO IN FOR SOME UNITS TO TRY AND INTERCEPT THEM DOWNTOWN.
MEANWHILE...
FINISH THEM OFF QUICKLY!
STOP HIM BEFORE WE ARE FURTHER DELAYED.
BRRRP
EXCELLENT. NOW IF WE MAY CONTINUE...
...OFFICER DOWN. OFFICER NEEDS ASSISTANCE. CORNER OF--
KRAK-KOOM
WHAT? O'TOOLE?!!

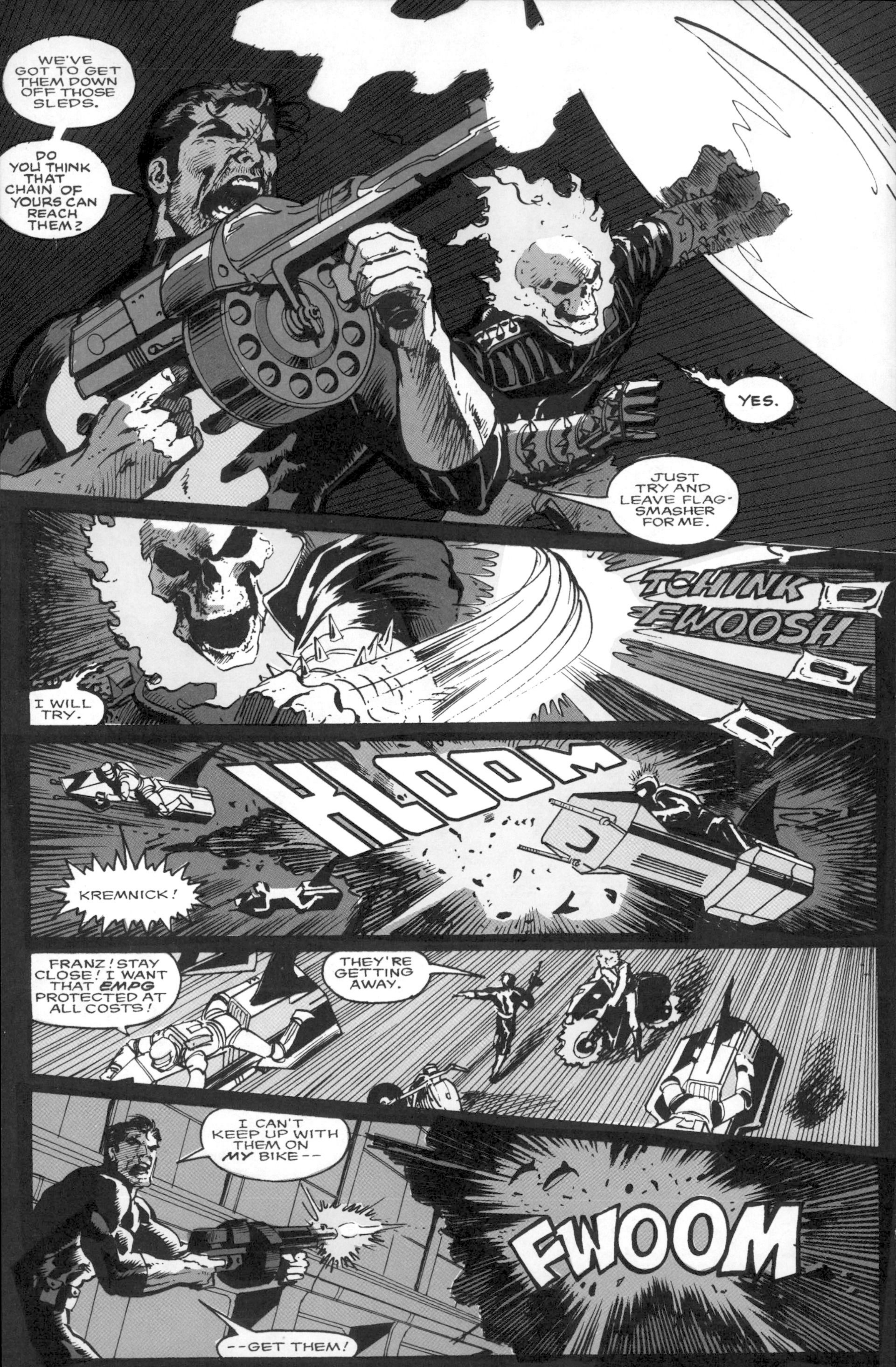
WE'VE GOT TO GET THEM DOWN OFF THOSE SLEDS.
DO YOU THINK THAT CHAIN OF YOURS CAN REACH THEM?
YES.
JUST TRY AND LEAVE FLAG-SMASHER FOR ME.
TCHINK
FWOOSH
I WILL TRY.
HOOM
KREMNICK!
FRANZ! STAY CLOSE! I WANT THAT EMPG PROTECTED AT ALL COSTS!
THEY'RE GETTING AWAY.
I CAN'T KEEP UP WITH THEM ON MY BIKE--
FWOOM
--GET THEM!

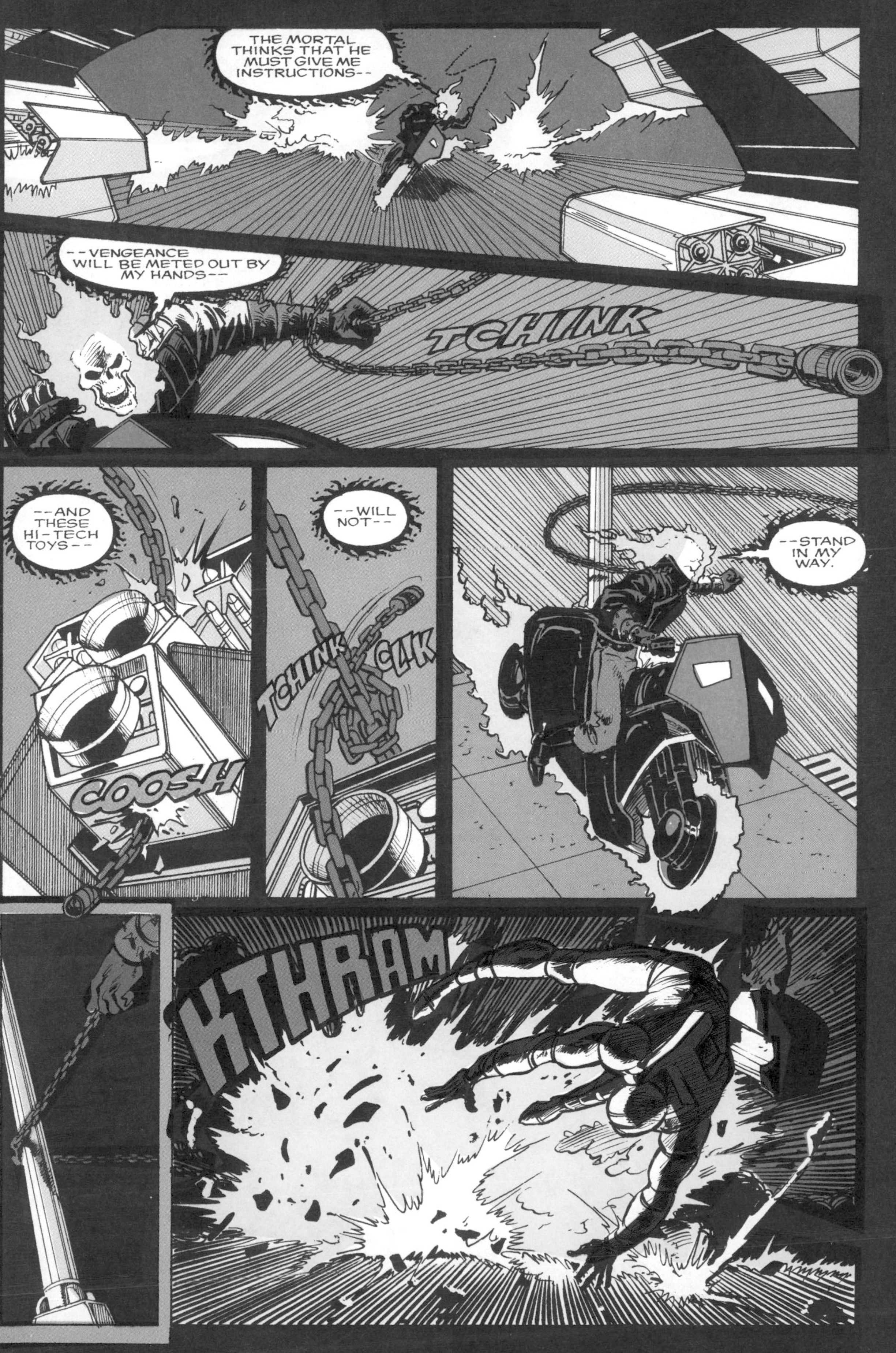
THE MORTAL THINKS THAT HE MUST GIVE ME INSTRUCTIONS--
--VENGEANCE WILL BE METED OUT BY MY HANDS--
TCHINK
--AND THESE HI-TECH TOYS--
COOSH
--WILL NOT--
TCHINK
CLIK
--STAND IN MY WAY.
KTHRAM

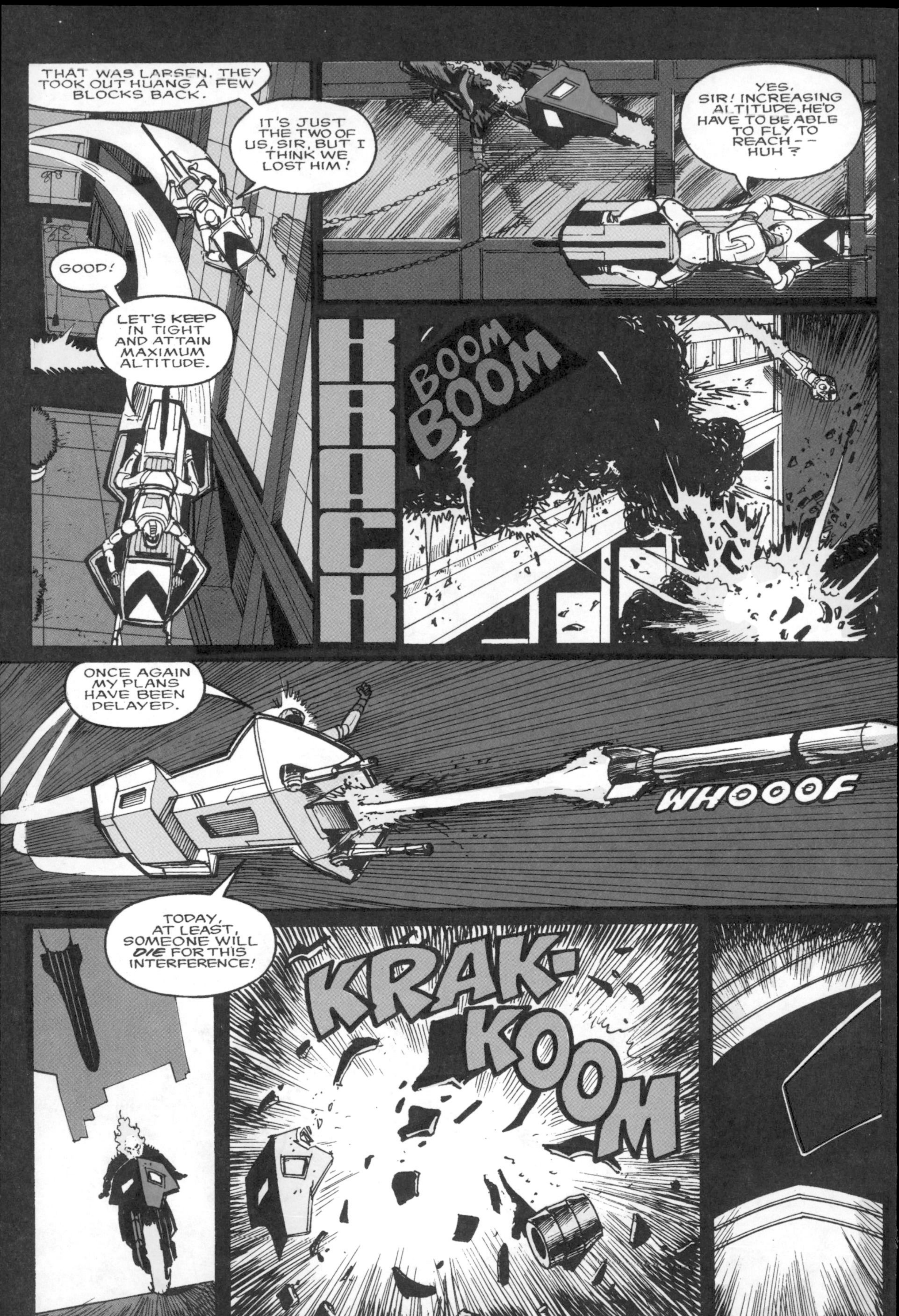
THAT WAS LARSEN. THEY TOOK OUT HUANG A FEW BLOCKS BACK.
IT'S JUST THE TWO OF US, SIR, BUT I THINK WE LOST HIM!
GOOD!
LET'S KEEP IN TIGHT AND ATTAIN MAXIMUM ALTITUDE.
YES, SIR! INCREASING ALTITUDE. HE'D HAVE TO BE ABLE TO FLY TO REACH-- HUH?
KRACK
BOOM BOOM
ONCE AGAIN MY PLANS HAVE BEEN DELAYED.
WHOOOF
TODAY, AT LEAST, SOMEONE WILL DIE FOR THIS INTERFERENCE!
KRAK-KOOOM

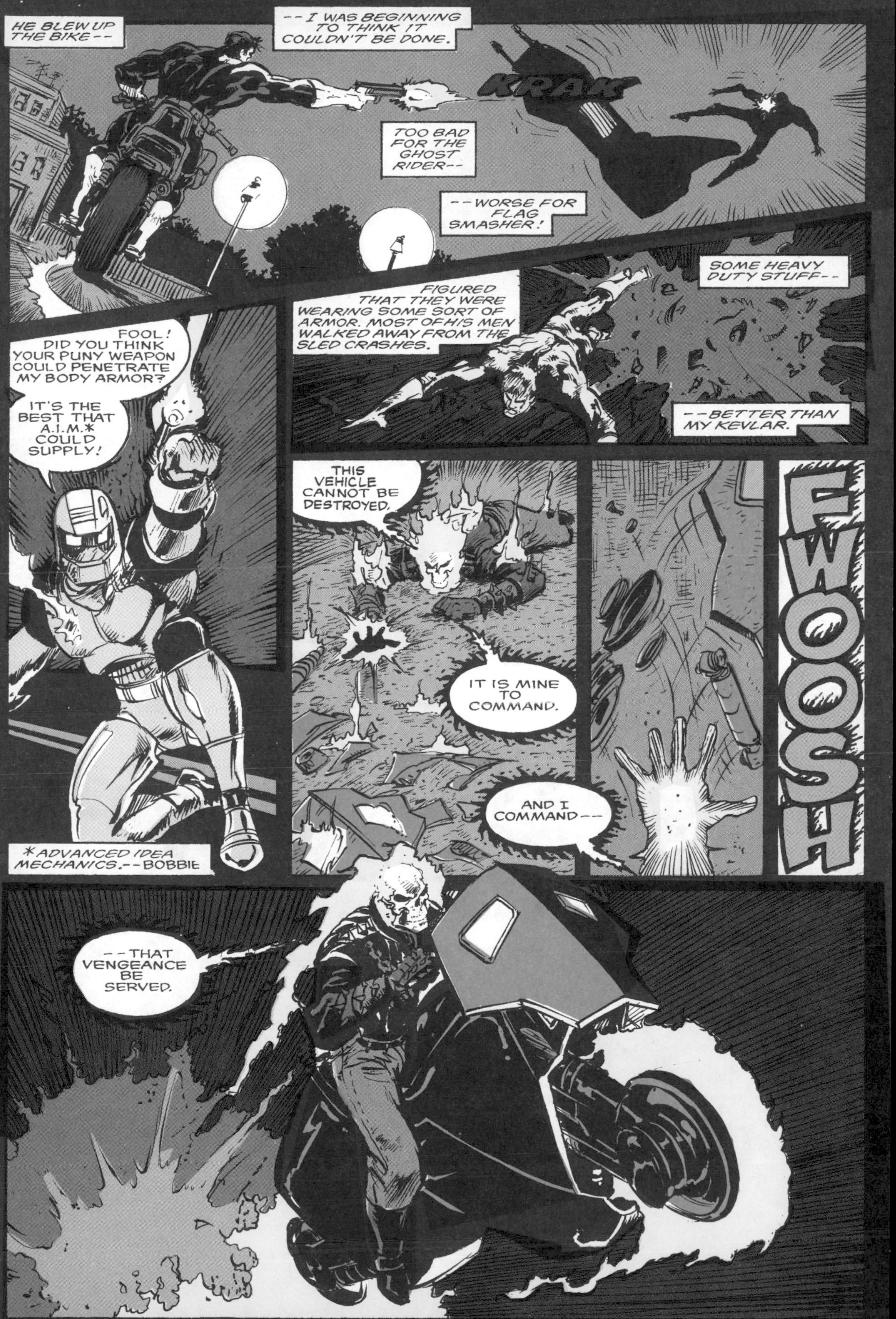

HE BLEW UP THE BIKE--
--I WAS BEGINNING TO THINK IT COULDN'T BE DONE.
KRAK
TOO BAD FOR THE GHOST RIDER--
--WORSE FOR FLAG SMASHER!
FOOL! DID YOU THINK YOUR PUNY WEAPON COULD PENETRATE MY BODY ARMOR?
IT'S THE BEST THAT A.I.M.* COULD SUPPLY!
*ADVANCED IDEA MECHANICS.--BOBBIE
FIGURED THAT THEY WERE WEARING SOME SORT OF ARMOR. MOST OF HIS MEN WALKED AWAY FROM THE SLED CRASHES.
SOME HEAVY DUTY STUFF--
--BETTER THAN MY KEVLAR.
THIS VEHICLE CANNOT BE DESTROYED.
IT IS MINE TO COMMAND.
AND I COMMAND--
FWOOOSH
--THAT VENGEANCE BE SERVED.

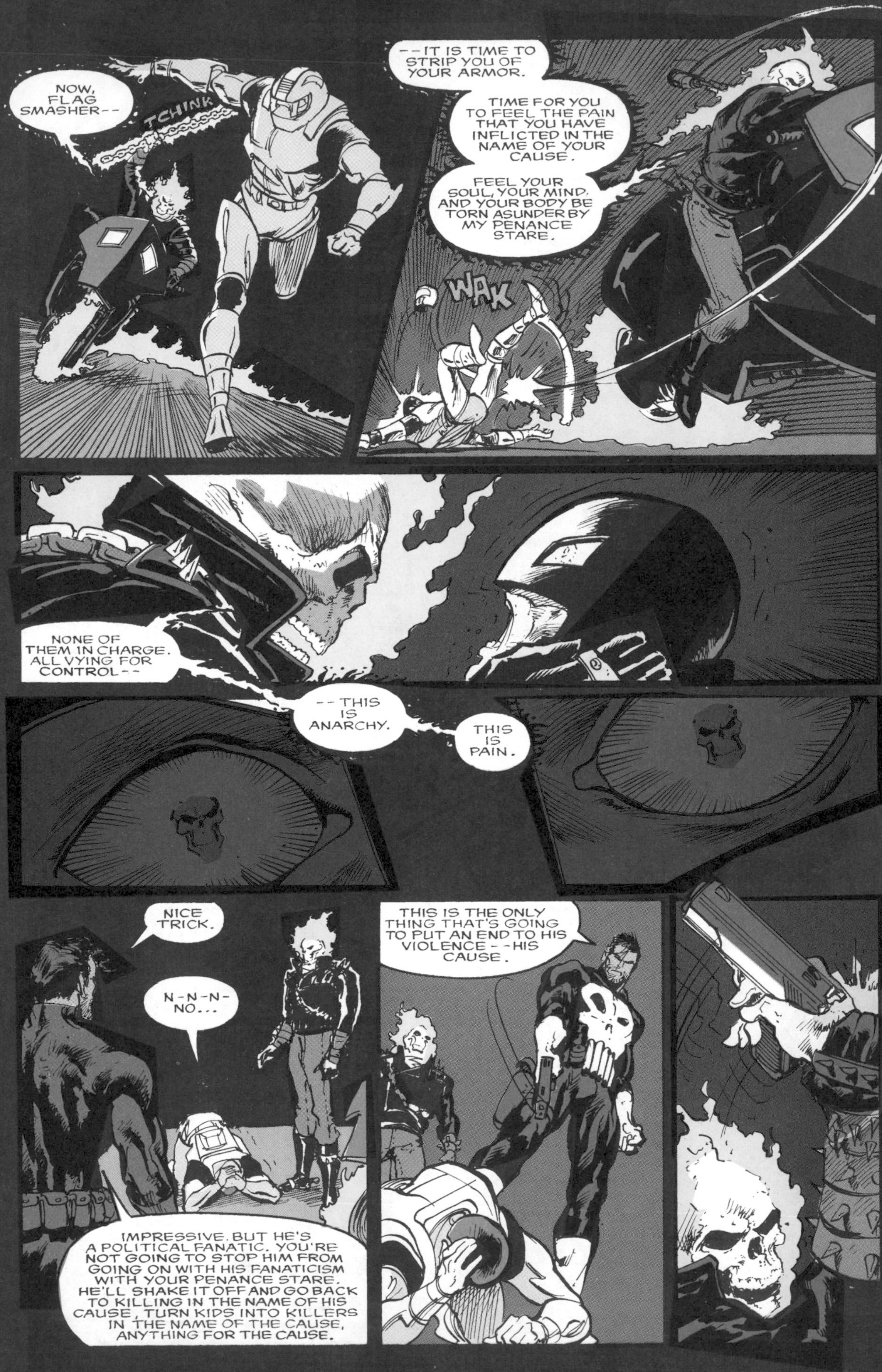
NOW, FLAG SMASHER--
TCHINK
--IT IS TIME TO STRIP YOU OF YOUR ARMOR.
TIME FOR YOU TO FEEL THE PAIN THAT YOU HAVE INFLICTED IN THE NAME OF YOUR CAUSE.
FEEL YOUR SOUL, YOUR MIND, AND YOUR BODY BE TORN ASUNDER BY MY PENANCE STARE.
WAK
NONE OF THEM IN CHARGE. ALL VYING FOR CONTROL--
--THIS IS ANARCHY.
THIS IS PAIN.
NICE TRICK.
N-N-N-NO...
IMPRESSIVE. BUT HE'S A POLITICAL FANATIC. YOU'RE NOT GOING TO STOP HIM FROM GOING ON WITH HIS FANATICISM WITH YOUR PENANCE STARE. HE'LL SHAKE IT OFF AND GO BACK TO KILLING IN THE NAME OF HIS CAUSE, TURN KIDS INTO KILLERS IN THE NAME OF THE CAUSE, ANYTHING FOR THE CAUSE.
THIS IS THE ONLY THING THAT'S GOING TO PUT AN END TO HIS VIOLENCE--HIS CAUSE.

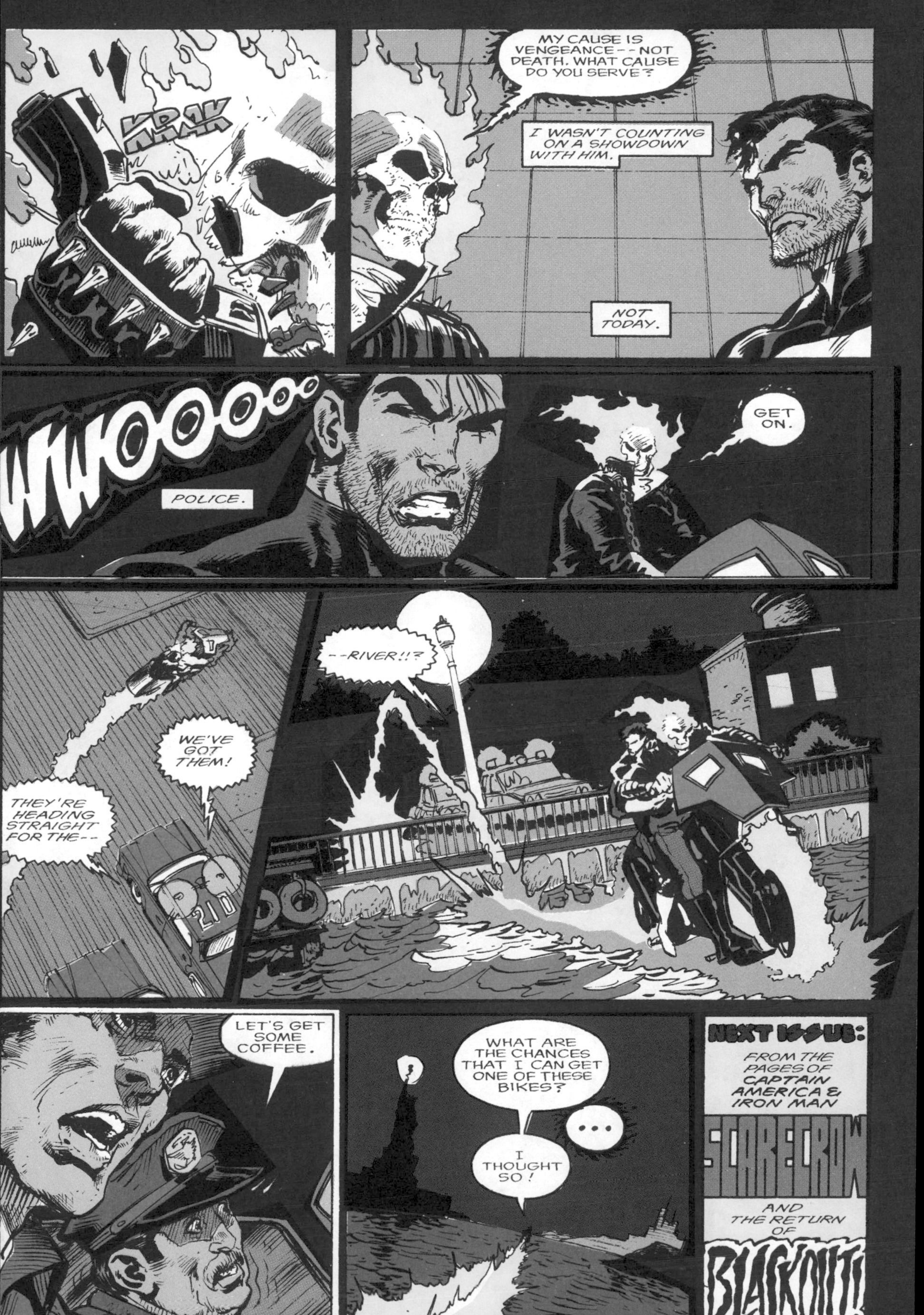
KRAK KRAK
MY CAUSE IS VENGEANCE--NOT DEATH. WHAT CAUSE DO YOU SERVE?
I WASN'T COUNTING ON A SHOWDOWN WITH HIM.
NOT TODAY.
WHOOOOOO
POLICE.
GET ON.
THEY'RE HEADING STRAIGHT FOR THE--
WE'VE GOT THEM!
--RIVER!!?
LET'S GET SOME COFFEE.
WHAT ARE THE CHANCES THAT I CAN GET ONE OF THESE BIKES?
...
I THOUGHT SO!
NEXT ISSUE:
FROM THE PAGES OF CAPTAIN AMERICA & IRON MAN
SCARECROW
AND THE RETURN OF
BLACKOUT!

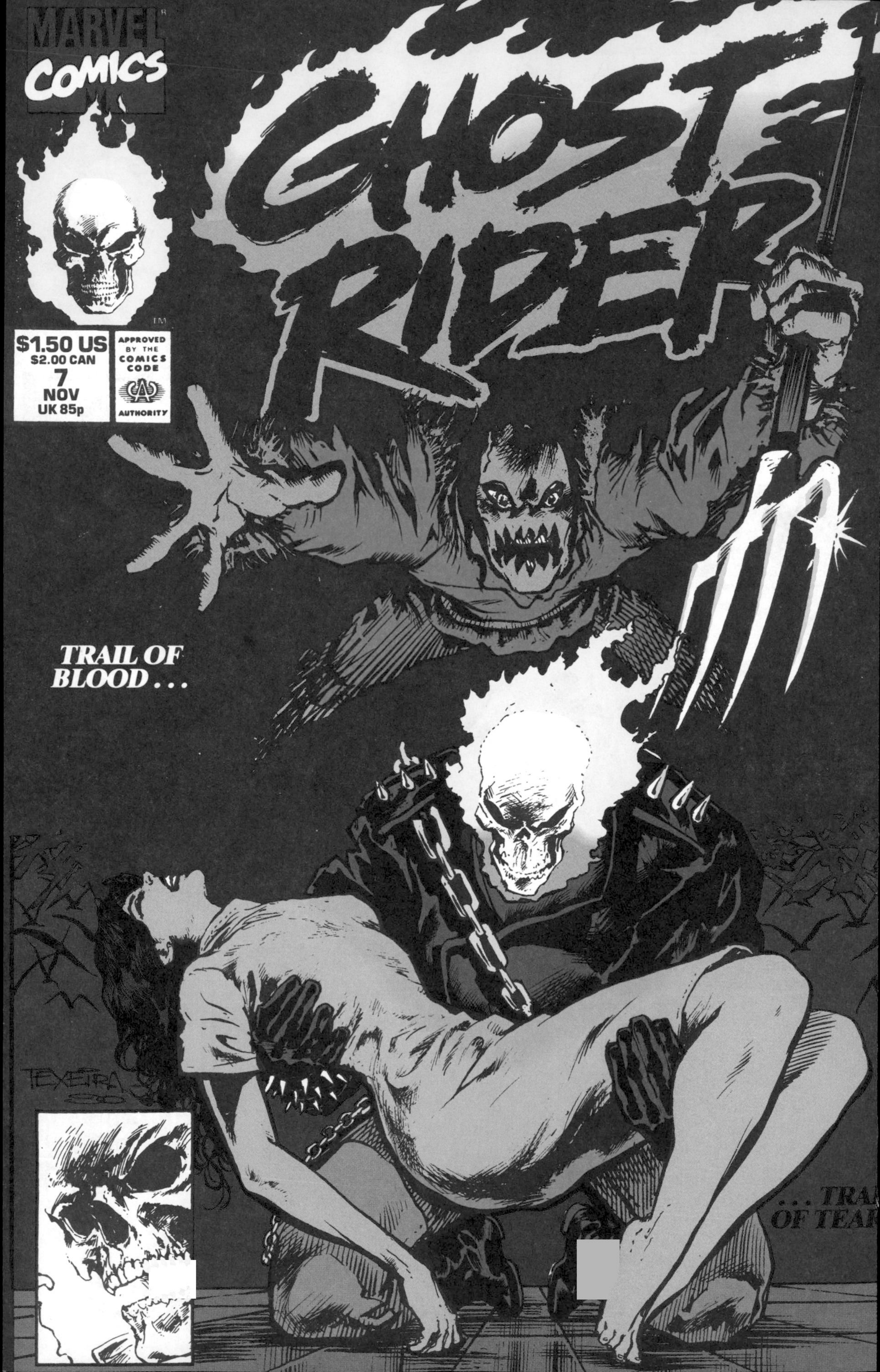

MARVEL COMICS
GHOST RIDER
$1.50 US
$2.00 CAN
7
NOV
UK 85p
APPROVED BY THE COMICS CODE AUTHORITY
TRAIL OF BLOOD . . .
. . . TRA
OF TEA
TEXEIRA

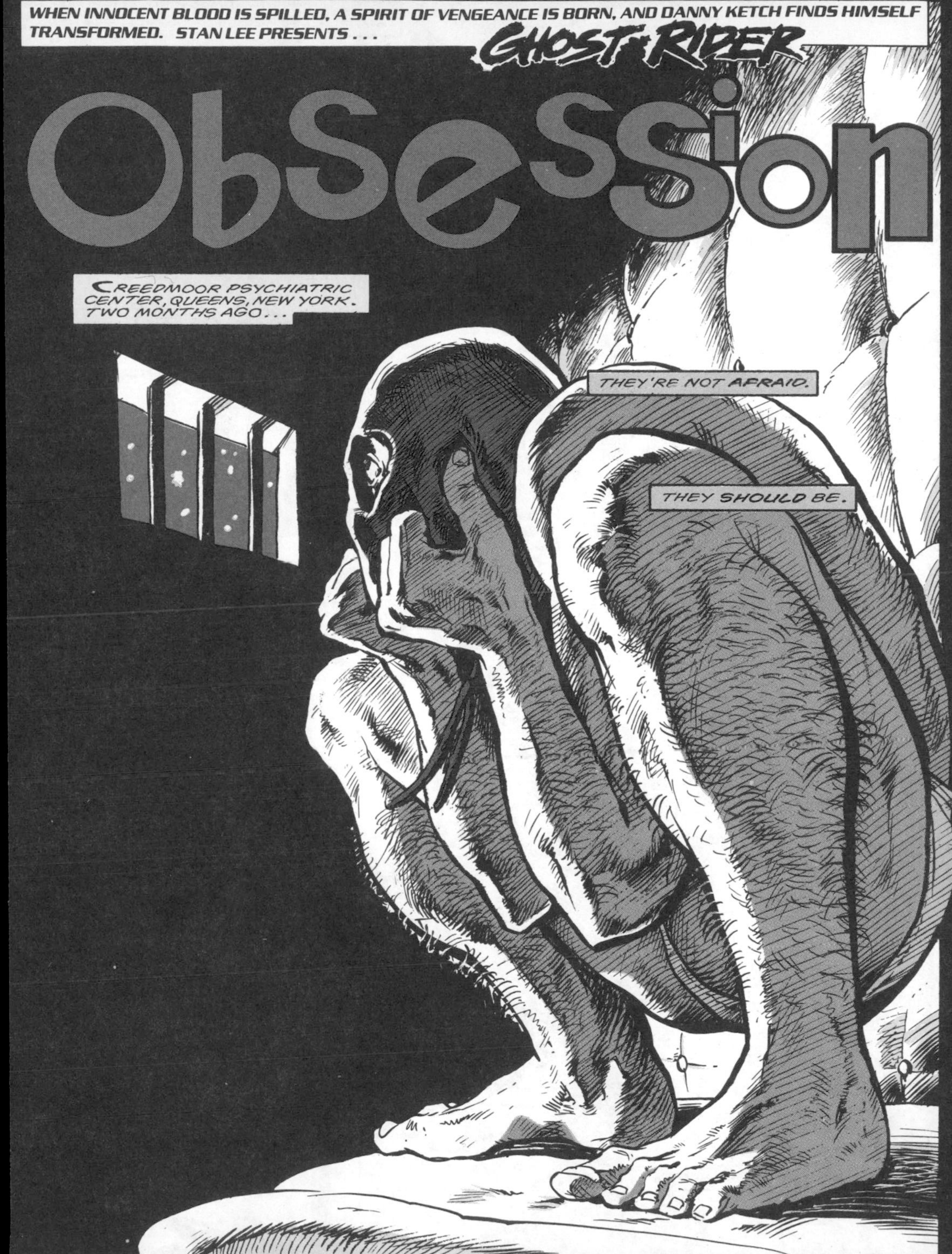
WHEN INNOCENT BLOOD IS SPILLED, A SPIRIT OF VENGEANCE IS BORN, AND DANNY KETCH FINDS HIMSELF TRANSFORMED. STAN LEE PRESENTS . . .
GHOST RIDER
OBSESSION
CREEDMOOR PSYCHIATRIC CENTER, QUEENS, NEW YORK. TWO MONTHS AGO . . .
THEY'RE NOT AFRAID.
THEY SHOULD BE.
HOWARD MACKIE WRITER • MARK TEXEIRA ARTIST • JANICE CHIANG LETTERER • GREGORY WRIGHT COLORIST • BOBBIE CHASE EDITOR • TOM DeFALCO EDITOR IN CHIEF

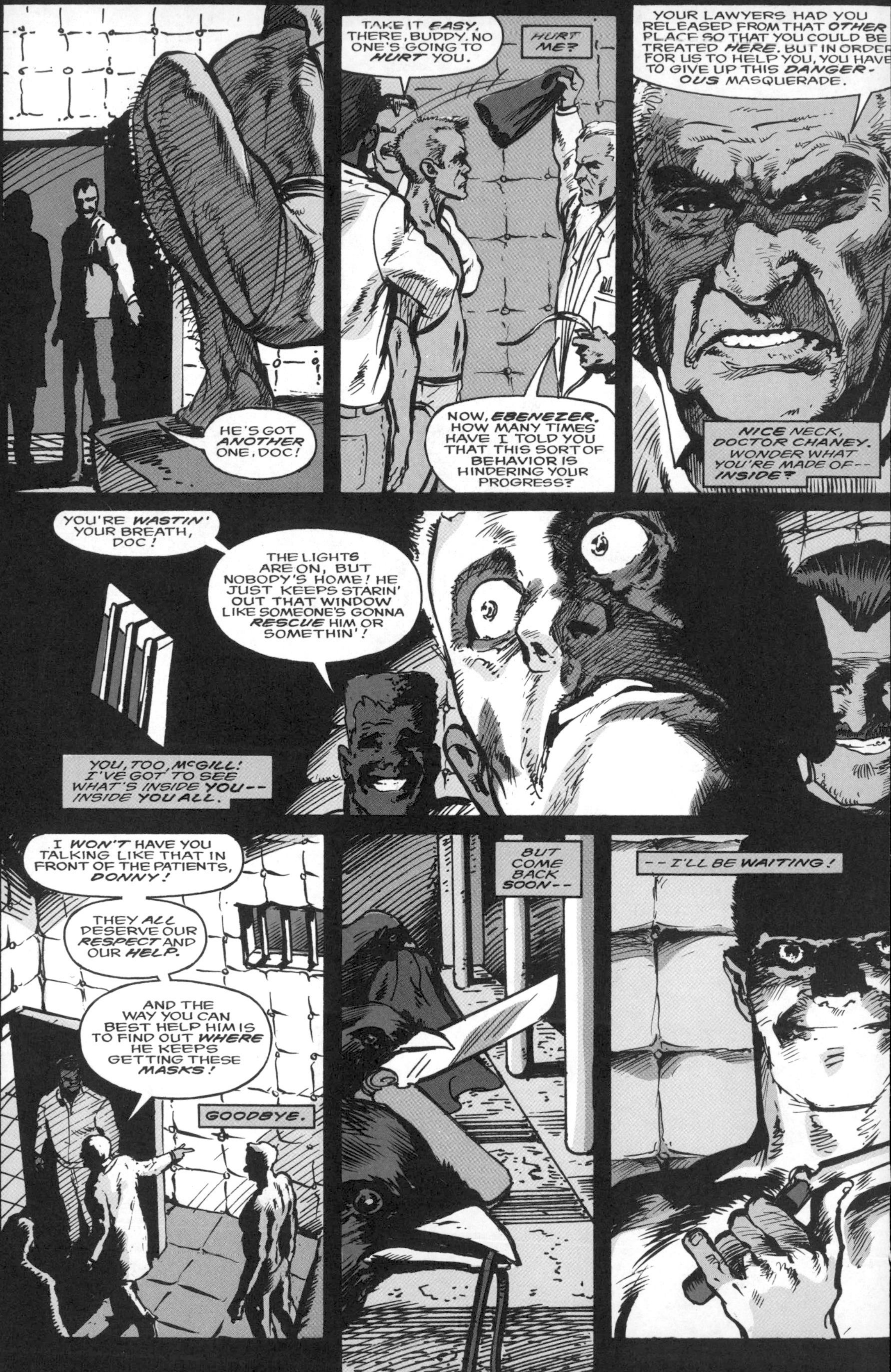
HE'S GOT ANOTHER ONE, DOC!
TAKE IT EASY, THERE, BUDDY. NO ONE'S GOING TO HURT YOU.
HURT ME?
NOW, EBENEZER. HOW MANY TIMES HAVE I TOLD YOU THAT THIS SORT OF BEHAVIOR IS HINDERING YOUR PROGRESS?
YOUR LAWYERS HAD YOU RELEASED FROM THAT OTHER PLACE SO THAT YOU COULD BE TREATED HERE. BUT IN ORDER FOR US TO HELP YOU, YOU HAVE TO GIVE UP THIS DANGEROUS MASQUERADE.
NICE NECK, DOCTOR CHANEY. WONDER WHAT YOU'RE MADE OF-- INSIDE?
YOU'RE WASTIN' YOUR BREATH, DOC!
THE LIGHTS ARE ON, BUT NOBODY'S HOME! HE JUST KEEPS STARIN' OUT THAT WINDOW LIKE SOMEONE'S GONNA RESCUE HIM OR SOMETHIN'!
YOU, TOO, McGILL! I'VE GOT TO SEE WHAT'S INSIDE YOU-- INSIDE YOU ALL.
I WON'T HAVE YOU TALKING LIKE THAT IN FRONT OF THE PATIENTS, DONNY!
THEY ALL DESERVE OUR RESPECT AND OUR HELP.
AND THE WAY YOU CAN BEST HELP HIM IS TO FIND OUT WHERE HE KEEPS GETTING THESE MASKS!
GOODBYE.
BUT COME BACK SOON--
--I'LL BE WAITING!

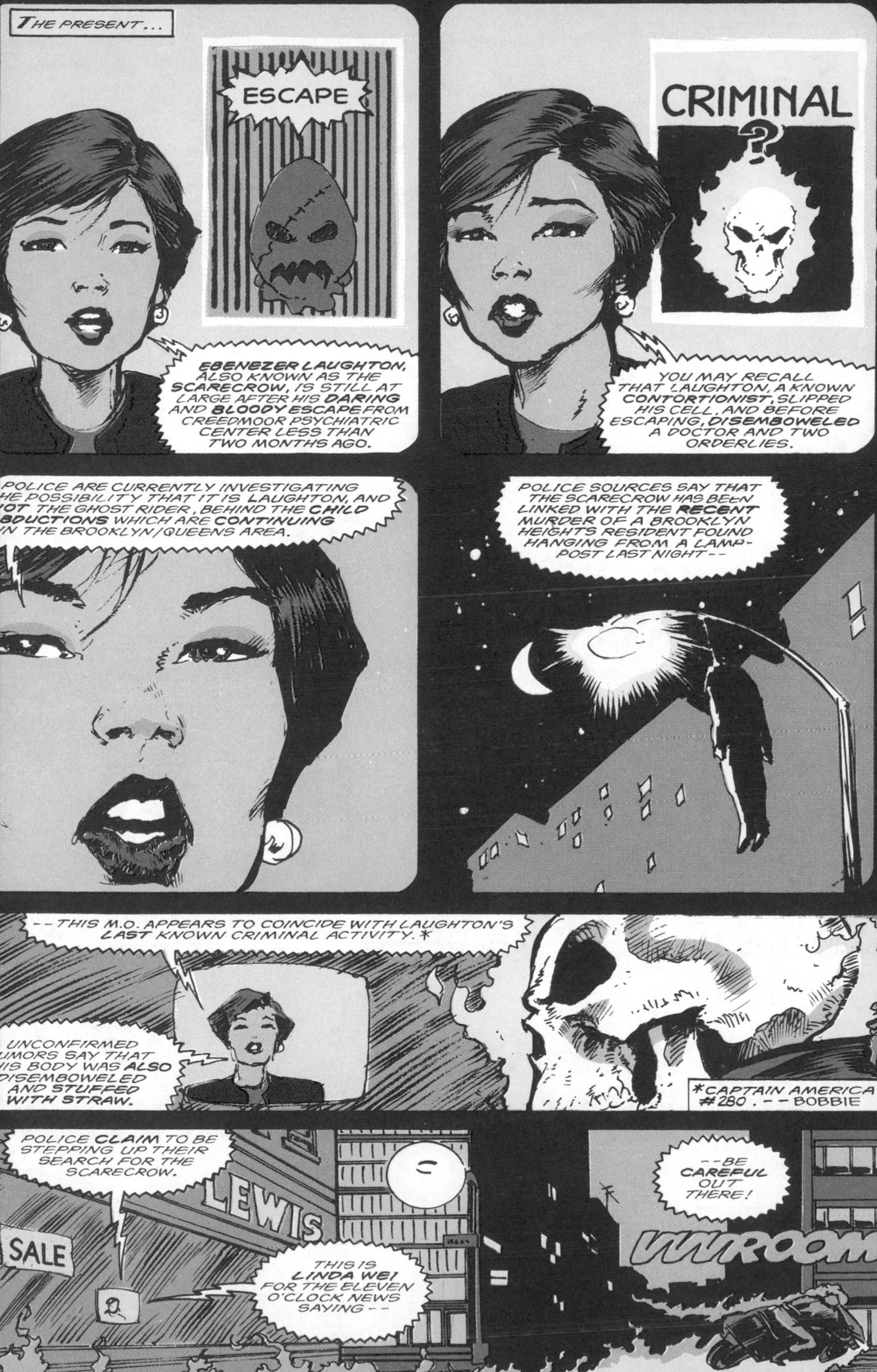

THE PRESENT...
ESCAPE
EBENEZER LAUGHTON, ALSO KNOWN AS THE SCARECROW, IS STILL AT LARGE AFTER HIS DARING AND BLOODY ESCAPE FROM CREEDMOOR PSYCHIATRIC CENTER LESS THAN TWO MONTHS AGO.
CRIMINAL
?
YOU MAY RECALL THAT LAUGHTON, A KNOWN CONTORTIONIST, SLIPPED HIS CELL, AND BEFORE ESCAPING, DISEMBOWELED A DOCTOR AND TWO ORDERLIES.
POLICE ARE CURRENTLY INVESTIGATING HE POSSIBILITY THAT IT IS LAUGHTON, AND OT THE GHOST RIDER, BEHIND THE CHILD BDUCTIONS WHICH ARE CONTINUING N THE BROOKLYN/QUEENS AREA.
POLICE SOURCES SAY THAT THE SCARECROW HAS BEEN LINKED WITH THE RECENT MURDER OF A BROOKLYN HEIGHTS RESIDENT FOUND HANGING FROM A LAMP-POST LAST NIGHT--
--THIS M.O. APPEARS TO COINCIDE WITH LAUGHTON'S LAST KNOWN CRIMINAL ACTIVITY.*
UNCONFIRMED UMORS SAY THAT HIS BODY WAS ALSO DISEMBOWELED AND STUFFED WITH STRAW.
*CAPTAIN AMERICA #280. --BOBBIE
POLICE CLAIM TO BE STEPPING UP THEIR SEARCH FOR THE SCARECROW.
LEWIS
SALE
THIS IS LINDA WEI FOR THE ELEVEN O'CLOCK NEWS SAYING--
--BE CAREFUL OUT THERE!
VVVROOM

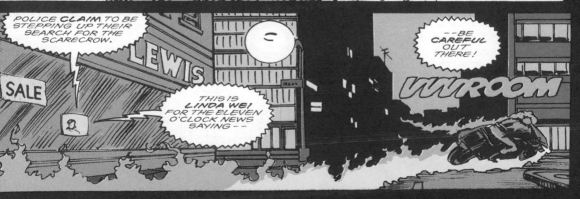

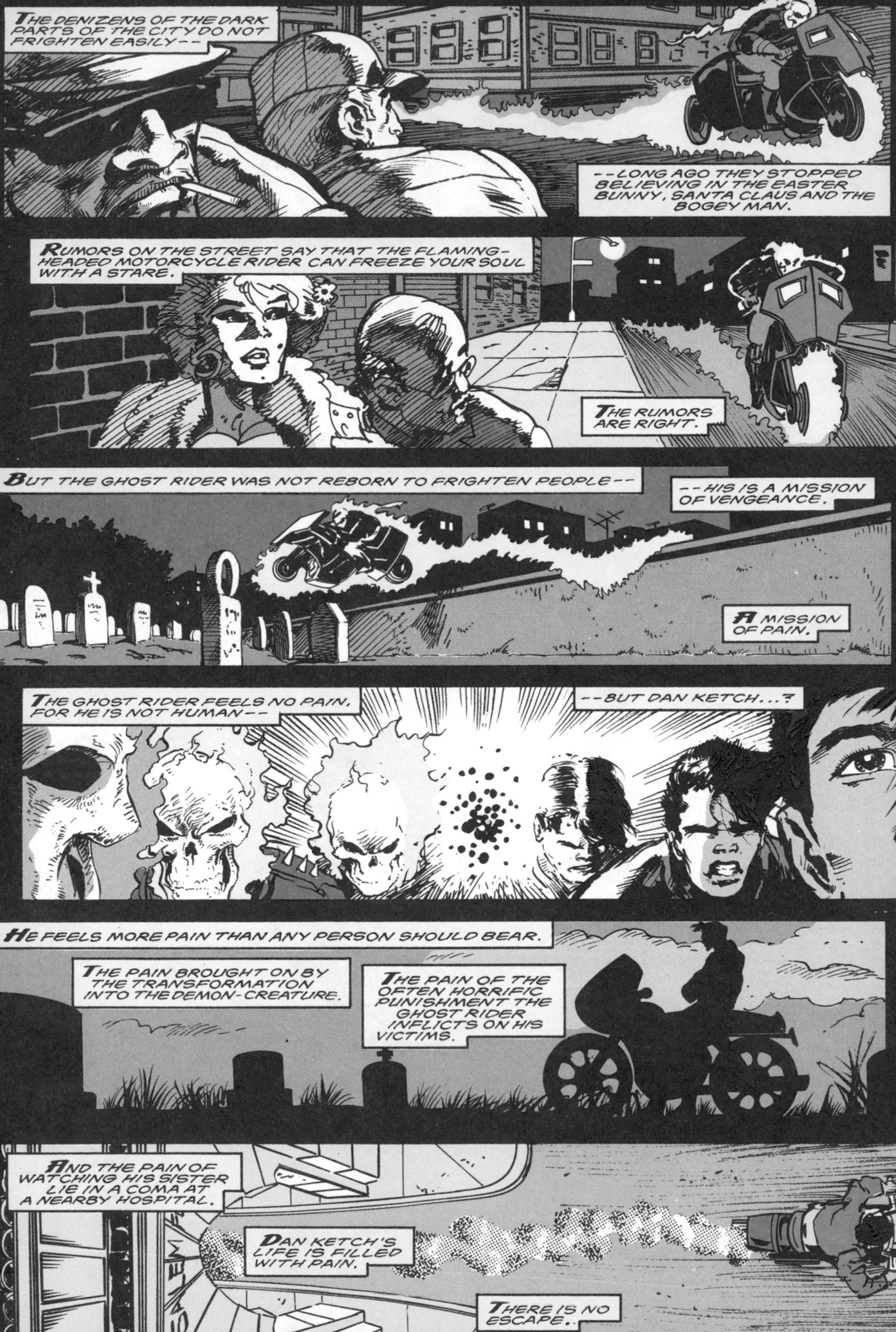
THE DENIZENS OF THE DARK PARTS OF THE CITY DO NOT FRIGHTEN EASILY--
--LONG AGO THEY STOPPED BELIEVING IN THE EASTER BUNNY, SANTA CLAUS AND THE BOGEY MAN.
RUMORS ON THE STREET SAY THAT THE FLAMING-HEADED MOTORCYCLE RIDER CAN FREEZE YOUR SOUL WITH A STARE.
THE RUMORS ARE RIGHT.
BUT THE GHOST RIDER WAS NOT REBORN TO FRIGHTEN PEOPLE--
--HIS IS A MISSION OF VENGEANCE.
A MISSION OF PAIN.
THE GHOST RIDER FEELS NO PAIN, FOR HE IS NOT HUMAN--
--BUT DAN KETCH...?
HE FEELS MORE PAIN THAN ANY PERSON SHOULD BEAR.
THE PAIN BROUGHT ON BY THE TRANSFORMATION INTO THE DEMON-CREATURE.
THE PAIN OF THE OFTEN HORRIFIC PUNISHMENT THE GHOST RIDER INFLICTS ON HIS VICTIMS.
AND THE PAIN OF WATCHING HIS SISTER LIE IN A COMA AT A NEARBY HOSPITAL.
DAN KETCH'S LIFE IS FILLED WITH PAIN.
THERE IS NO ESCAPE.

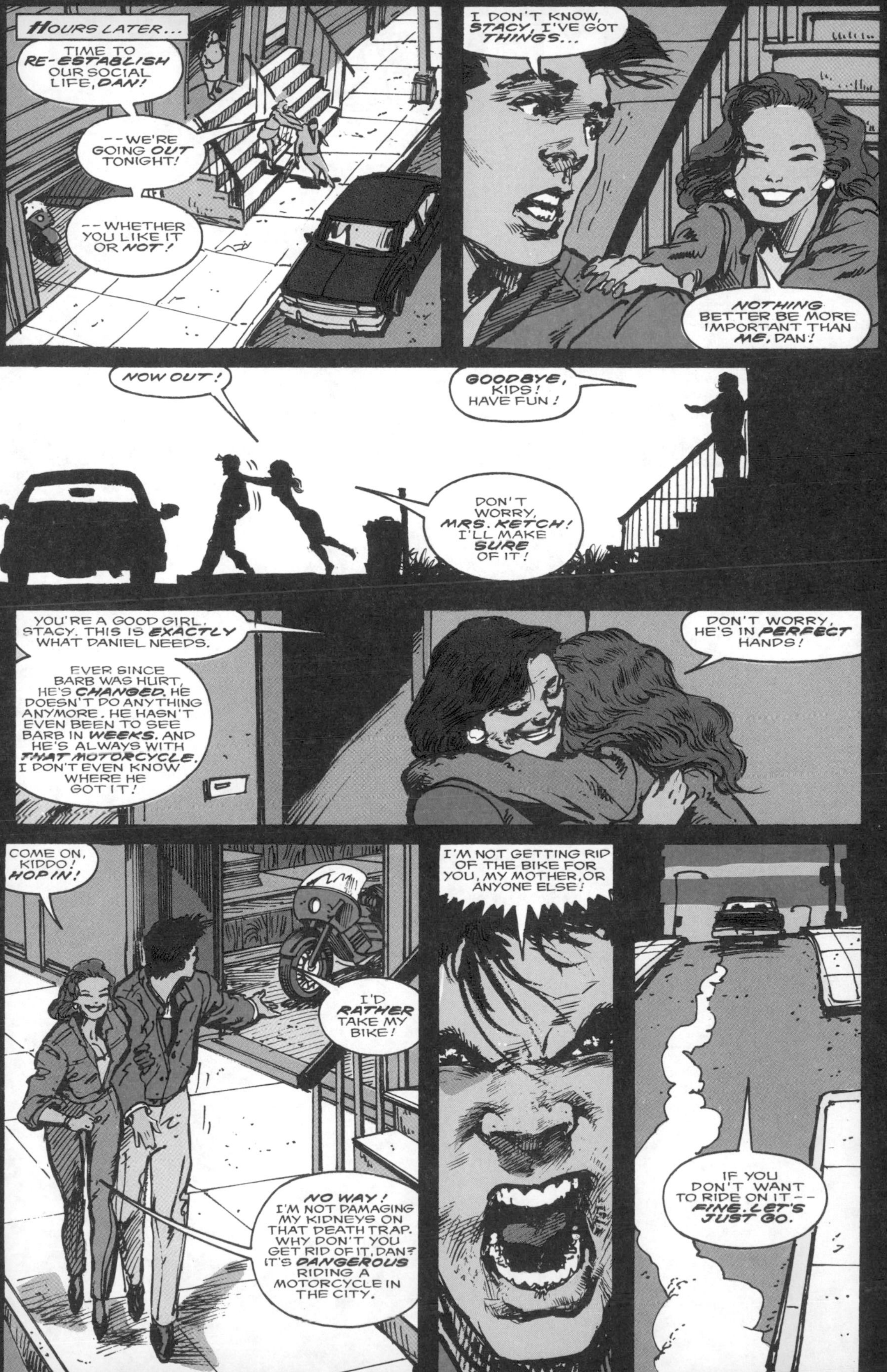
HOURS LATER...
TIME TO RE-ESTABLISH OUR SOCIAL LIFE, DAN!
--WE'RE GOING OUT TONIGHT!
--WHETHER YOU LIKE IT OR NOT!
I DON'T KNOW, STACY, I'VE GOT THINGS...
NOTHING BETTER BE MORE IMPORTANT THAN ME, DAN!
NOW OUT!
GOODBYE, KIDS! HAVE FUN!
DON'T WORRY, MRS. KETCH! I'LL MAKE SURE OF IT!
YOU'RE A GOOD GIRL, STACY. THIS IS EXACTLY WHAT DANIEL NEEDS.
EVER SINCE BARB WAS HURT, HE'S CHANGED. HE DOESN'T DO ANYTHING ANYMORE. HE HASN'T EVEN BEEN TO SEE BARB IN WEEKS. AND HE'S ALWAYS WITH THAT MOTORCYCLE. I DON'T EVEN KNOW WHERE HE GOT IT!
DON'T WORRY, HE'S IN PERFECT HANDS!
COME ON, KIDDO! HOP IN!
I'D RATHER TAKE MY BIKE!
NO WAY! I'M NOT DAMAGING MY KIDNEYS ON THAT DEATH TRAP. WHY DON'T YOU GET RID OF IT, DAN? IT'S DANGEROUS RIDING A MOTORCYCLE IN THE CITY.
I'M NOT GETTING RID OF THE BIKE FOR YOU, MY MOTHER, OR ANYONE ELSE!
IF YOU DON'T WANT TO RIDE ON IT-- FINE. LET'S JUST GO.

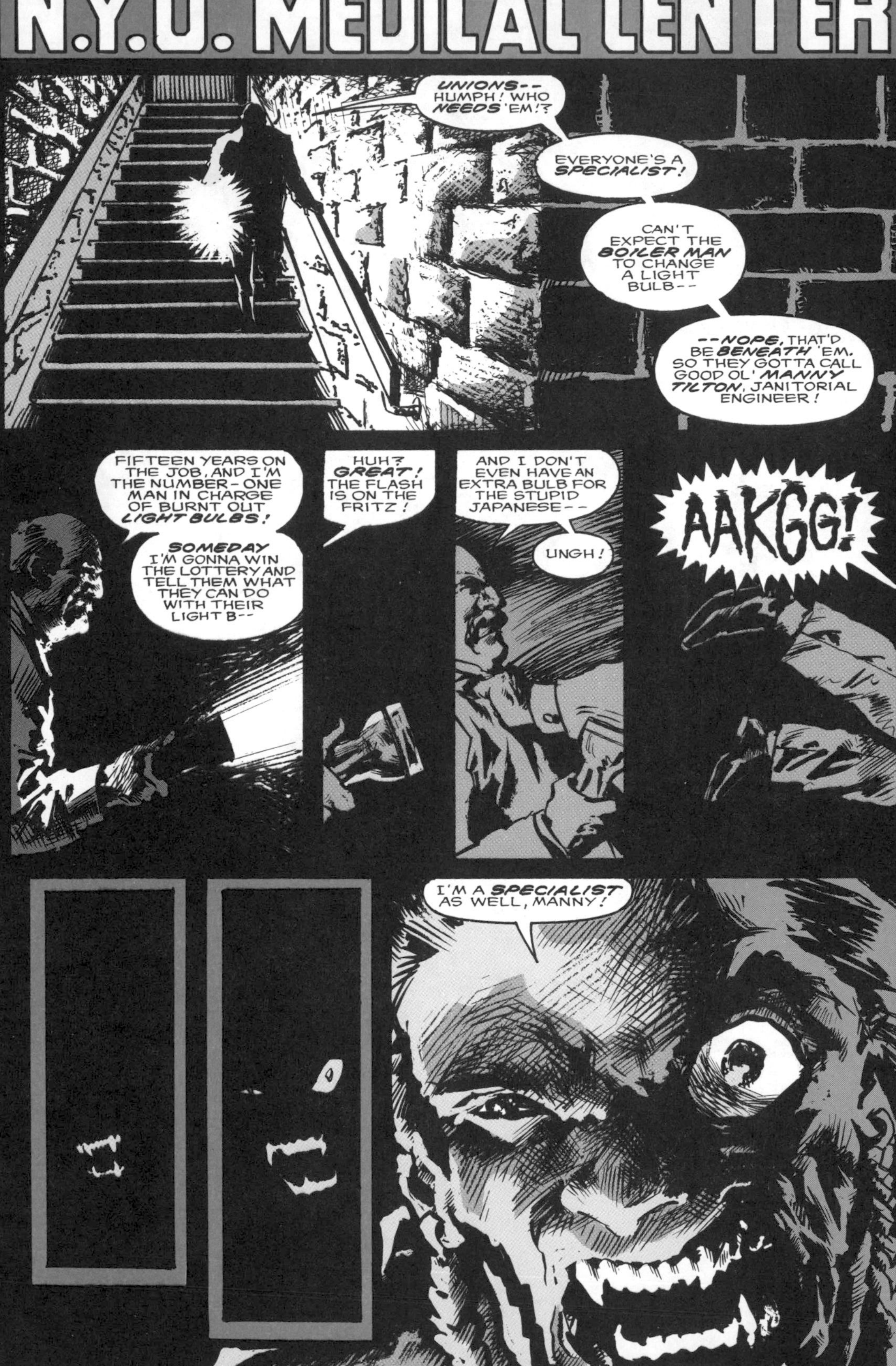
N.Y.U. MEDICAL CENTER
UNIONS-- HUMPH! WHO NEEDS 'EM!?
EVERYONE'S A SPECIALIST!
CAN'T EXPECT THE BOILER MAN TO CHANGE A LIGHT BULB--
--NOPE, THAT'D BE BENEATH 'EM. SO THEY GOTTA CALL GOOD OL' MANNY TILTON, JANITORIAL ENGINEER!
FIFTEEN YEARS ON THE JOB, AND I'M THE NUMBER-ONE MAN IN CHARGE OF BURNT OUT LIGHT BULBS!
SOMEDAY I'M GONNA WIN THE LOTTERY AND TELL THEM WHAT THEY CAN DO WITH THEIR LIGHT B--
HUH? GREAT! THE FLASH IS ON THE FRITZ!
AND I DON'T EVEN HAVE AN EXTRA BULB FOR THE STUPID JAPANESE--
UNGH!
AAKGG!
I'M A SPECIALIST AS WELL, MANNY!

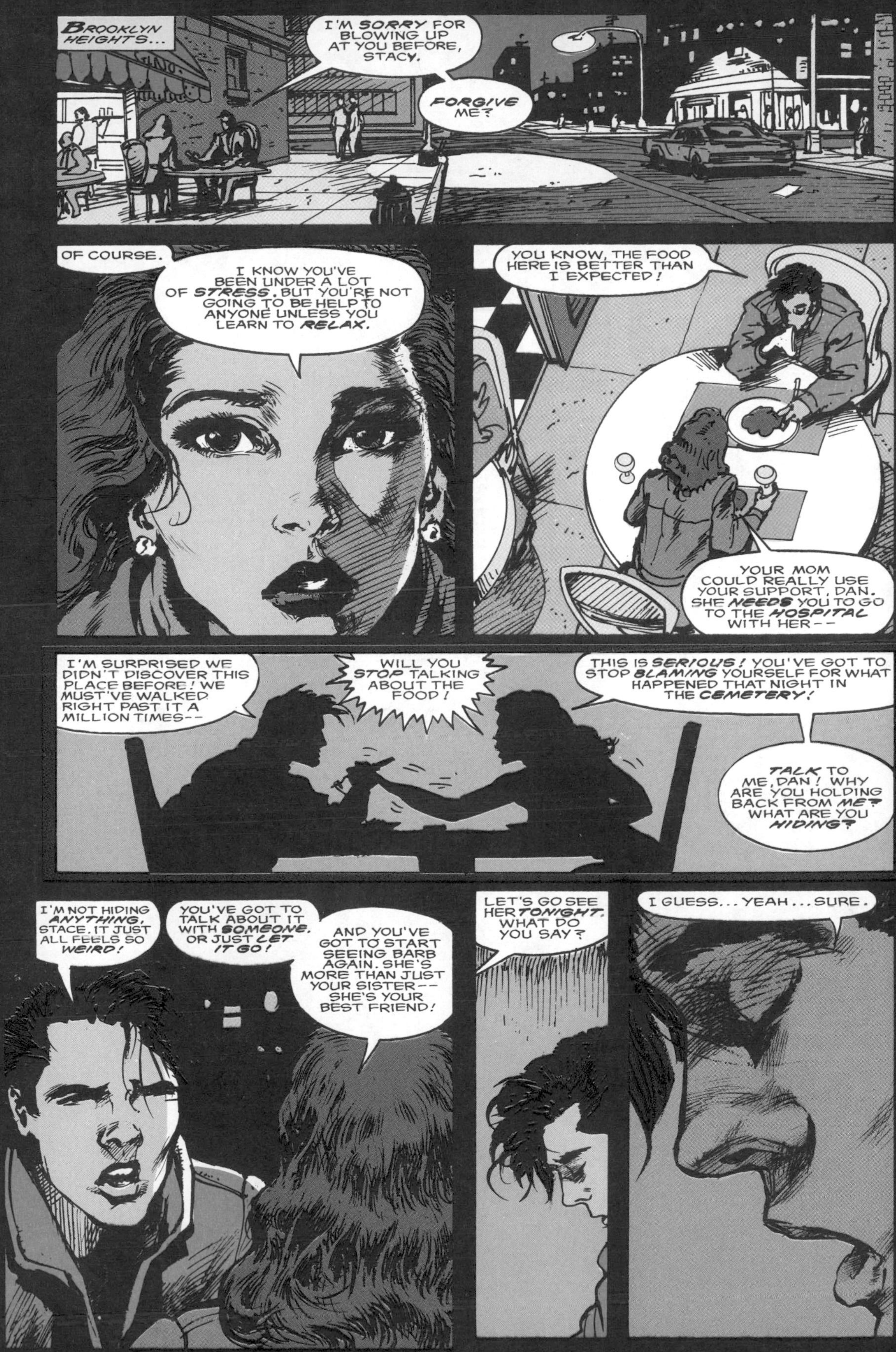
BROOKLYN HEIGHTS...
I'M SORRY FOR BLOWING UP AT YOU BEFORE, STACY.
FORGIVE ME?
OF COURSE.
I KNOW YOU'VE BEEN UNDER A LOT OF STRESS. BUT YOU'RE NOT GOING TO BE HELP TO ANYONE UNLESS YOU LEARN TO RELAX.
YOU KNOW, THE FOOD HERE IS BETTER THAN I EXPECTED!
YOUR MOM COULD REALLY USE YOUR SUPPORT, DAN. SHE NEEDS YOU TO GO TO THE HOSPITAL WITH HER--
I'M SURPRISED WE DIDN'T DISCOVER THIS PLACE BEFORE! WE MUST'VE WALKED RIGHT PAST IT A MILLION TIMES--
WILL YOU STOP TALKING ABOUT THE FOOD!
THIS IS SERIOUS! YOU'VE GOT TO STOP BLAMING YOURSELF FOR WHAT HAPPENED THAT NIGHT IN THE CEMETERY!
TALK TO ME, DAN! WHY ARE YOU HOLDING BACK FROM ME? WHAT ARE YOU HIDING?
I'M NOT HIDING ANYTHING, STACE. IT JUST ALL FEELS SO WEIRD!
YOU'VE GOT TO TALK ABOUT IT WITH SOMEONE. OR JUST LET IT GO!
AND YOU'VE GOT TO START SEEING BARB AGAIN. SHE'S MORE THAN JUST YOUR SISTER-- SHE'S YOUR BEST FRIEND!
LET'S GO SEE HER TONIGHT. WHAT DO YOU SAY?
I GUESS... YEAH... SURE.

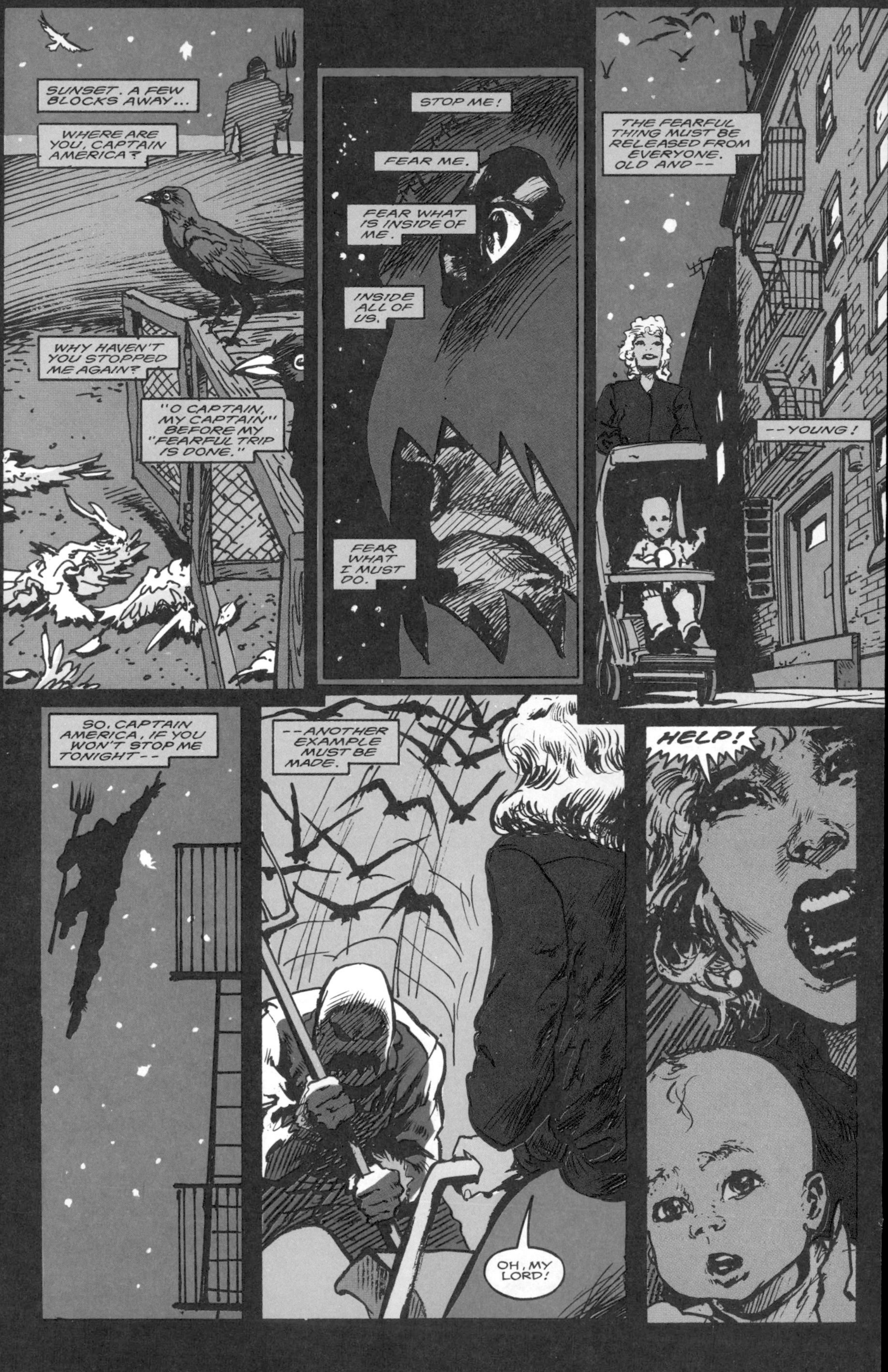
SUNSET. A FEW BLOCKS AWAY...
WHERE ARE YOU, CAPTAIN AMERICA?
WHY HAVEN'T YOU STOPPED ME AGAIN?
"O CAPTAIN, MY CAPTAIN" BEFORE MY "FEARFUL TRIP IS DONE."
STOP ME!
FEAR ME.
FEAR WHAT IS INSIDE OF ME.
INSIDE ALL OF US.
FEAR WHAT I MUST DO.
THE FEARFUL THING MUST BE RELEASED FROM EVERYONE. OLD AND--
--YOUNG!
SO, CAPTAIN AMERICA, IF YOU WON'T STOP ME TONIGHT--
--ANOTHER EXAMPLE MUST BE MADE.
OH, MY LORD!
HELP!

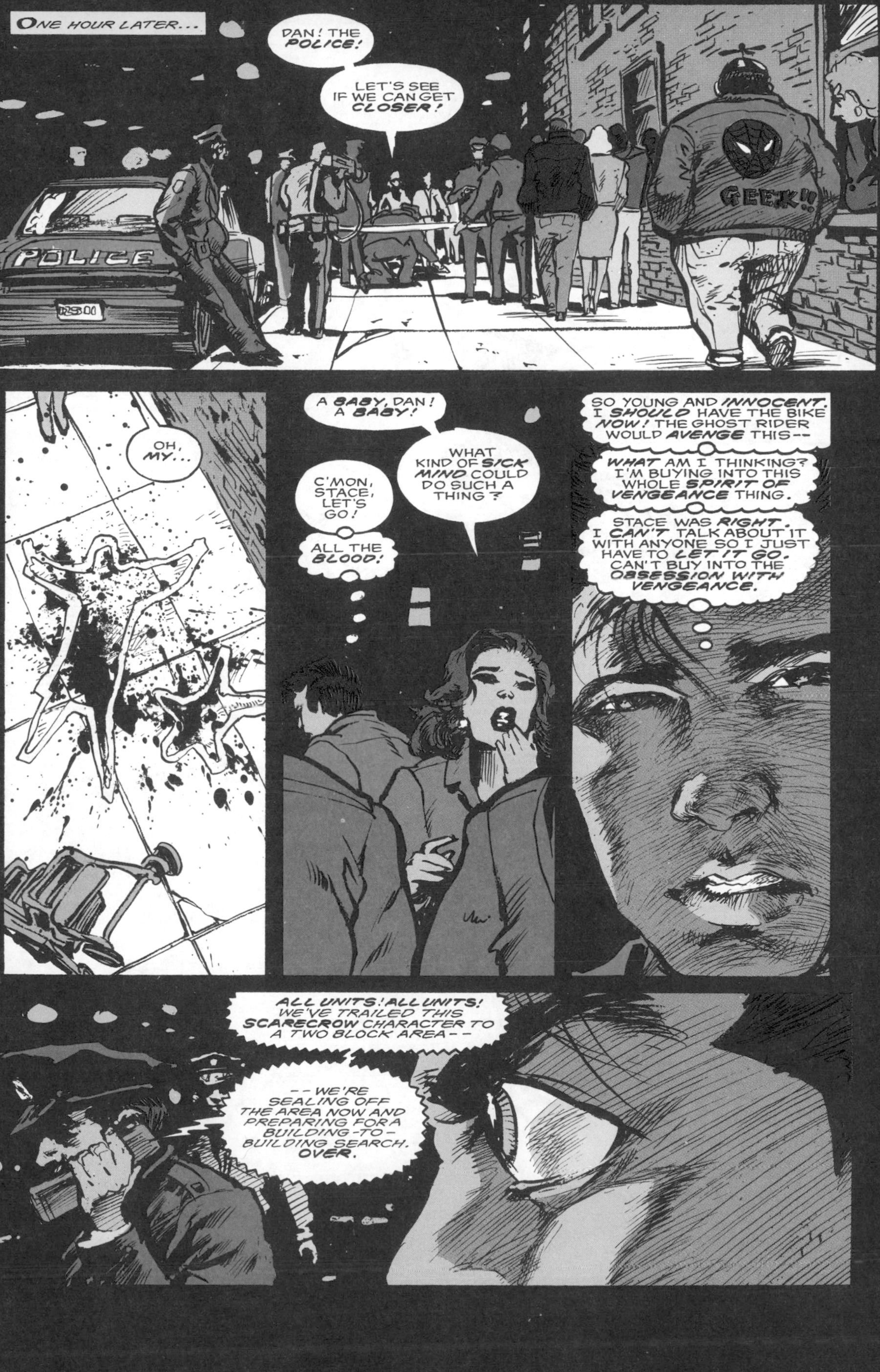
ONE HOUR LATER...
DAN! THE POLICE!
LET'S SEE IF WE CAN GET CLOSER!
POLICE
GEEK!!
OH, MY...
A BABY, DAN! A BABY!
WHAT KIND OF SICK MIND COULD DO SUCH A THING?
C'MON, STACE, LET'S GO!
ALL THE BLOOD!
SO YOUNG AND INNOCENT. I SHOULD HAVE THE BIKE NOW! THE GHOST RIDER WOULD AVENGE THIS--
WHAT AM I THINKING? I'M BUYING INTO THIS WHOLE SPIRIT OF VENGEANCE THING.
STACE WAS RIGHT. I CAN'T TALK ABOUT IT WITH ANYONE SO I JUST HAVE TO LET IT GO. CAN'T BUY INTO THE OBSESSION WITH VENGEANCE.
ALL UNITS! ALL UNITS! WE'VE TRAILED THIS SCARECROW CHARACTER TO A TWO BLOCK AREA--
--WE'RE SEALING OFF THE AREA NOW AND PREPARING FOR A BUILDING-TO-BUILDING SEARCH. OVER.

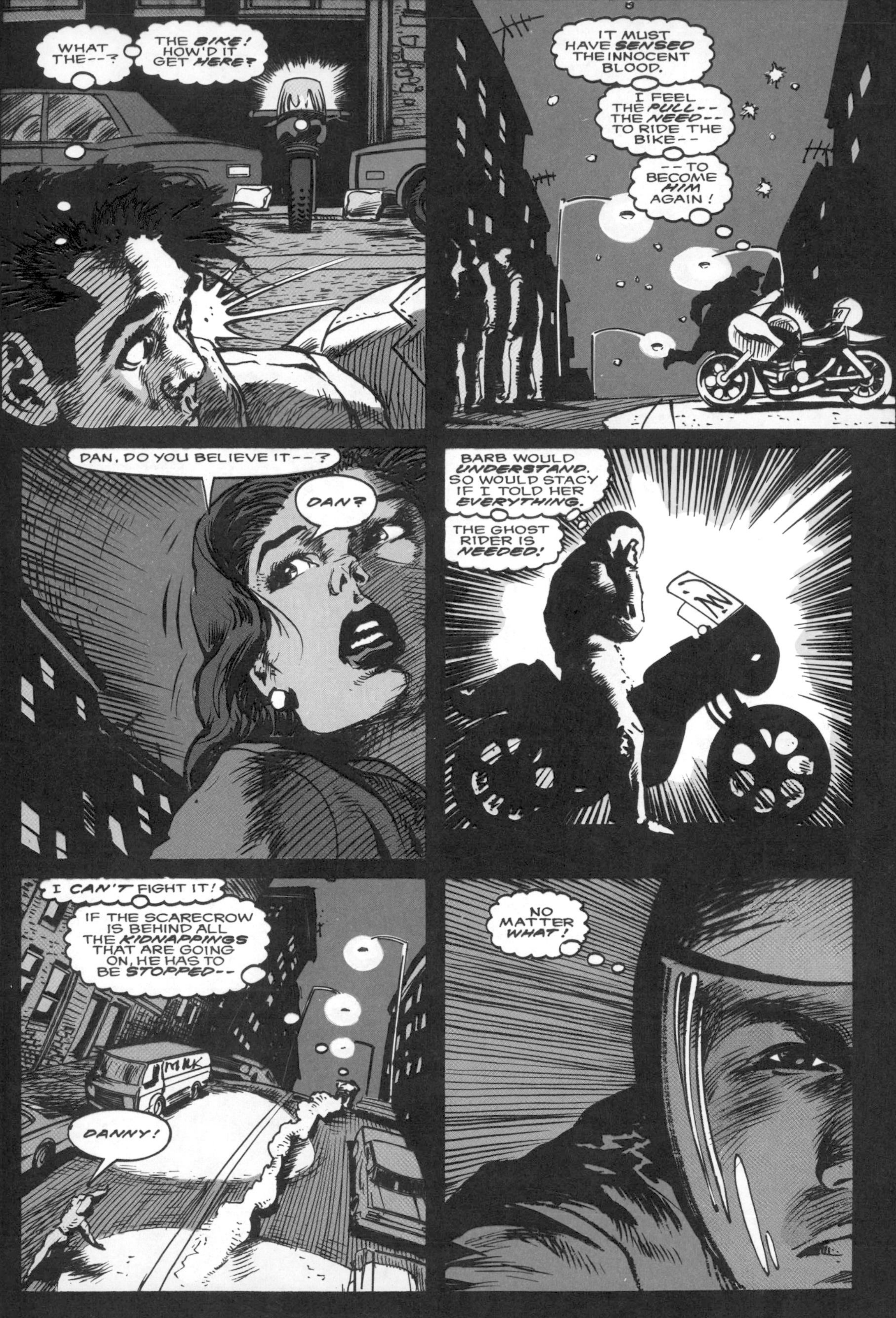
WHAT THE--?
THE BIKE! HOW'D IT GET HERE?
IT MUST HAVE SENSED THE INNOCENT BLOOD.
I FEEL THE PULL-- THE NEED-- TO RIDE THE BIKE--
--TO BECOME HIM AGAIN!
DAN, DO YOU BELIEVE IT--?
DAN?
BARB WOULD UNDERSTAND. SO WOULD STACY IF I TOLD HER EVERYTHING.
THE GHOST RIDER IS NEEDED!
I CAN'T FIGHT IT!
IF THE SCARECROW IS BEHIND ALL THE KIDNAPPINGS THAT ARE GOING ON, HE HAS TO BE STOPPED--
DANNY!
NO MATTER WHAT!

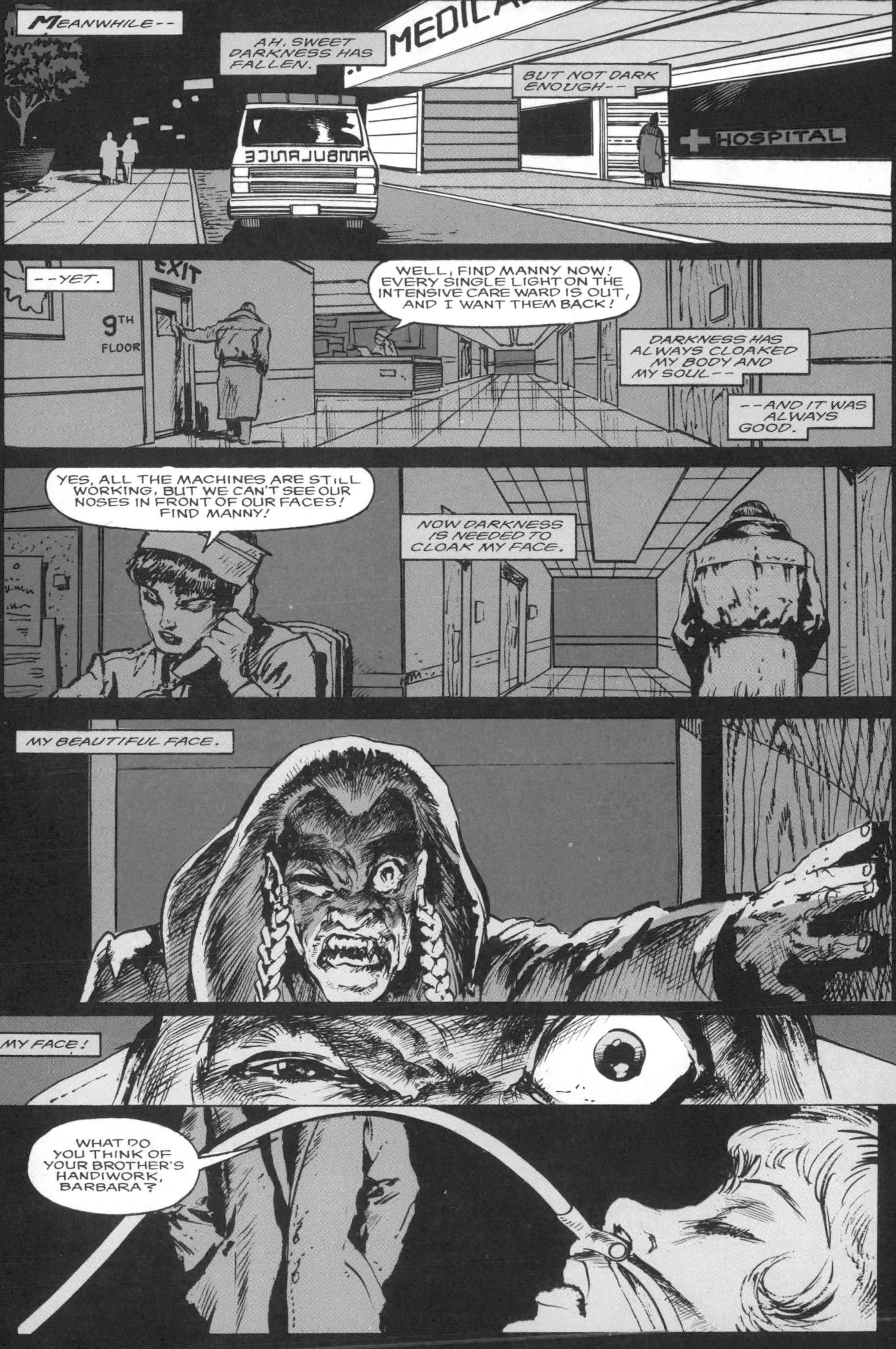
MEANWHILE--
AH, SWEET DARKNESS HAS FALLEN.
MEDICAL
BUT NOT DARK ENOUGH--
AMBULANCE
HOSPITAL
--YET.
EXIT
9TH FLOOR
WELL, FIND MANNY NOW! EVERY SINGLE LIGHT ON THE INTENSIVE CARE WARD IS OUT, AND I WANT THEM BACK!
DARKNESS HAS ALWAYS CLOAKED MY BODY AND MY SOUL--
--AND IT WAS ALWAYS GOOD.
YES, ALL THE MACHINES ARE STILL WORKING, BUT WE CAN'T SEE OUR NOSES IN FRONT OF OUR FACES! FIND MANNY!
NOW DARKNESS IS NEEDED TO CLOAK MY FACE.
MY BEAUTIFUL FACE.
MY FACE!
WHAT DO YOU THINK OF YOUR BROTHER'S HANDIWORK, BARBARA?

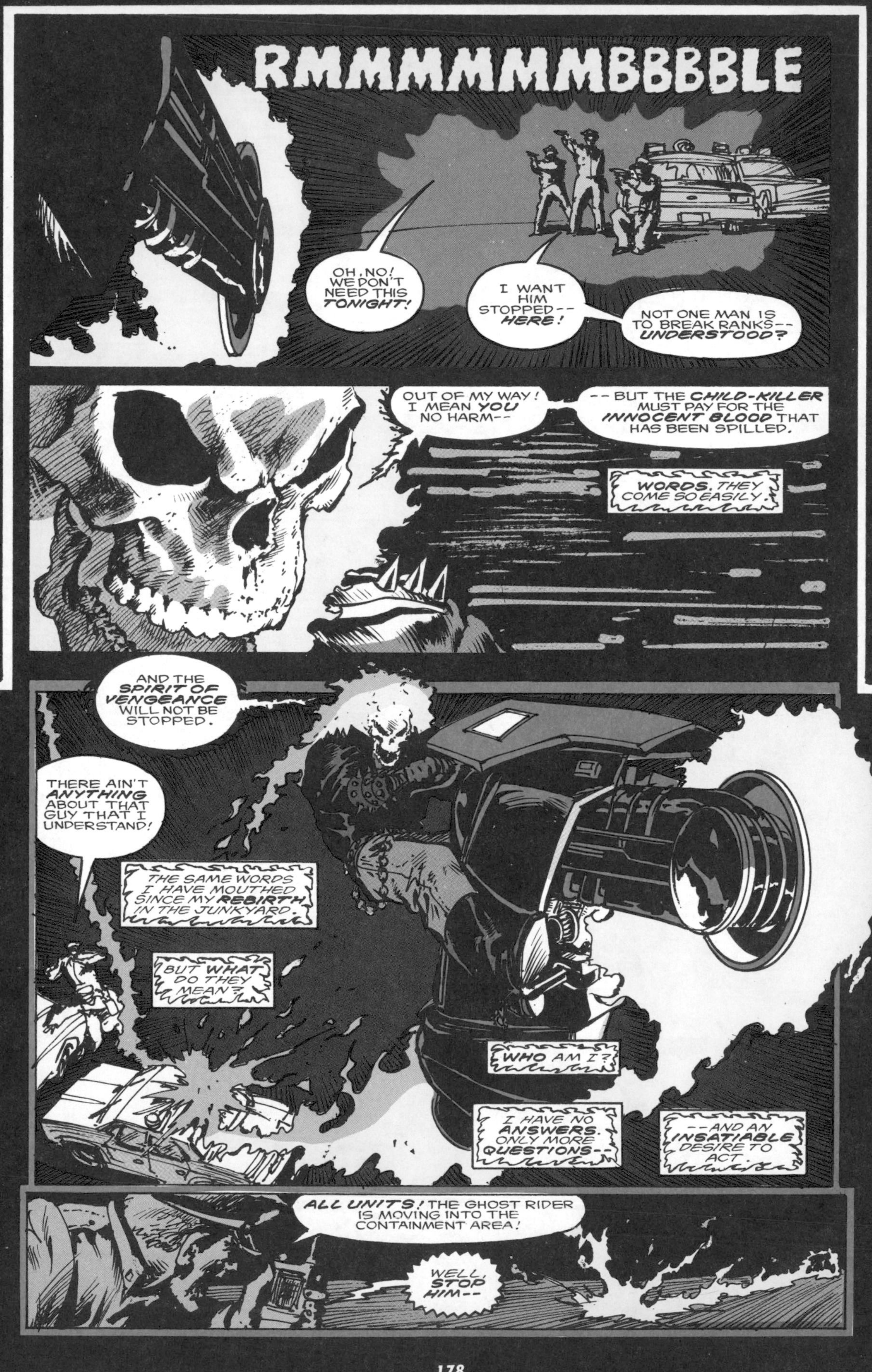

RMMMMMMMBBBBLE
OH, NO! WE DON'T NEED THIS TONIGHT!
I WANT HIM STOPPED -- HERE!
NOT ONE MAN IS TO BREAK RANKS -- UNDERSTOOD?
OUT OF MY WAY! I MEAN YOU NO HARM--
-- BUT THE CHILD-KILLER MUST PAY FOR THE INNOCENT BLOOD THAT HAS BEEN SPILLED.
WORDS. THEY COME SO EASILY.
AND THE SPIRIT OF VENGEANCE WILL NOT BE STOPPED.
THERE AIN'T ANYTHING ABOUT THAT GUY THAT I UNDERSTAND!
THE SAME WORDS I HAVE MOUTHED SINCE MY REBIRTH IN THE JUNKYARD.
BUT WHAT DO THEY MEAN?
WHO AM I?
I HAVE NO ANSWERS. ONLY MORE QUESTIONS--
--AND AN INSATIABLE DESIRE TO ACT
ALL UNITS! THE GHOST RIDER IS MOVING INTO THE CONTAINMENT AREA!
WELL, STOP HIM--

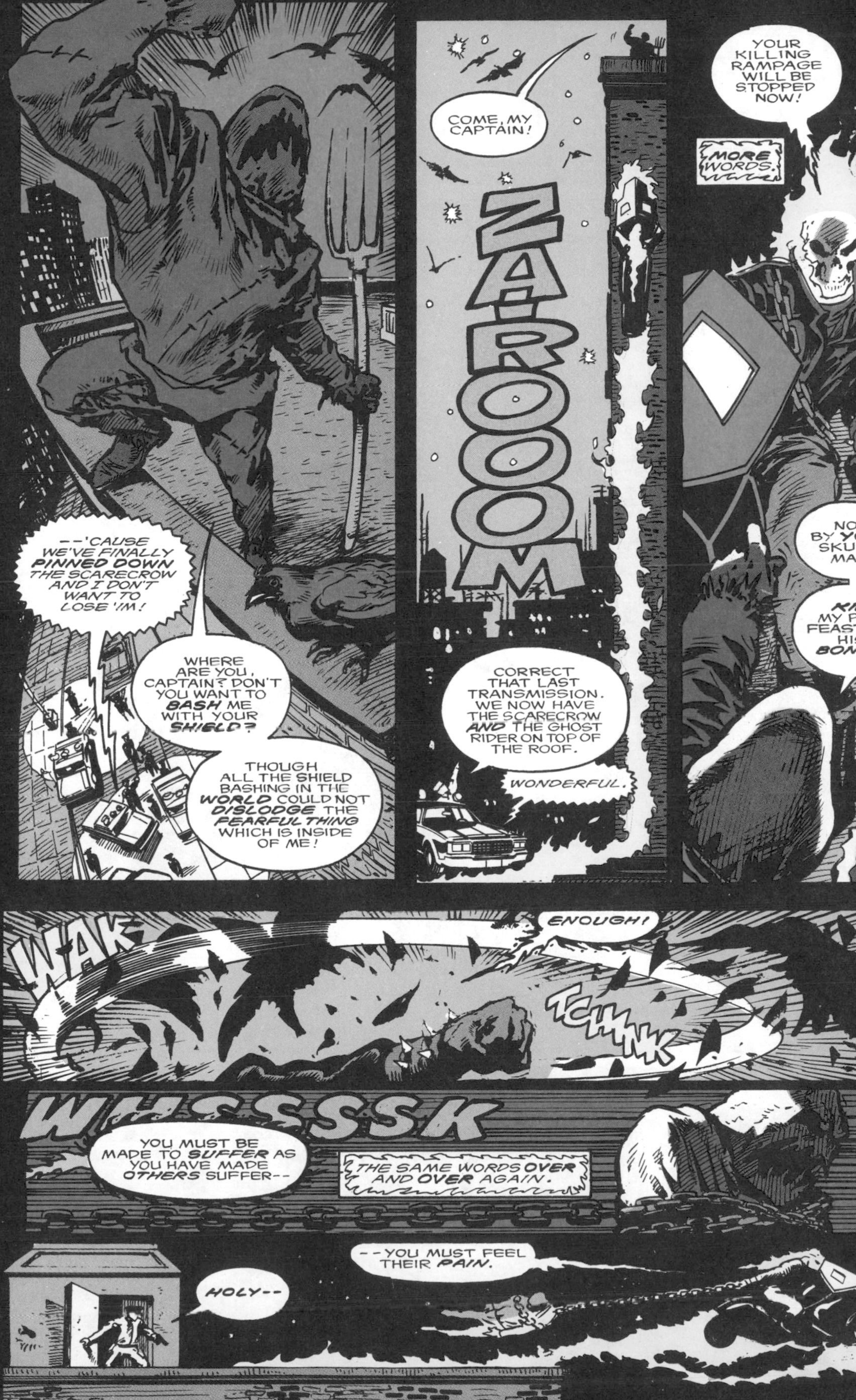
--'CAUSE WE'VE FINALLY PINNED DOWN THE SCARECROW AND I DON'T WANT TO LOSE 'IM!
WHERE ARE YOU, CAPTAIN? DON'T YOU WANT TO BASH ME WITH YOUR SHIELD?
THOUGH ALL THE SHIELD BASHING IN THE WORLD COULD NOT DISLODGE THE FEARFUL THING WHICH IS INSIDE OF ME!
COME, MY CAPTAIN!
ZAROOOOM
CORRECT THAT LAST TRANSMISSION. WE NOW HAVE THE SCARECROW AND THE GHOST RIDER ON TOP OF THE ROOF.
WONDERFUL.
YOUR KILLING RAMPAGE WILL BE STOPPED NOW!
MORE WORDS.
NOT BY YOU, SKULL-MAN!
KILL, MY PETS! FEAST ON HIS BONES!
WAK
ENOUGH!
TCHUNK
WHSSSSK
YOU MUST BE MADE TO SUFFER AS YOU HAVE MADE OTHERS SUFFER--
THE SAME WORDS OVER AND OVER AGAIN.
--YOU MUST FEEL THEIR PAIN.
HOLY--

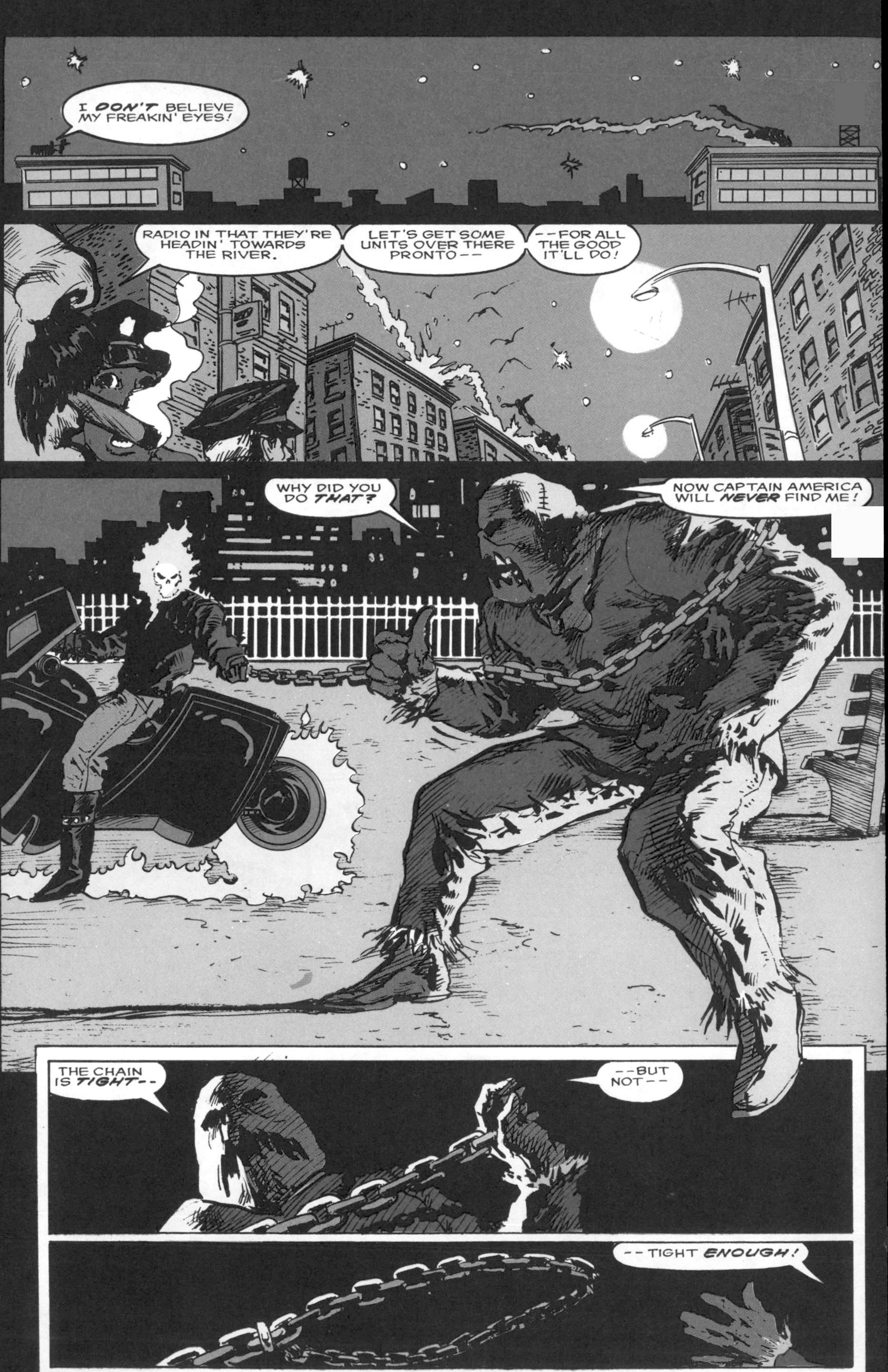
I DON'T BELIEVE MY FREAKIN' EYES!
RADIO IN THAT THEY'RE HEADIN' TOWARDS THE RIVER.
LET'S GET SOME UNITS OVER THERE PRONTO--
--FOR ALL THE GOOD IT'LL DO!
WHY DID YOU DO THAT?
NOW CAPTAIN AMERICA WILL NEVER FIND ME!
THE CHAIN IS TIGHT--
--BUT NOT--
--TIGHT ENOUGH!

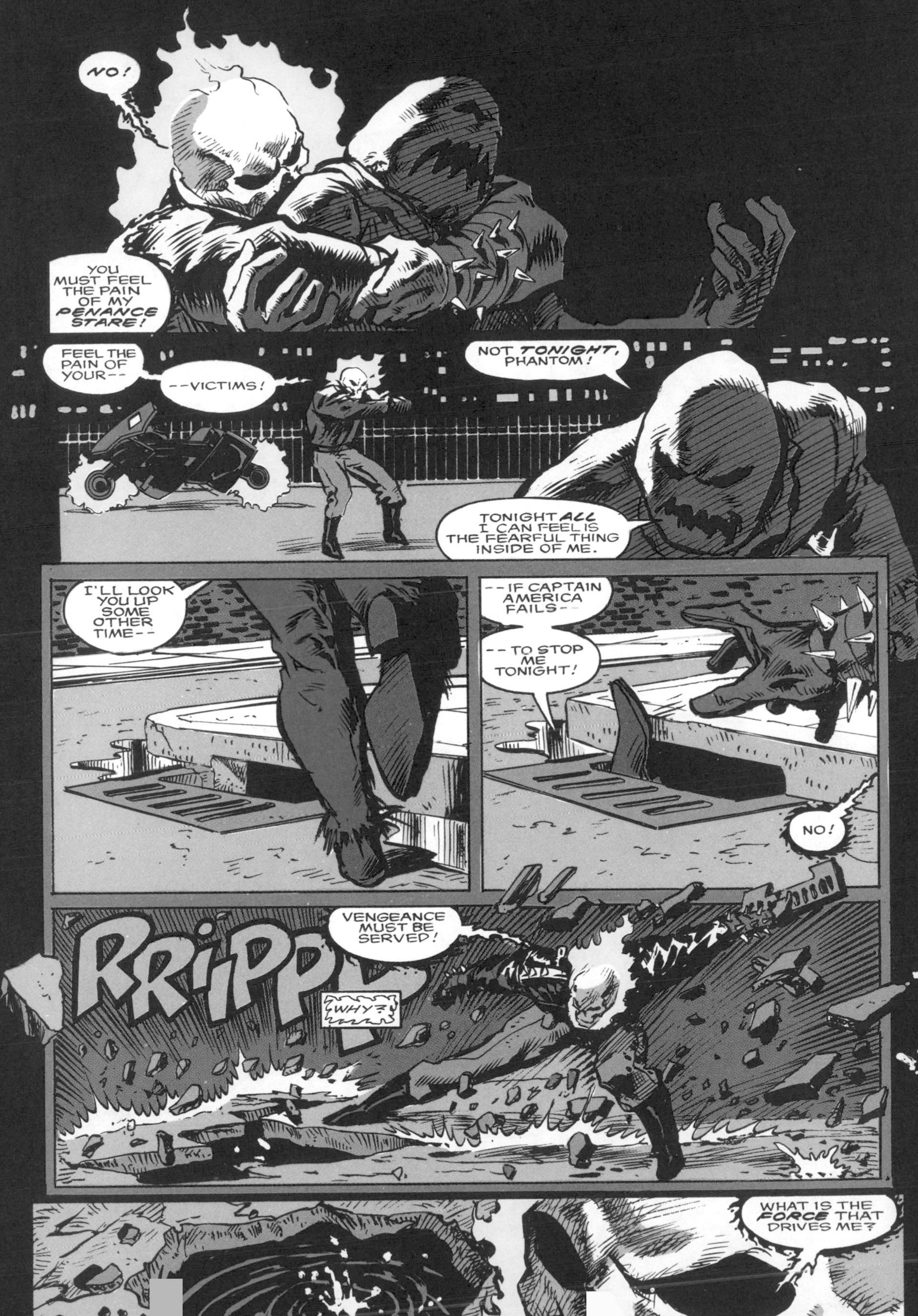
NO!
YOU MUST FEEL THE PAIN OF MY PENANCE STARE!
FEEL THE PAIN OF YOUR--
--VICTIMS!
NOT TONIGHT, PHANTOM!
TONIGHT ALL I CAN FEEL IS THE FEARFUL THING INSIDE OF ME.
I'LL LOOK YOU UP SOME OTHER TIME--
--IF CAPTAIN AMERICA FAILS--
--TO STOP ME TONIGHT!
NO!
RRIPP
VENGEANCE MUST BE SERVED!
WHY?
WHAT IS THE FORCE THAT DRIVES ME?

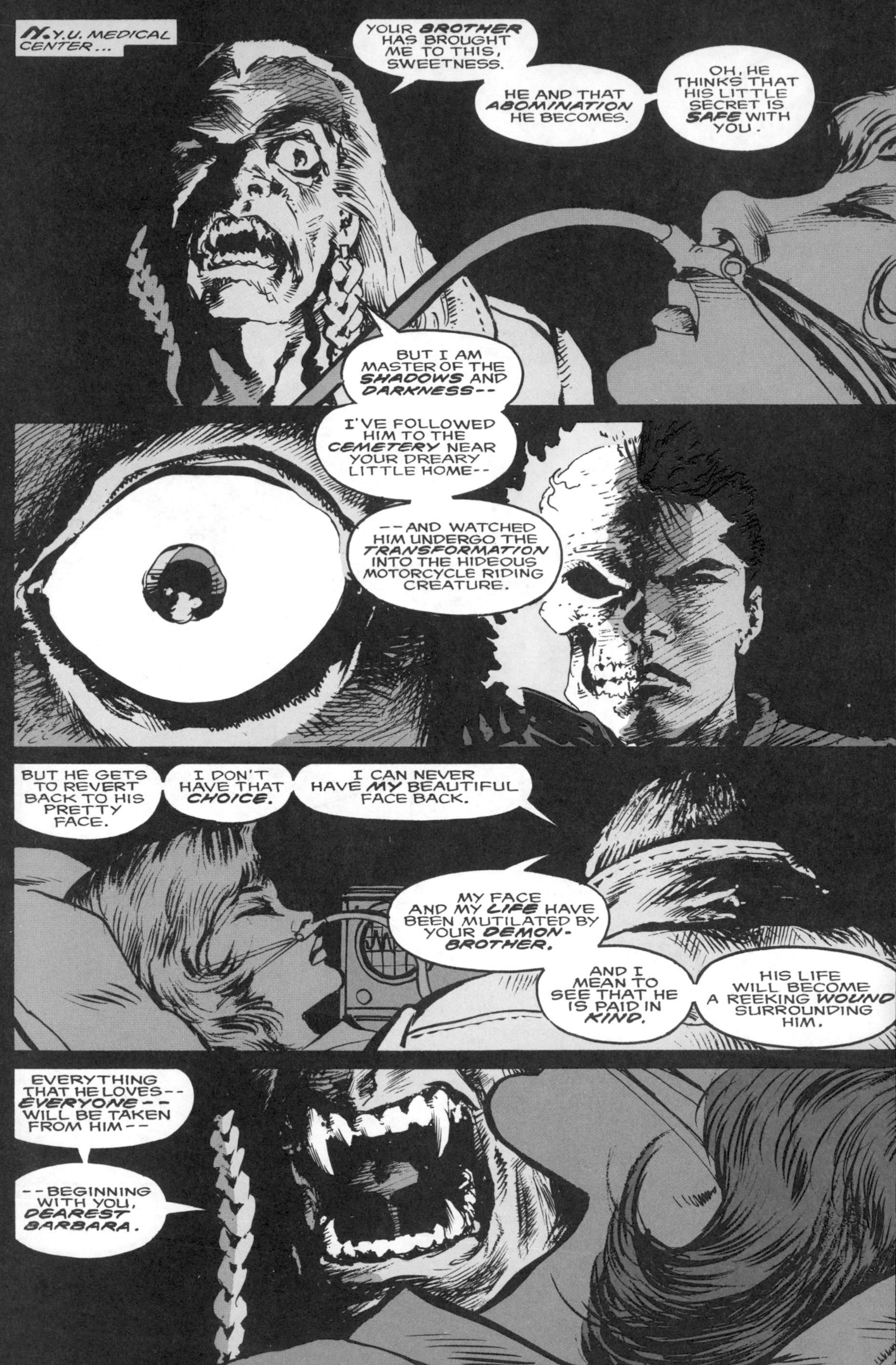
N.Y.U. MEDICAL CENTER...
YOUR BROTHER HAS BROUGHT ME TO THIS, SWEETNESS.
HE AND THAT ABOMINATION HE BECOMES.
OH, HE THINKS THAT HIS LITTLE SECRET IS SAFE WITH YOU.
BUT I AM MASTER OF THE SHADOWS AND DARKNESS--
I'VE FOLLOWED HIM TO THE CEMETERY NEAR YOUR DREARY LITTLE HOME--
--AND WATCHED HIM UNDERGO THE TRANSFORMATION INTO THE HIDEOUS MOTORCYCLE RIDING CREATURE.
BUT HE GETS TO REVERT BACK TO HIS PRETTY FACE.
I DON'T HAVE THAT CHOICE.
I CAN NEVER HAVE MY BEAUTIFUL FACE BACK.
MY FACE AND MY LIFE HAVE BEEN MUTILATED BY YOUR DEMON-BROTHER.
AND I MEAN TO SEE THAT HE IS PAID IN KIND.
HIS LIFE WILL BECOME A REEKING WOUND SURROUNDING HIM.
EVERYTHING THAT HE LOVES--EVERYONE--WILL BE TAKEN FROM HIM--
--BEGINNING WITH YOU, DEAREST BARBARA.

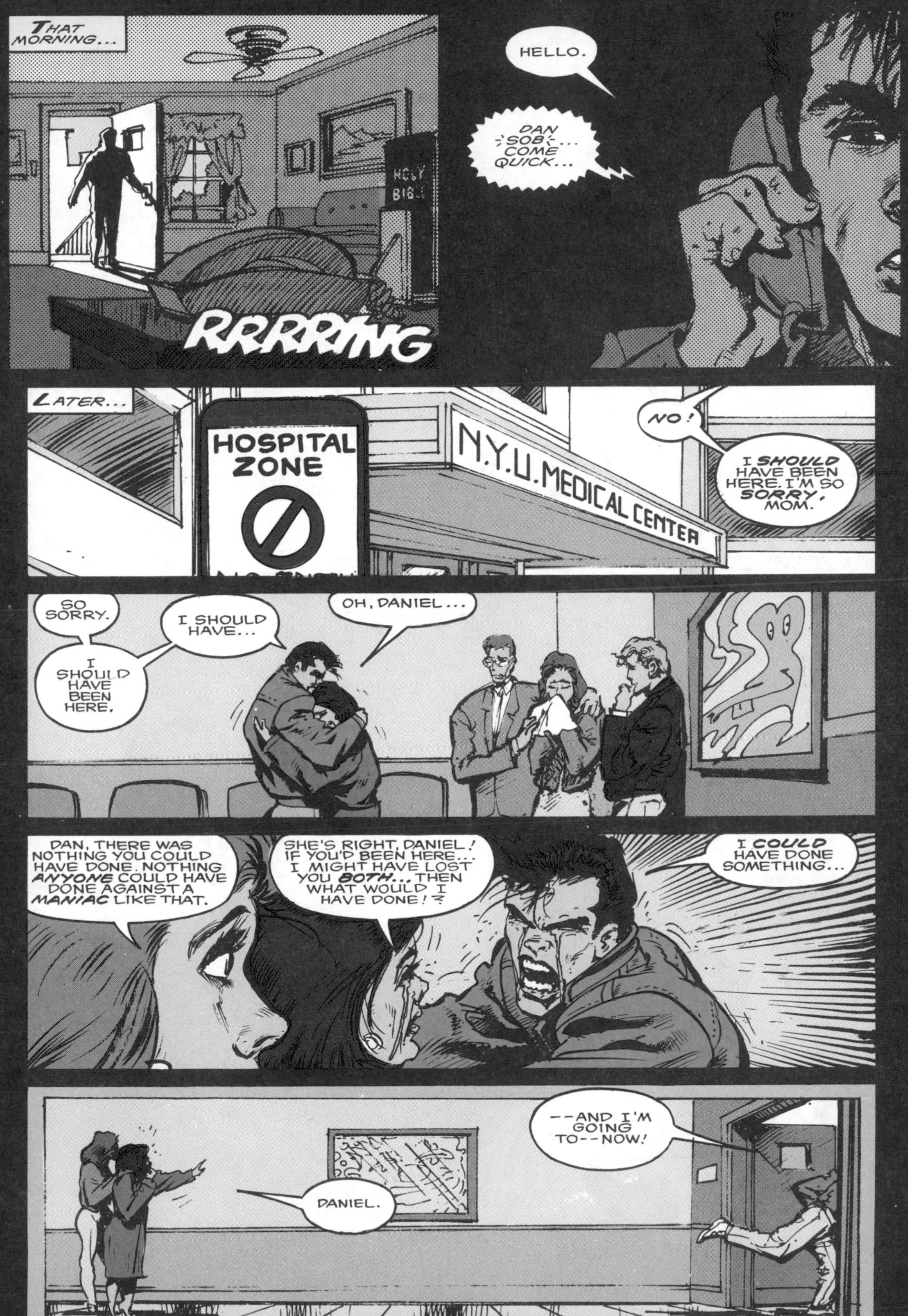
THAT MORNING...
RRRRING
HELLO.
DAN -SOB-... COME QUICK...
LATER...
HOSPITAL ZONE
N.Y.U. MEDICAL CENTER
NO!
I SHOULD HAVE BEEN HERE. I'M SO SORRY, MOM.
SO SORRY.
I SHOULD HAVE BEEN HERE.
I SHOULD HAVE...
OH, DANIEL...
DAN, THERE WAS NOTHING YOU COULD HAVE DONE. NOTHING ANYONE COULD HAVE DONE AGAINST A MANIAC LIKE THAT.
SHE'S RIGHT, DANIEL! IF YOU'D BEEN HERE... I MIGHT HAVE LOST YOU BOTH... THEN WHAT WOULD I HAVE DONE!?
I COULD HAVE DONE SOMETHING...
--AND I'M GOING TO--NOW!
DANIEL.

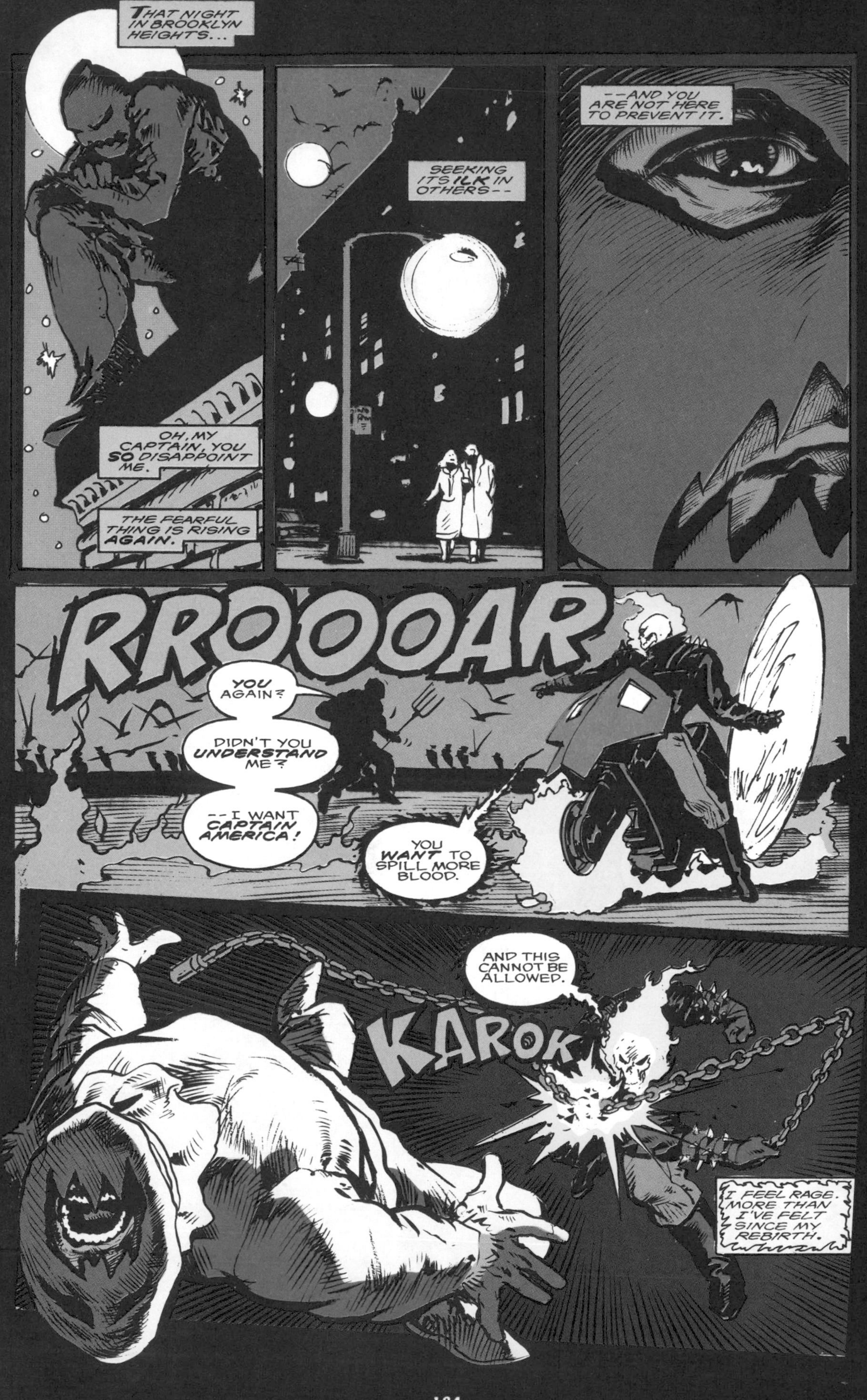
THAT NIGHT IN BROOKLYN HEIGHTS...
OH, MY CAPTAIN, YOU SO DISAPPOINT ME.
THE FEARFUL THING IS RISING AGAIN.
SEEKING ITS ILK IN OTHERS--
--AND YOU ARE NOT HERE TO PREVENT IT.
RROOOAR
YOU AGAIN?
DIDN'T YOU UNDERSTAND ME?
--I WANT CAPTAIN AMERICA!
YOU WANT TO SPILL MORE BLOOD.
AND THIS CANNOT BE ALLOWED.
KAROK
I FEEL RAGE. MORE THAN I'VE FELT SINCE MY REBIRTH.

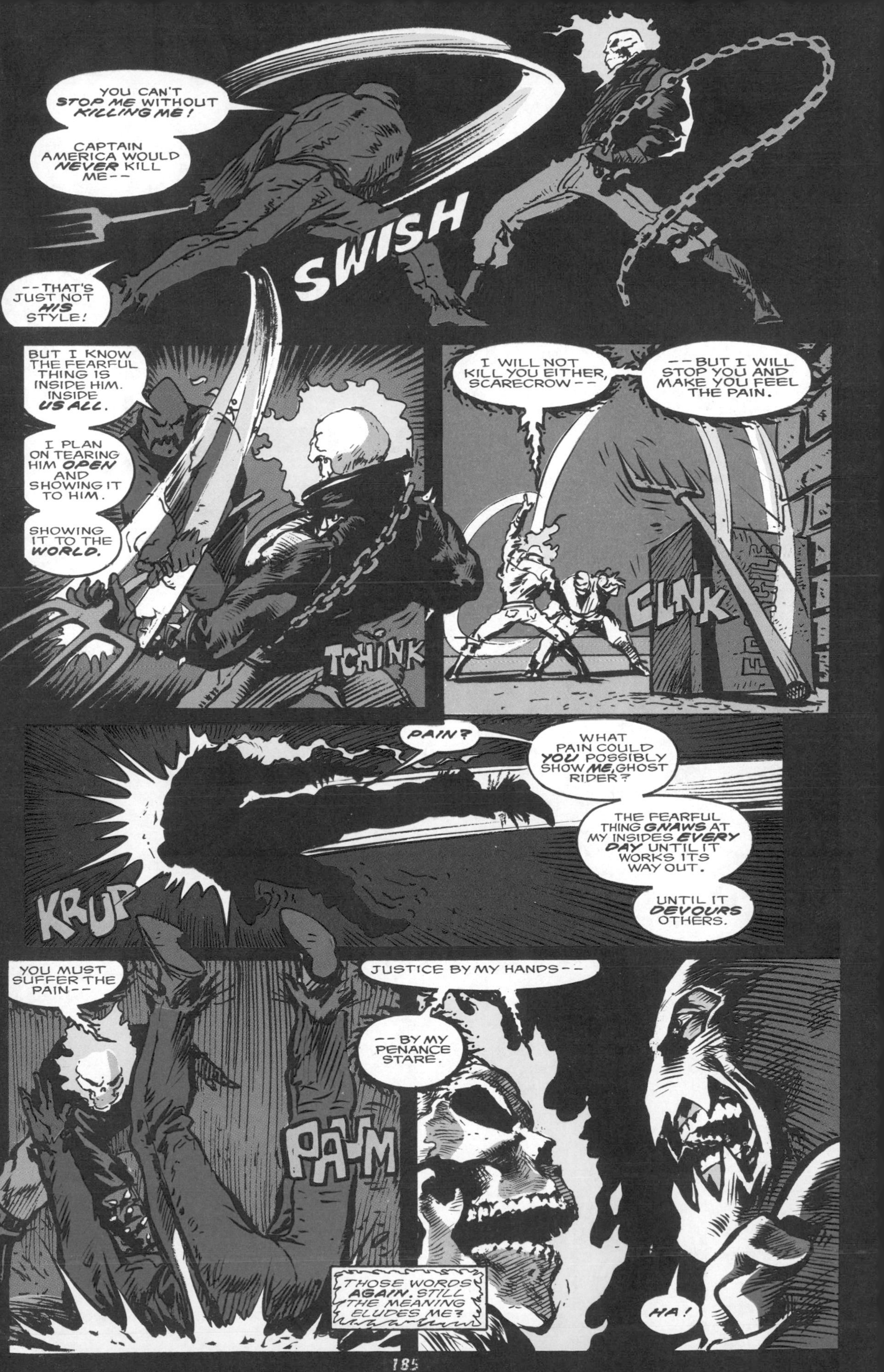
YOU CAN'T STOP ME WITHOUT KILLING ME!
CAPTAIN AMERICA WOULD NEVER KILL ME--
SWISH
--THAT'S JUST NOT HIS STYLE!
BUT I KNOW THE FEARFUL THING IS INSIDE HIM. INSIDE US ALL.
I PLAN ON TEARING HIM OPEN AND SHOWING IT TO HIM.
SHOWING IT TO THE WORLD.
TCHINK
I WILL NOT KILL YOU EITHER, SCARECROW--
--BUT I WILL STOP YOU AND MAKE YOU FEEL THE PAIN.
CLNK
PAIN?
WHAT PAIN COULD YOU POSSIBLY SHOW ME, GHOST RIDER?
THE FEARFUL THING GNAWS AT MY INSIDES EVERY DAY UNTIL IT WORKS ITS WAY OUT.
UNTIL IT DEVOURS OTHERS.
KRUP
YOU MUST SUFFER THE PAIN--
JUSTICE BY MY HANDS--
--BY MY PENANCE STARE.
PA-M
THOSE WORDS AGAIN. STILL THE MEANING ELUDES ME?
HA!

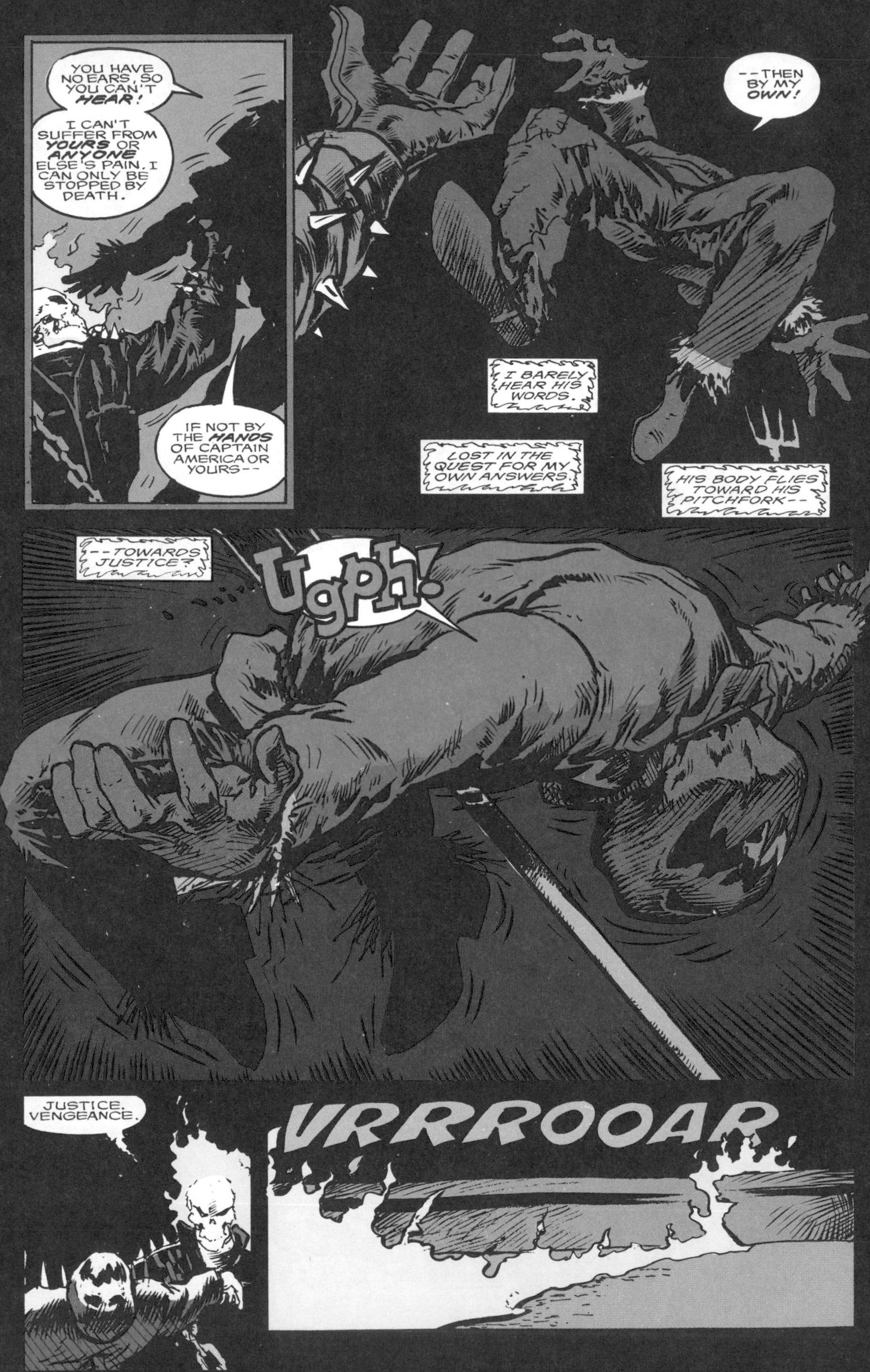
YOU HAVE NO EARS, SO YOU CAN'T HEAR!
I CAN'T SUFFER FROM YOURS OR ANYONE ELSE'S PAIN. I CAN ONLY BE STOPPED BY DEATH.
IF NOT BY THE HANDS OF CAPTAIN AMERICA OR YOURS--
--THEN BY MY OWN!
I BARELY HEAR HIS WORDS.
LOST IN THE QUEST FOR MY OWN ANSWERS.
HIS BODY FLIES TOWARD HIS PITCHFORK--
--TOWARDS JUSTICE?
UGPH!
JUSTICE. VENGEANCE.
VRRROOAR

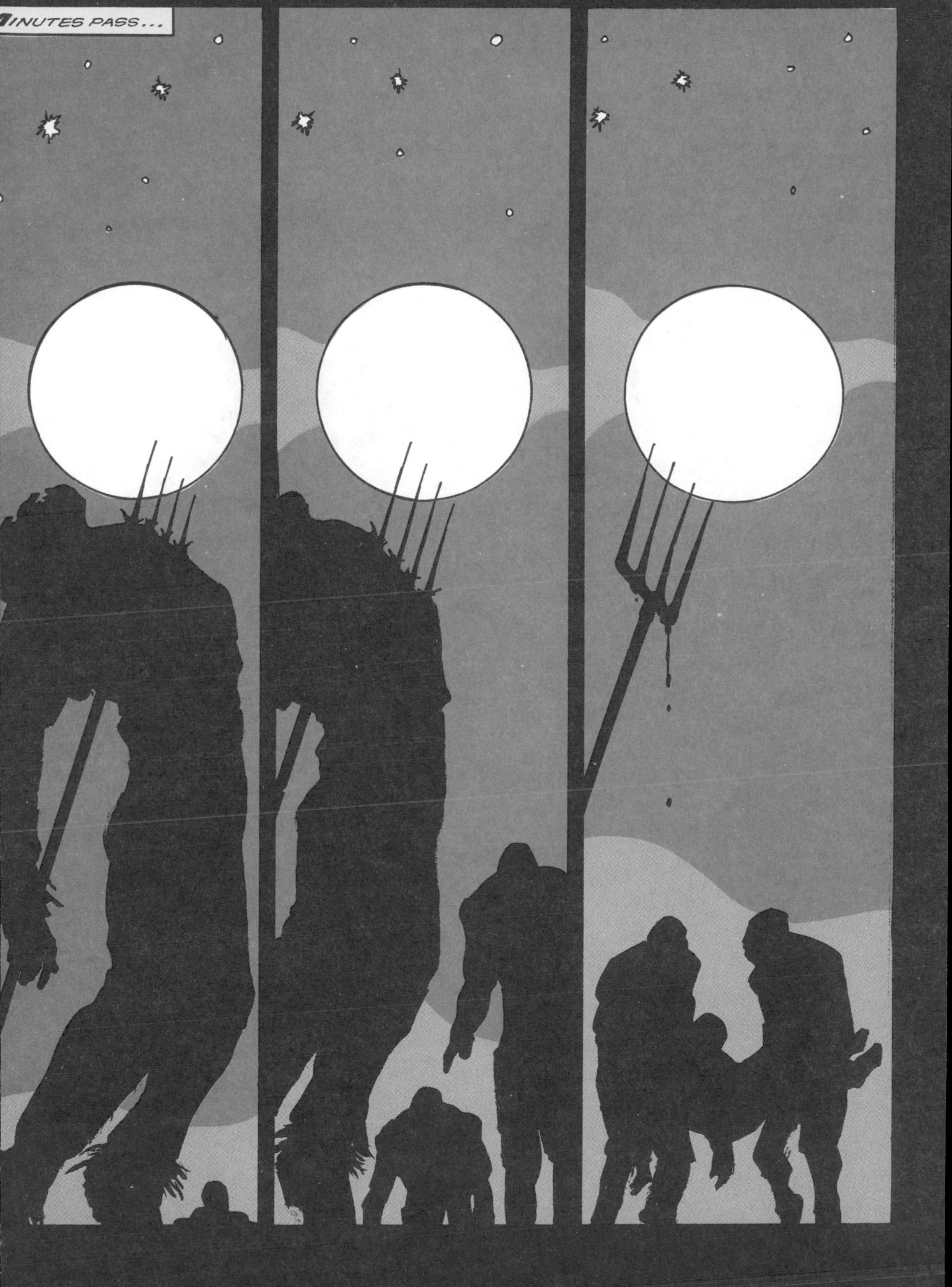
MINUTES PASS...

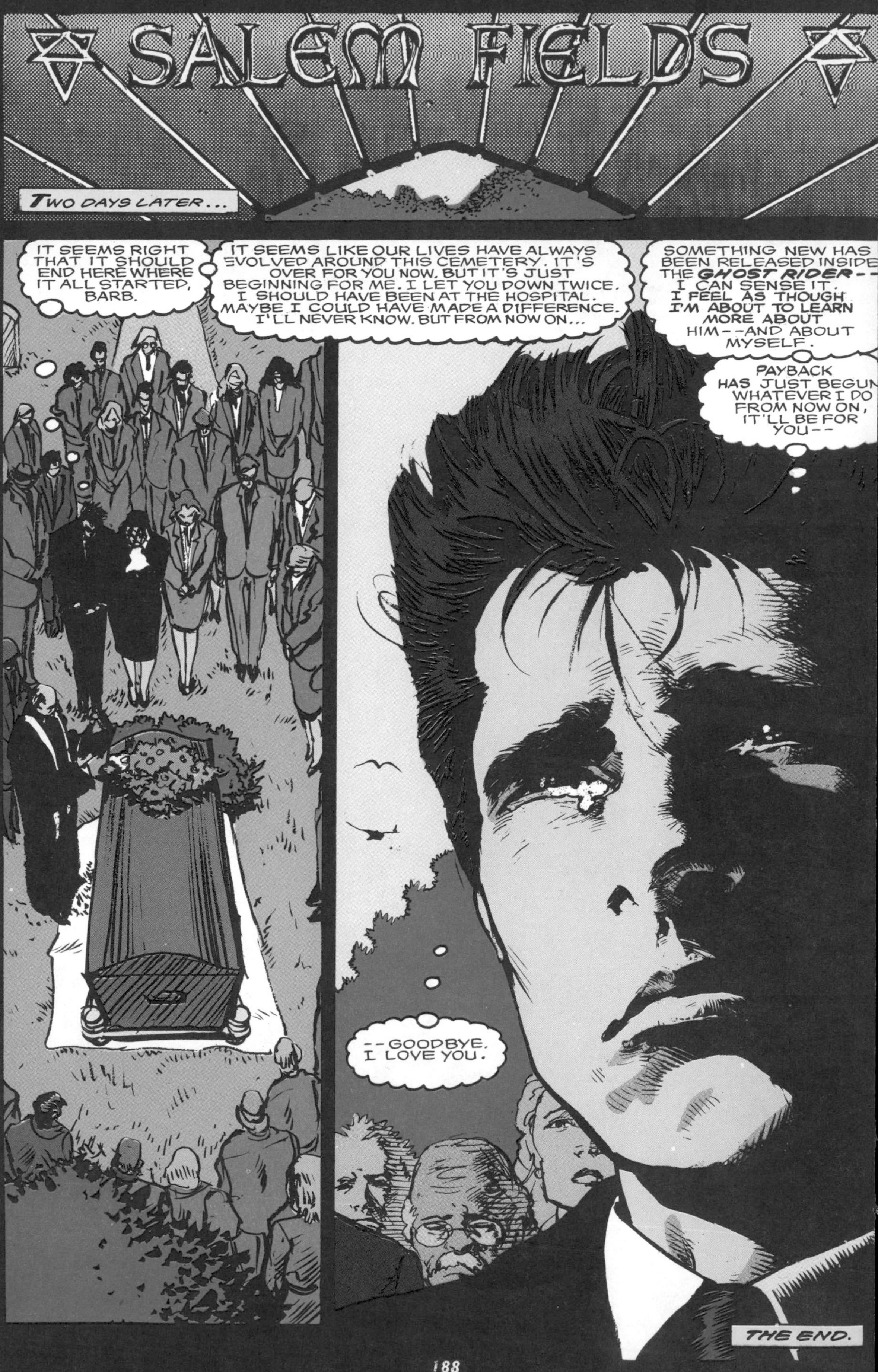
SALEM FIELDS
TWO DAYS LATER...
IT SEEMS RIGHT THAT IT SHOULD END HERE WHERE IT ALL STARTED, BARB.
IT SEEMS LIKE OUR LIVES HAVE ALWAYS EVOLVED AROUND THIS CEMETERY. IT'S OVER FOR YOU NOW. BUT IT'S JUST BEGINNING FOR ME. I LET YOU DOWN TWICE. I SHOULD HAVE BEEN AT THE HOSPITAL. MAYBE I COULD HAVE MADE A DIFFERENCE. I'LL NEVER KNOW. BUT FROM NOW ON...
SOMETHING NEW HAS BEEN RELEASED INSIDE THE GHOST RIDER-- I CAN SENSE IT. I FEEL AS THOUGH I'M ABOUT TO LEARN MORE ABOUT HIM--AND ABOUT MYSELF.
PAYBACK HAS JUST BEGUN. WHATEVER I DO FROM NOW ON, IT'LL BE FOR YOU--
--GOODBYE. I LOVE YOU.
THE END.

I read that someone had been arrested for digging up graves and decapitating the corpses. He claimed to be getting thousands of dollars a head. What kind of sick mind would do a thing like this? And where? Salem Fields. In the heart of the Cypress Hills Cemeteries. Dan Ketch's cemetery! Ghost Rider's cemetery. My cemetery!

The neighborhood I grew up in had changed. This kind of thing just didn't happen when my friends and I were hanging out there. We had respect for the cemeteries that we had adopted as our stomping grounds.

Cypress Hills, Brooklyn is a cemetery. You live there and you're never more than a couple of blocks away from one. They were our schoolyard, park and playground rolled into one gigantic tree-covered hangout.

Hey, trees and grass are rare commodities in Brooklyn! The cemetery was an all around good deal for us. We considered ourselves lucky. Our friends, from outside the neighborhood, considered us brave (or was it stupid?) for going into the graveyard at night. For us it was just the most obvious place for us to hang out and let our imaginations, and ourselves, run wild. Boy, did they run! And on many nights so did we!

Strange lights dancing in the dark, mausoleum doors swinging open unaided and the odd ear-piercing shriek through the shadows of the night. Shadows that played tricks of the eye and on the mind — or were they tricks? I'm still not totally convinced that some of the bizarre things I witnessed weren't real. If you want to know what kind of things I'm talking about, read the book.

All of this in a place of rest for the dead. And I considered all this normal. I was sure everybody had the same experiences. Didn't they?

Not that I wasn't scared — I was petrified — and so were all of the Brooklyn tough guys (male and female) with whom I hung out. The security and comfort of the cemetery combined with the occasional frights was the entire appeal. We loved it. And more importantly, we respected it!

These are the memories that I tried to dig up years later when I was given the privilege of writing a comic book about the rebirth of the Spirit of Vengeance. In his previous incarnation the GHOST RIDER rode throughout the western part of the United States dispensing his own form of vengeance. Was he a good guy? A bad guy? It depended.

Since I had rarely been further west than the Hudson River, I decided to stay away from the supernatural cowboy motif that had attracted me to the character in the first place. "Write what you know" say the books. What did I know? Cemeteries. Brooklyn/Queens. And the kind of people who live near and around them.

It was fun to reread all the old Ghost Rider comic books. The works of Roger Stern, J.M. DeMatteis et al. I was able to relive my childhood in two ways. The first by returning to one of my all-time favorite comic book characters. And the second by returning to the old neighborhood, in thought and in deed.

I went back to take reference photos for two of the best artists in the business, JAVIER SALTARES and MARK TEXEIRA. These two have been instrumental in the re-creation of my old neighborhood — or at least the way I remember it. Cypress Hills is real. The cemeteries are real. Ghost Rider. . .? If the Spirit of Vengeance was hanging out in my old neighborhood, the book you're holding in your hands is the best representation of how he would look and act.

The people of Brooklyn are no-nonsense types. They give no garbage and expect none in return. I like that kind of person.

Dan Ketch is a composite of many of my old buddies. Almost every supporting character has a little of my old friends in them. A little of the old neighborhood. A little of Brooklyn.

Ghost Rider. I never actually met anyone quite like him, but I know he is a hero. There is no doubt in my mind (even though there is some doubt in his and those supporting characters in the book). He wants vengeance. Vengeance for all the pain that has been inflicted on all the innocents that have ever been hurt. And he's getting it one person at a time.

If I were to meet a guy like Ghost Rider, I'm sure he'd be hanging out in a cemetery in Brooklyn. And there would certainly be no grave robbing going on. He is a Brooklyn-born hero.

Thanks for reading about the old neighborhood.

H.W. Mackie '91

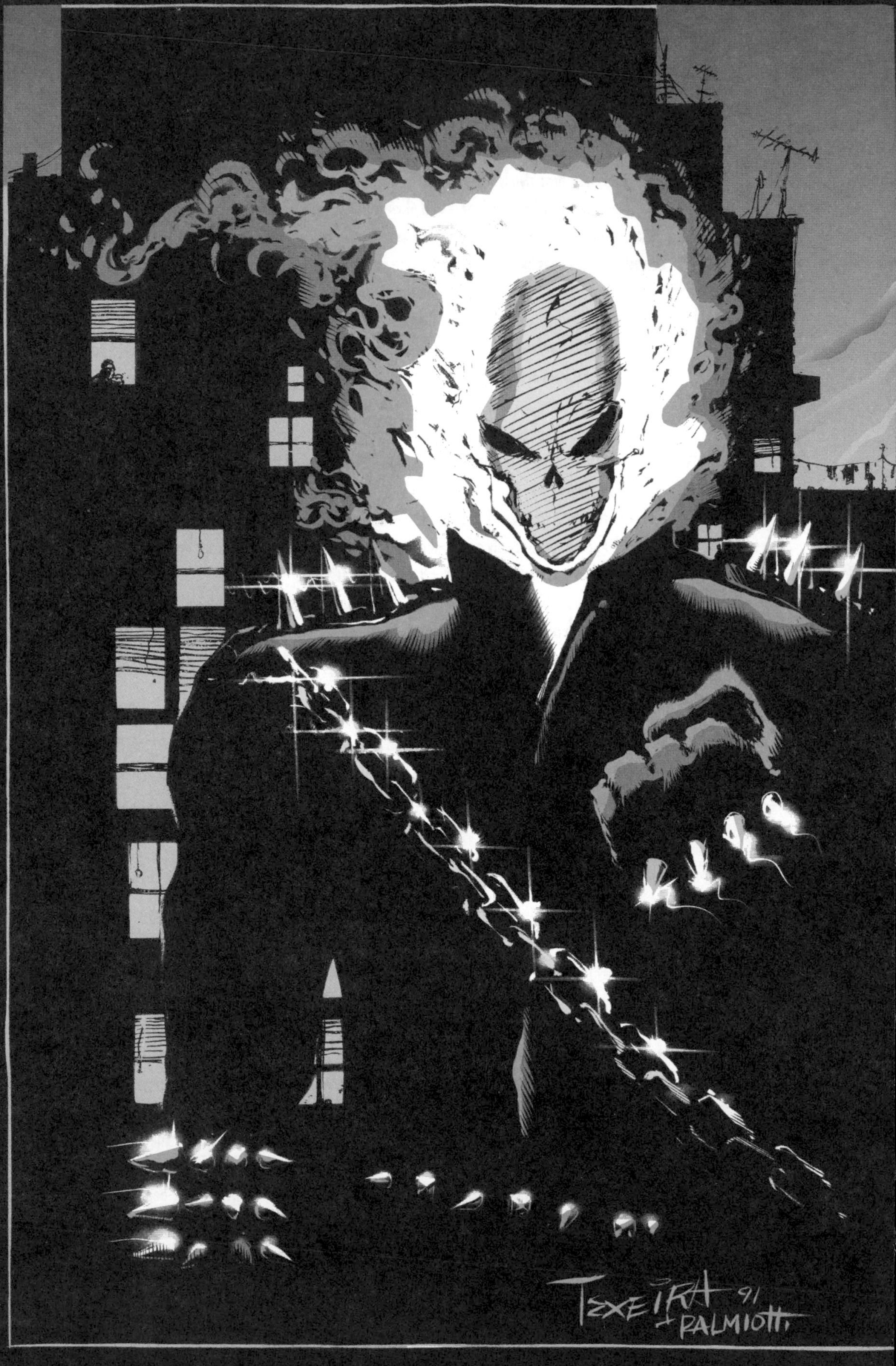
TEXEIRA 91
PALMIOTTI

JAVIER SALTARES 91

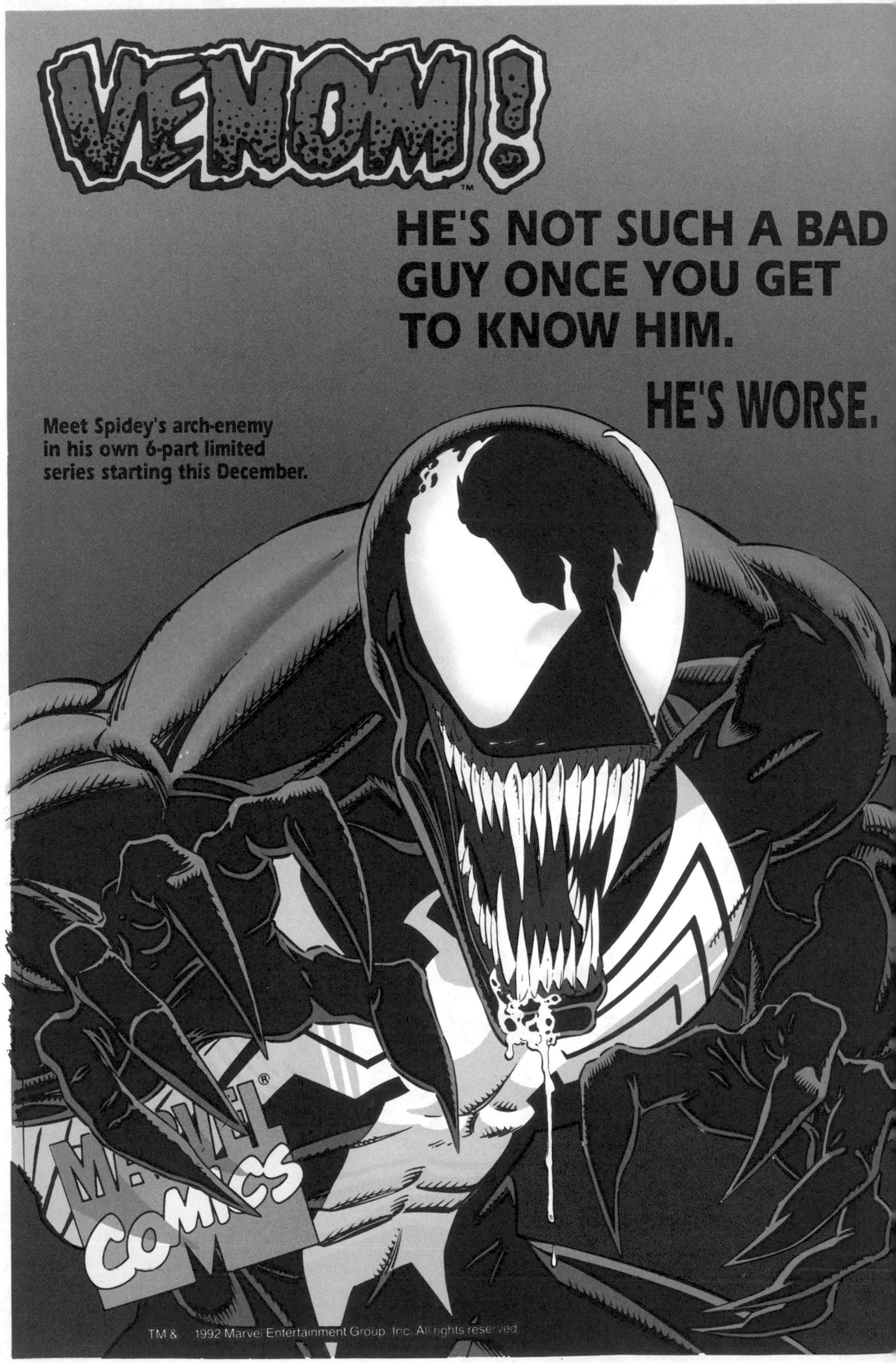
VENOM!™
HE'S NOT SUCH A BAD GUY ONCE YOU GET TO KNOW HIM.
HE'S WORSE.
Meet Spidey's arch-enemy in his own 6-part limited series starting this December.
MARVEL® COMICS
TM & 1992 Marvel Entertainment Group, Inc. All rights reserved.